Award Winning Architecture
International Yearbook 1997

Frontcover: Brigitte Shim and Howard Sutcliffe, Craven Road House, Toronto, Canada (see page 28)

Prestel books are available worldwide. Please contact your nearest bookseller or write to either of the following addresses for information concerning your local distributor:

Prestel Verlag, Mandlstrasse 26, D-80802 Munich, Germany
Phone (89) 38 17 09-0, Fax (89) 38 17 09-35
Prestel Verlag, 16 West 22nd Street, New York, N.Y. 10010, USA
Phone (212) 627 81 99, Fax (212) 627 98 66

Library of Congress Cataloging-in-Publication Data is available.

Die Deutsche Bibliothek – CIP-Einheitsaufnahme
Award Winning Architecture ... : AWA ; international yearbook ...
- Engl. Orig-Ausg. - Munich ; New York : Prestel.
Erscheint jährl. - Aufnahme nach 1996
ISSN 1430-9459
NE: AWA ; international yearbook ...
Engl. Orig. – Ausg.
1996 –

Editorial coordination Diana Wessling, Bettina Schimmer

Design WIGEL, Munich
Offset lithography Fischer Repro Technik GmbH, Frankfurt
Printing and binding Bawa Print + Partner GmbH, Munich
Printed on acid-free paper
ISBN 3-7913-1833-0
ISSN 1430-9459

International Yearbook

Award Winning Architecture

AAA 1997

Edited by
Frantisek Sedlacek

in cooperation with
Christine Waiblinger-Jens

Advisory Board
**Thomas Herzog, Vittorio Magnago Lampugnani,
Manfred Sack, Werner Strodthoff**

Patron
**UIA
(Union Internationale des Architectes)**

Prestel Munich · New York

Contents

SELECTED PROJECTS

Audaces fortuna iuvat

Most schools of philosophy are in agreement that what distinguishes human beings from animals — apart from man's linguistic abilities and his capacity to use implements — is the faculty for creative thinking; and that is precisely what design is, not only in a general sense, but also particularly in the field of architecture. In spite of the complexity of a building and the long, occasionally endless, path it follows from idea to realization, its quality will ultimately depend on the quality of its design. A building cannot be better than its design. But how can one evaluate something that is immeasurable — an idea?

In my opinion, the greatest difference between human beings and animals is the fact that we can consciously LAUGH, that we have a sense of humour.

Our brain can be broadly divided into two parts. One segment is responsible for logical, rational thought. It acts as a kind of "store" that absorbs pragmatic information and is subject to a constant process of programming and reprogramming. In the present case, this means the whole range of specialist architectural and constructional knowledge. The other segment of our brain accommodates our feelings. It is responsible for our tears and our LAUGHTER; it is the realm of the senses. It is here that the powers for creative activity and the sense of beauty reside; in other words, this is the realm that determines the quality of design.

Form – the outcome of the process of design — cannot be comprehended purely in rational terms such as function, construction or economic viability. If form is the decisive criterion of design and thus of architecture, non-measurable aspects such as individuality, imagination, poetry and, of course, LAUGHTER, assume a special significance in our modern over-technicized world with its paucity of human qualities. The quest for spirituality, for a more discriminating way of thinking, gathers momentum. In our present state of surfeit, material needs play an increasingly subordinate role. It is again possible, indeed there is a growing desire, to cultivate the realm of the senses, which had long seemed to be redundant. What is meant here is allowing a new latitude to mystical qualities such as the playful, irrational, intuitive, emotional sides of our nature.

Architecture may be seen as an image of life: building forms that reflect the complexity of life and in which the two basic needs of man find a visible, built counterpart — the need for ties, order, orientation and security on the one hand, and the desire for liberty, openness, freedom of choice on the other. It is an architecture based on the love of life and, therefore, reflecting the polarities of life.

In reality, what seem like pairs of opposites — reason and intuition, pragmatism and idealism, hard and soft, poetic and prosaic, order and chaos, calculation and spontaneity — are merely complementary sets of relations. A design will be perceived as successful only if, in a certan aspect, it exhibits some token of its opposite. Perception depends on contrasts. Anything without contrast will be experienced as

little more than a formless, scarcely perceptible background.
Tears and LAUGHTER: no, preferably LAUGHTER here, for that is probably the most beautiful emotion of our lives and of architecture, too. In other words, our quest is for an architecture that is full of laughter and humour, that is endowed with wit and elements of surprise, that is eventful and entertaining.

In this book, I shall present a series of objects that have already received the highest accolades on a national level. Any comparisons based on traditional criteria would be both impossible and superfluous. Only if measured against a higher or exceptional scale of quality, as described above, can a comparison of this kind capture our interest.

The world is turned on its head — inverted inwardly rather than outwardly, because its distances have shrunk. The media have come to replace reason. Prague in Bohemia is only a few fax minutes from New York City.

The media have put an end to the idea of a locally relevant architectural culture. The pursuit of quality has become more international. That, too, legitimates and justifies the drawing of comparisons.

To assist me in this work, I invited a number of people to serve on an advisory board. It comprised the following members.

Thomas Herzog, architect, BDA, who has his own architectural practice in Munich and is professor for design and building construction at the University for Technology, Munich. In 1993, Thomas Herzog was awarded the BDA gold medal and in 1996 the Auguste Perret Prize of the International Union of Architects (UIA).

Vittorio Magnago Lampugnani, professor for the history of urban planning at the ETH in Zurich.

Manfred Sack, architectural critic of the German weekly newspaper *Die Zeit*. Manfred Sack lives in Hamburg.

Werner Strodthoff, who is also an architectural critic and lives in Cologne.

A commentary on the selection of schemes made for the main project section of this book can be found on page ten.

KEEP SMILING is a sound philosophy.
KEEP SMILING ARCHITECTURE could be the seal of quality for the future.

Frantisek D. Sedlacek
Editor

Preface from the UIA

Without any doubt, we are living in a stimulating age, with our sights and hopes focused on 21st century.

We only need to read a newspaper, stop at a newsstand, simply listen to the radio or watch television, to be aware of how small the world has become thanks to technology.

For all of us, access to simultaneous information on events happening in practically all corners of the world has become a matter of fact.

Satellites, global communication via Internet and other similar resources have made this possible.

But one important question has to be asked.

If we are capable of such fast and efficient communication, if we are trying to discover the secrets of the Universe, and witness the constant use of new materials, then why have we not been successful in applying this technology in arousing a greater awareness, emphasizing the value of the spaces where we live and work, and lead our daily lives?

In this sense, it is undeniable that in the promotion, knowledge, study, analysis and critical appraisal of architecture, books continue to have a transcendental role. Going back to the 15th or 16th centuries, when the great treatises on architecture were published, they were the only tool for familiarizing oneself with the buildings and constructions of other times and places.

Today, in spite of all the technological resources available, books continue to be fundamental in this *rapprochement* and in our knowledge of architecture.

In fact communicating architecture is a complicated challenge. Space in Architecture is to be experienced physically, it is a psychobiological experience.

Therefore, beyond actually visiting to the building, books are the closest way to communicate architecture. Through the eyes of the narrator we perceive the sequence of images, plans, perspectives and descriptive texts, creating the sequence of these psychobiological spaces, and recreating time and space. Books give us the opportunity of analyzing plans by relating them to sections, façades and photos, with the aim of making the language of architecture accessible to the general public.

This encourages the importance and transcendence of a global view of award-winning projects in every country and stimulates architects and public alike to recognize the diversity, creativity and plurality of today's architectural output.

Publications like this are important tools in our aim in promoting architects and architecture, and the meaningful values in our daily lives.

Sara Topelson de Grinberg
President of the Union Internationale des Architectes

Notes on the Second Volume of this Yearbook

AWA '97, the second volume of this review of international architecture, is now complete — reason enough to look back briefly at the inception of this work.

At the outset, let us recall the aims of this publication. AWA presents an international selection of the buildings that, in the course of the previous year, were awarded official prizes by the various national institutions for architecture that are members of the world umbrella organization, the International Union of Architects (UIA). In other words, they are prizes awarded to architects by their fellow architects, not by industrial interest groups. The present volume, published under the aegis of the UIA, can, therefore, truly claim to provide an almost complete review of the best works of architecture realized throughout the world in the previous year. Establishing contacts with the individual national organizations and convincing those responsible of the importance of their collaboration proved to be a laborious task in preparing AWA '96. The positive response we received to this first volume, however, encouraged and strengthened us in our endeavours; and our partners now show great commitment to this venture and make every effort themselves to ensure that their prize-winning schemes, chosen by juries appointed from their own ranks, are presented in our current compendium of the most important works of international architecture. At this point, therefore, we should like to express our thanks to all the architectural organizations that approached us immediately after their prize-giving ceremonies to help us establish contact with the award-winning architects. In some cases, the organizations themselves compiled the illustrations and drawings for all the schemes they submitted for publication. This was not only of enormous help for the team of editors; it also allowed the individual architectural institutes to present their prize-winning projects in the form they wished and to bring out the special significance of the schemes from their own point of view. It is to be hoped that other organizations will follow suit, so that their award-winning projects may be presented fully and in the right light.

The general approval and acceptance with which AWA has met have made it a great success. This has led to a further positive development. In AWA '96, it was possible to illustrate and document some 150 projects. Exactly twice that number of architectural schemes from all countries that awarded prizes to architects last year have been submitted for the present issue.

AWA '97, therefore, presents a global review of prize-winning architecture.

Despite the great volume of material submitted, the slightly revised layout allows a clear presentation of the work, a quick orientation and the inclusion of a wealth of information. Some countries that, for political reasons, had hitherto not seen themselves in a position to award prizes for buildings have followed the example of other national organizations and brought a greater degree of transparency to their native architecture by instituting awards and approaching us directly. In other words, they have remedied the situation by drawing attention to the buildings in their countries in an international context.

As one would expect of any painstaking documentation such as this, it should not go unmentioned that, in the course of the pioneering work that went into compiling this comprehensive and complex publication, certain unfortunate mishaps occured. The Chamber of Architects and Civil Engineers of Malta informed us that it does not award prizes. Instead, it gave us the name of an architectural office whose work could be seen to represent current Maltese architecture. We should like to apologize at this point to the Chamber of Architects and Civil Engineers of Malta that it was no longer possible, in view of the pressures of time shortly before copy deadline, to clarify whether the Maltese chamber would recognize the inclusion of a project by this office in AWA '96 as an official recommendation. We wish to make clear that the Maltese scheme included in AWA '96 had neither received a prize from the Chamber of Architects and Civil Engineers of Malta nor been given a written recommendation.

Finally, we should like to extend special thanks to the UIA world organization for agreeing to bestow its patronage on this project, as well as to all the national federations for their commitment in helping to ensure the realization of AWA '97. Thanks are also due to the many individual architects without whose contributions it would not have been possible to complete this publication. We hope we shall be able to count on this support in the future.

We are delighted to present the second, enlarged volume of our international yearbook of award-winning architecture, AWA '97. We hope we may rely on your continued support in the form of valuable suggestions for AWA '98.

Christine Waiblinger-Jens

A Tendency to Lightness

Entries from more than 60 countries and almost 400 architects throughout the world make it no easy task to define what it is about their prizewinning buildings that evidently interests so many colleagues and contemporaries so keenly: in other words, what trends one has to keep an eye on in the world of architecture. There is no unequivocal answer to this that points in any single direction. There is no all-embracing "style", merely a number of related phenomena that are usually identifiable in the form of construction or the materials used. In this respect, the situation today is no different from that 20 years ago, as documented in an extremely interesting exhibition with the title "Transformations in Modern Architecture", which was shown in the Museum of Modern Art in New York. In a series of examples that were as diverse and singular as the architects who had designed them, the exhibition depicted the second phase of modernism almost 30 years after the Second World War. The list of contents in the catalogue included first, "Sculptural Form — Brutalism, Imagery, Black Boxes, Planes and Volumes, Expressionism, Organic Form"; second, "Structure — Cages, Cantilevers, Design by System, Glass Skins, Greenhouses and Other Public Spaces"; and third, "Hybrids". Finally, three equally distinctive yet quite different architects were presented: Louis Kahn, James Stirling (the "modern" works rather than the "sculptural" ones criticized as historicist) and Robert Venturi. The final section of the catalogue bore the title "Historicizing".

From all this, one could only conclude that architects did not follow a single, dominant (post-war) style, but designed their own highly individual forms of architecture. Each one of them revealed him or herself to be a unique personality who followed a distinctly personal line. In other words, there were as many "styles", as many personal architectural and structural forms of expression as there were architects.

Not even the ephemeral period of so-called Postmodernism with its historicist, decorative, surface architecture has changed anything in this respect. Concerned with superficial appearances, it was for the most part a fashion in architecture that was evidently necessary for a time: a kind of loosening-up exercise after the Modern Movement had lost its vigour and become stiff and degenerate. It was Charles Jencks who coined this striking term to describe an architectural means of escape, before it was adopted by science (in west European philosophy) and given a completely different, but equally fleeting meaning.

What of the present, though? It is not easy to find a single term to describe the architecture of the past year.

In some countries, tradition quite clearly manifests itself in modern architecture, somewhat uncertainly, for example, in South Africa, but with astounding vigour in Mexico. In other countries, one senses that current trends are gradually tending towards a stylistic consensus, however overstated they may seem at present. In Europe, one can observe a reavowal of the principles of the classical modernism of the first quarter of this century, but now treated more freely than ever before and reinterpreted in the light of new structural techniques, improved materials and new scope for their application. On the other hand, there are architects who evidently find it difficult to express their own identity through their buildings and who resort instead to stylistic imports.

It is also interesting to note that, among last year's prize- winning schemes, there are very few examples in which innovative structural forms or new technologies played an important role. This applies even to those genuine attempts to use conventional sources of energy more economically or to exploit solar energy: in other words, schemes that sought to create a form of architecture specifically inspired by these goals.

There is another striking aspect, too: a striving not only for greater transparency — as one knows it from the Modern Movement with its obsession for light — but for lightness of weight. This applies not only to buildings in steel and glass, but to solid stone structures with a clear geometry. They no longer appear to be monolithically heavy, but seem almost to have been assembled from a series of parts. This is particularly evident in buildings with a skeleton frame, which are far more common now than they used to be.

Disburdened by means of their stable structural frame, these buildings seem to enjoy a greater degree of freedom: the materials allow more openness, and the façades are more elegant. This is probably linked to some new optimistic architectural virtuosity that it is difficult to define. One notices it in the intensity with which the details are worked out. As a result, this kind of architecture does not reveal its formal intentions at a glance or at a great distance. The closer one comes to it, the richer it appears.

In this, perhaps, lies the explanation for the fact that virtually none of the top international architectural achievements of the last year reveals a boldness of design that immediately takes one's breath away, quite apart from exhibiting eccentrically daring features. Equally, there are no examples of social concepts directly translated into architecture. Only occasionally does one come across new building types that have not been encountered before. Is a greater degree of architectural invention simply not possible?

Manfred Sack
on behalf of the Advisory Board

**DETAILED DESCRIPTIONS
OF SELECTED PROJECTS:
A REPRESENTATIVE CROSS-SECTION**

Architects **Denton Corker Marshall Pty Ltd, Melbourne**

Award Winning Building **Melbourne Exhibition Centre**

Location **Clarendon Street, Southbank, Melbourne, Australia**

Design and Construction Period **1993–1996**

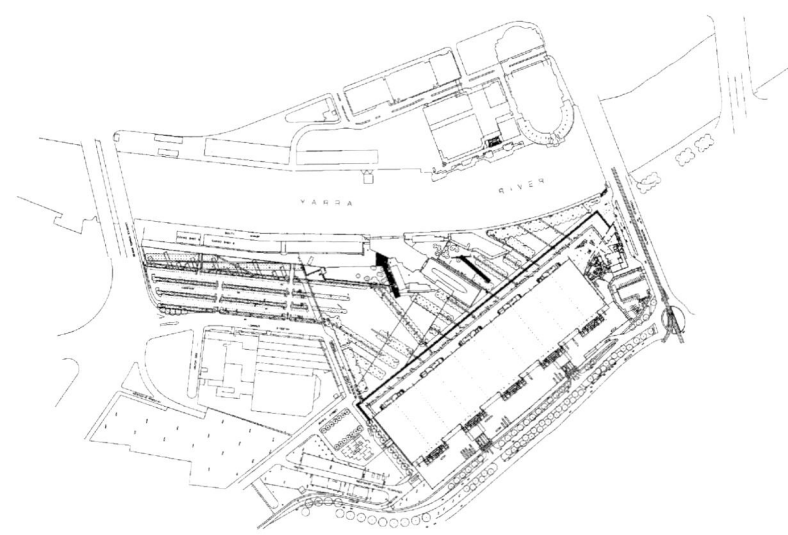

Award 1) National RAIA Sir Zelman Cowen Award for Public Buildings 1996;
   2) RAIA Victorian Chapter Sir Osborne McCutcheon Award for Commercial
   Architecture; 3) RAIA Gold Medal 1996

Given by The Royal Australian Institute of Architects

Prize Presentation 1) June / 26 / 1996

Members of the Jury 1) Peter Gargett (Chair), Ric Butt, Lindsay Clare,
   Yvonne von Hartel, Jenny Kee

Design Team Denton Corker Marshall Pty Ltd

Structural Engineering Ove Arup & Partners

Civil Engineering Ove Arup & Partners

Mechanical Engineering Connell Wagner Rankine and Hill

Electrical Engineering Connell Wagner Rankine and Hill

Acoustic Engineering Watson Moss Growcott

Air Conditioning Consultant Connell Wagner Rankine and Hill

Lighting Consultant Connell Wagner Rankine and Hill

Graphic Design Emery Vincent Associates

Interior Design Denton Corker Marshall Pty Ltd

Landscape Architecture Denton Corker Marshall Pty Ltd

Quantity Surveying WT Partnership

Approximate Cost A$ 129,000,000

Site Area 14 ha

Building Area 45,000 m^2

Total Floor Area 80,000 m^2

Photographer John Gollings

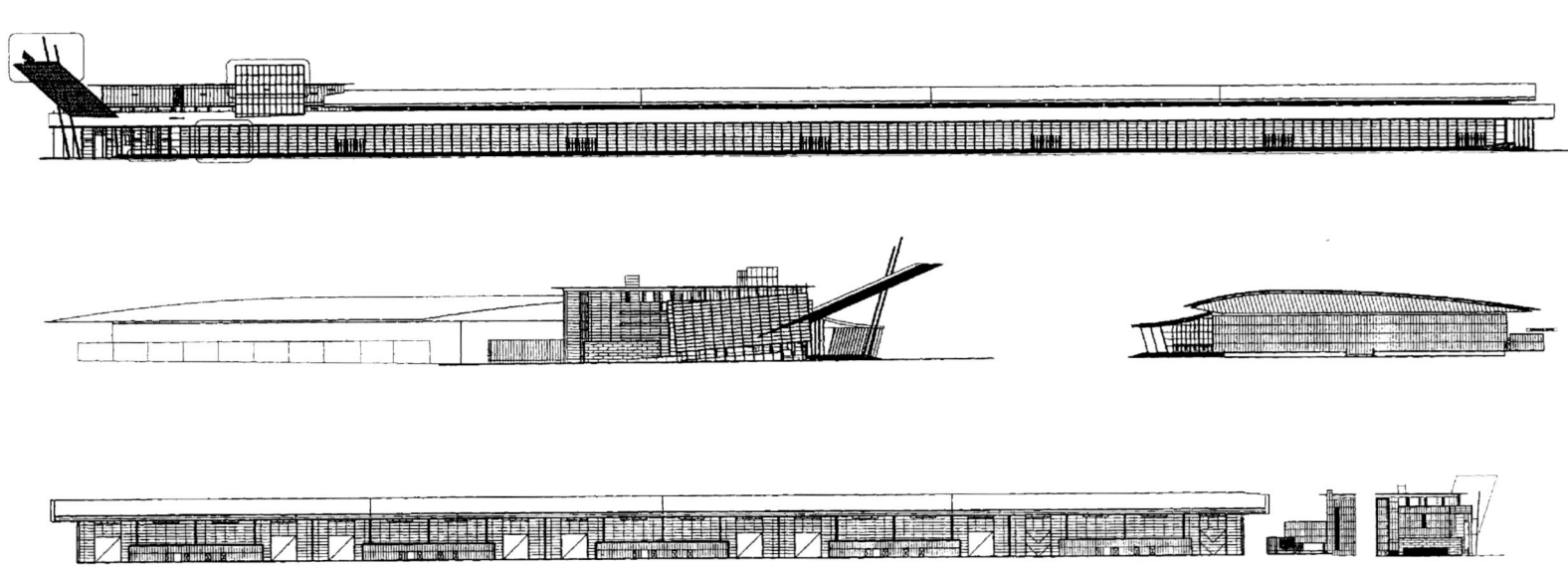

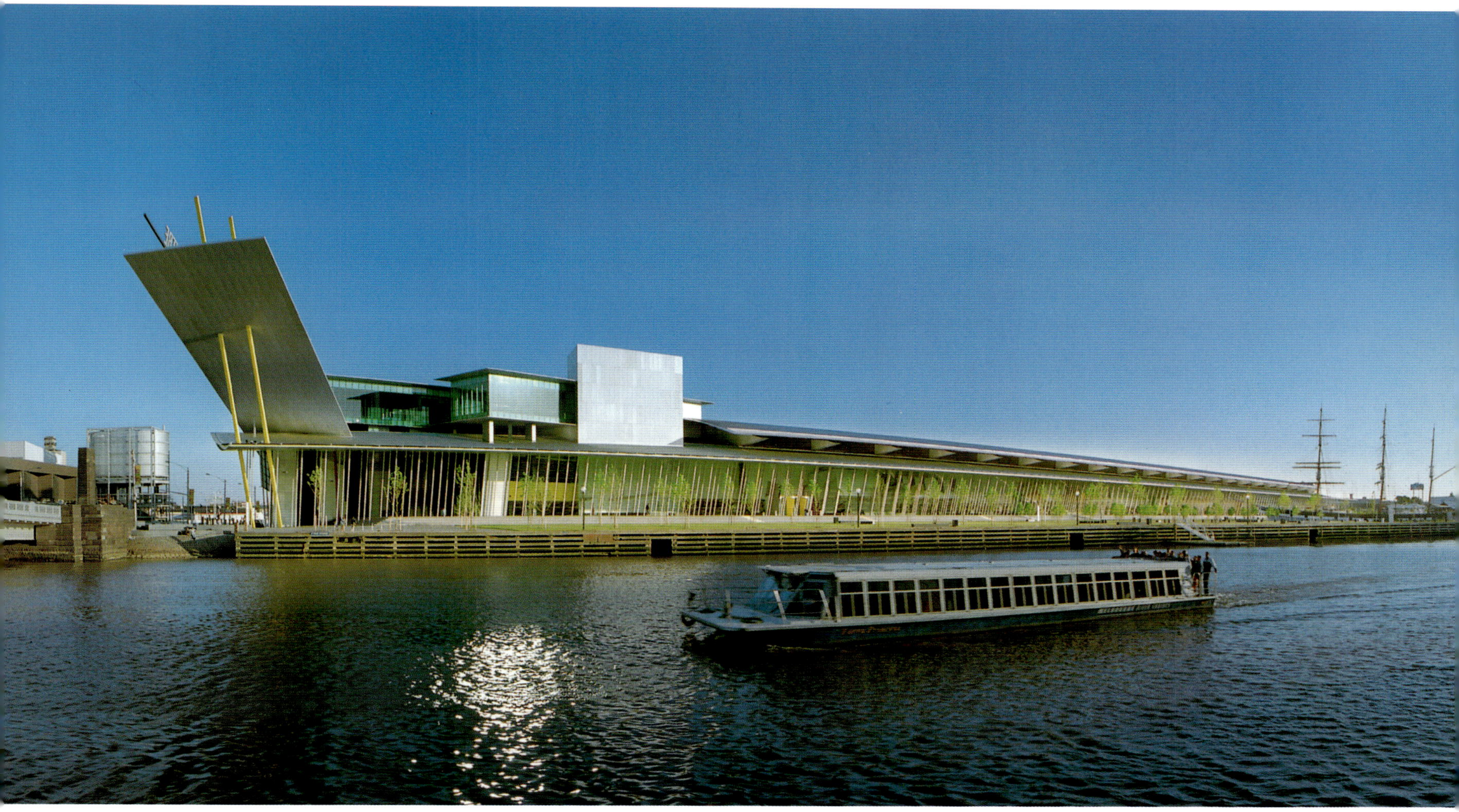

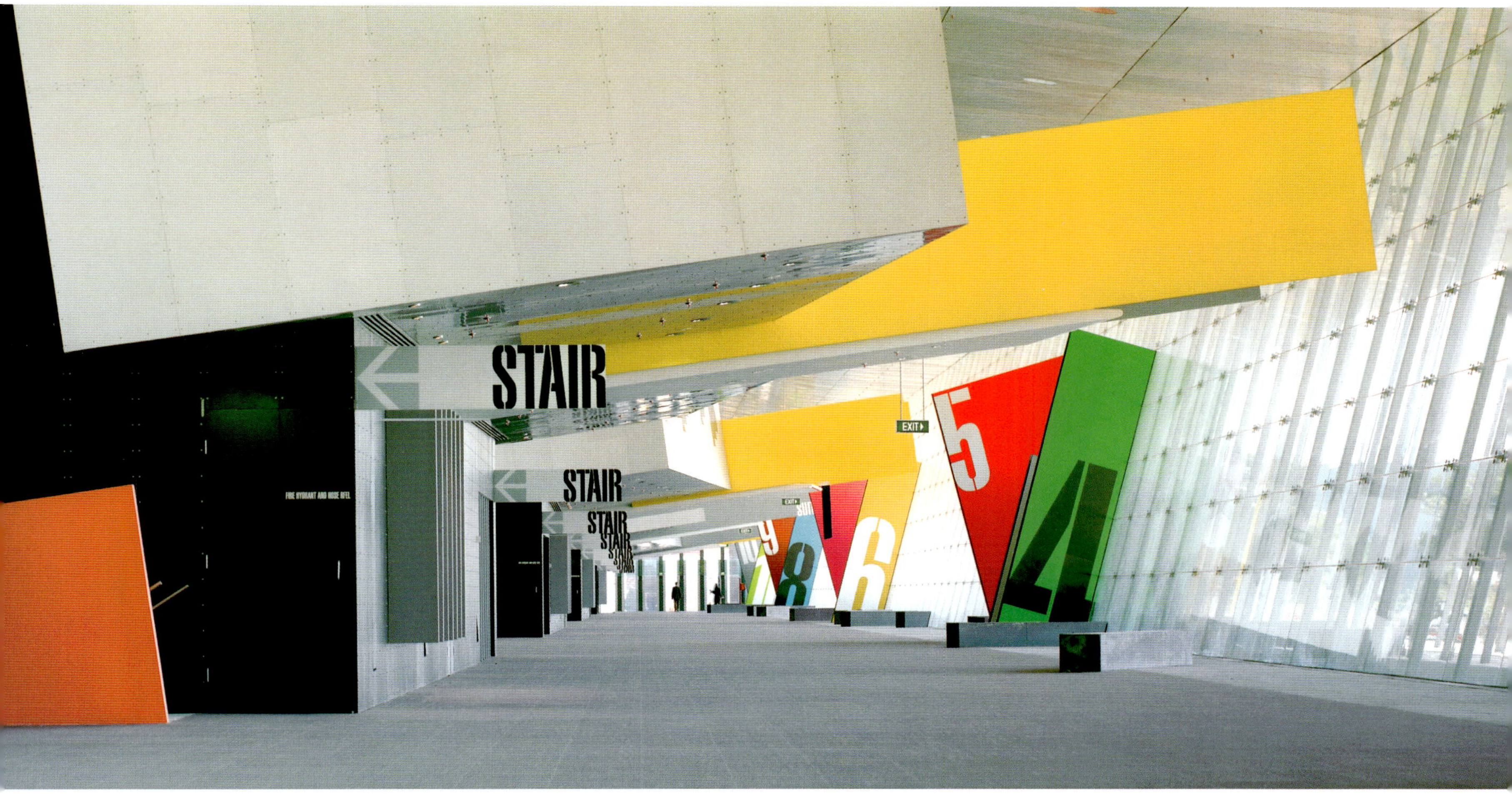
STAIR
STAIR
EXIT

Architect   **Fernando de Mello Franco, São Paulo**

Associated Architects   **Marta Moreira, Milton Braga, São Paulo**

Award Winning Building   **DPTO Propaganda & Marketing Building**

Location   **Rua Pio XI, 1473 São Paulo, Brazil**

Design and Construction Period   **1994**

Award   Best Built for Commercial Buildings

Given by   Instituto de Arquitetos do Brasil

Prize Presentation   March / 22 / 1995

Members of the Jury   Abrahão Sanovicz, Gianfranco Vanuchi, Wilis Myasaka,
   Décio Tozzi, Marília Santana de Almeida, Tio Lívio Frascino

Architecture and Interior Design   Fernando de Mello Franco, Marta Moreira,
   Milton Braga

Reinforced Pre-Cast Concrete   Consid

Containing Wall   Eling WallCast Conc

Metalwork   Rocha e Alves Engenharia e Consultoria de Projetos

Mechanical Engineering   Guimaro e Associados

Electrical Engineering   Guimaro e Associados

Approximate Cost   US$ 1,000,000

Site Area   500 m^2

Total Floor Area   800 m^2

Photographer   Walter Abreu

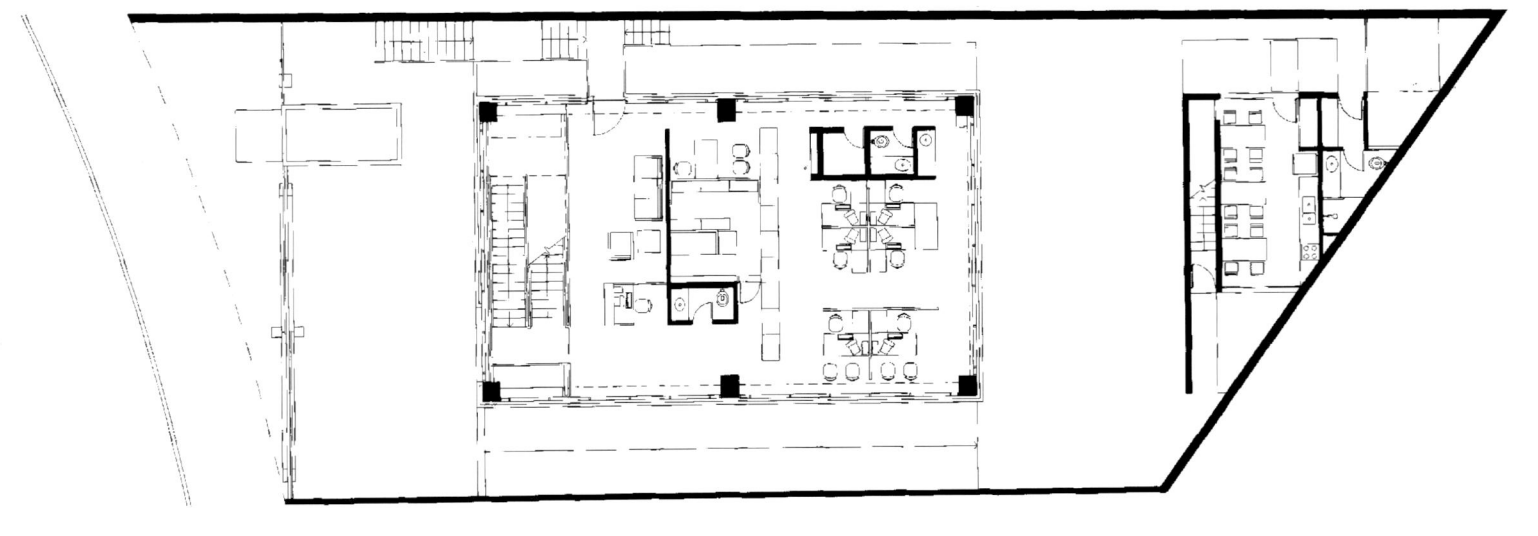

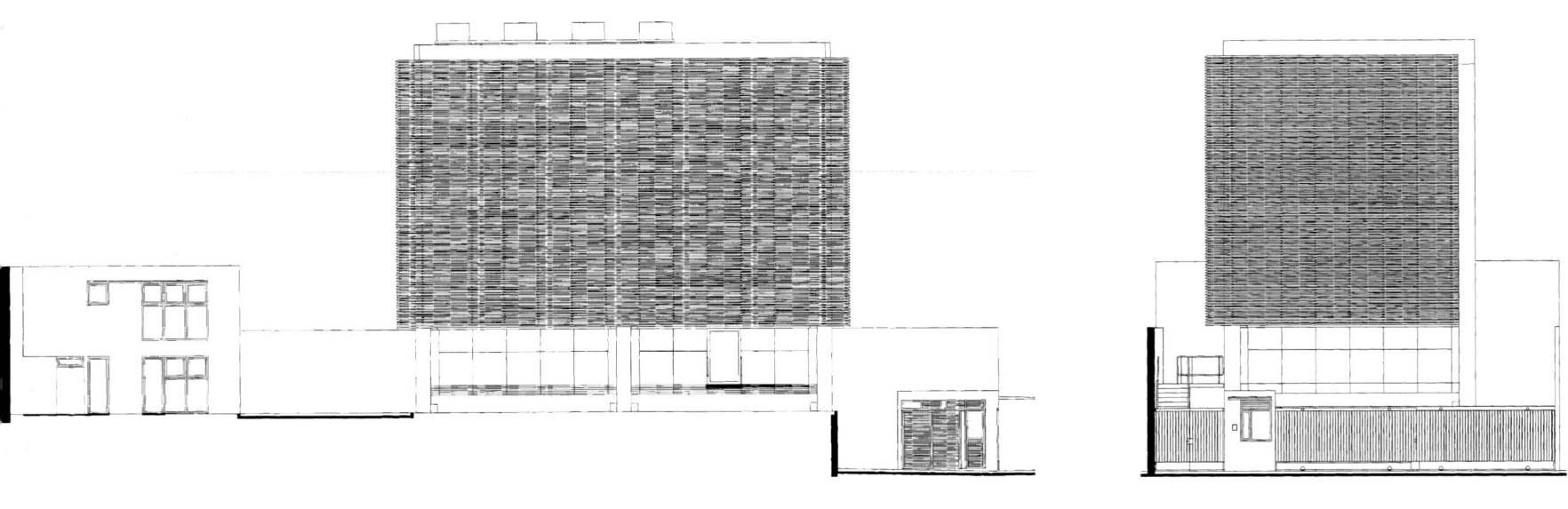

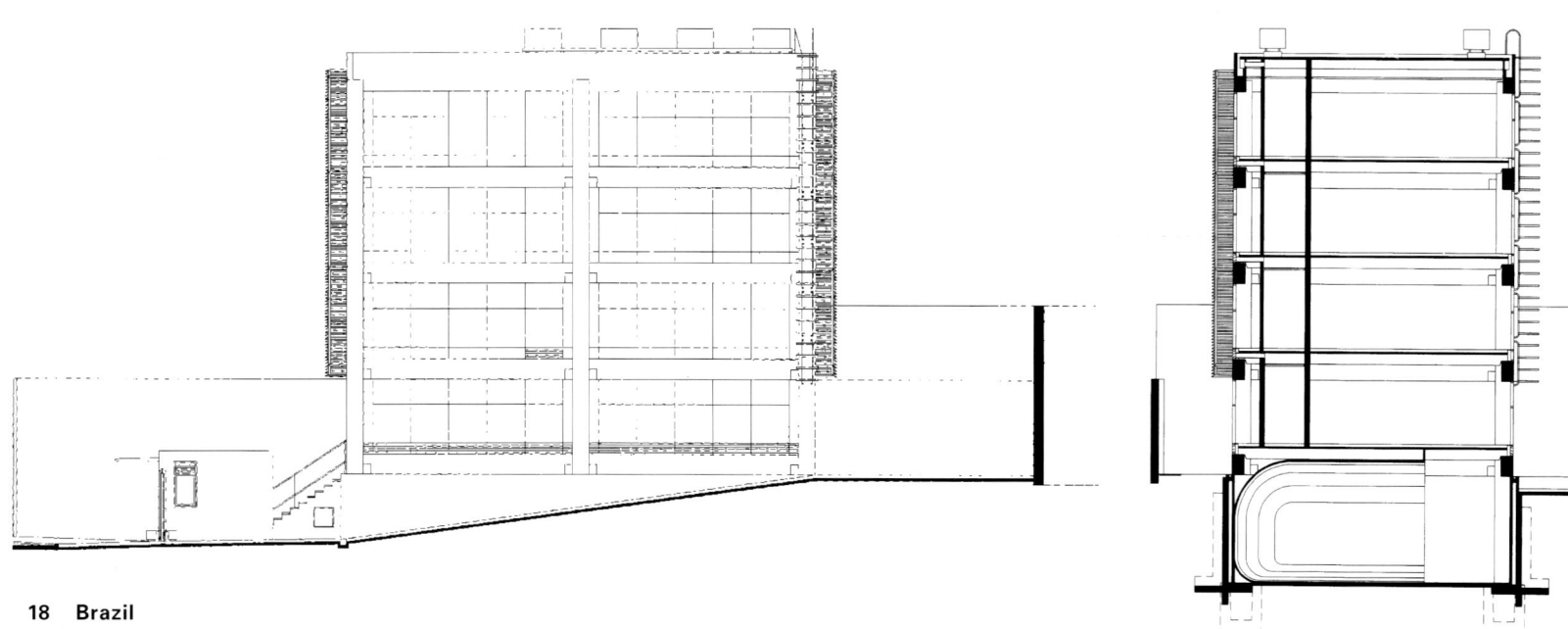

Architect **Otavio Leonídio Ribeiro, Rio de Janeiro**
Award Winning Building **Casa Pacelli**
Location **Búzios, Rio de Janeiro, Brazil**
Design and Construction Period **1994–1996**

Award Arquiteto Hélio Uchôa
Given by Instituto de Arquitetos do Brasil
Prize Presentation December / 13 / 1996
Members of the Jury Flávio Carsalade, Lilian Fessler Vaz, Nireu Cavalcanti,
   Túlio Mariante, Ernani Freire
Design Team Otavio Leonídio Ribeiro, assisted by Beatriz Rocha
Structural Engineering Paulo Cesar Soares
Civil Engineering Conchas Ltda. (George Clark)
Electrical Engineering Conchas Ltda. (George Clark)
Lighting Consultant Otavio Leonídio Ribeiro
Interior Design Otavio Leonídio Ribeiro
Landscape Architecture Otavio Leonídio Ribeiro
Approximate Cost US$ 250,000
Site Area 1,650 m²
Building Area 522 m²
Total Floor Area 700 m²

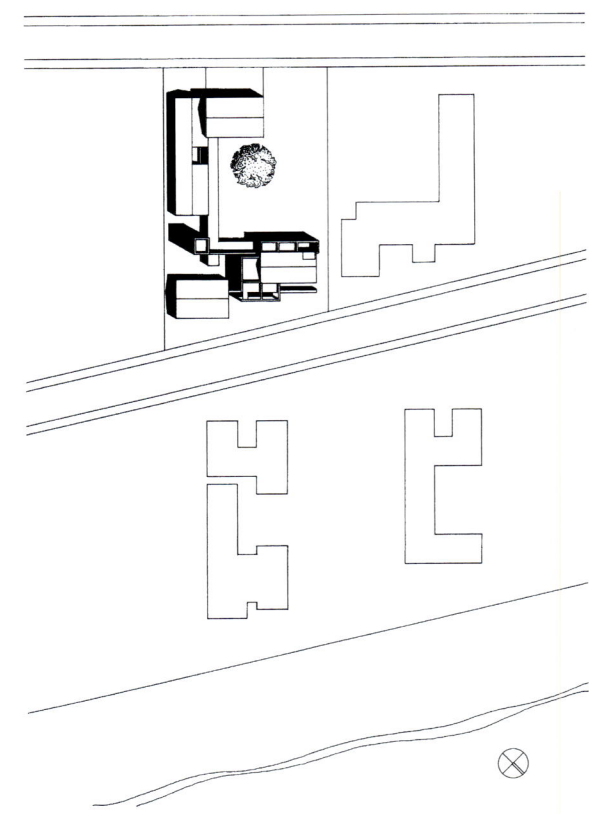

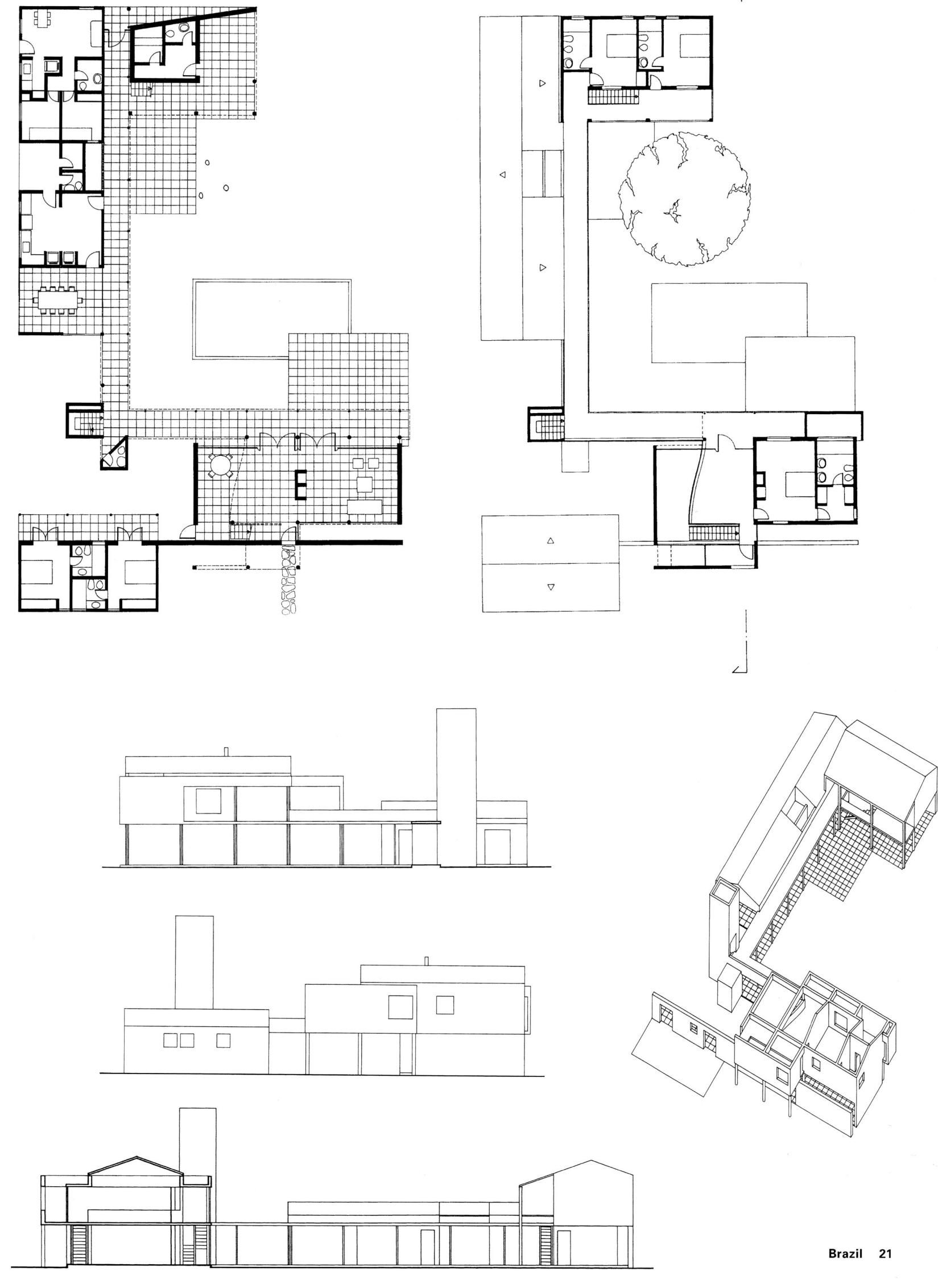

Architects **Les Architectes Boutros et Pratte, Montreal**

Award Winning Building **Plaza Laurier (Laurier Avenue)**

Location **Laurier Avenue, Montreal, Quebec, Canada**

Design and Construction Period **1992–1994**

Award 1997 Governor General's Award for Architecture

Given by The Royal Architectural Institute of Canada

Prize Presentation June 1997

Project Team Raouf Boutros (Principal in Charge), Normand Pratte,
 Christine Gervais, Robert Abou, Albert De Coen, Jean-Jacques Binoux

Structural Engineering Toutant, Ladouceur & Ass.

General Contractor Construction Cogerex, Montreal

Mechanical Engineering St-Amant, Vézina, Vinet, Brassard et ass.

Electrical Engineering St-Amant, Vézina, Vinet, Brassard et ass.

Site Area 630 m²

Building Area 410 m²

Total Floor Area 1,230 m²

Photographer Yves Lefebvre

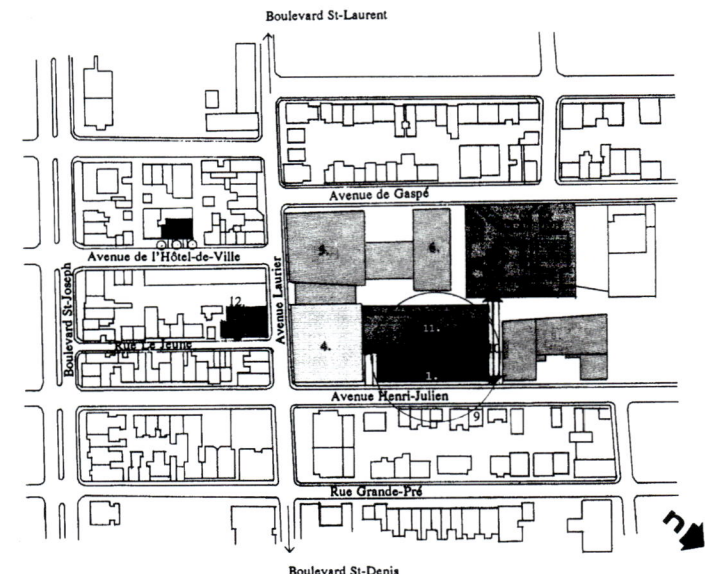

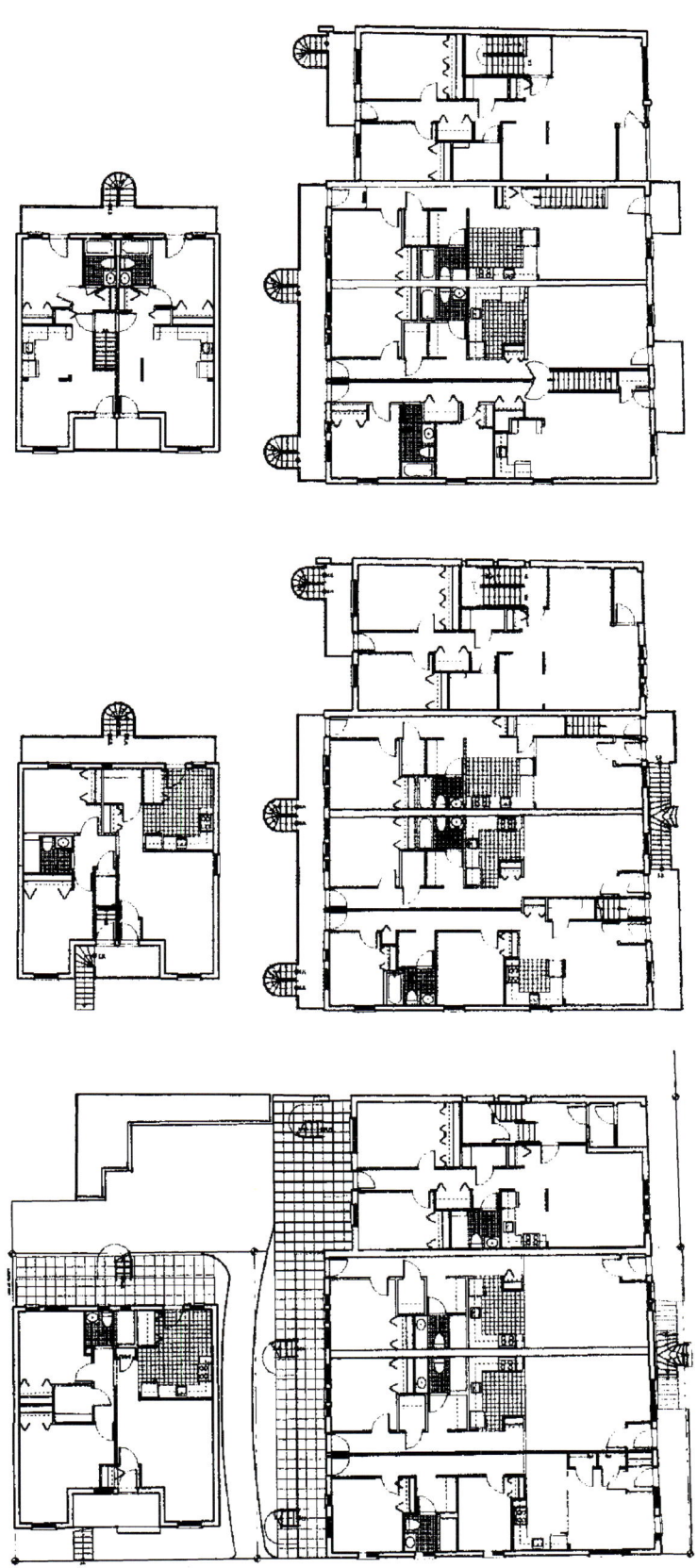

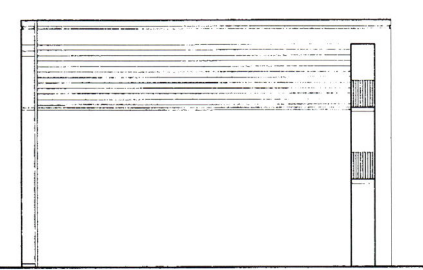

Architects **Montgomery and Sisam Architects, Toronto**

Award Winning Building **The Humber River Bicycle Pedestrian Bridge**

Location **Toronto, Ontario, Canada**

Design and Construction Period **1992–1994**

Award 1997 Governor General's Award for Architecture

Given by The Royal Architectural Institute of Canada

Prize Presentation June 1997

Members of the Jury Douglas Cardinal, Ken Greenberg, Dan Hanganu,
  Phyllis Lambert, Christine Macy, Abraham Zabludovsky

Design Team Terry Montgomery, David Sisam, Robert Davies, Santiago Kunzle

Structural Engineering Delcan Corporation

Civil Engineering Delcan Corporation

Landscape Architecture Ferris and Quinn Associates Inc.

Artists Brad Golden and Lynne Eichenberg

Length of clear arch span 100 m

Length of deck (distance between abutments) 115.2 m

Total length of bridge including approach plazas 139.2 m

Width of deck between railings 6.5 m

Diameter of steel tubes 1.22 m

Wall thickness of steel tubes (varies) 18-25 mm

Diameter of stainless steel hanger rods 51 mm

Height of arch above arch base 21 m

Height of deck above water (based on 100 year flood) 4.8 m

Photographer Design Archive (Robert Burley)

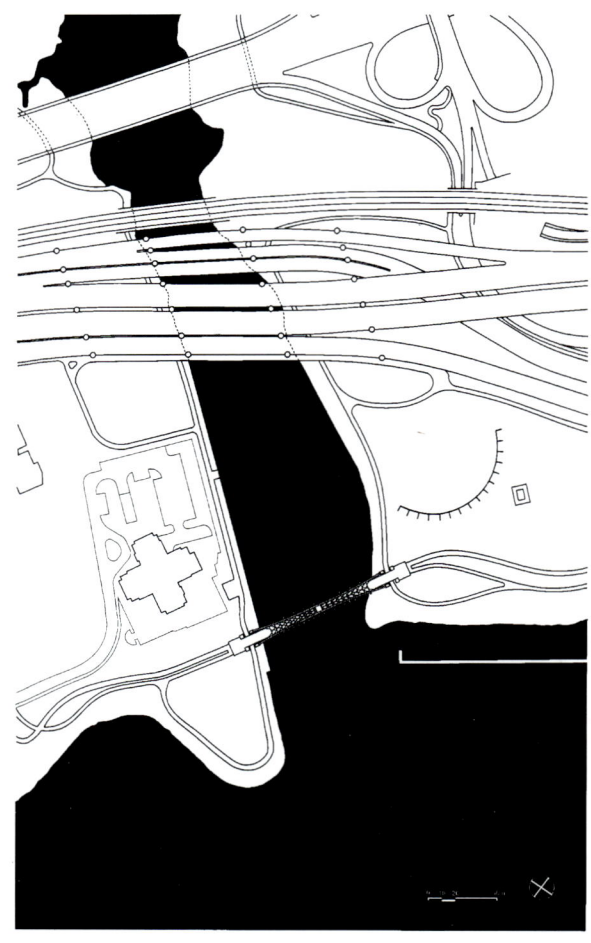

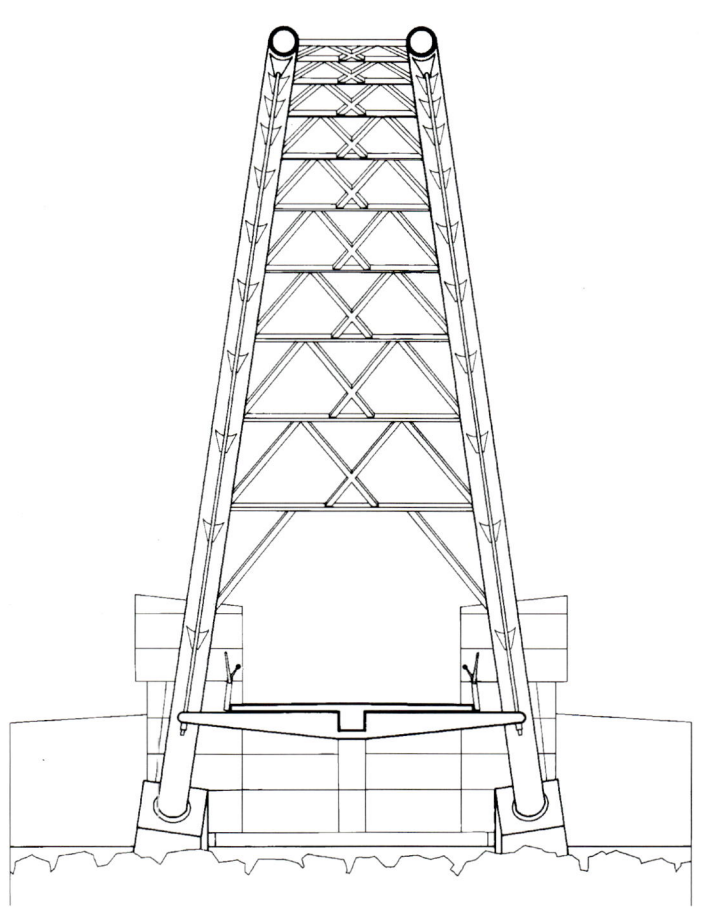

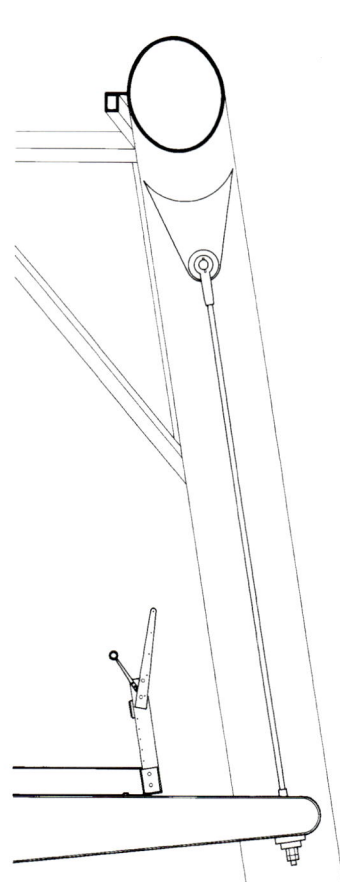

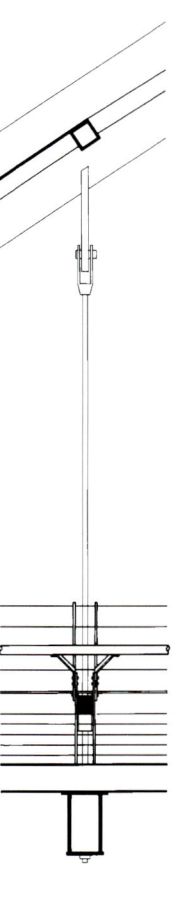

Architect **Pierre Thibault, Quebec**
Award Winning Building **Queen of Heart Theatre /**
  Théâtre de la Dame de Cœur
Location **Upton, Quebec, Canada**
Design and Construction Period **1995**

Award 1997 Governor General's Award for Architecture
Given by The Royal Architectural Institute of Canada
Prize Presentation June 1997
Members of the Jury Phyllis Lambert, Dan Hanganu
Design Team Pierre Thibault, Eric Thibodeau, Jean-François Fortin,
  André Limoge
Structural Engineering Groupe Technika
Civil Engineering Groupe Technika
Landscape Architecture Pierre Thibault
Approximate Cost CAN$ 1,200,000
Site Area 10,000 m²
Building Area 1,500 m²
Photographer Alain Laforest

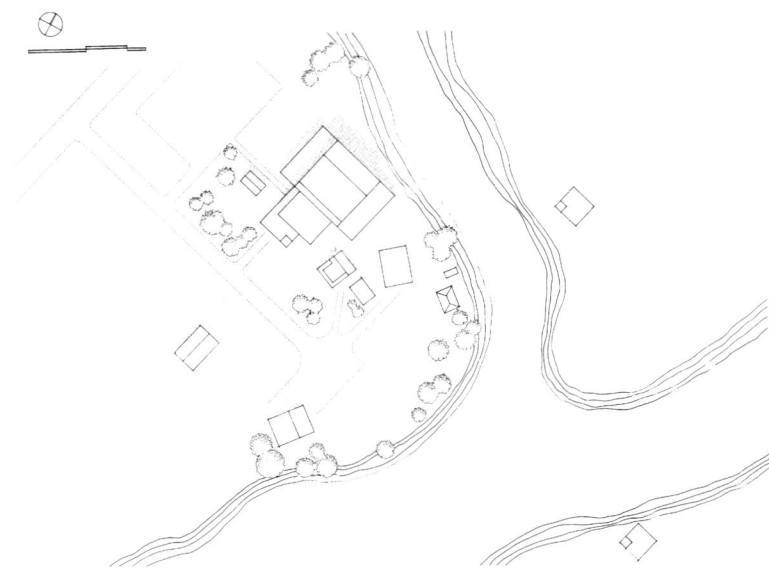

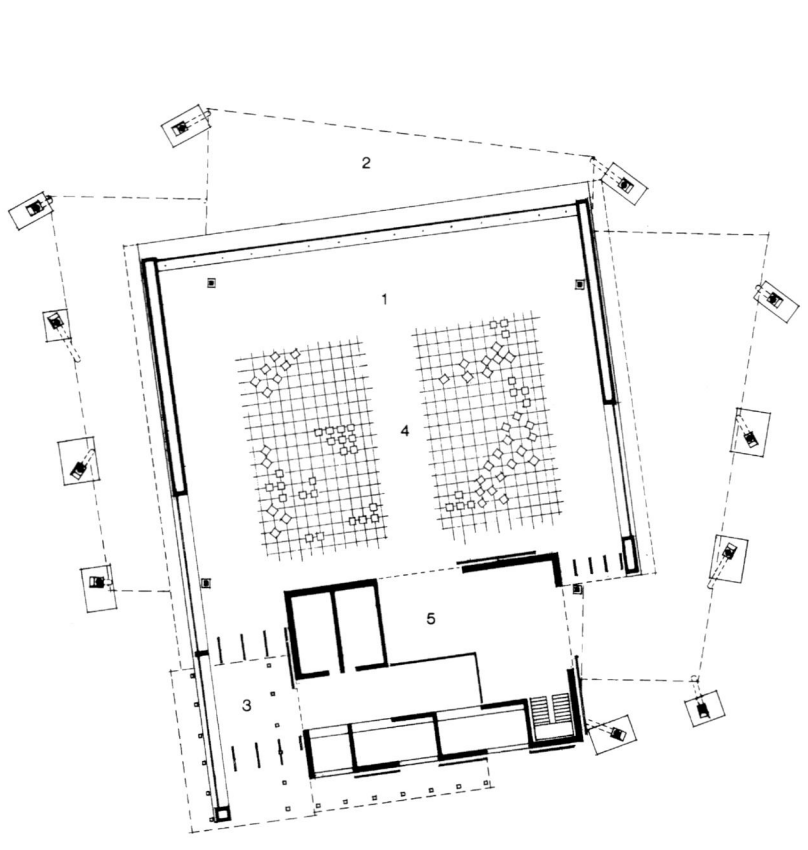

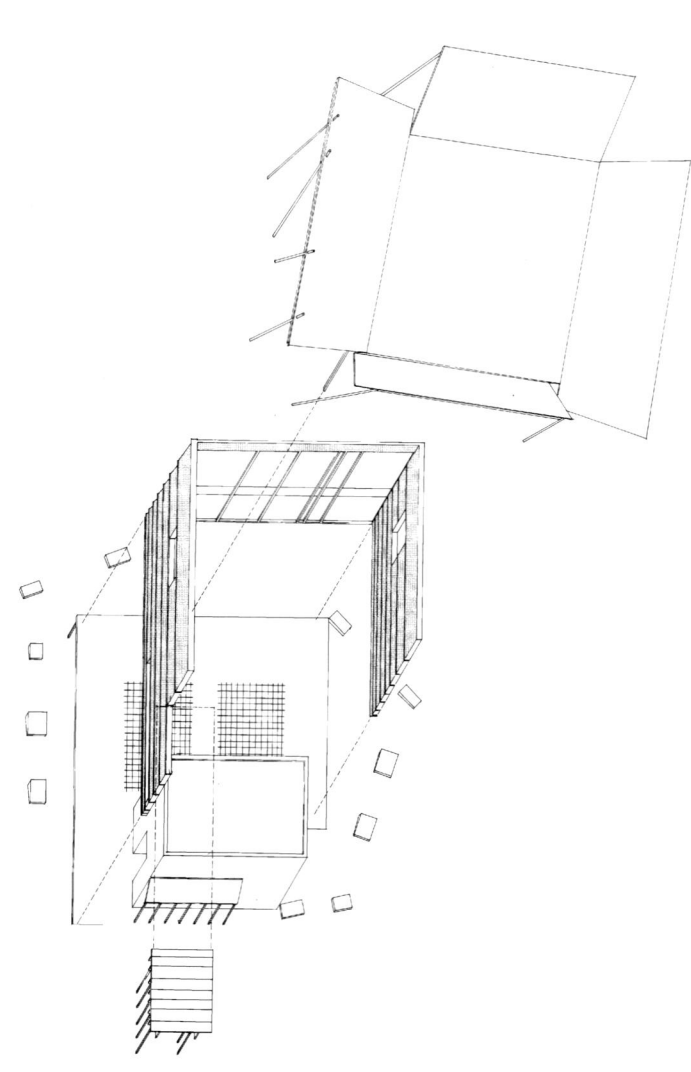

Architects   **Brigitte Shim and Howard Sutcliffe, Toronto**
Award Winning Building   **Craven Road House**
Location   **Toronto, Canada**
Design and Construction Period   **1995–1996**

Award   1997 Governor General's Award for Architecture
Given by   The Royal Architectural Institute of Canada
Prize Presentation   June 1997
Members of the Jury   Douglas Cardinal, Ken Greenberg, Dan Hanganu,
   Phyllis Lambert, Christine Macy, Abraham Zabludovsky
Design Team   Brigitte Shim and Howard Sutcliffe
Structural Engineering   Ned Onen
Millwork   Radiant City Millwork
Approximate Cost   CAN$ 100,000
Site Area   25 ft. by 90 ft.
Total Building Area   1,100 sq. ft.
Photographer   Michael Award Architecture / Photography, Robert Hill

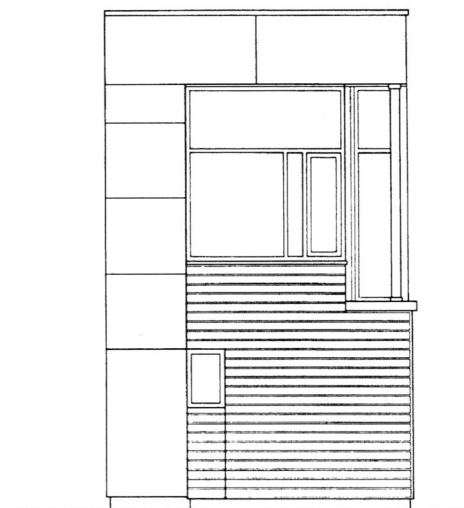
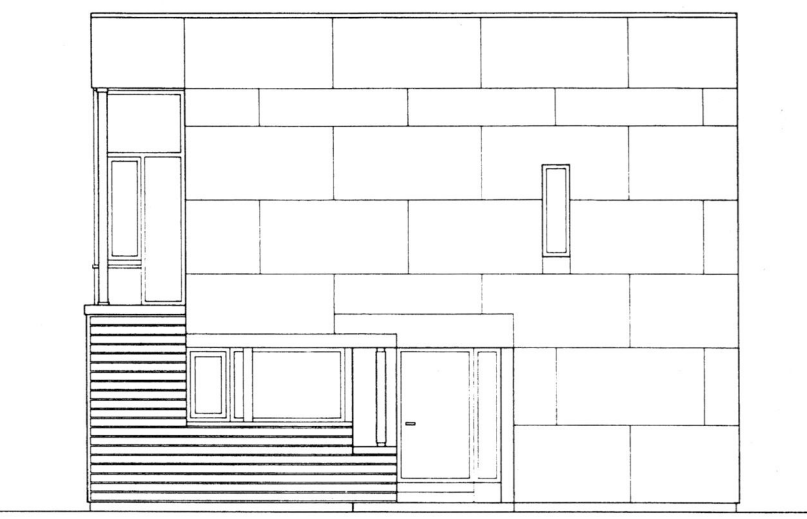

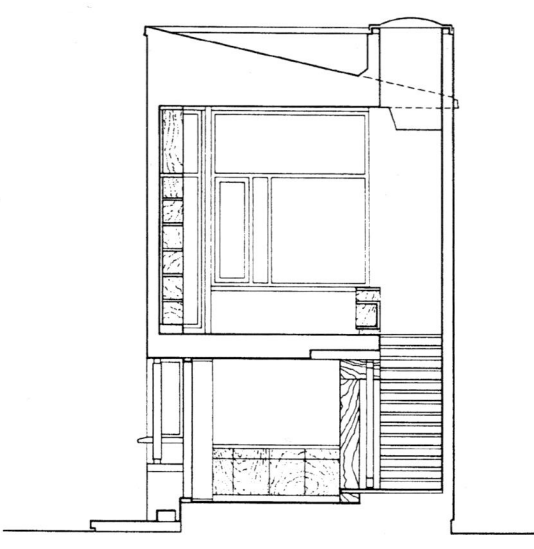
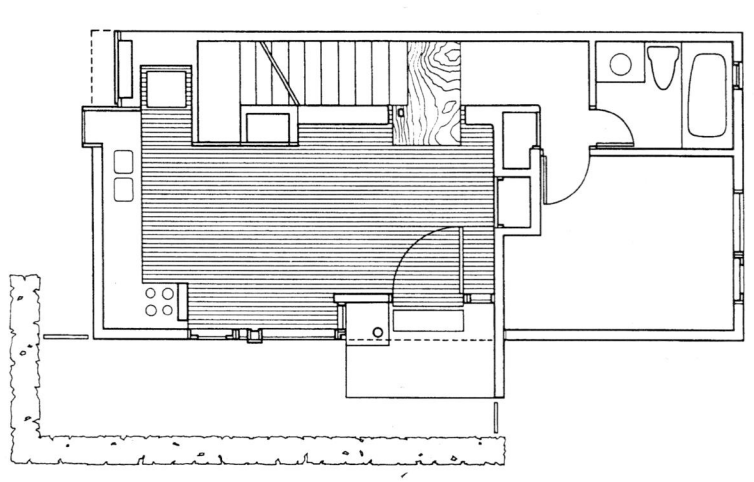

Architects **Jiménez & Cortés Boshell, Bogota**

Award Winning Building **Edificio Av. 82**

Location **Av. 82 No. 7-42, Bogota, Colombia**

Design and Construction Period **1993–1996**

Award Premio Nacional de Diseño Arquitectonico, XV Bienal De Arquitectura

Given by Sociedad Colombiana de Arquitectos

Prize Presentation May / 24 / 1996

Members of the Jury Antonio Cruz Villalón (Spain), Carlos Jiménez Cordero
(Costa Rica), German Samper Gnecco (Colombia), Rodrigo Tascón (Colombia),
Juan Felipe Gomez (Colombia)

Design Team Ernesto Jiménez, Tatiana Meléndez

Structural Engineering P & D Ingenieros

Mechanical Engineering Hisan Ltda

Electrical Engineering Coeleng Ltda

Air Conditioning Consultant Alvaro Tapias

Approximate Cost US$ 6,500,000

Site Area 2,304 m²

Building Area 1,080 m²

Total Floor Area 11,000 m²

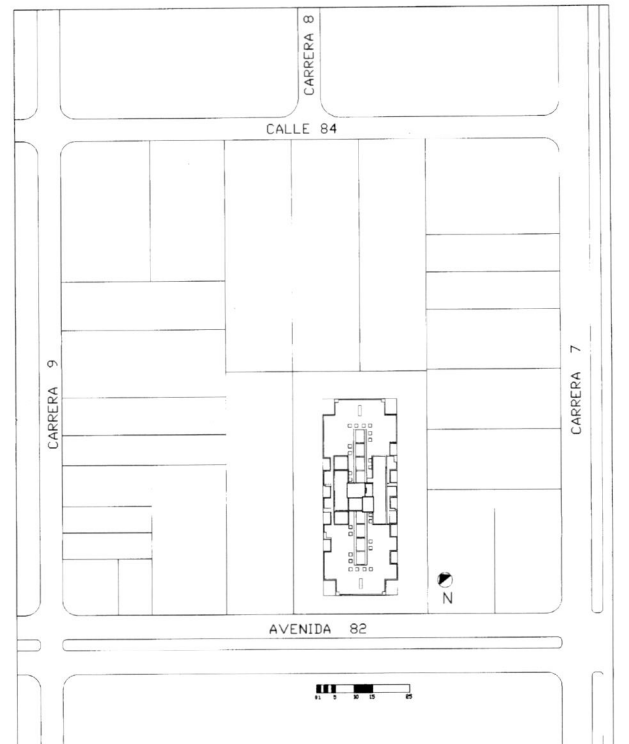

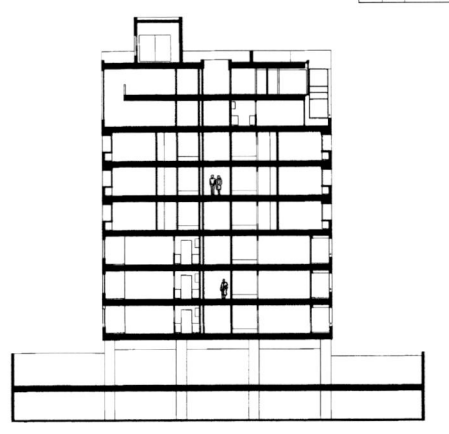

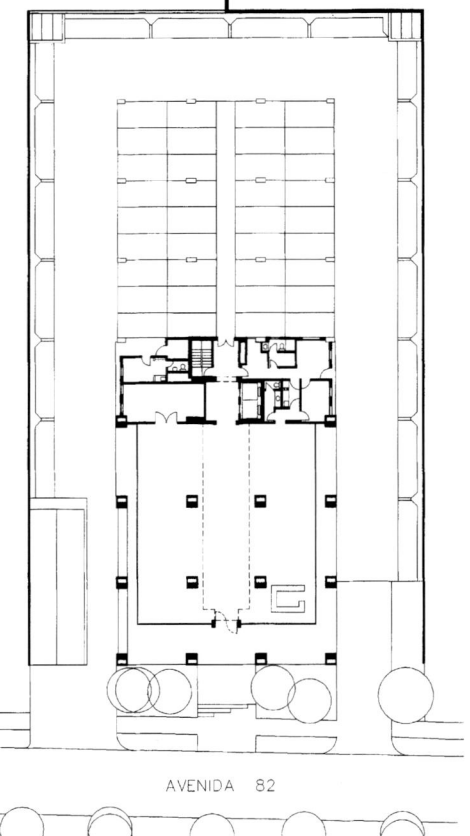

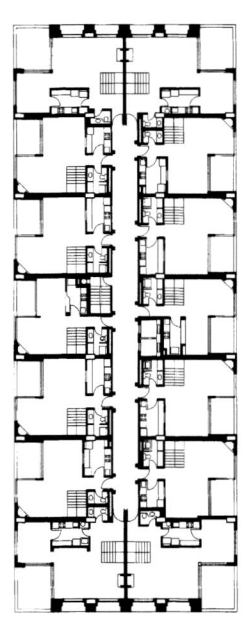

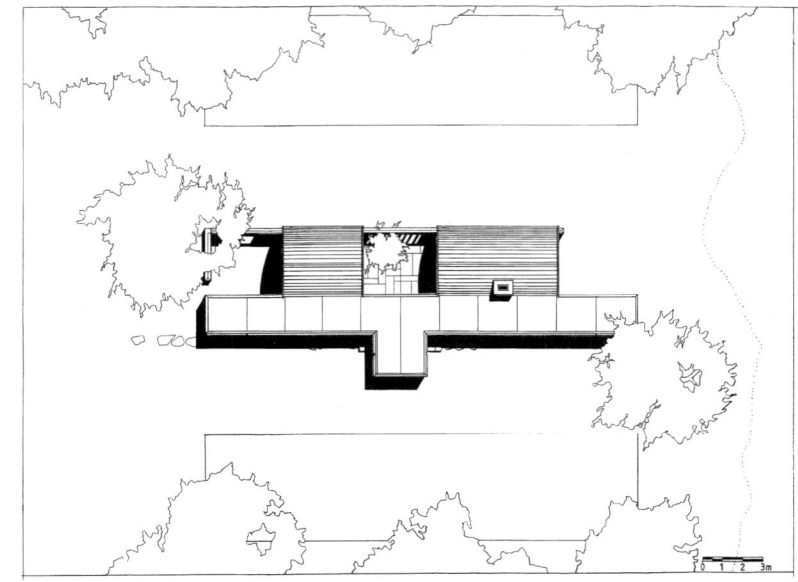

Architect **Sverre Fehn, Oslo**

Award Winning Building **Eco House**

Location **Mauritzberg, Sweden**

Design and Construction Period **1991–1992**

Award Den Grønne Nål

Given by Danske Arkitekters Landsforbund / Akademisk Arkitektforenings
(DAL / AA)

Prize Presentation Spring 1996

Members of the Jury Charlotte Weile (Chair), Bodil Vilholm Henningsen,
Mogens Harttung, Peter Dahl Nielsen, Cris Fløe Svenningsen

Design Team Sverre Fehn in collaboration with Henrik Hille

Civil Engineering Terje Orlien

Mechanical Engineering Terje Orlien

Lighting Consultant Sverre Fehn

Interior Design Sverre Fehn

Landscape Architecture Sverre Fehn

Building Area 52 m²

Total Floor Area 52 m²

Photographer Henrik Hille

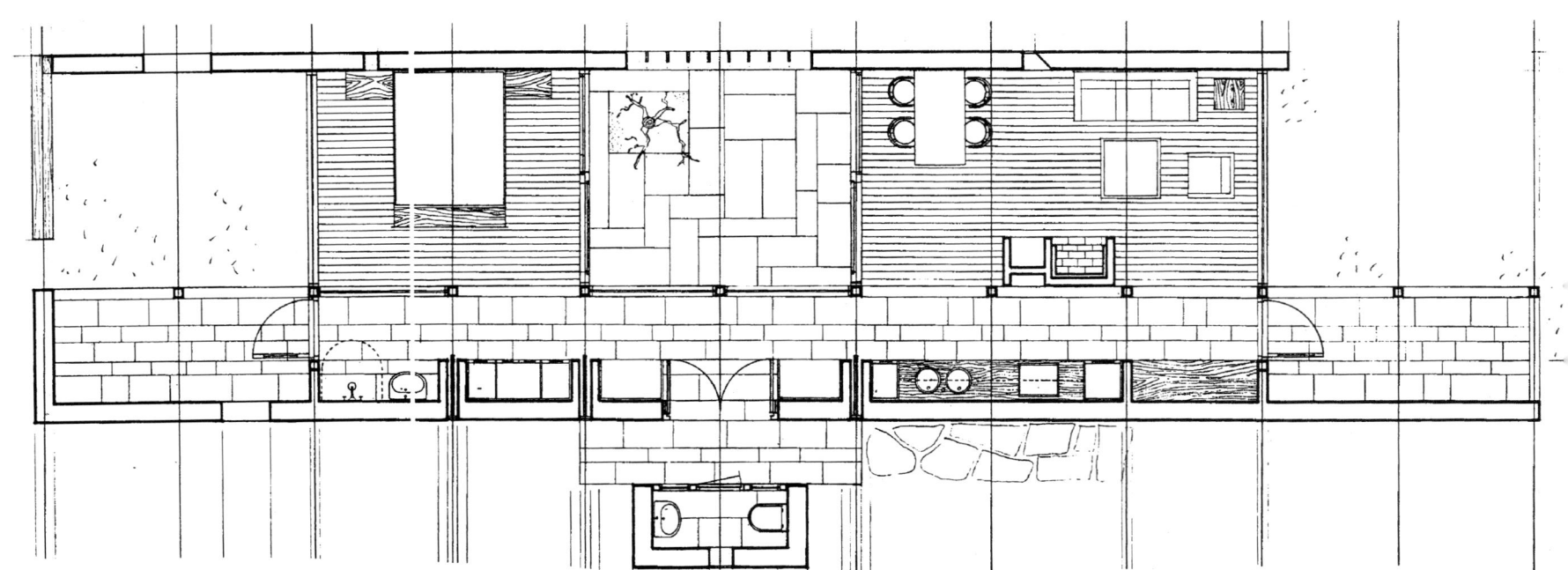

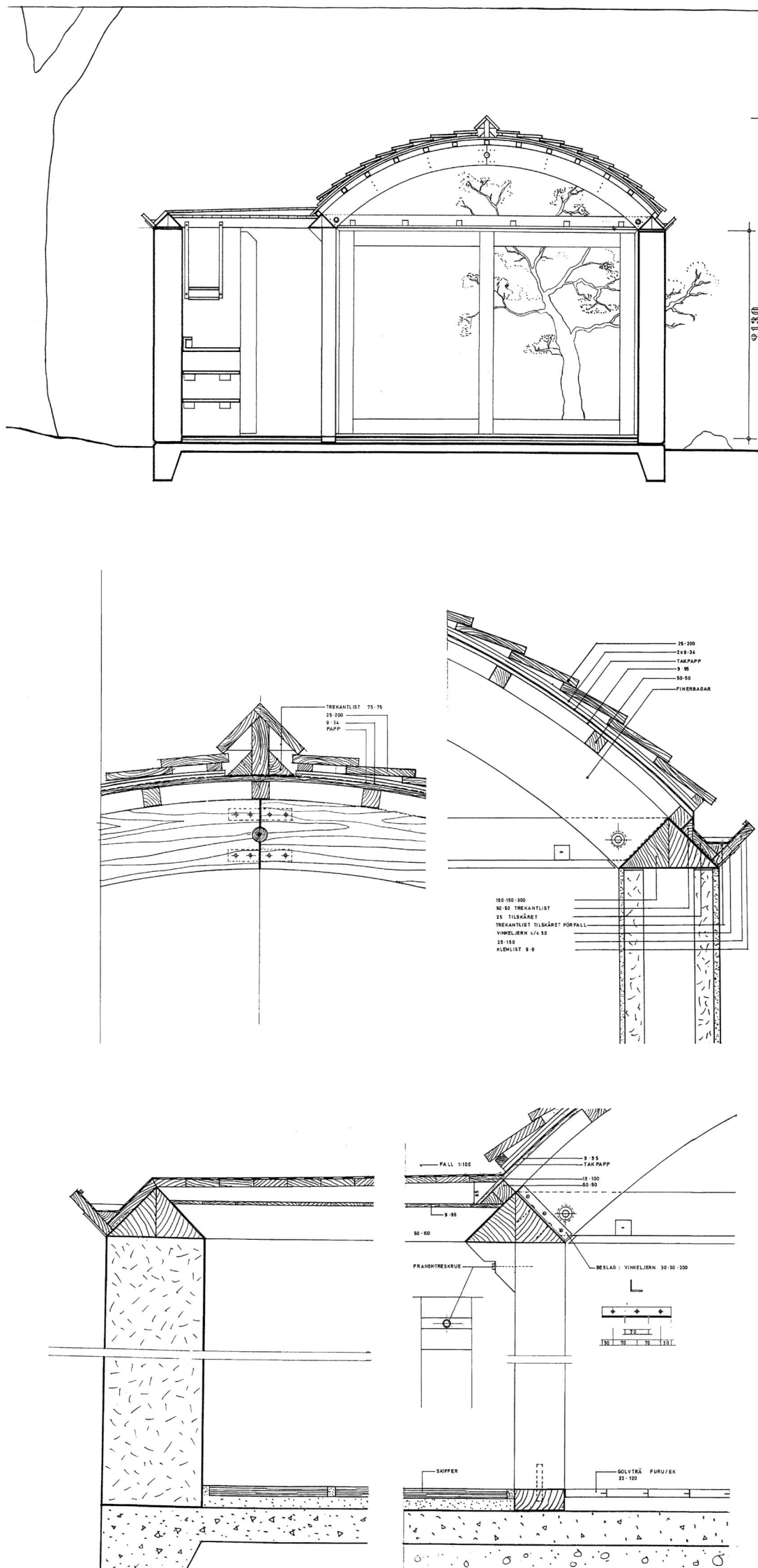

TREKANTLIST 75·75
25·200
9·34
PAPP

25·200
2×9·34
TAKPAPP
9·95
50·50
FINERBÄGAR

150·150·300
50·50 TREKANTLIST
25 TILSKÅRET
TREKANTLIST TILSKÅRET FÖR FALL
VINKELJERN c/c 50
25·150
KLEMLIST 9·9

FALL 1:100

9·95
TAK.PAPP
·19·100
50·50

9·95

50·100

FRANSK:TRESKRUE

BESLAG : VINKELJERN 30·30·200

SKIFFER

GOLVTRÄ FURU/EK
22·120

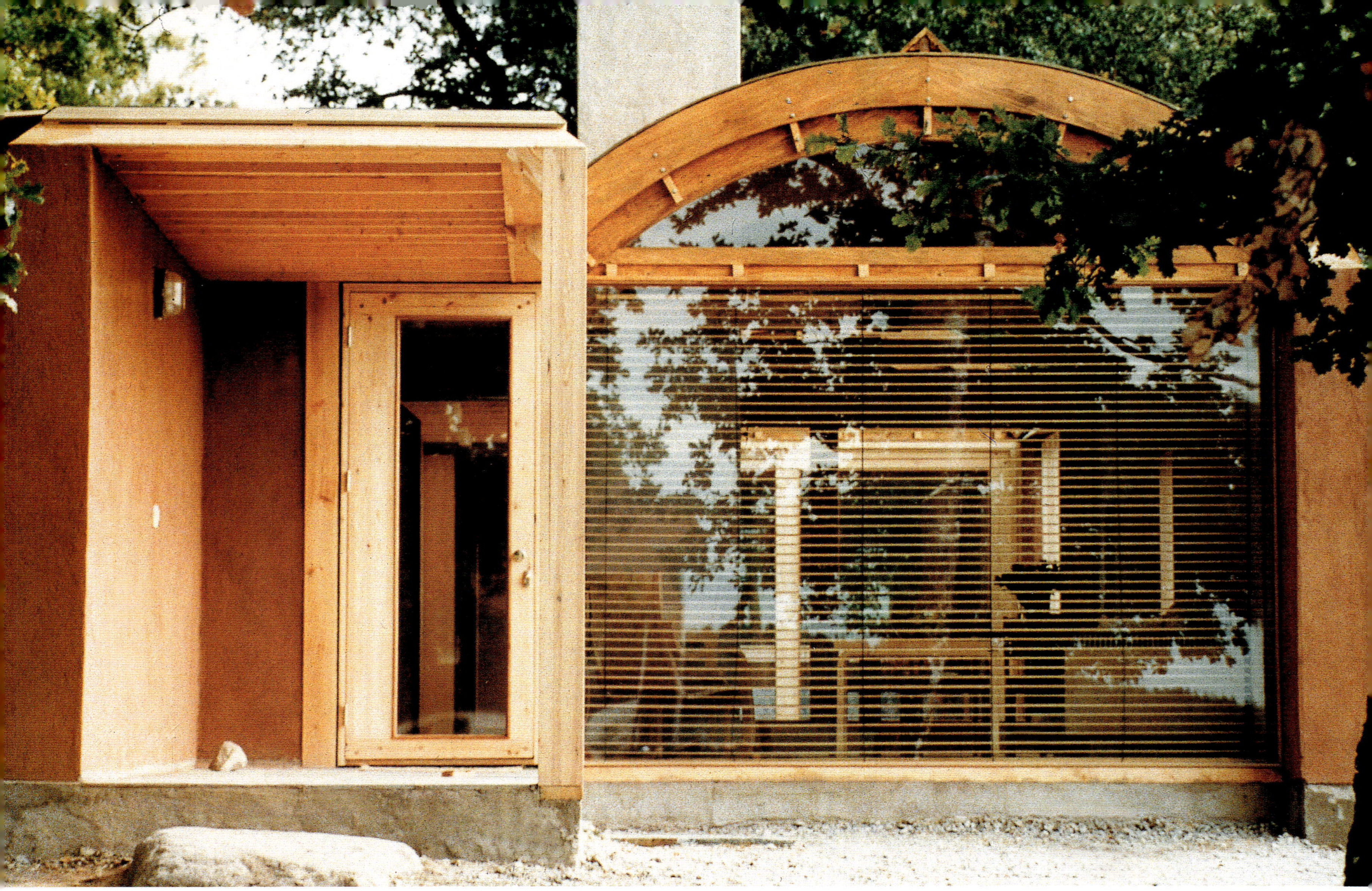

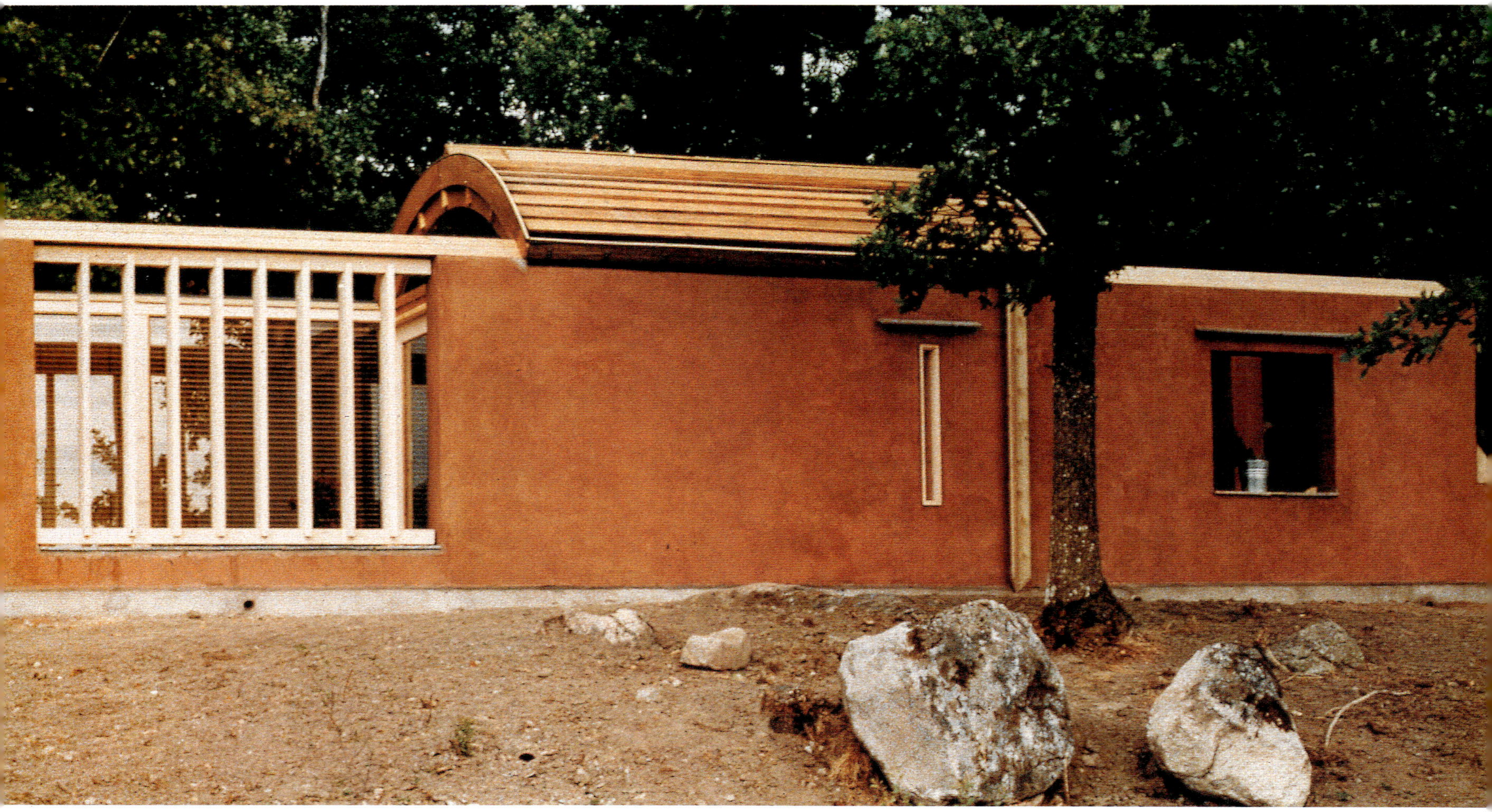

Architects   **Boje Lundgaard & Lene Tranberg ApS, Copenhagen**

Award Winning Building   **Apartment House (urban renewal)**

Location   **Dannebrogsgade 18, 1660 Copenhagen V, Denmark**

Design and Construction Period   **1992**

Award   Den Grønne Nål

Given by   Danske Arkitekters Landsforbund (DAL)

Prize Presentation   April / 25 / 1996

Members of the Jury   Charlotte Weile (Chair), Bodil Vilholm Hennigsen,
   Mogens Harttung, Peter Dahl Nielssen, Cris Fløe Svenningsen

Design Team   Erik Frandsen, Filip Heiberg, Ole Justesen, Peter Thorsen

Glass Facade   Danluk, Ølstykke, and Boje Lundgaard & Lene Tranberg

Solar Collector   Batec A/S, Herfølge

Rain Reception System   Dominia A/S, Copenhagen

Structural Engineering   Dominia A/S, Copenhagen

Civil Engineering   Dominia A/S, Copenhagen

Mechanical Engineering   Dominia A/S, Copenhagen

Electrical Engineering   Dominia A/S, Copenhagen

Environmental Engineering   Dominia A/S, Copenhagen

Acoustic Engineering   Dominia A/S, Copenhagen

Air Conditioning Consultant   Dominia A/S, Copenhagen

Lighting Consultant   Dominia A/S, Copenhagen

Life Safety Consultant   Dominia A/S, Copenhagen

Interior Design   Boje Lundgaard & Lene Tranberg (Kitchens and bathrooms)

Approximate Cost   DKR 12,000,000

Building Area   186 m²

Total Floor Area   902 m²

Photographers   Jens Lindhe, Søren Kuhn, Morten Kjærgaard,
   Eva Kjærgaard

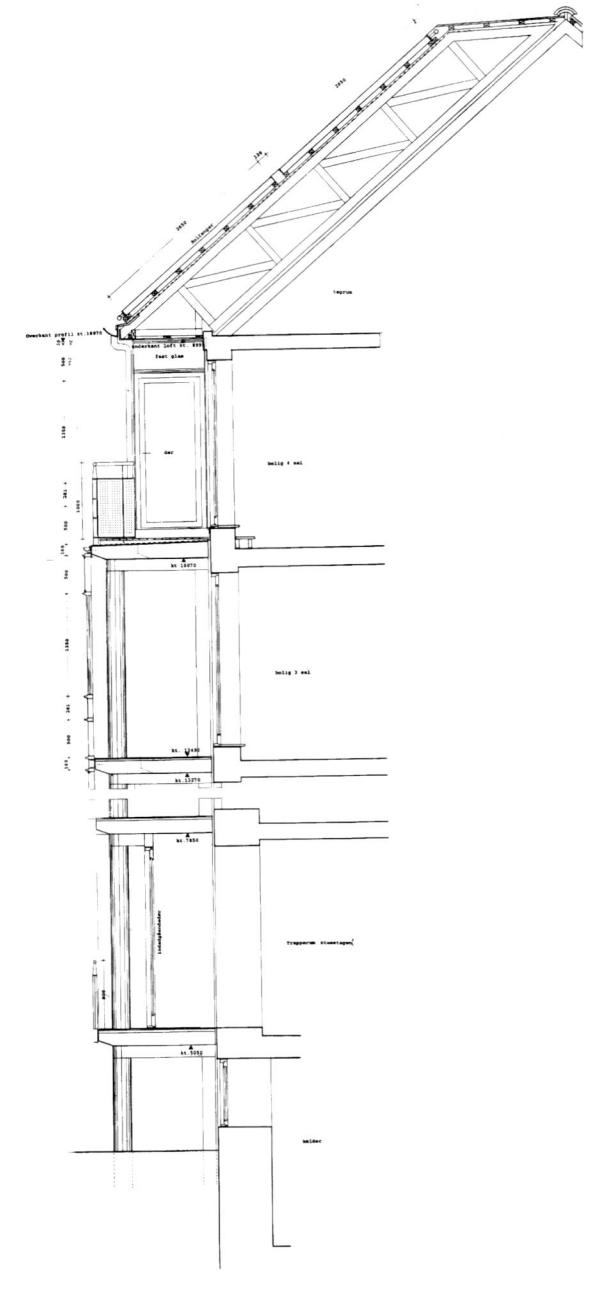

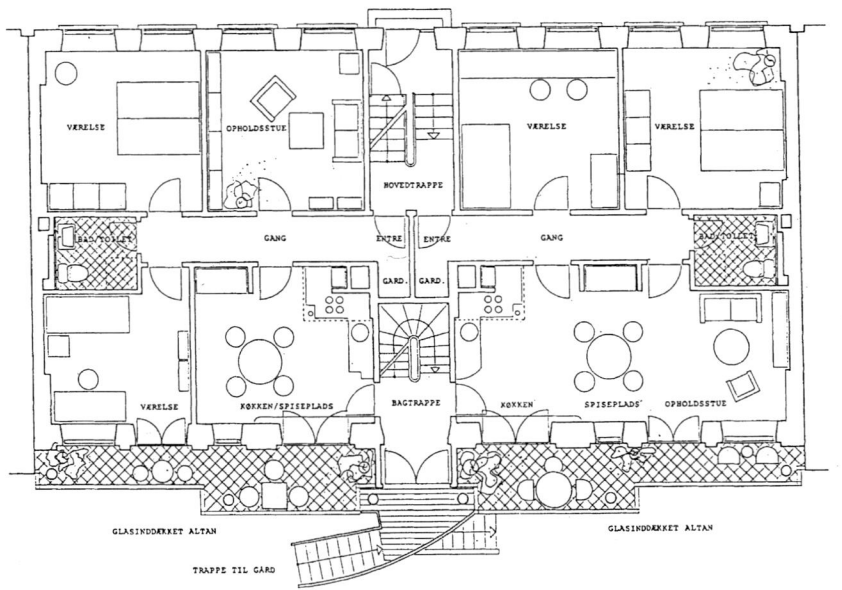

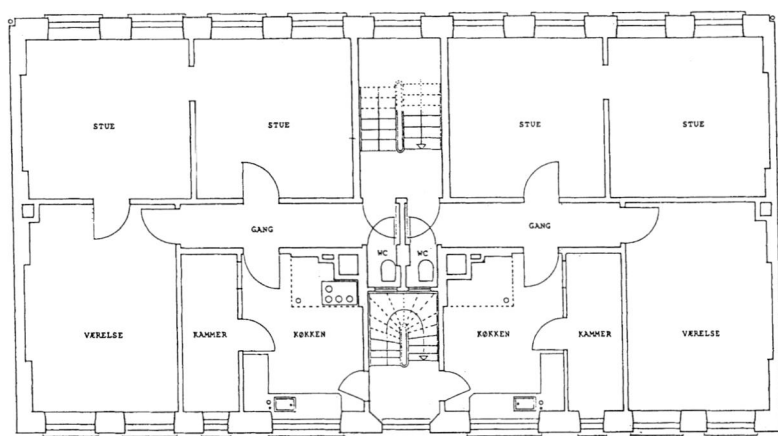

r=3900
kt.5090
35,75°
kt.3470
r=3900
2803,5
A
A
B
B
250
C
C

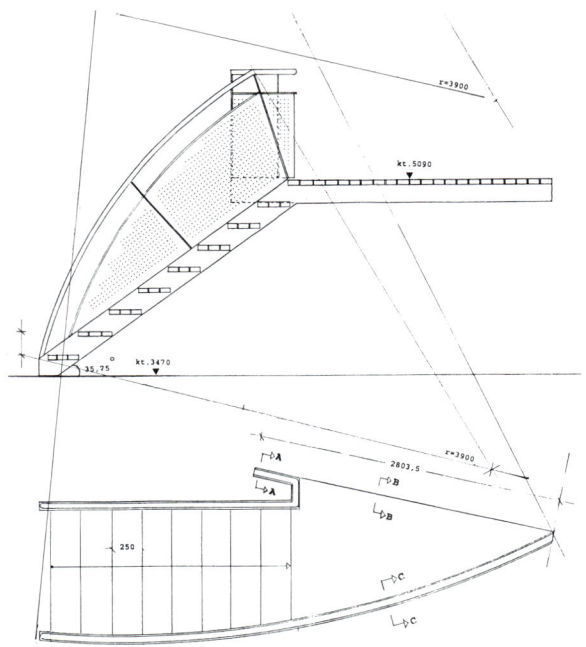

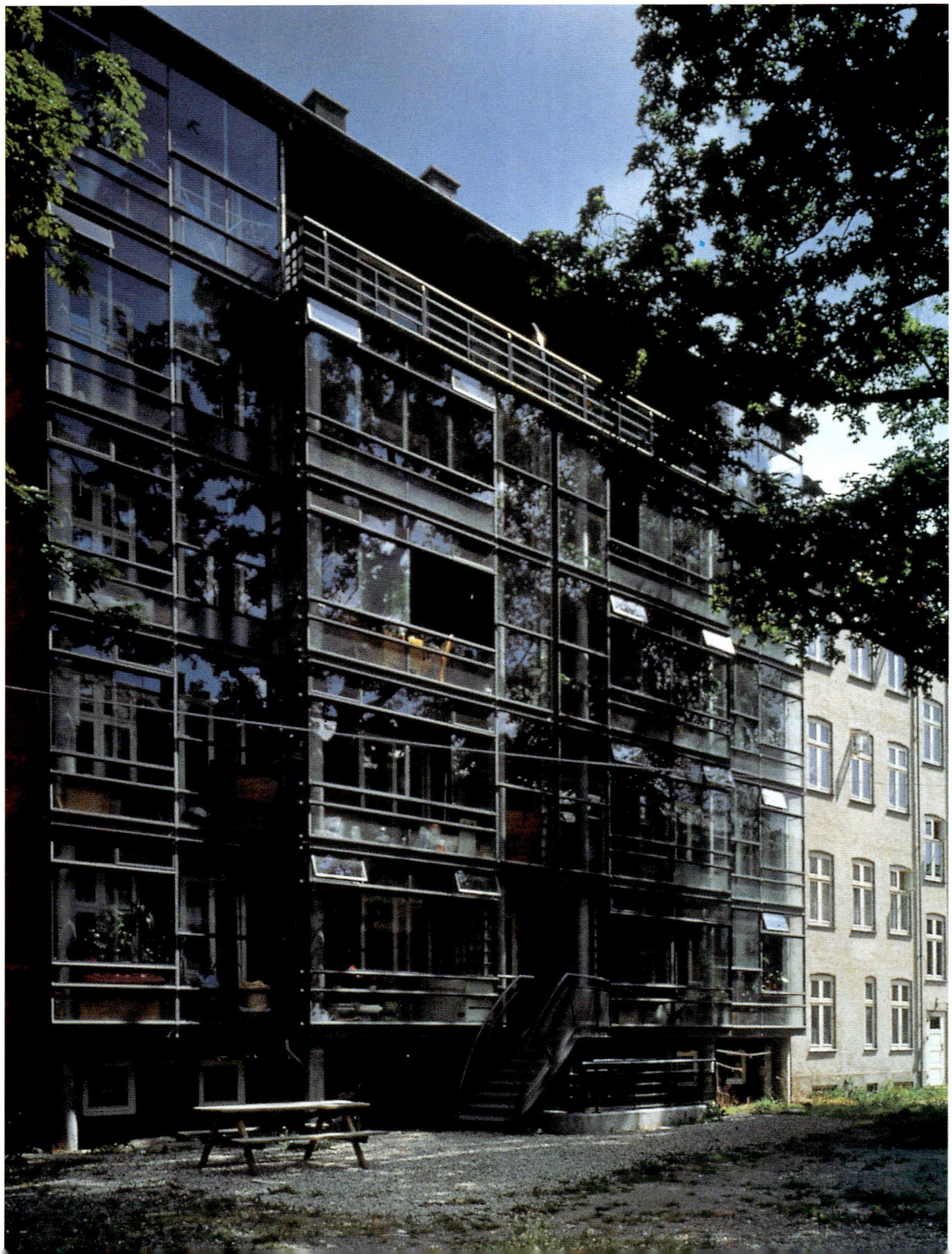

Architects **Fabrice Dusapin & François Leclercq, Paris**

Award Winning Building **CNP Service Centre and Public Garden**

Location **Angers, France**

Design and Construction Period **1990–1996**

Award Prix Special du Jury

Given by Le Moniteur

Prize Presentation November 1996

Members of the Jury Marc-Noël Vigier (Président, Le Moniteur), Architects:
  Christian De Portzamparc, Bernard Tschumi, Jacques Lucan and Jeremy
  Dixon, Critics: Manuel Gausa (Quaderns), Geert Bekaert (Archis), Bertrand
  Lemoine (AMC), Professional: Francis Ampe (Agence de Développement et
  d'Urbanisme de la Communauté Urbaine de Lille)

Design Team Fabrice Dusapin & François Leclercq, Philippe Croisier et
  Bernard Tournier Lasserve

Structural Engineering Marc Mimram Ingénierie

Civil Engineering Noble Ingénierie

Mechanical Engineering Noble Ingénierie

Electrical Engineering Noble Ingénierie

Environmental Engineering Fabrice Dusapin & François Leclercq

Acoustic Engineering Capri Acoustique

Air Conditioning Consultant Noble Ingénierie

Lighting Consultant Roger Narboni

Life Safety Consultant Socotec

Interior Design Fabrice Dusapin & François Leclercq

Landscape Architecture Phusis

Quantity Surveying Marc Mimram Ingénierie

Approximate Cost FF 149,000,000

Site Area 10,560 m^2

Building Area 4,312 m^2 (building) + 5,033 m^2 (parking and technical area)

Total Floor Area 17,000 m^2

Photographer Jean-Marie Monthiers

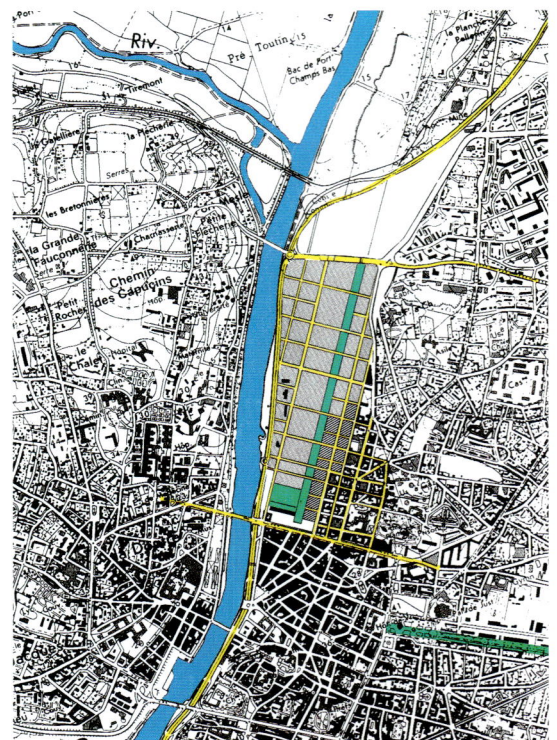

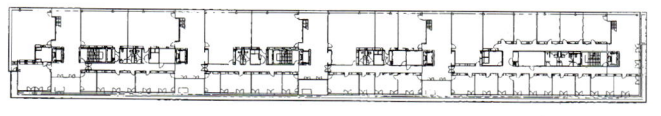

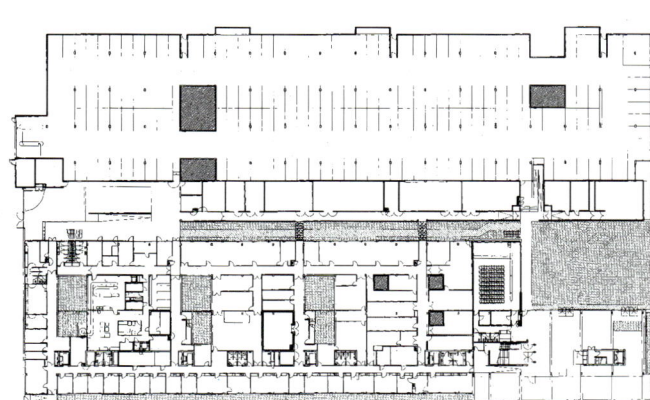

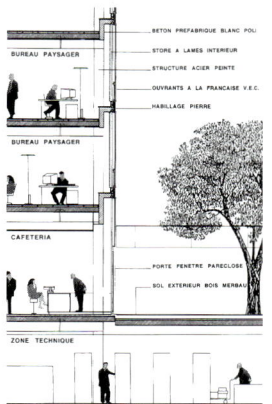

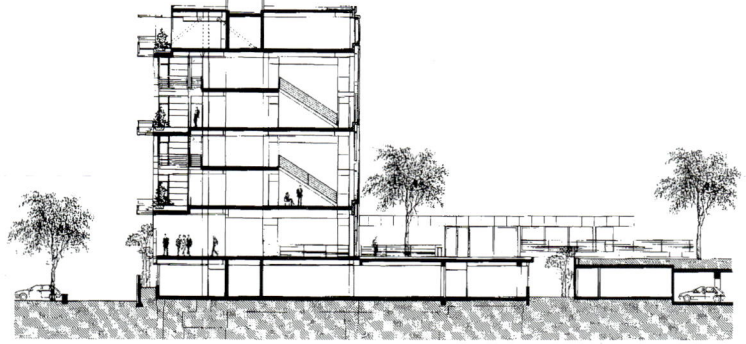

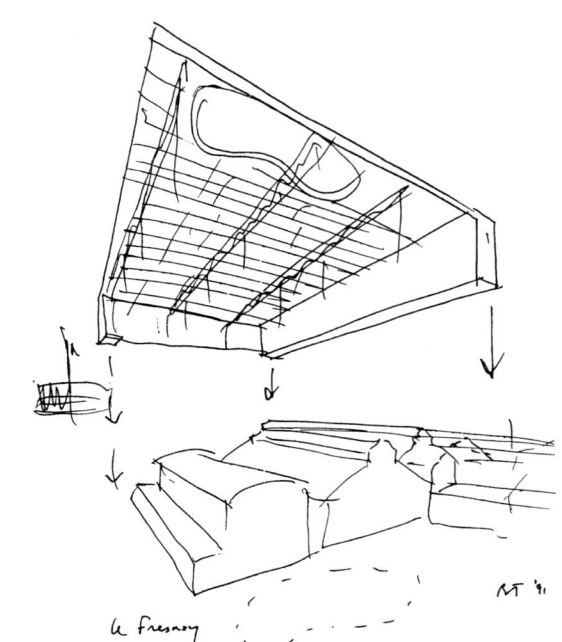

Architect **Bernard Tschumi, Paris**

Award Winning Building **Le Fresnoy, National Studio for Contemporary Arts, Le Fresnoy**

Location **Tourcoing, France**

Design and Construction Period **1991–1997**

Award 1996 Grand Prix National d'Architecture

Given by French Ministry of Culture (Region Nord, Pas-de Calais)

Prize Presentation December 1996

Design Team Bernard Tschumi, Tom Kowalski, Jean-François Erhel, Véronique Descharriéres, François Gillet, Yannis Aesopos, Henning Ehrhart

Mechanical Engineering Choulet

Approximate Cost US$ 17,500,000

Site Area 10,000 m²

Photographer Bernard Tschumi Architects and Peter Mauss, ESTO

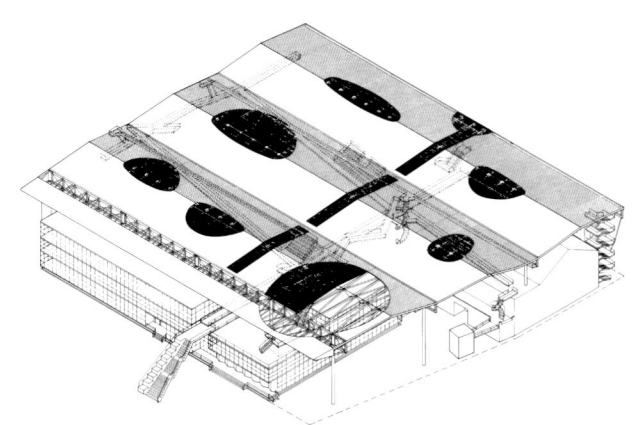

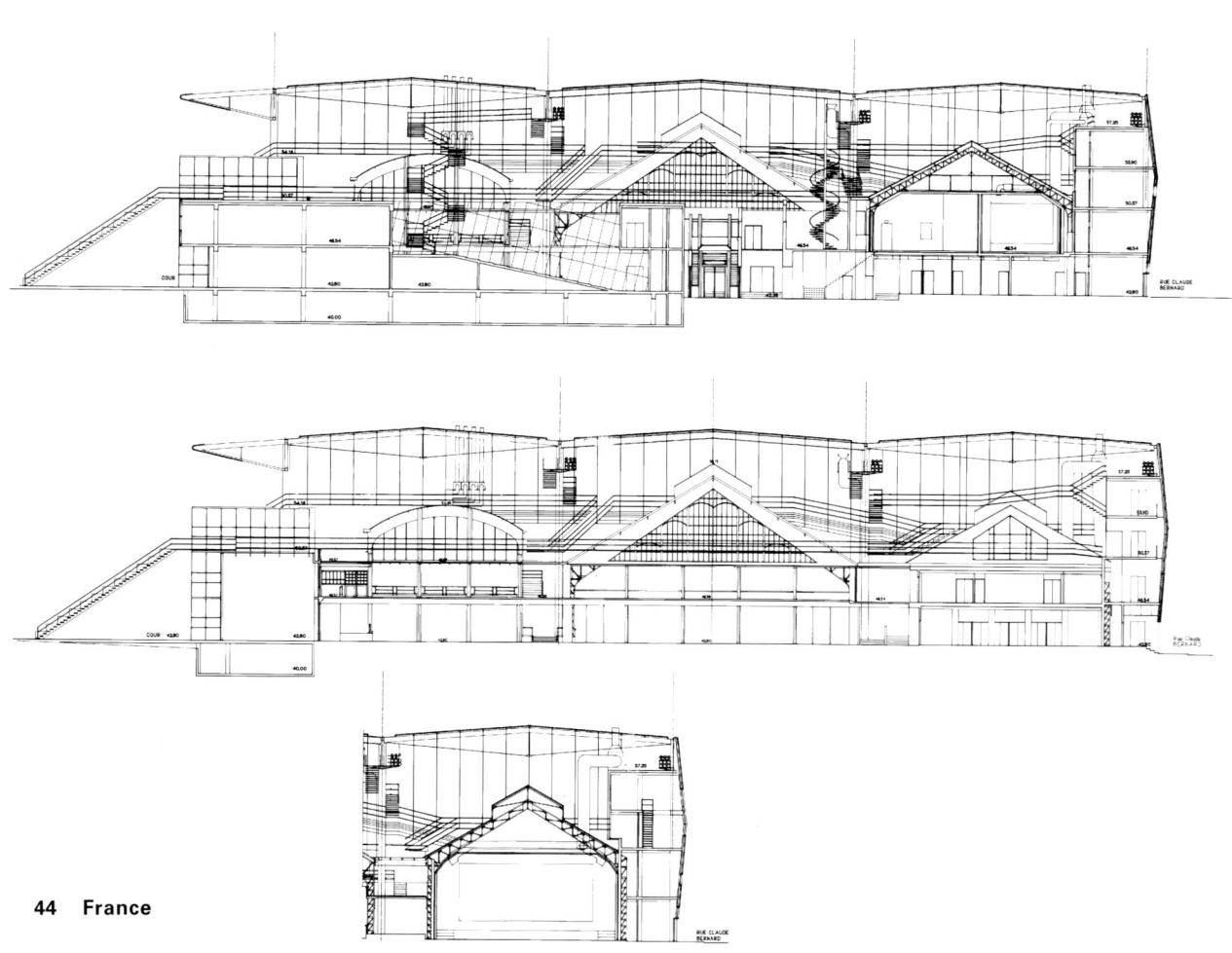

Architect   **Heinz Bienefeld †, Swisttal-Ollheim**

Representative Building   **Kindergarten**

Location   **Lahnstein, Germany**

Design and Construction Period   **1992–1995**

Award   Der Große BDA Preis for the complete work of Heinz Bienefeld

Given by   BDA Bund Deutscher Architekten

Prize Presentation   May / 17 / 1996

Design Team   Sándor Forgó, Joachim Siller

Structural Engineering   Ingenieurbüro Müller, Lahnstein

Interior Design   Heinz Bienefeld

Landscape Architecture   Heinz Bienefeld

Site Area   4028 m^2

Building Area   685 m^2

Total Floor Area   541 m^2

Photographers   Susanne Trappmann, Köln; Christian Richters, Münster

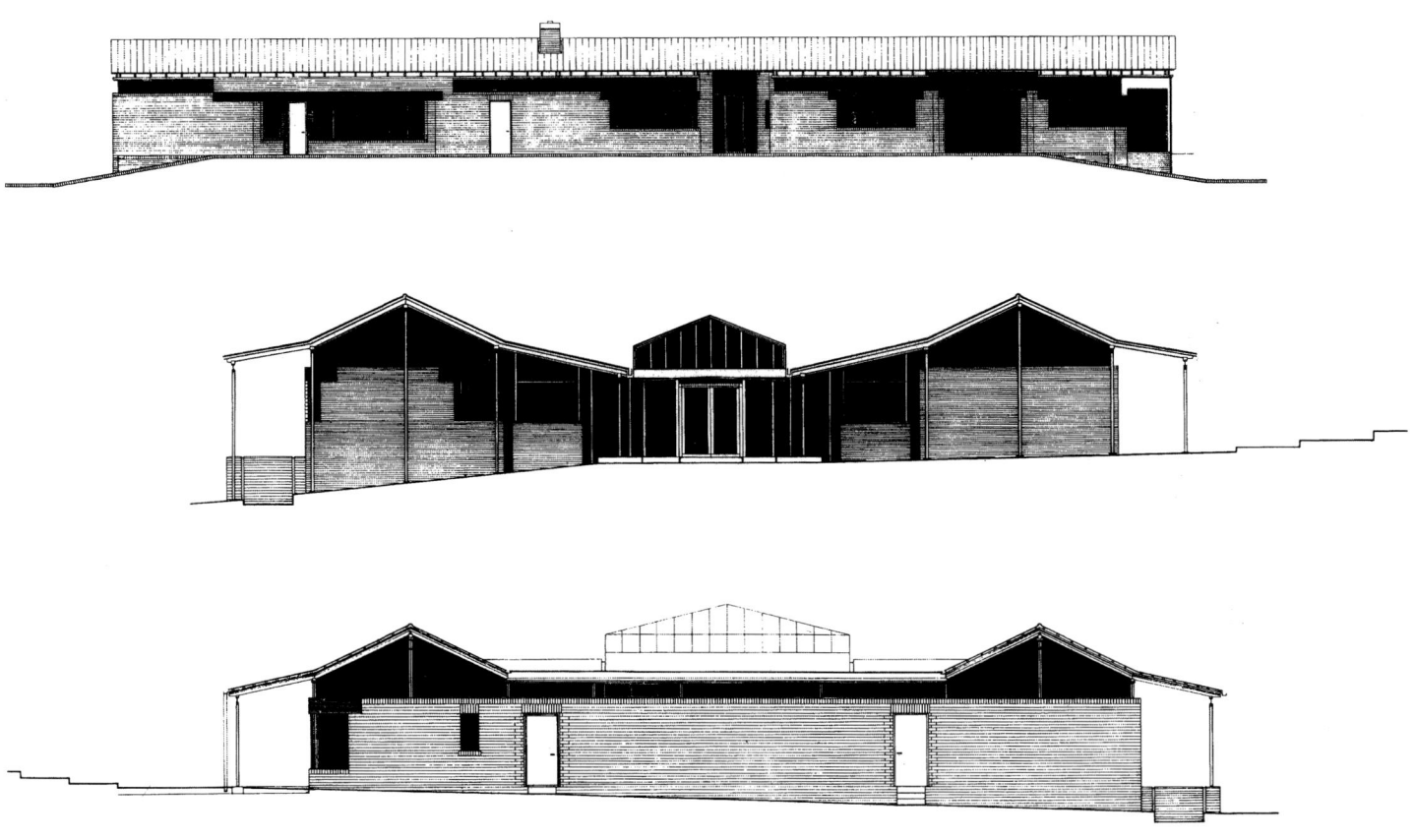

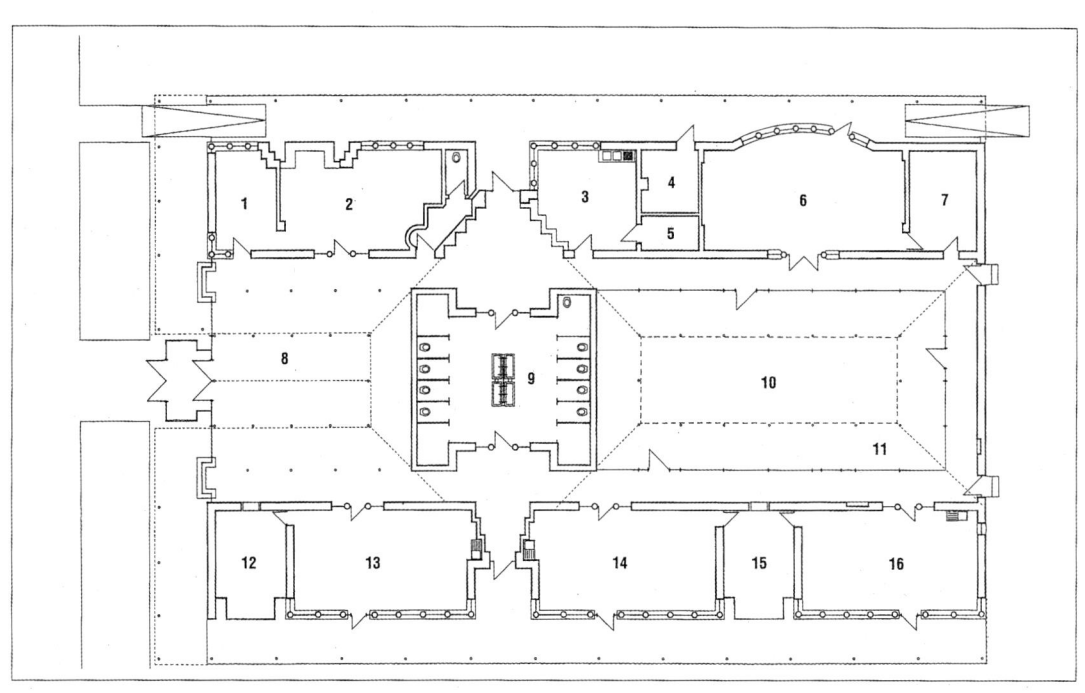

Architects **Jürgen Böge und Ingeborg Lindner-Böge, Hamburg**
Award Winning Building **Office Building Heidenkampsweg**
Location **Heidenkampsweg 40, Hamburg, Germany**
Design and Construction Period **1992–1995**

Award BDA Hamburg Architekturpreis 1996
Given by BDA Bund Deutscher Architekten Hamburg
Prize Presentation November / 14 / 1996
Members of the Jury Dietmar Eberle (Austria), Charlotte Frank (Germany), Hilde
  Léon (Chair, Germany), Carsten Lorenzen (Denmark), Manfred Sack (Germany)
Design Team Volker Fuchs, Markus Leben, Lars Christensen, Jakob Bronsted
Structural Engineering Windels, Timm, Morgen, Hamburg
Lighting Consultant Ulrike Brandi, Hamburg
Interior Design Jürgen Böge und Ingeborg Lindner-Böge, Hamburg
Landscape Architecture Jürgen Böge und Ingeborg Lindner-Böge, Hamburg
Site Area 2,677 m^2
Building Area 2,517 m^2
Total Floor Area 12,386 m^2
Photographer Klaus Frahm

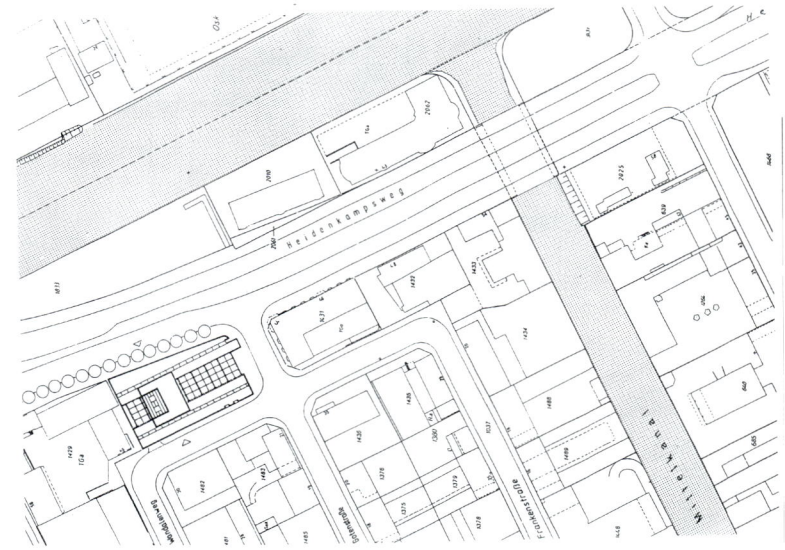

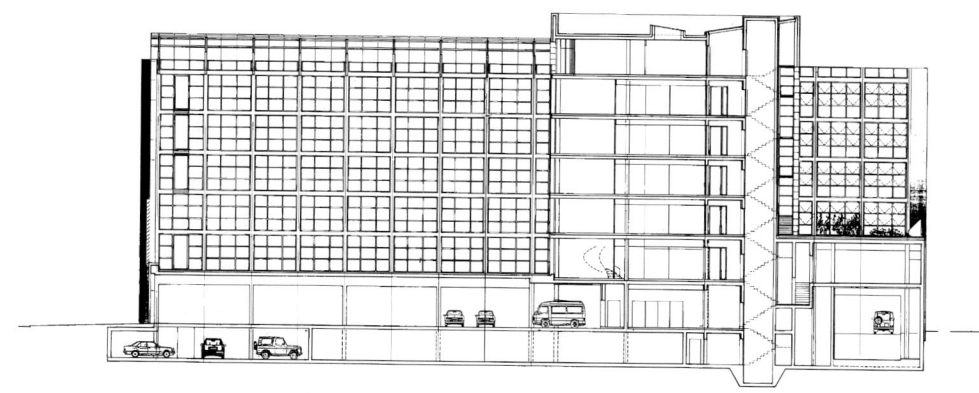

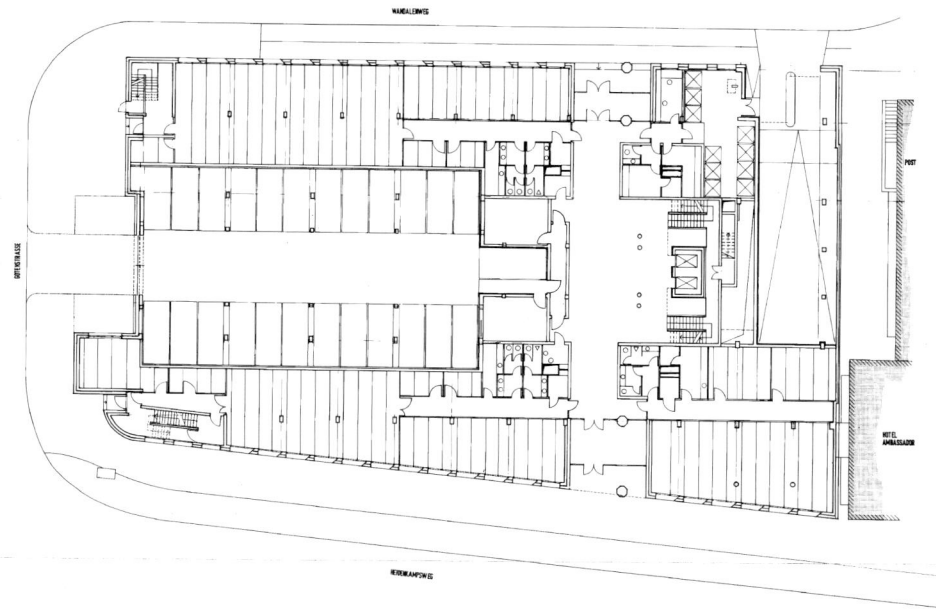

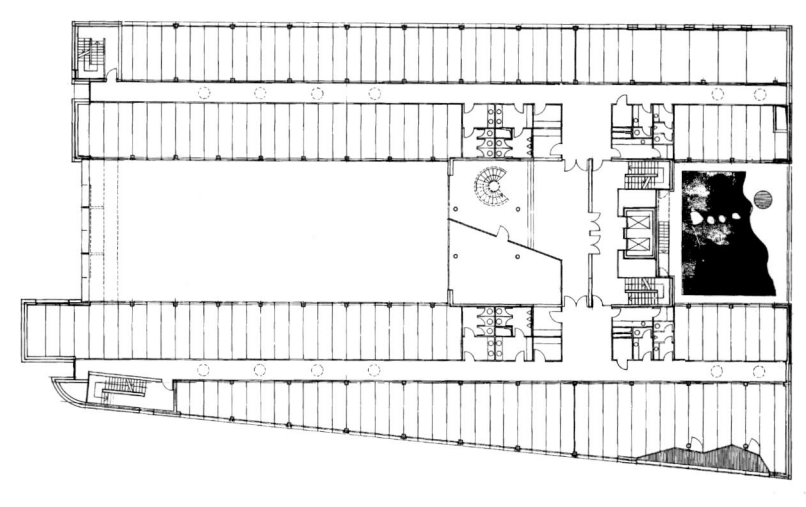

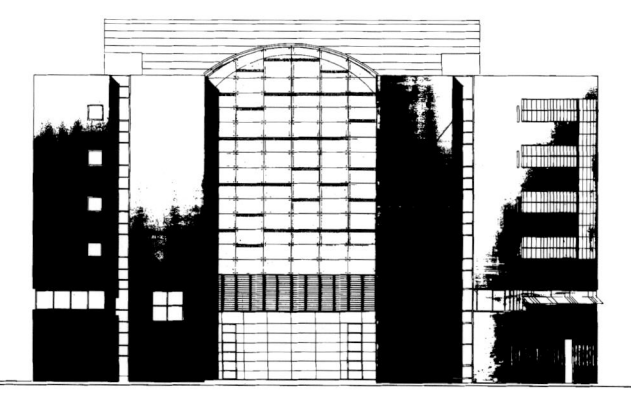

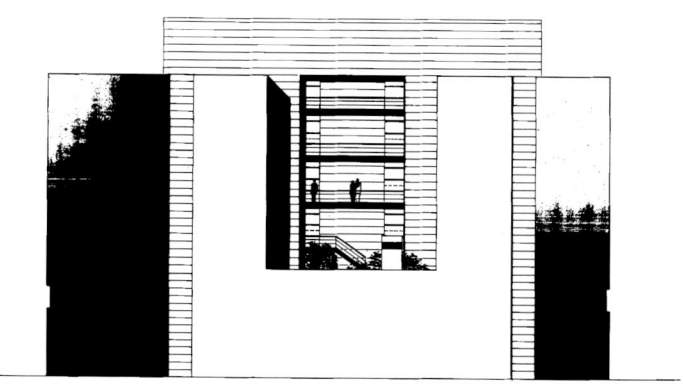

Architects **Rebecca E. Chestnutt, Robert Niess, Berlin**

Award Winning Building **Luisenbad Library**

Location **Travemünderstr. 2, Berlin-Wedding, Germany**

Design and Construction Period **1988–1995**

Award BDA Berlin Architekturpreis 1996 (Honorable Mention)

Given by BDA Bund Deutscher Architekten Berlin

Prize Presentation October / 11 / 1996

Members of the Jury Julia Bolles-Wilson, Kees Christiaanse, Manfred Eichel,
  Falk Jaeger, Otto Steidle, Eva Krings, Mathias Sauerbruch

Design Team Rebecca E. Chestnutt, Robert Niess

Structural Engineering Manleitner

Civil Engineering Vermessungsamt Wedding, Berlin

Mechanical Engineering Bohn & Hock GmbH; Juul

Electrical Engineering Hochbauamt Wedding, Berlin

Acoustic Engineering Ing.-Büro Moll

Air Conditioning Consultant Alfred Eichelberger GmbH & Co

Lighting Consultant Louis Poulsen; Sill

Interior Design Rebecca E. Chestnutt, Robert Niess

Landscape Architecture Garten- und Landschaftsarchitektur Müller
  Knippschild, Wehberg

Approximate Cost DM 30,000,000

Site Area 3,209 m^2

Building Area 3,245 m^2

Total Floor Area 2,650 m^2

Photographer Ulrich Schwarz, Reinhard Görner

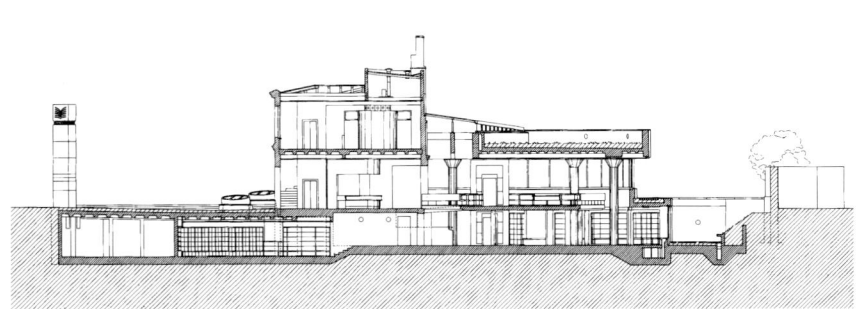

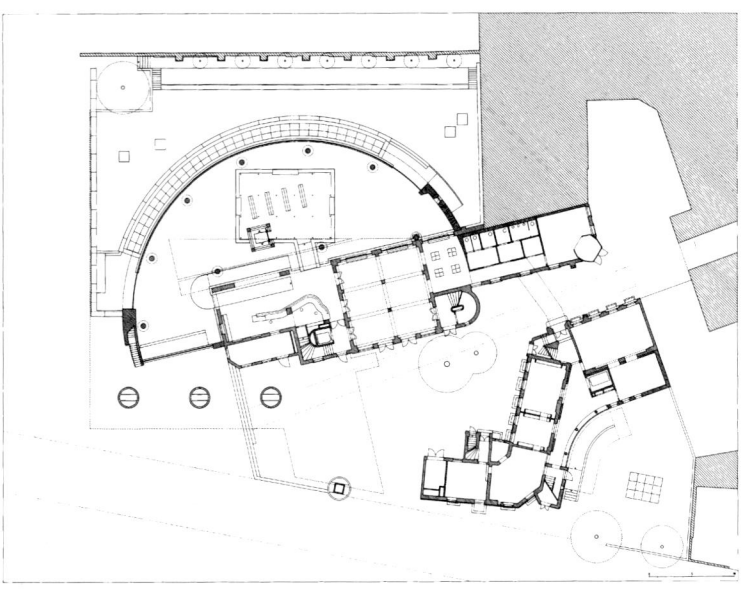
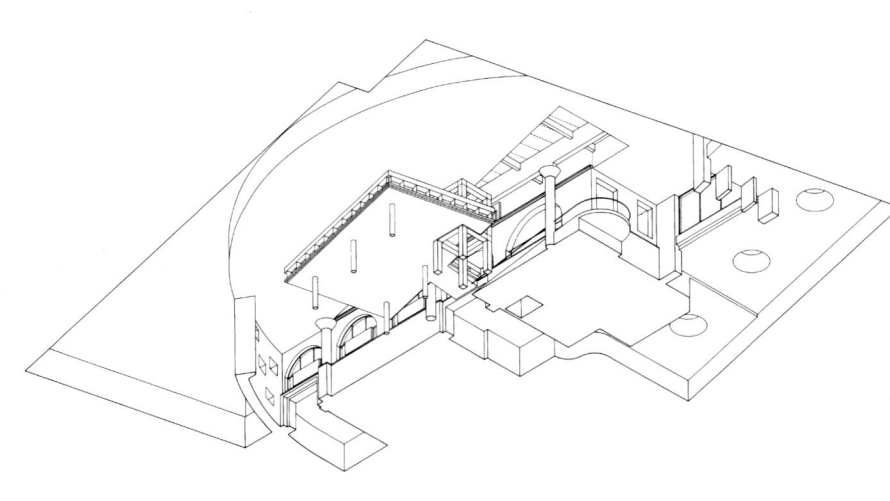

Architects **Hermann & Valentiny, Remerschen, Luxembourg**
Award Winning Building **Hotel and Service Center**
Location **Magistralen Carré, Halle-Neustadt, Germany**
Design and Construction Period **1992–1995**

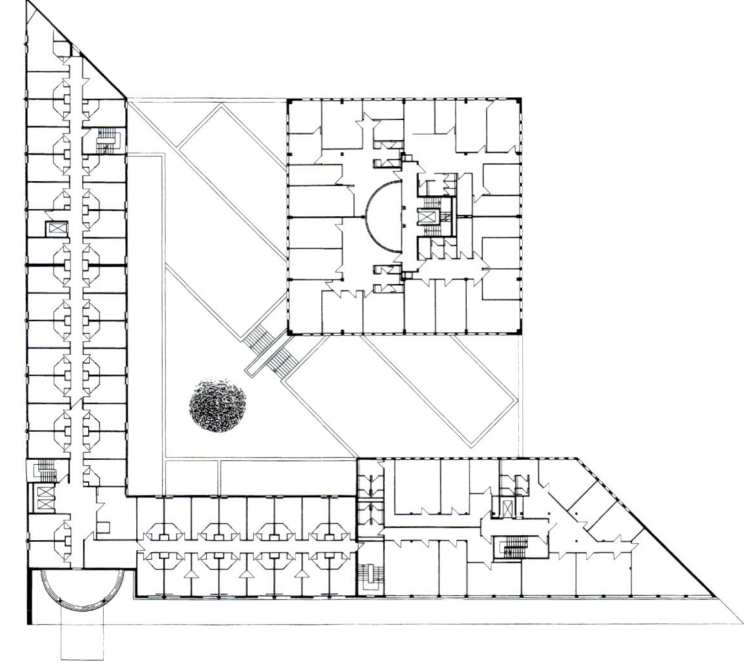

Award Architekturpreis des Landes Sachsen-Anhalt 1995
Given by Ministerium für Wohnungswesen, Städtebau und Verkehr and
   Architektenkammer Sachsen-Anhalt in Magdeburg
Prize Presentation December / 11 / 1995
Members of the Jury Karl-Heinz Wolf, Jürgen Heyer, Walter Lütz, Jutta Geikler,
   Barbara Jakubeit, Claudia Schrader, Daniel Libeskind, Thomas Freytag
Design Team Hermann & Valentiny, Architect Christmann (Responsible Project),
   Architect Reinert (Responsible Planning), K. Appelt, T. Carentz, G. Connerth,
   U. Holler, B. Kathoffer, T. Knedel, C. Luzi, S. Reiser, A. Schnitzer, V. Schulke,
   S. Winkler (Staff)
Structural Engineering TBH Hochtief AFG, Köln, Correns & Adams (Responsible)
Mechanical Engineering Ing. Büro Goblet & Lavandier, Luxembourg, Dehner
   (Responsible); Krantz TKT, Mannheim, Utsch (Responsible)
Electrical Engineering Ing. Büro Kaufmann, Schkeuditz-Leipzig, Großkopf
Environmental Engineering Ing. Büro Fuhrmann, Halle, Fuhrmann (Responsible)
Acoustic Engineering Von Rekowski & Partner, Weinheim, Janke (Responsible)
Air Conditioning Consultant Ing. Büro Goblet & Lavandier, Luxembourg, Dehner
   (Responsible); Krantz TKT, Mannheim, Utsch (Responsible)
Lighting Consultant Ing. Büro Kaufmann, Schkeuditz-Leipzig, Großkopf
   (Responsible)
Life Safety Consultant Halfkan, Heister & Kirchner, Erkelenz, Eger (Responsible)
Interior Design Designer's House, Frankfurt, Moes (Responsible)
Landscape Architecture Ing. Büro Ernst, Trier, Ernst (Responsible)
Quantity Surveying Promaco, Luxembourg, Verwimp (Responsible)
Approximate Cost DM 34,500,000
Site Area 8,925 m^2
Building Area 4,030 m^2
Total Floor Area 6,550 m^2 (hotel), 6,650 m^2 (offices), 3,270 m^2 (garage)
Photographer GG Kirchner, H. Roth, Köln

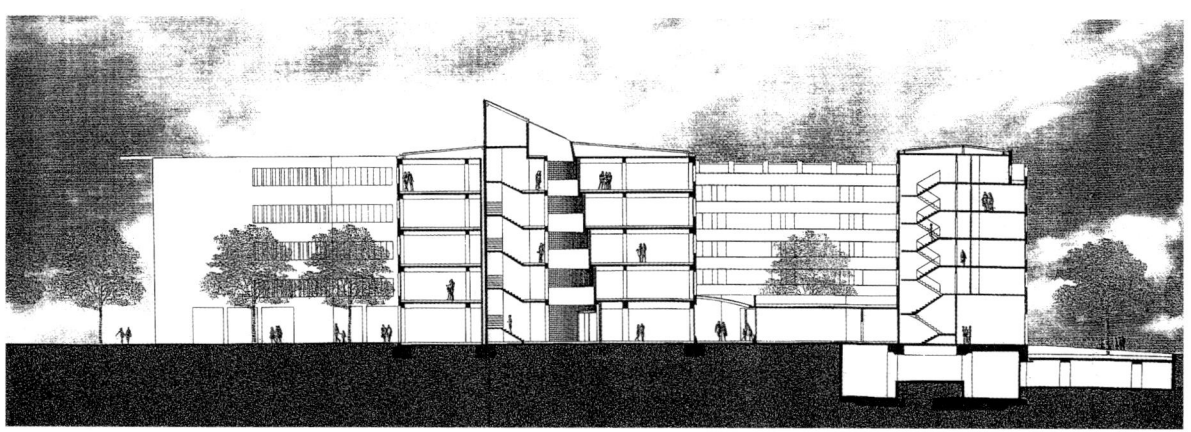

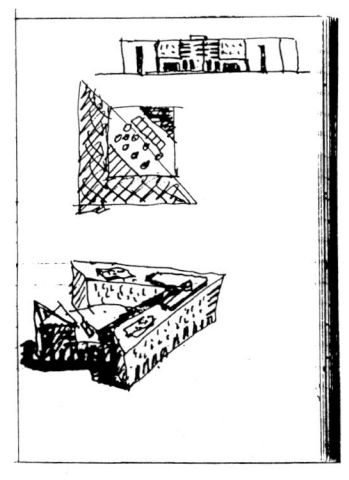
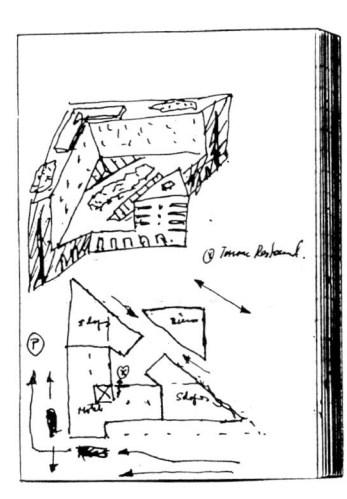

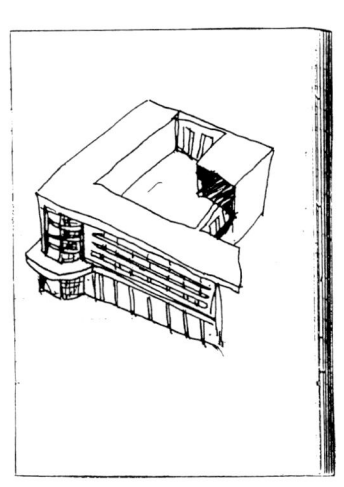

Architect **Thomas Herzog, Munich**
Representative Building **Wilkhahn Production Hall and Energy Plant**
Location **Bad Münder, Germany**
Design and Construction Period **1989–1992**

Award Auguste-Perret-Prize 1996 for the complete work of Thomas Herzog
Given by UIA International Union of Architects
Prize Presentation July / 4 / 1996
Members of the Jury Jaime Duro Pifarre (President, Spain), Vassilis Sgoutas
(Secretary General, Greece), Enrico Milone (Treasurer, Italy), and UIA Vice
Presidents: Gunnel Adlercreutz (Finland), Moshe Zarhy (Israel), Sara Topelson
de Grinberg (Mexico), Kok Leon Chia (Singapore), Salah Zaky Said (Egypt)
Design Team Thomas Herzog with Bernd Steigerwald,
Holger Gestering in Haag, von Ohlen, Rüffer and Partners
Structural Engineering Sailer und Stepan
Landscape Architecture Anneliese and Peter Latz
Building Area 3,300 m²
Photographer Dieter Leistner

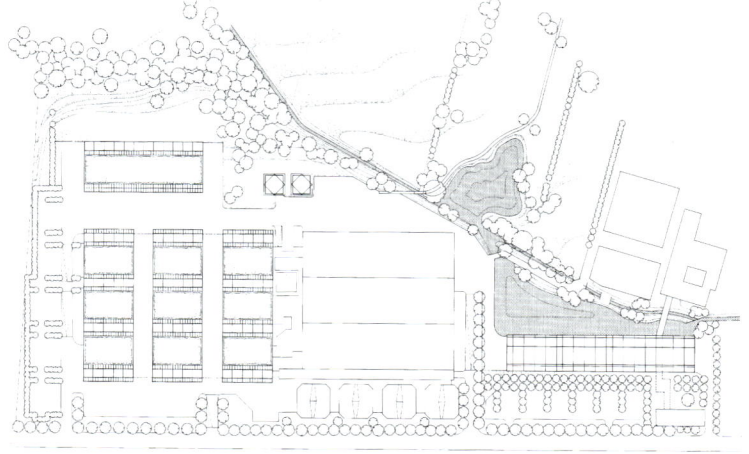

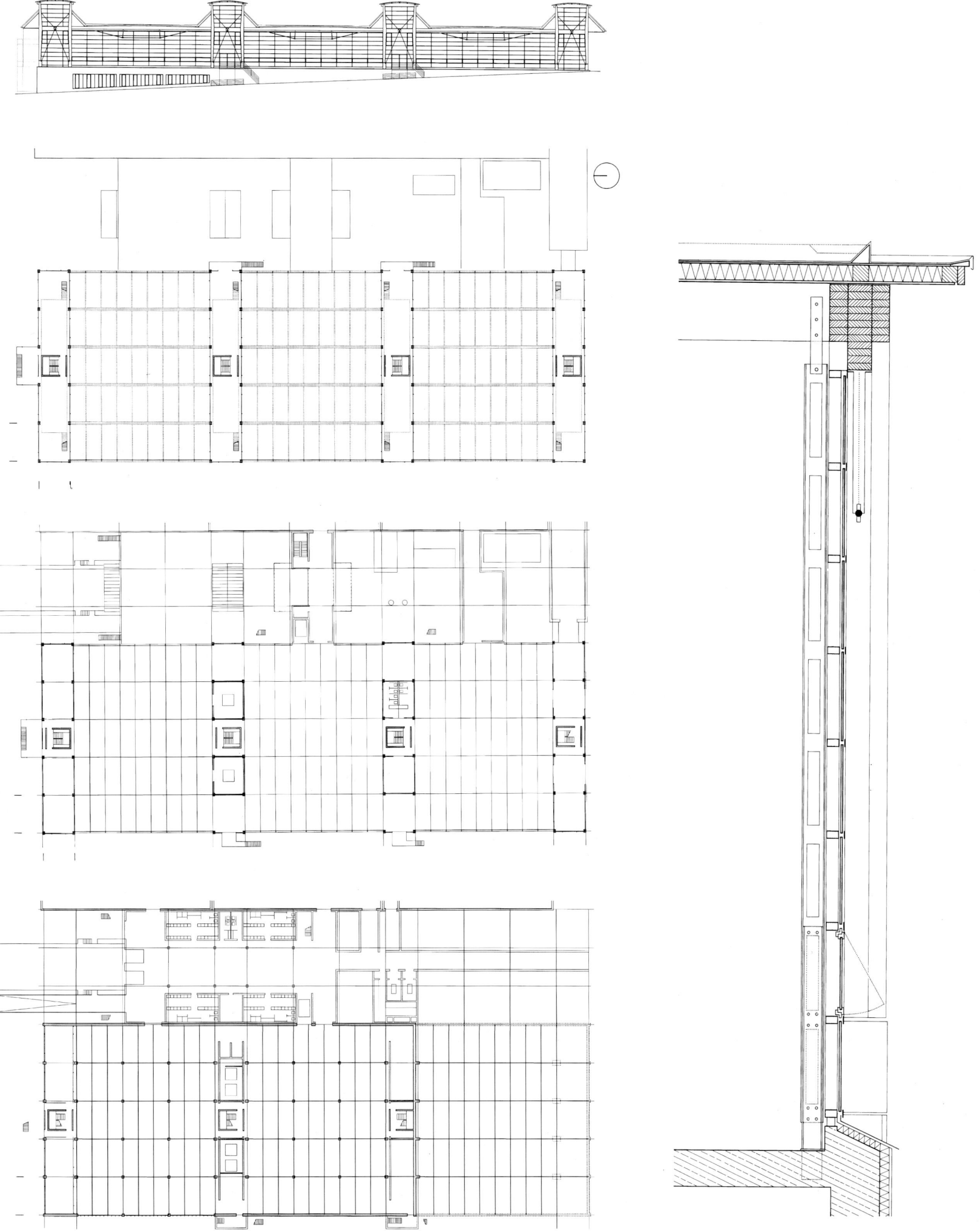

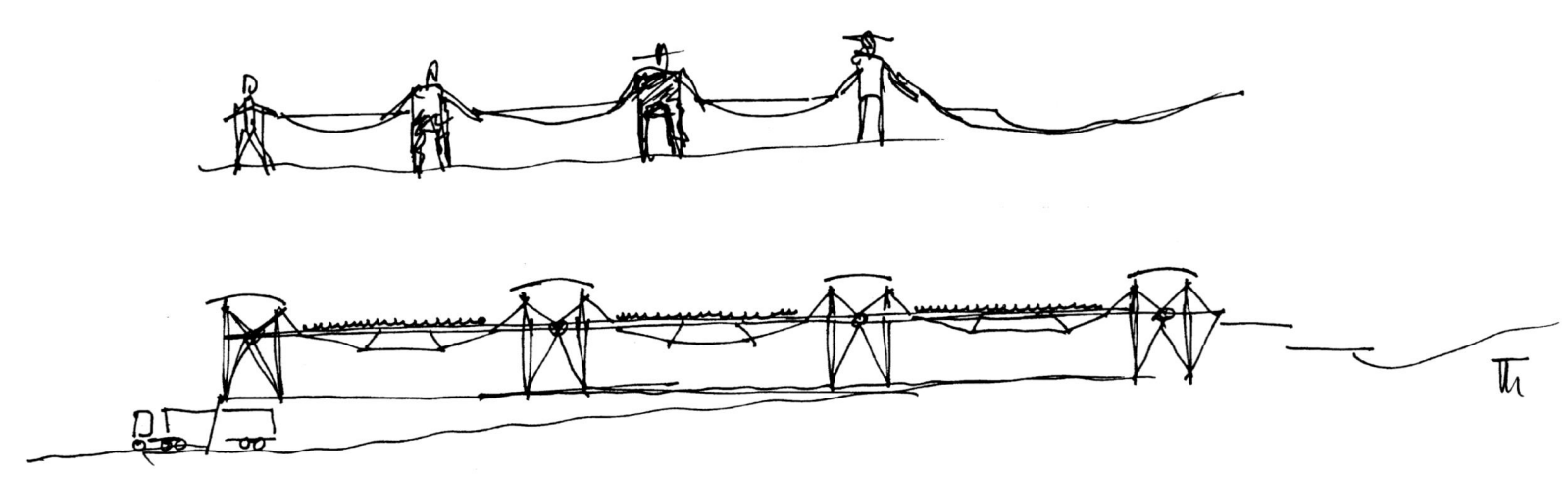

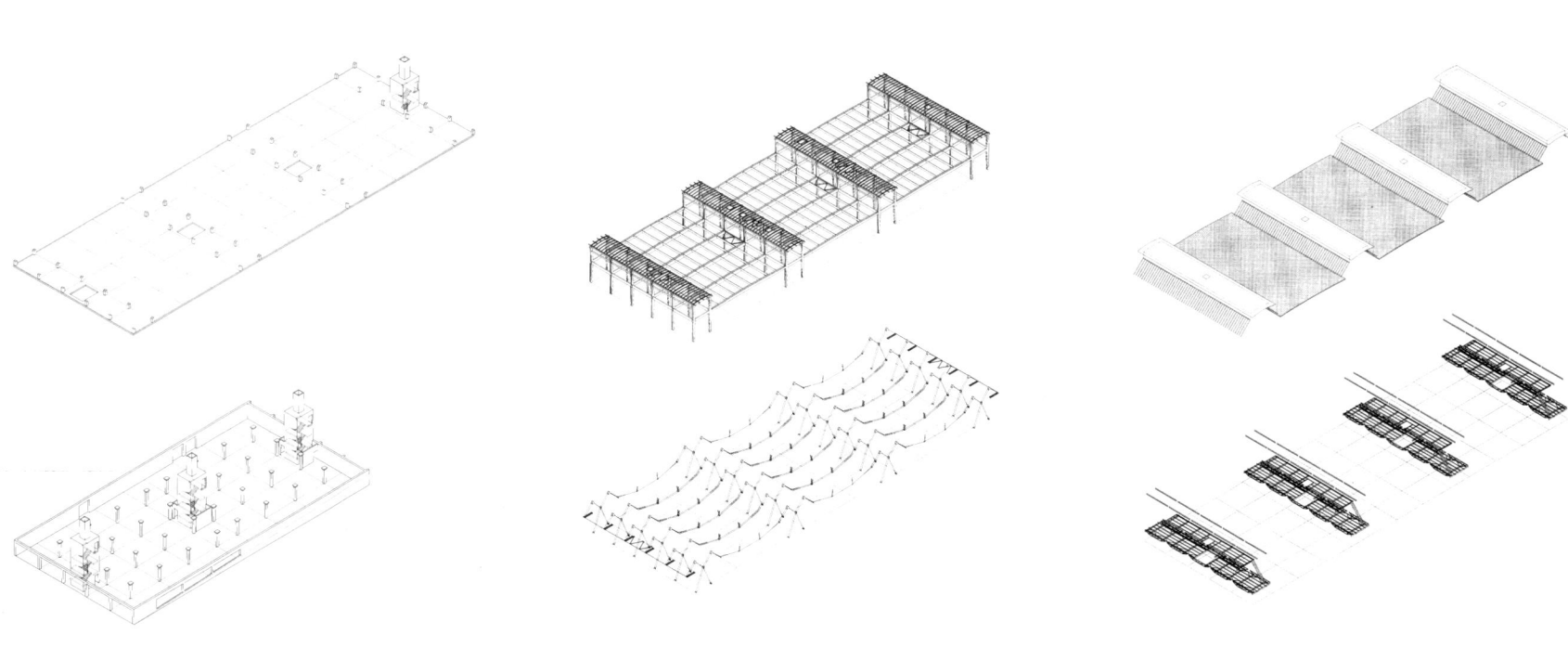

Architects **Kahlfeldt Architekten, Berlin**

Award Winning Building **Engelhardt Hof**

Location **Danckelmannstr. 9, Berlin-Charlottenburg, Germany**

Design and Construction Period **1993–1996**

Award BDA Berlin Architekturpreis 1996 (Honorable Mention)

Given by BDA Bund Deutscher Architekten Berlin

Prize Presentation 1996

Design Team Petra and Paul Kahlfeldt with Anja Herold (Project Leader:
   Design), Christoph Haag (Project Leader: Realization), Yves Minssart,
   Michael Fuchs, Jörn Pötting, Thomas Kälber, Conor Moran, Frauke Hellweg,
   Martin Oestlund

Structural Engineering Ingenieurbüro Fink, Berlin

Mechanical Engineering Ingenieurbüro Rahn, Berlin

Lighting Consultant Licht Kunst Licht, Berlin / Bonn

Landscape Architecture TOPOS, Stefan Buddatsch, Berlin

Site Area 26,299.62 m^2

Total Floor Area 6,501.49 m^2 (without cellar)

Photographer Stefan Müller

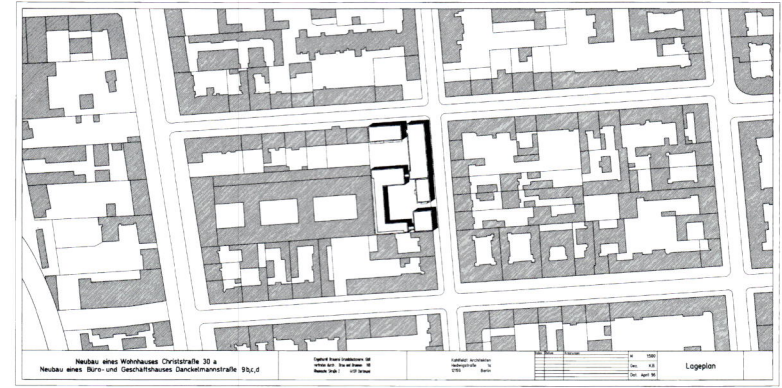

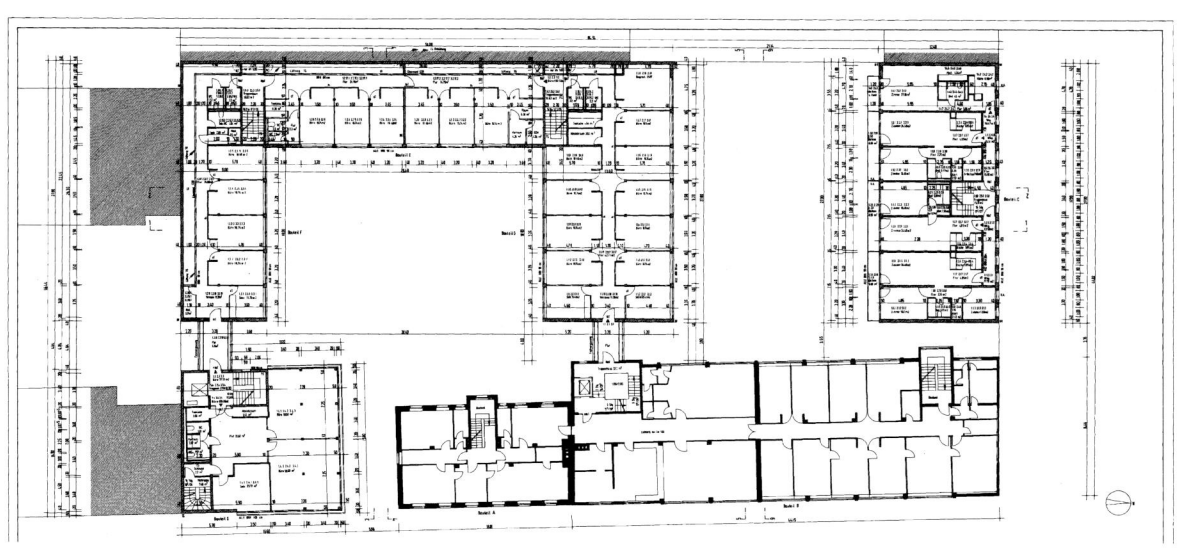

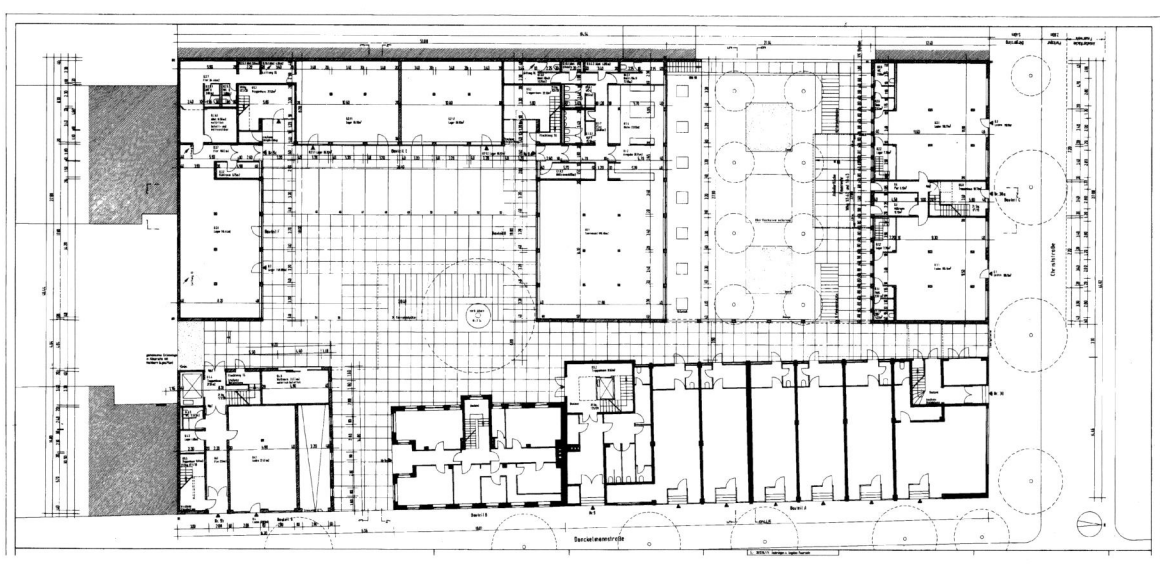

Architect **Marc-Olivier Mathez, Hamburg**

Award Winning Building **Rehrstieg Housing Complex, Hamburg**

   (renewal and addition)

Location **Hamburg-Neuwiedental, Germany**

Design and Construction Period **1992–1995**

Award BDA Hamburg Architekturpreis 1996 (1. Preisrang)

Given by BDA Bund Deutscher Architekten Hamburg

Prize Presentation November / 14 / 1996

Members of the Jury Dietmar Eberle (Austria), Charlotte Frank (Germany),

   Hilde Léon (Chair, Germany), Carsten Lorenzen (Denmark), Manfred Sack

   (Germany)

Design Team Marc-Olivier Mathez and Ralf Kunze, Elke Goebel,

   Roman Schlueter, Karl Heinz Wulf (Site Supervisor)

Structural Engineering Ingenieurbüro Puszies, Hamburg

Civil Engineering Ingenieurbüro Otto, Hamburg

Electrical Engineering Ingenieurbüro Kohn, Barmstedt

Landscape Architecture Verena Pechter, Hamburg

Approximate Cost DM 2,520/m^2

Site Area 10,000 m^2

Building Area 2,132.90 m^2

Total Floor Area 4,333 m^2

Photographer Michael Wortmann

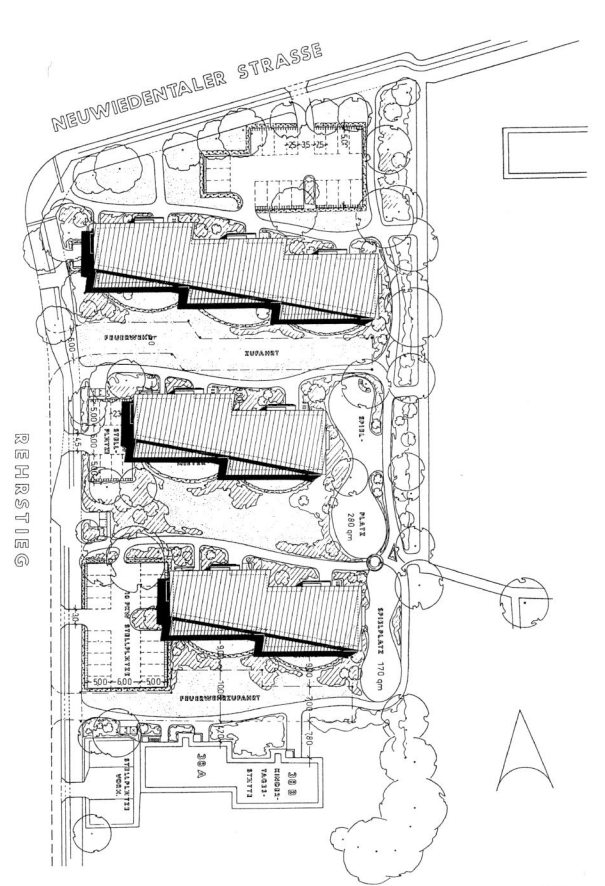

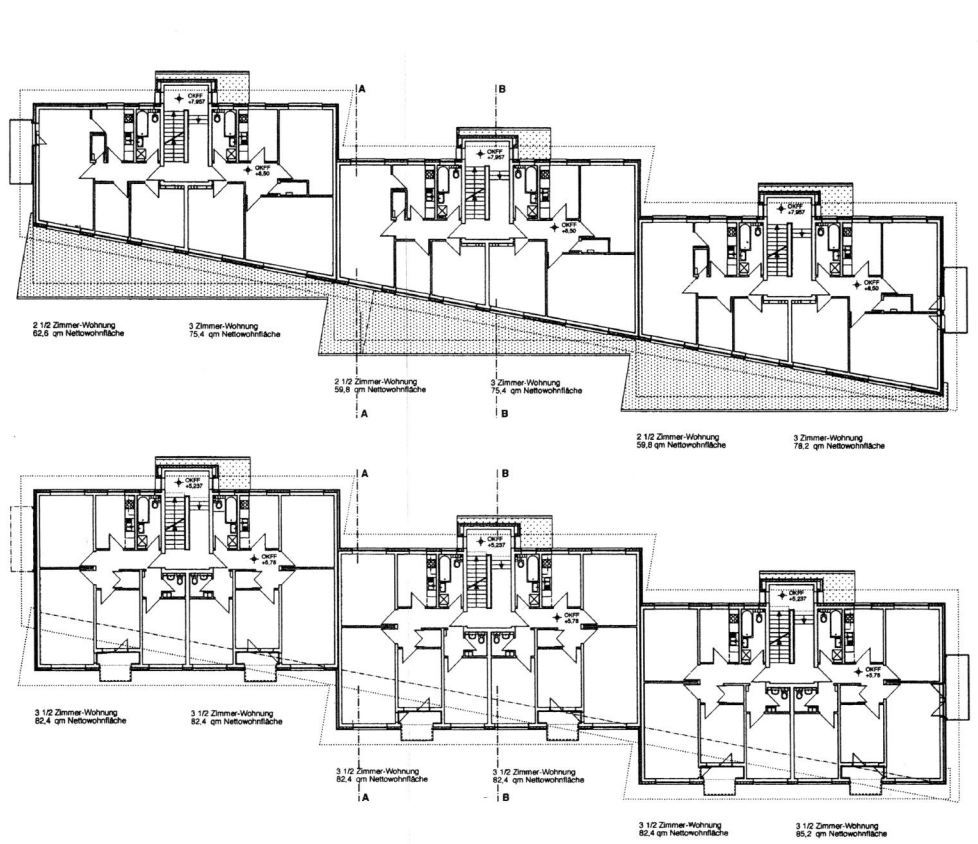

Architects **Schneider und Schumacher, Frankfurt**

Award Winning Building **Info-Box**

Location **Potsdamer Platz, Berlin, Germany**

Design and Construction Period **1995**

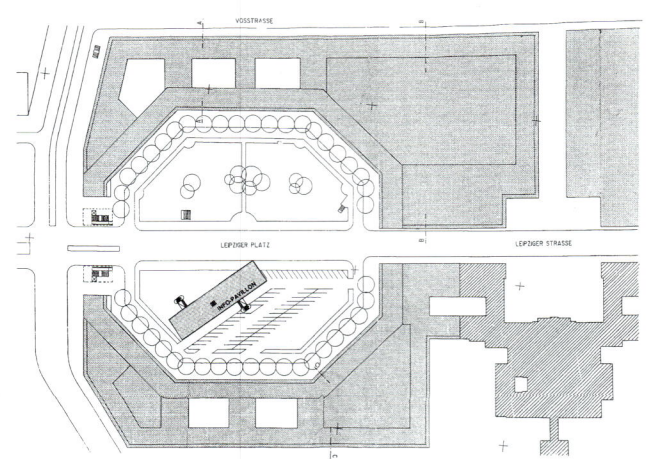

Award BDA Berlin Architekturpreis 1996 (Honorable Mention)

Given by BDA Bund Deutscher Architekten Berlin

Prize Presentation November 1996

Members of the Jury Julia Bolles-Wilson, Kees Christiaanse, Manfred Eichel, Falk Jaeger, Otto Steidle, Eva Krings, Mathias Sauerbruch

Design Team Peter Begon, Kristin Dirschl, Petra Pfeiffer, Philipp Schiffer, Christian Simons, Susanne Widmer, Thomas Zürcher (Schneider und Schumacher)

Structural Engineering Bollinger und Grohmann, Frankfurt am Main

Acoustic Engineering Emch und Berger GmbH, Berlin

Air Conditioning Consultant Emch und Berger GmbH, Berlin

Lighting Consultant Emch und Berger GmbH, Berlin

Quantity Surveying Emch und Berger GmbH, Berlin

Approximate Cost DM 10,000,000

Total Floor Area 2,230 m^2

Photographer Waltraud Krase, Jörg Hempel, Oltmann Reuter

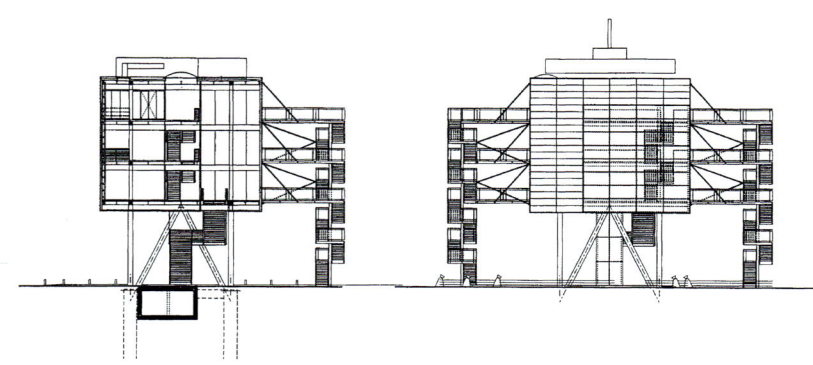

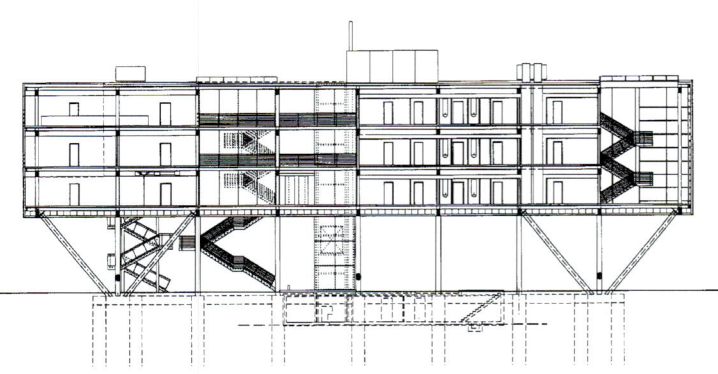

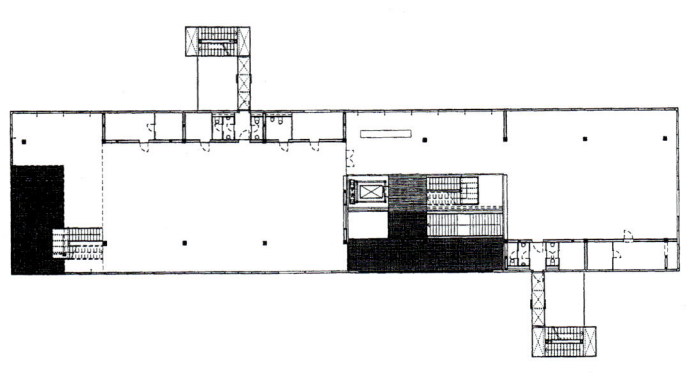

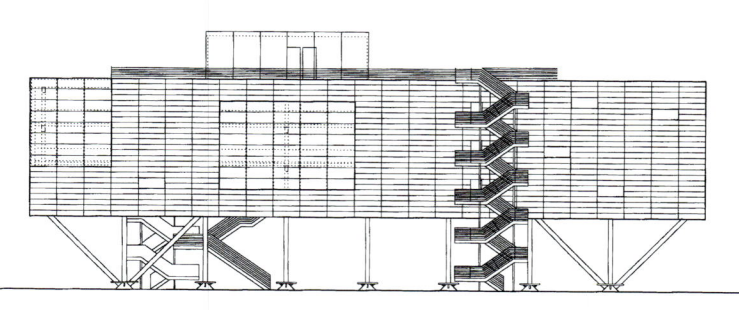

Architects **Schneider und Schumacher, Frankfurt**

Award Winning Building **Office Building for Thompson Advertising Agency**

Location **Schwedlerstr. 6, 60314 Frankfurt, Germany**

Design and Construction Period **1994–1995**

Award 1) BDA Berlin Architekturpreis 1996; 2) Honorable Mention for
   Excellent Building in Hessen

Given by BDA Bund Deutscher Architekten Hessen

Prize Presentation March 1996

Members of the Jury Alfram Edler von Hoessle, Cornelia Issmer-Pfromm,
   Christoph Mäckler, Klaus Trojan, Monika Weber-Pahl, Peter Welbergen,
   Marlies Hauber, Sabine Brinitzer

Design Team Karen Ehlers, Petra Pfeiffer, Beate Hoyer, Kristin Dirschl,
   Matthew O'Malia, Richard Voss, Marcel Eckert, Heike Heinzelmann
   (Schneider und Schumacher)

Structural Engineering Philip Holzmann; ARUP (façade)

Electrical Engineering ARUP

Acoustic Engineering ARUP

Air Conditioning Consultant ARUP

Lighting Consultant ARUP

Interior Design Schneider und Schumacher, VITRA

Quantity Surveying Hans Pfefferkorn

Approximate Cost DM 20,000,000

Site Area 2,366 m^2

Building Area 1,424 m^2

Total Floor Area 5,915 m^2

Photographer Waltraud Krase, Jörg Hempel, H.G. Esch

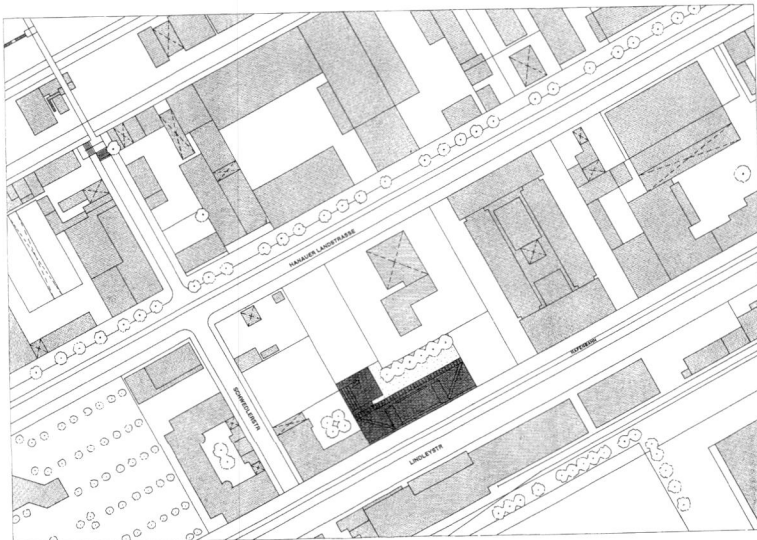

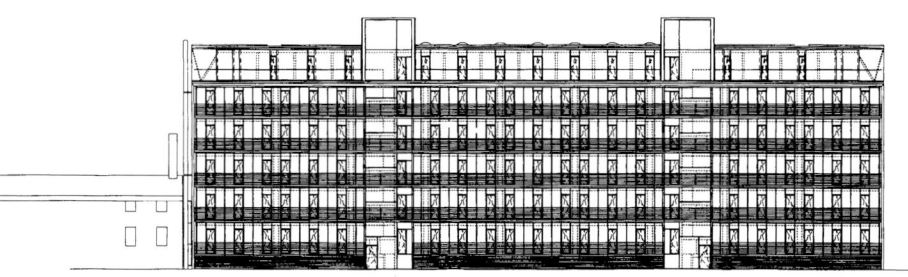

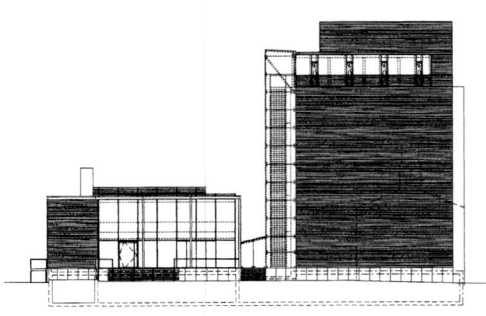

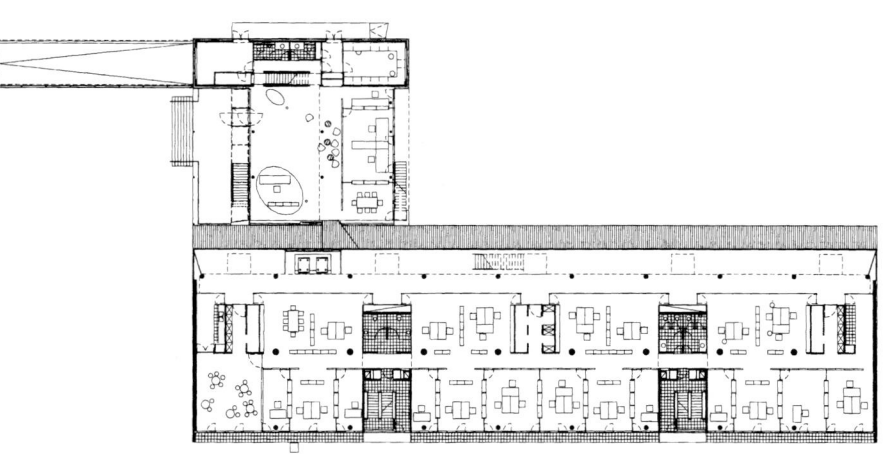

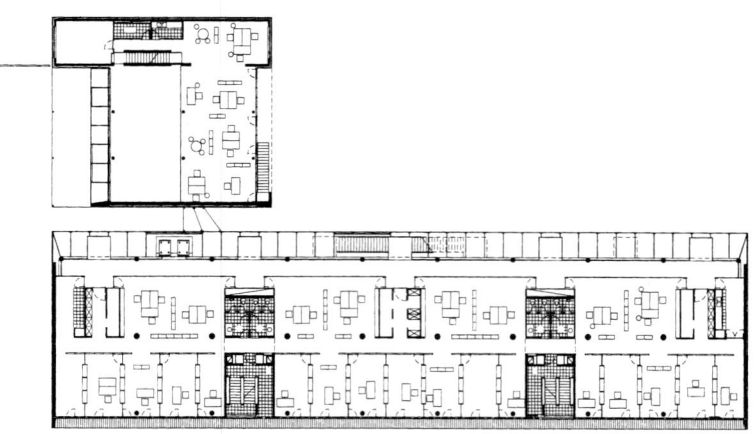

Architects **D. Reznik Architects, Jerusalem, Israel; Fowler, Ferguson, Kingston, Ruben Architects, Salt Lake City, USA**
Award Winning Building **The Jerusalem Center for Near Eastern Studies (Mormon University in Jerusalem)**
Location **Jerusalem, Israel**
Design and Construction Period **1981–1986**

Award The Zeev Rechter Prize
Given by Association of Architects and City Planners in Israel
Prize Presentation December / 17 / 1996
Members of the Jury Ulrich Plesner, Chaim Dotan, Gabriela Nusbaum
Structural Engineering A. Warshawsky
Civil Engineering Construction Management and Supervision E. Rahat
Mechanical Engineering Doron-Shachar, Tel-Aviv
Electrical Engineering Ramor, Tel-Aviv
Acoustic Engineering D. Klepper, New York
Air Conditioning Consultant Doron-Shachar, Tel-Aviv
Lighting Consultant Mac-Alister, Tel-Aviv
Life Safety Consultant I. Blaiberg, Haifa
Interior Design D. Reznik Architects; Fowler, Ferguson, Kingston, Ruben Architects with Adina Preuss Architect
Landscape Architecture L. Yahalom – D. Zur, Landscape Architects
Quantity Surveying E. Rahat
Approximate Cost US$ 18,000,000
Site Area 17,000,000 m²
Building Area 15,000 m²
Total Floor Area 12,000 m²
Photographer Yoram Lehman, Werner Braun (general view)

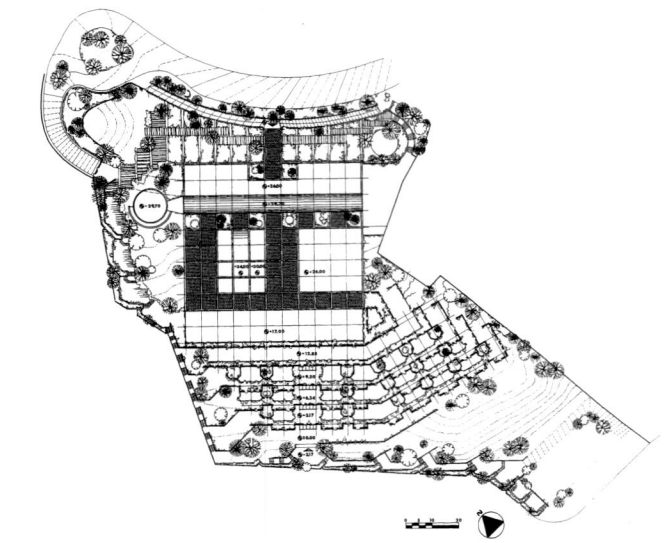

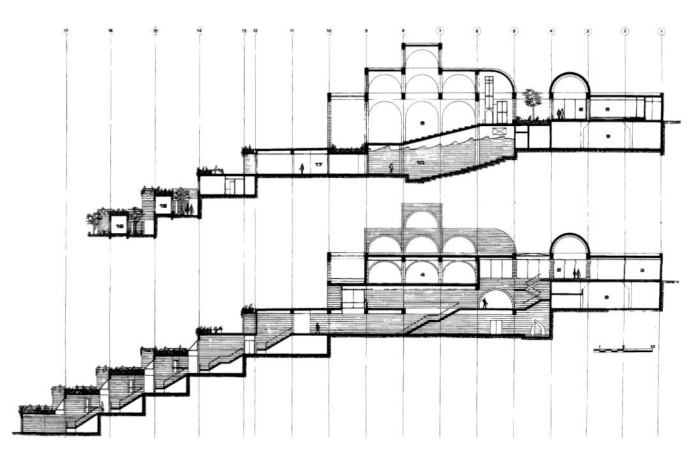

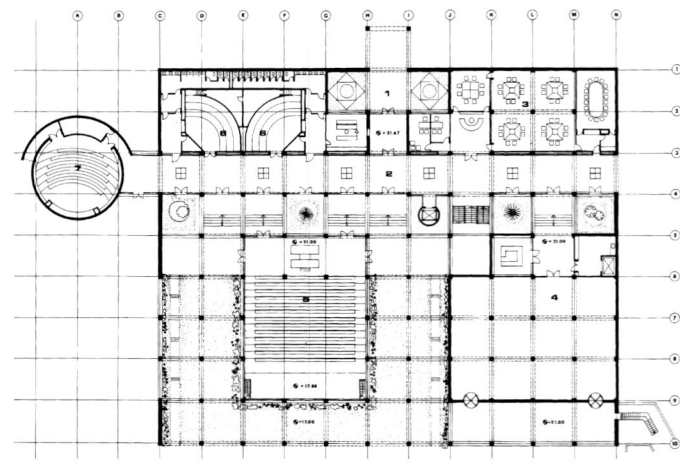

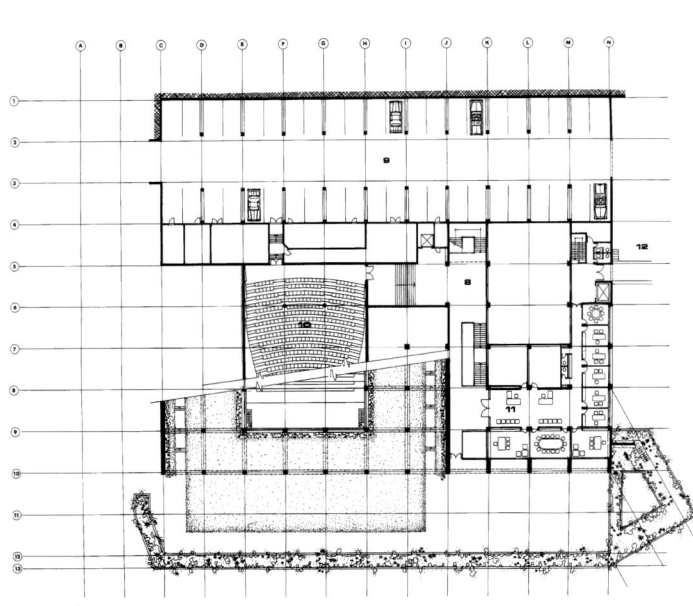

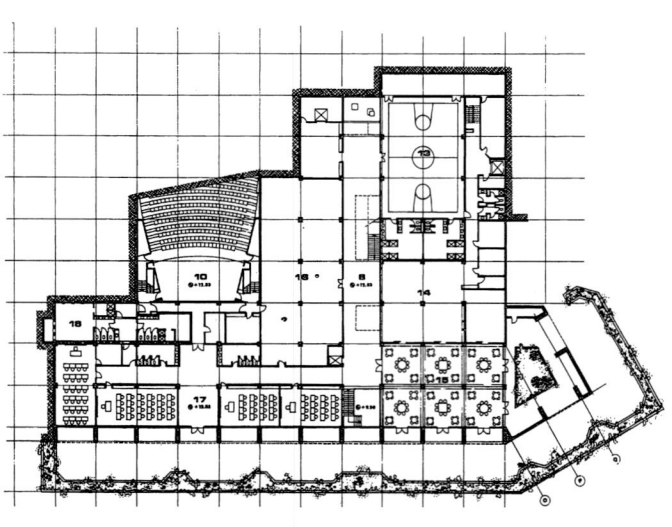

Architect **Takasaki Masaharu, Tokyo**
Award Winning Building **Kihoku Astronomical Museum**
Location **Uwaba Park 1660-3, Ichinari Kihoku-cho, Kagoshima-ken, Japan**
Design and Construction Period **1989–1995**

Award JIA Award for the Best Young Architects of the Year 1996
Given by JIA The Japan Institute of Architects
Prize Presentation September / 5 / 1996
Members of the Jury Uchida, Ito, Naito
Design Team Takasaki Masaharu Architects
Structural Engineering Tanaka Institute, Waseda University
Civil Engineering Takasaki Masaharu Architects
Mechanical Engineering Takasaki Masaharu Architects
Electrical Engineering Nihon Dengyo Corporation
Environmental Engineering Takasaki Masaharu Architects
Acoustic Engineering Takasaki Masaharu Architects
Air Conditioning Consultant Takasaki Masaharu Architects
Lighting Consultant Takasaki Masaharu Architects
Life Safety Consultant Penta – Ocean Construction Co., Ltd.
Interior Design Takasaki Masaharu Architects
Landscape Architecture Takasaki Masaharu Architects
Quantity Surveying Penta – Ocean Construction Co., Ltd. Harazonogumi
Approximate Cost ¥ 394,570,000
Site Area 5,288 m^2
Building Area 425.54 m^2
Total Floor Area 427.60 m^2
Photographers Takasaki Masaharu, Kida Katsuhisa, Shinkenchiku GA
  Photographers

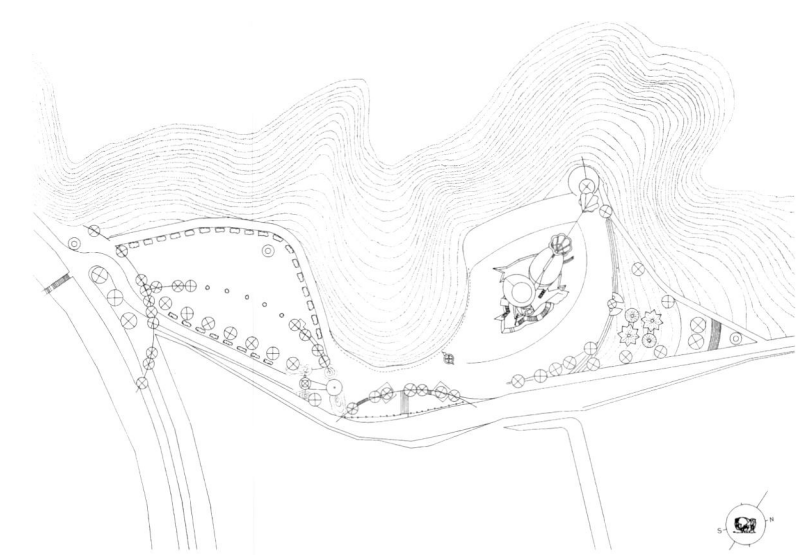

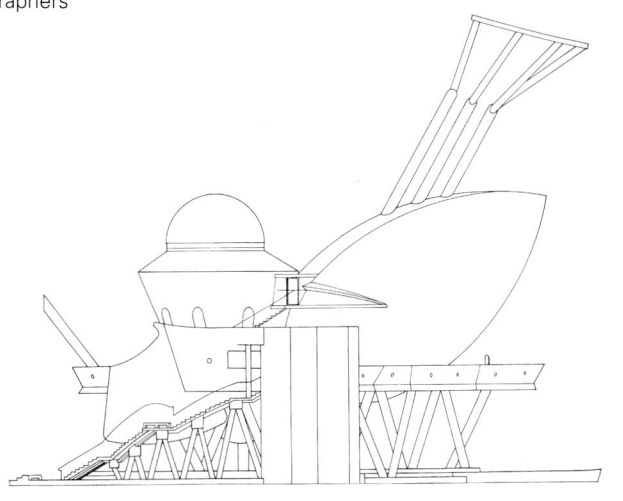

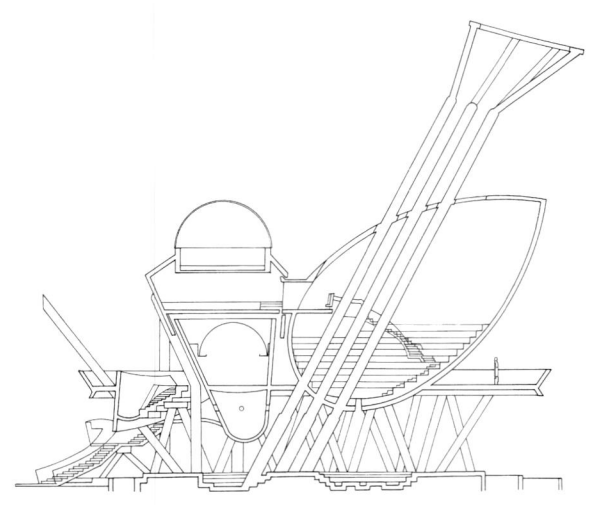

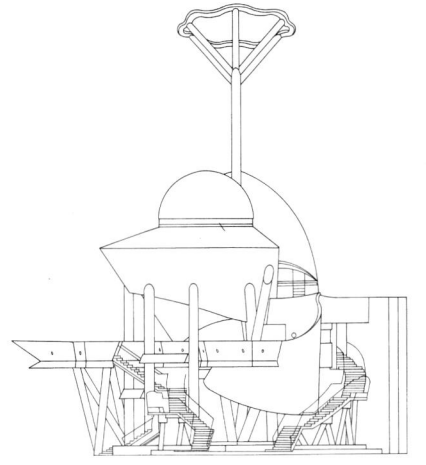

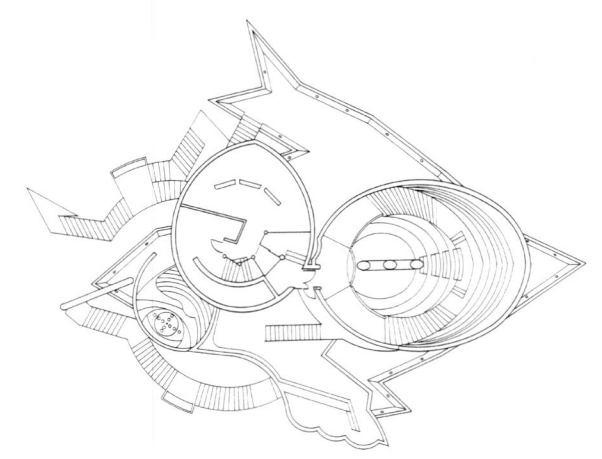

Architect **Toshiaki Ishida, Tokyo**

Award Winning Building **NOS-h, a second house for an artisan**

Location **Shiraoi, Hokkaido, Japan**

Design and Construction Period **1992–1993**

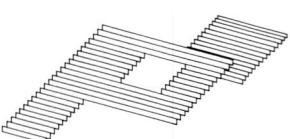

Award JIA Award for the Best Young Architects of the Year 1996

Given by JIA The Japan Institute of Architects

Prize Presentation September / 5 / 1996

Members of the Jury Yoshitika Utida, Toyo Ito, Hiroshi Naito

Design Team Toshiaki Ishida Architect & Associates

Structural Engineering STUDY Structure Technical Design Architect's Office

Site Area 242.12 m²

Building Area 115.93 m²

Total Floor Area 115.93 m²

Photographer Hiroyuki Hirai

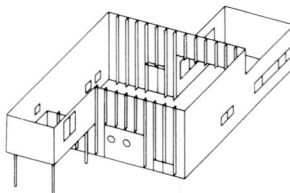

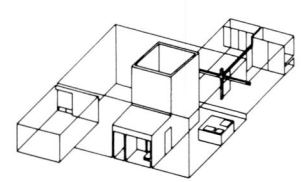

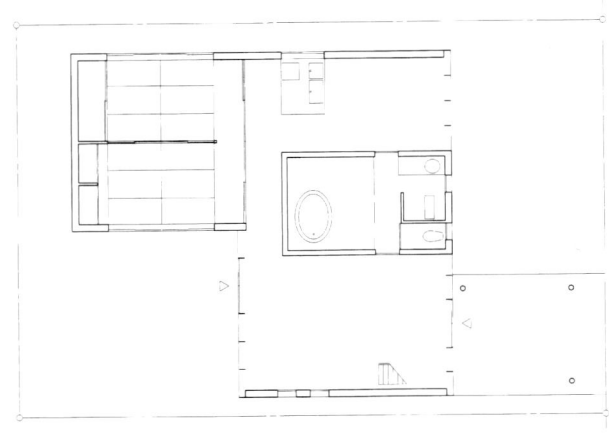

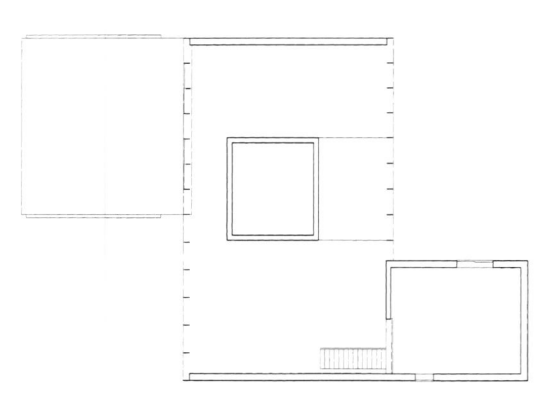

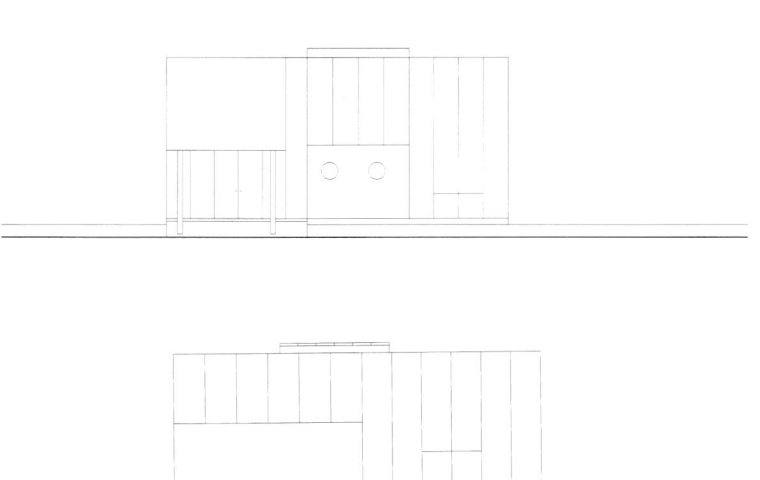

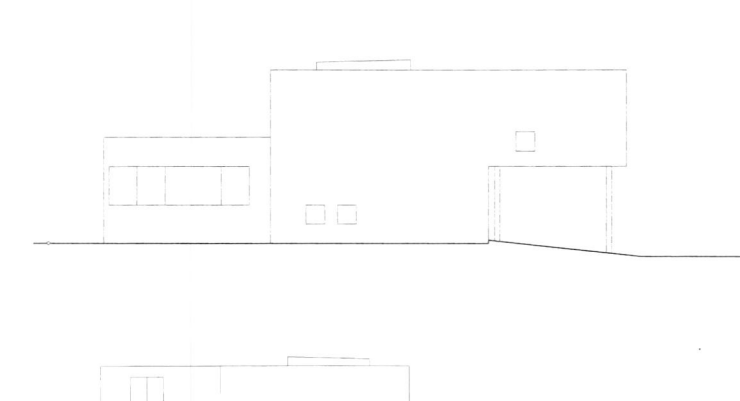

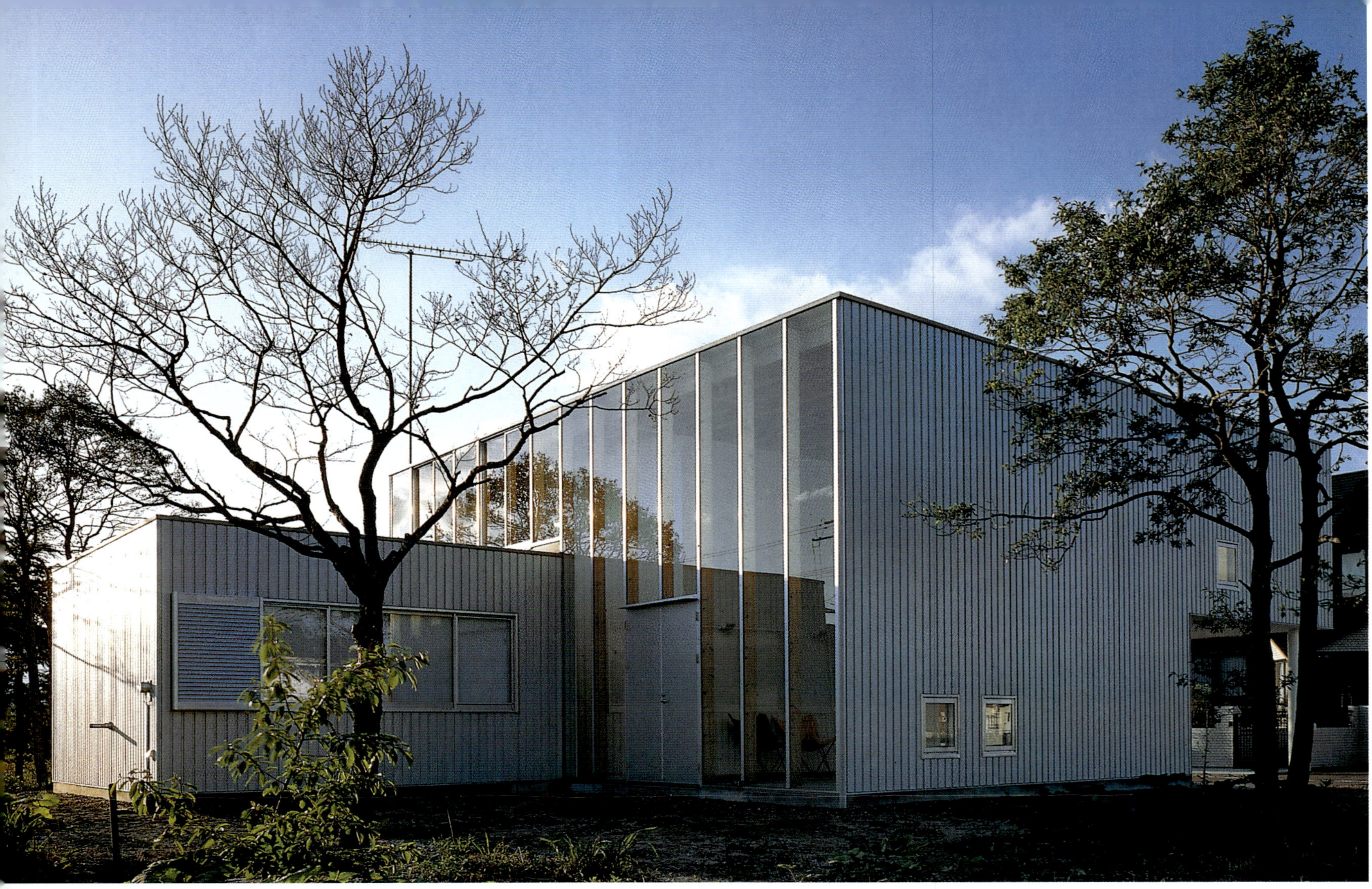

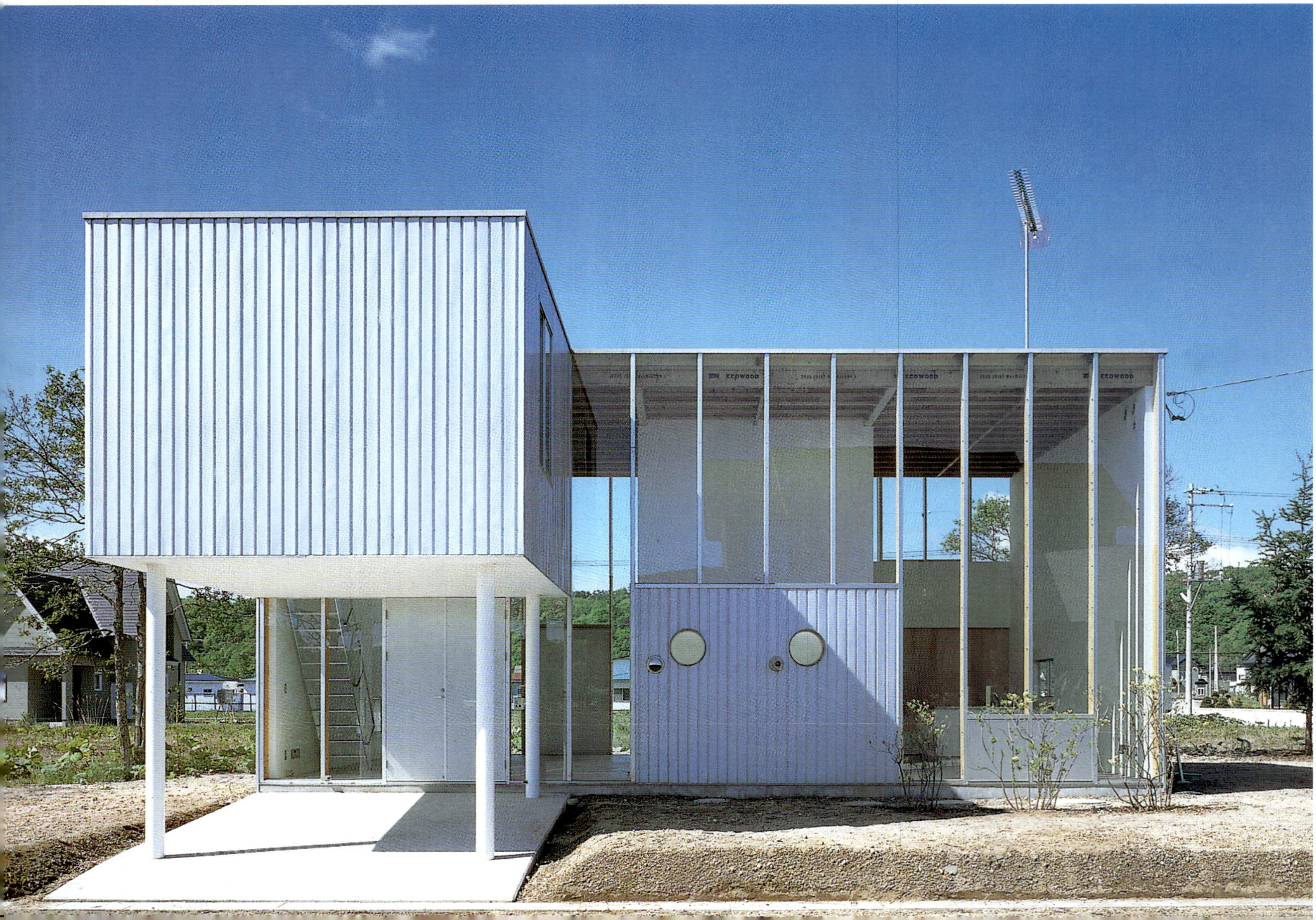

Architects   **Kazutoshi Katayama / DIK Architects & Associates, Tokyo**
Award Winning Building   **Sainokuni Chichibu Forest Lodge and Study Center**
Location   **Ootaki-Mura, Chichibu-Gun, Saitama-Prefecture, Japan**
Design and Construction Period   **1990–1993**

Award   JIA Award for the Best Young Architects of the Year 1995
Given by   JIA The Japan Institute of Architects
Prize Presentation   October / 26 / 1995
Members of the Jury   Yoshiro Ikehara, Takebumi Aida, Atushi Kitagawara
Design Team   Kazutoshi Katayama / DIK Architects & Associates
Structural Engineering   MASUDA Structural Engineering Office
Mechanical Engineering   TETENS Engineering Co Ltd
Electrical Engineering   TETENS Engineering Co Ltd
Air Conditioning Consultant   TETENS Engineering Co Ltd
Lighting Consultant   TETENS Engineering Co Ltd
Landscape Architecture   Kazutoshi Katayama / DIK Architects & Associates;
   YAGI Landscape Architects Inc.
Quantity Surveying   RAIRA Quantity Surveying
Approximate Cost   ¥ 1,300,000,000 (including land development)
Site Area   26,108 m^2
Building Area   2,502 m^2
Total Floor Area   2,431 m^2
Photographer   Yasuhiko Kidera

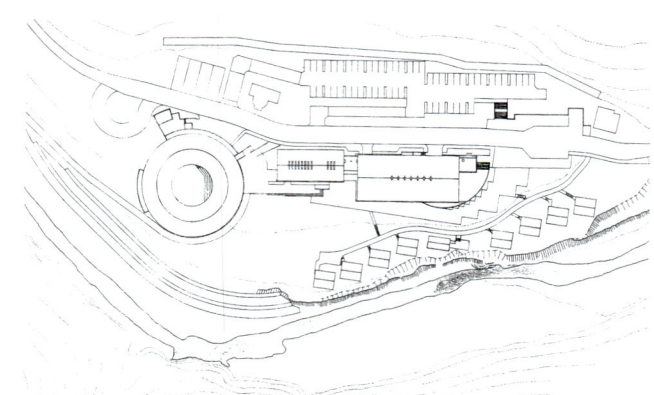

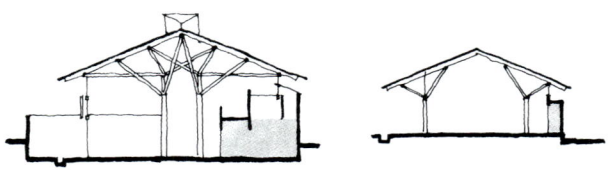

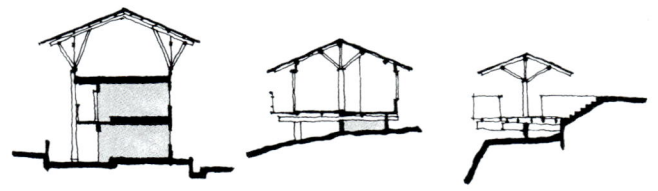

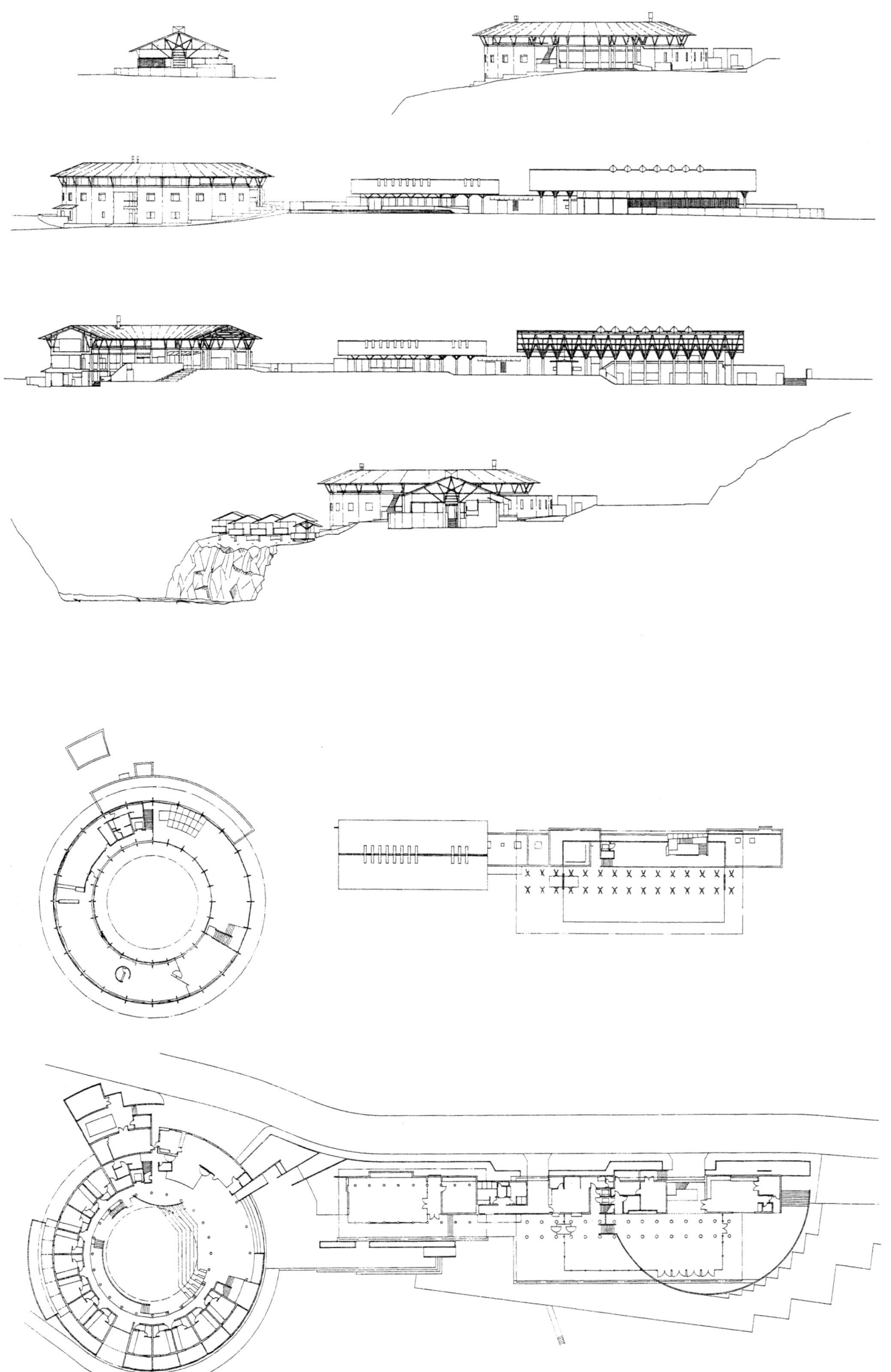

Architects **Christian Bauer Architectes, Bridel**

Award Winning Building **House Bauer**

Location **Luxembourg, Luxembourg**

Design and Construction Period **1992–1994**

Award 1995 Prix Luxembourgeois d'Architecture (Honorable Mention)

Given by Fondation de l'Architecture et de l'Ingénierie

Prize Presentation November / 10 / 1995

Members of the Jury Stephane Beel, Jean Flammang, Enrico Lunghi,
   Bohdan Paczowski, Dominique Perrault

Design Team Christian Bauer

Civil Engineering Gehl, Jacoby & Associates

Mechanical Engineering Jean Schmit Engineering

Interior Design Christian Bauer

Landscape Architecture Latz & Partner – Freising, Germany

Site Area 1,600 m²

Building Area 240 m²

Total Floor Area 420 m²

Photographer Lukas Roth, Köln

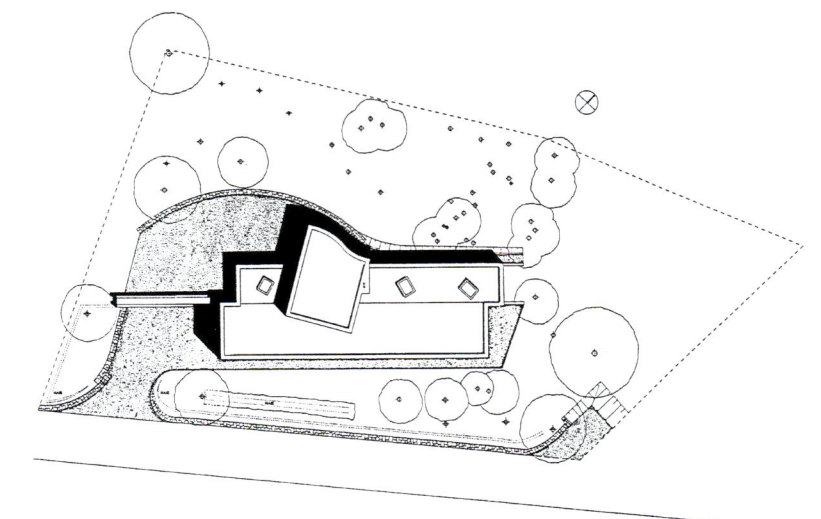

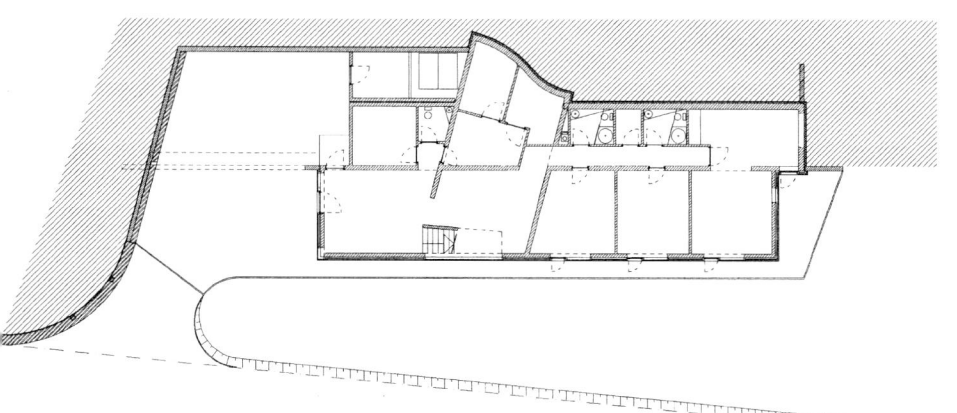

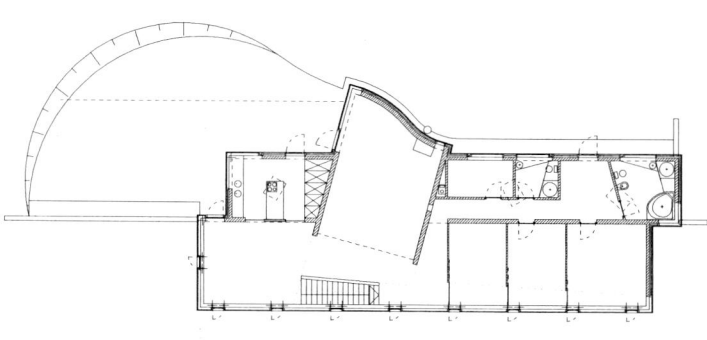

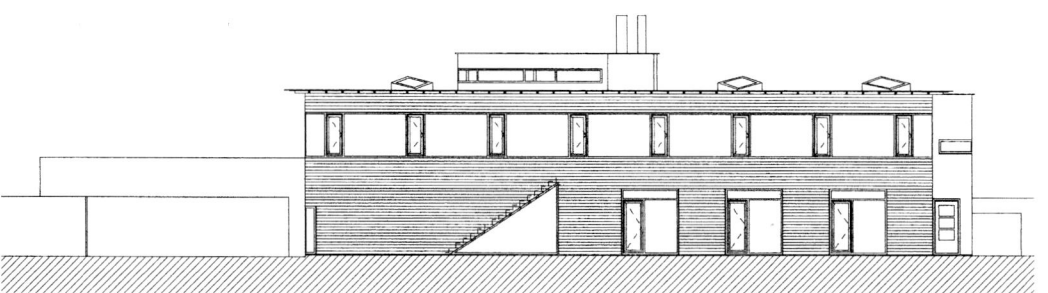

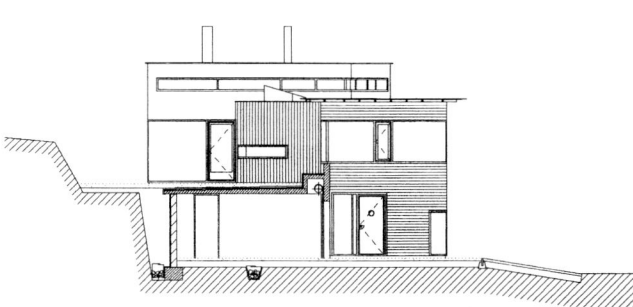

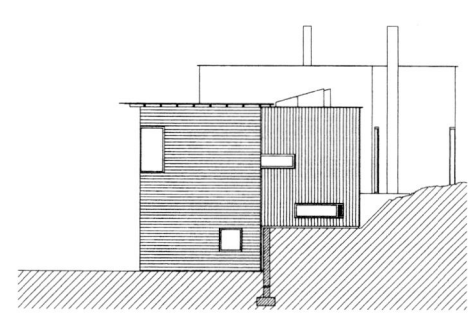

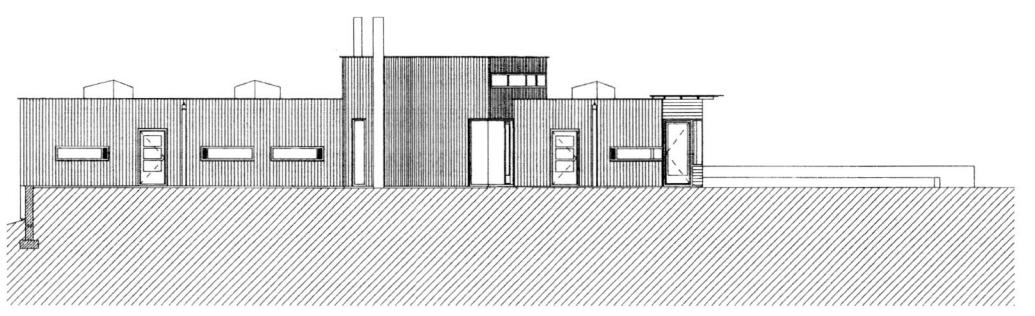

Architect **Nico Steinmetz, Luxembourg**

Award Winning Building **House & Workshop Malakoff**

Location **Luxembourg, Luxembourg**

Design and Construction Period **1990–1995**

Award 1) 1995 Prix Luxembourgois d' Architecture (Lauréat); 2) Distinguished
  Finalist Benedictus – Du Pont Award

Given by 1) Fondation de l'Architecture et de l'Ingénierie; 2) ACSA – Du Pont

Prize Presentation 1) November / 10 / 1995; 2) April / 15 / 1996

Members of the Jury 1) Stephane Beel, Jean Flammang, Enrico Lunghi,
  Bohdan Paczowski, Dominique Perrault; 2) Dominique Perrault, Robert
  J. Berkebile, Randolph Croxton

Design Team Nico Steinmetz

Structural Engineering Fior Livio Steel & Sermelux Glass

Approximate Cost F. LUX. 3,500,000

Site Area 123 m²

Building Area 99 m²

Total Floor Area 158 m²

Photographer Frank Weber, Nico Steinmetz

Architects **Leon Glodt, Regina Pizzinini, Bridel**

Award Winning Building **Villa Petite**

Location **Bridel, Luxembourg**

Design and Construction Period **1992–1995**

Award 1995 Prix Luxembourgois d'Architecture

Given by Fondation de l'Architecture et de l'Ingénierie

Prize Presentation November / 10 / 1995

Members of the Jury Stéphane Beel, Jean Flammang, Enrico Lunghi, Bohdan Paczowski, Dominique Perrault

Design Team Padraic Cassidy, Richard Griswold

Structural Engineering Jean-Paul Heinen

Mechanical Engineering Cenid

Electrical Engineering De Caro

Interior Design Leon Glodt, Regina Pizzinini

Landscape Architecture Existing Park

Approximate Cost US$ 150,000

Building Area 36 m²

Total Floor Area 72 m²

Photographer Gert von Bassewitz

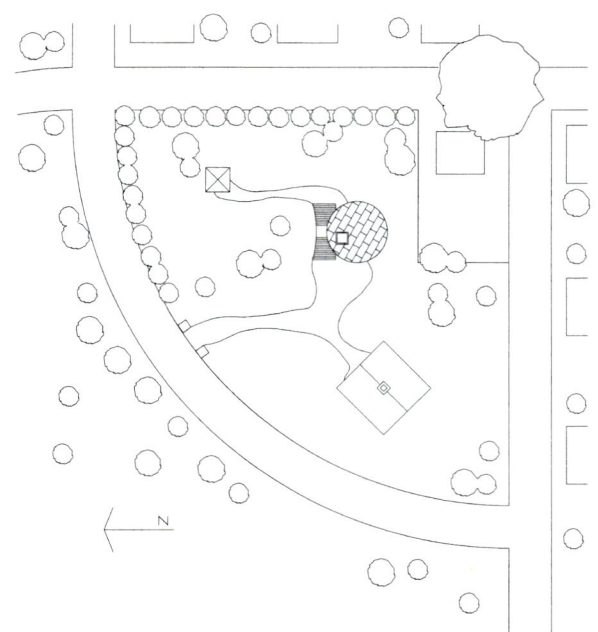

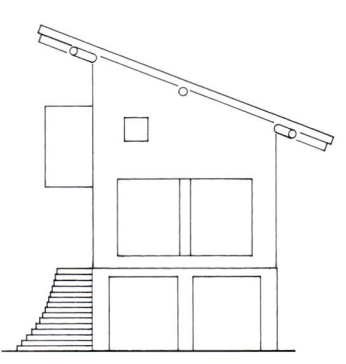

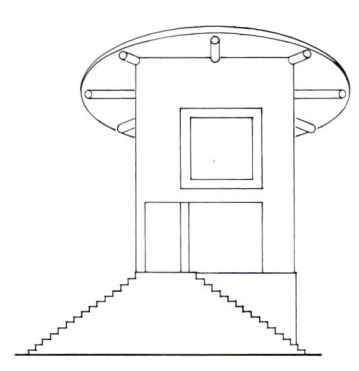

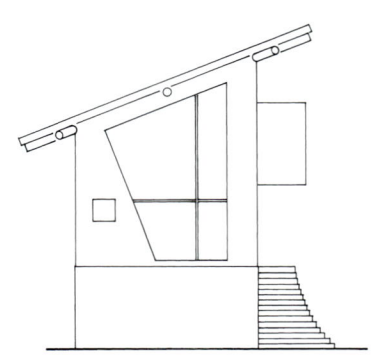

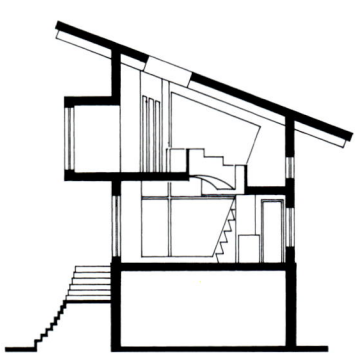

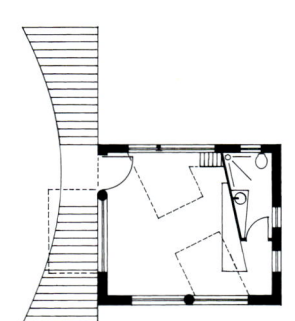

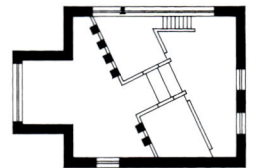

Architect **Moises Becker Kabachnik, Mexico City**

Award Winning Building **Taller de Arquitectura Becker Arquitectos**

Location **Mexico City, Mexico**

Design and Construction Period **1994**

Award Award of Mexican Architecture 1996 (IV Biennale of Architecture,
   Honorable Mention)

Given by Federación de Colegios de Arquitectos de la República Mexicana

Prize Presentation December / 13 / 1996

Members of the Jury Julio de la Peña Lomelin, Mauricio Romano del Valle,
   Félix Sánchez Aguilar, Antonio Toca Fernandez, Ramón Torres Martinez,
   Francisco Treviño Loustaunau, Héctor Velázquez Moreno, José Luis Cortez
   Delgado, Rutilo Malacara de Léon

Design Team Eugenio Romero Contreras, Benjamin Villeda Trejo, Oscar
   Muñoz Perez, Salomon Ison Zaga, Augusto Fernandez Mas

Electrical Engineering Rito Puga Perez

Air Conditioning Consultant Ing. Félix Cruz

Lighting Consultant Cecilia Valencia

Interior Design Design Team

Approximate Cost US$ 100,000

Site Area 150 m^2

Photographer Fernando Cordero

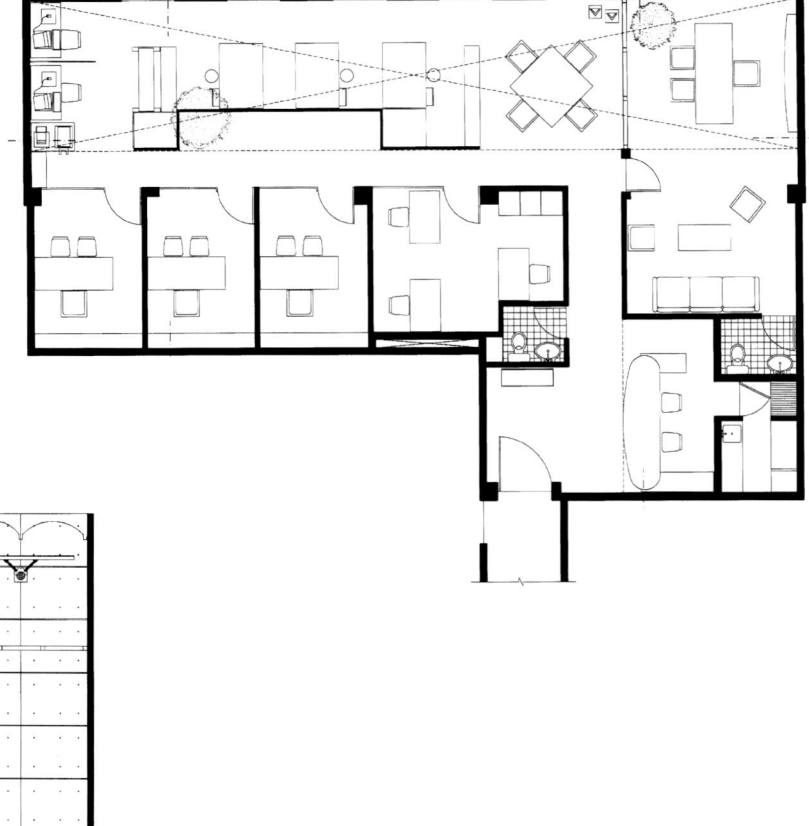

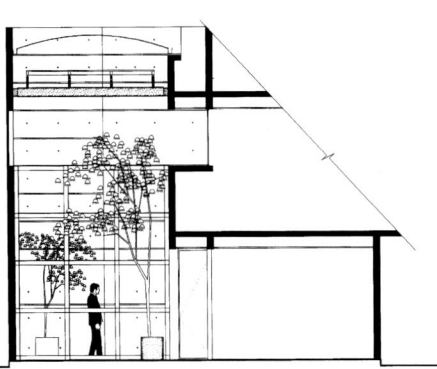

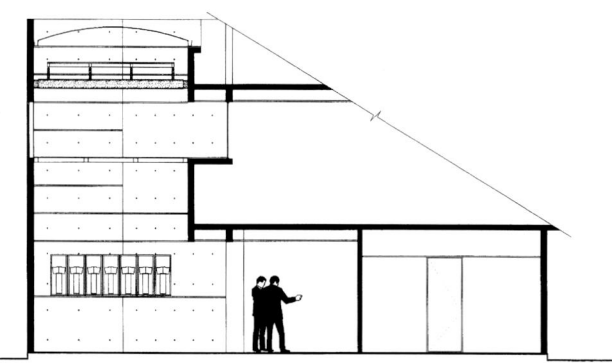

Architect   **Teodoro González de Leon**

Award Winning Building   **Conservatorio Nacional de Música
de la Ciudad de las Artes**

Location   **Mexico City, Mexico**

Design and Construction Period   **1993–1994**

Award   Award of Mexican Architecture 1996 (IV Biennale of Architecture,
Honorable Mention)

Given by   Federación de Colegios de Arquitectos de la República Mexicana

Prize Presentation   November 1996

Members of the Jury   Julio de la Peña Lomelin, Mauricio Romano del Valle,
Félix Sánchez Aguilar, Antonio Toca Fernández, Ramón Torres Martinez,
Francisco Treviño Constannan, Héctor Velázquez Moreno, José Luis Cortez
Delgado, Rutilo Malacara de Léon

Collaborator   Architect Ernesto Betancourt

Structural Engineering   Diseño y Supervision, S.C.

Hydraulics and Sanitary Engineering   Tecnoproyectos, S.C.

Electrical Engineering   Tecnoproyectos, S.C.

Acoustic Engineering   Jaffe Holden Scarbrough Acoustics Inc.

Air Conditioning Consultant   Tecnoproyectos, S.C.

Site Area   7,800 m^2

Building Area   8,950 m^2

Photographer   Pedro Hiriart

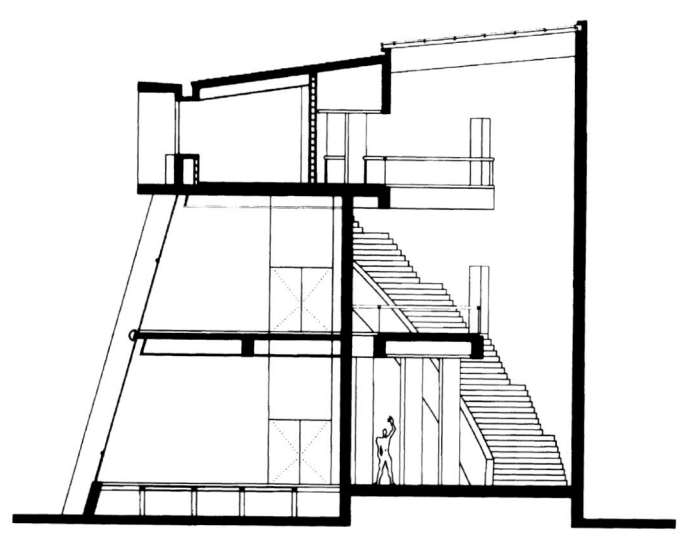

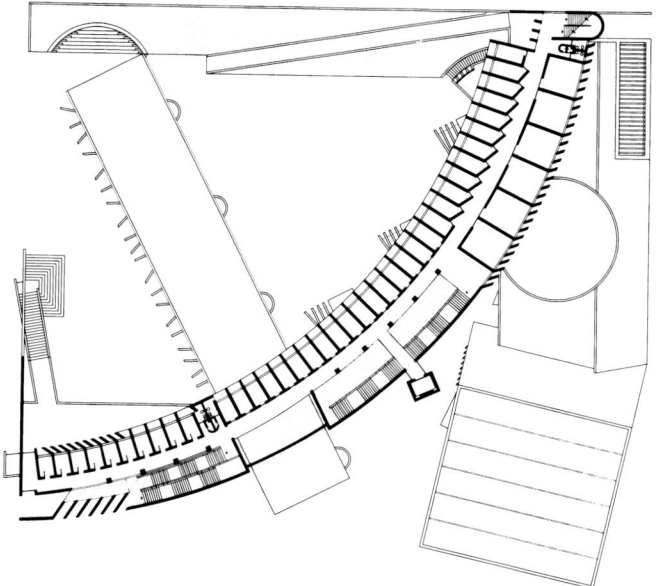

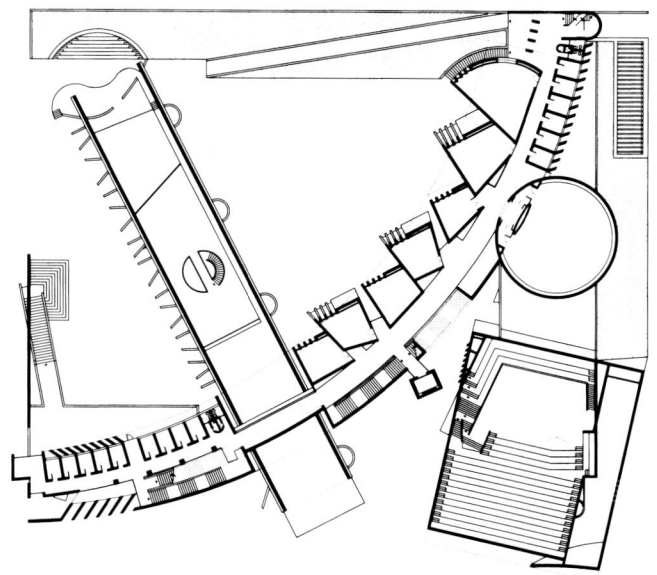

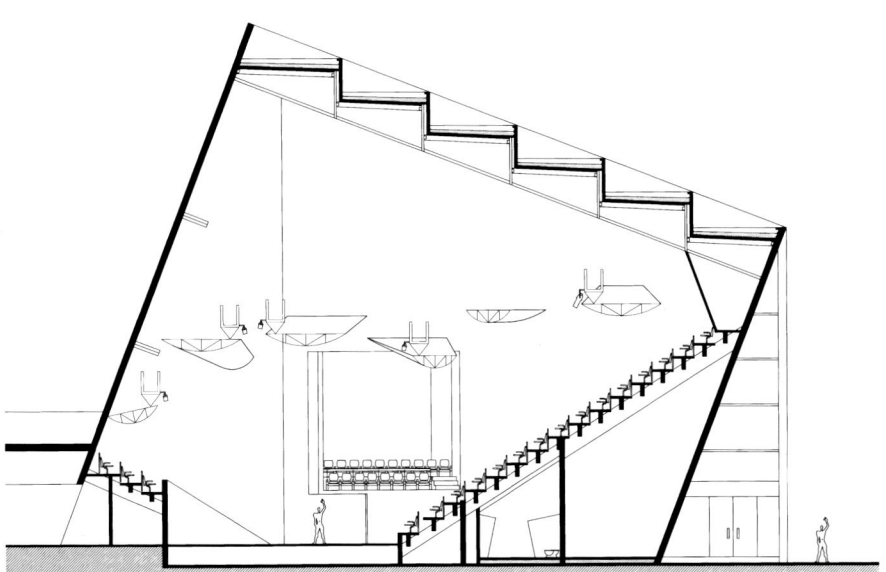

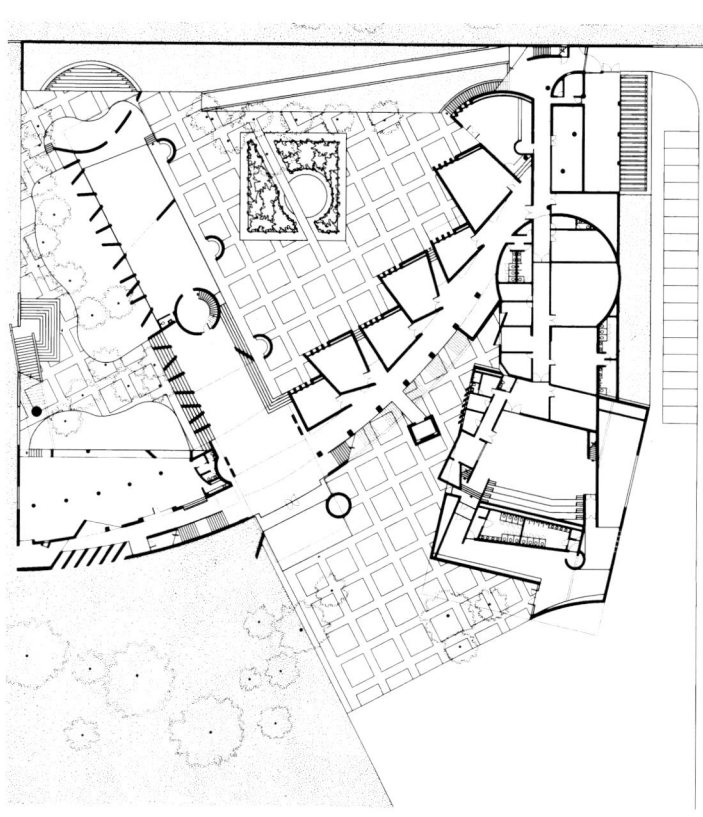

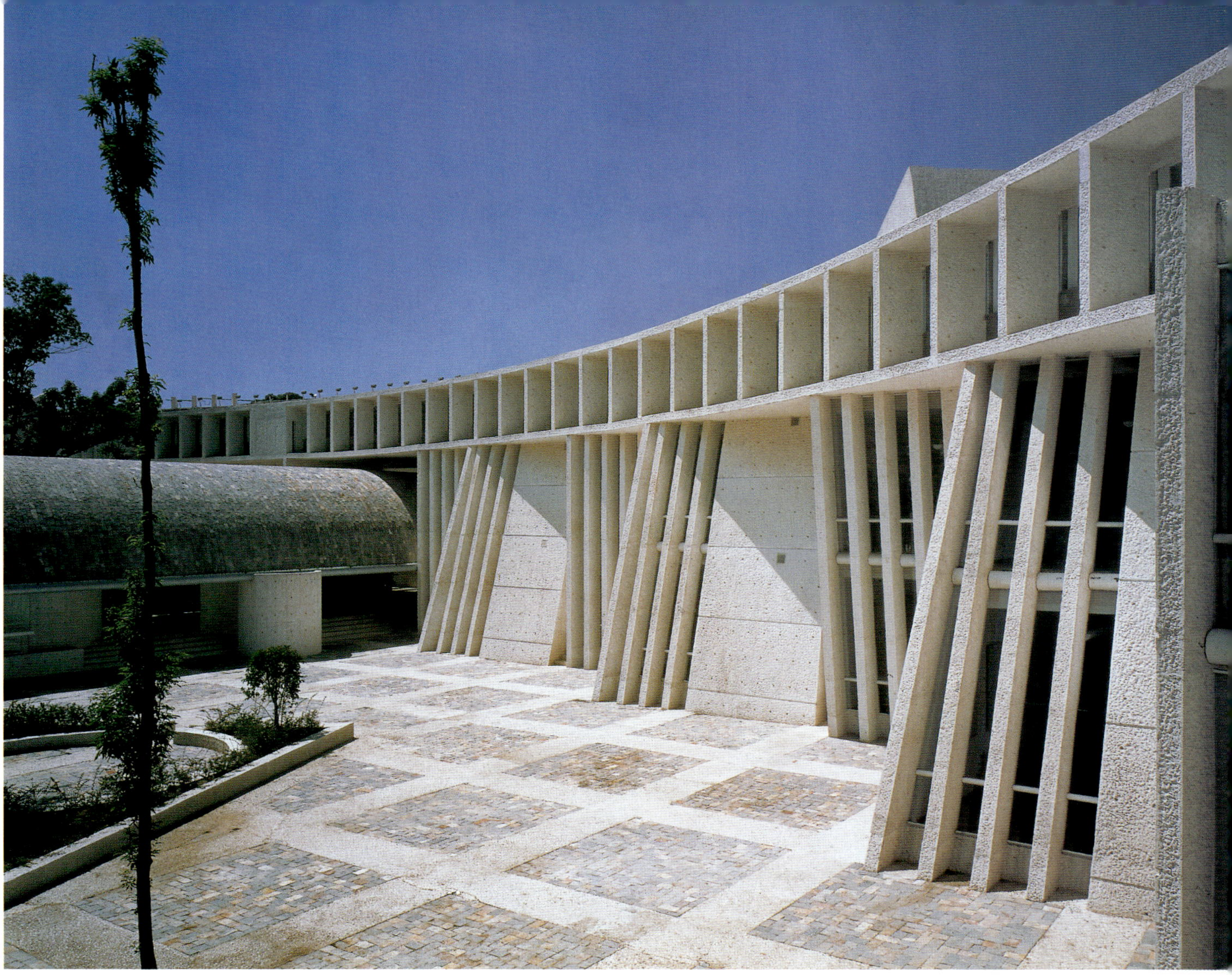

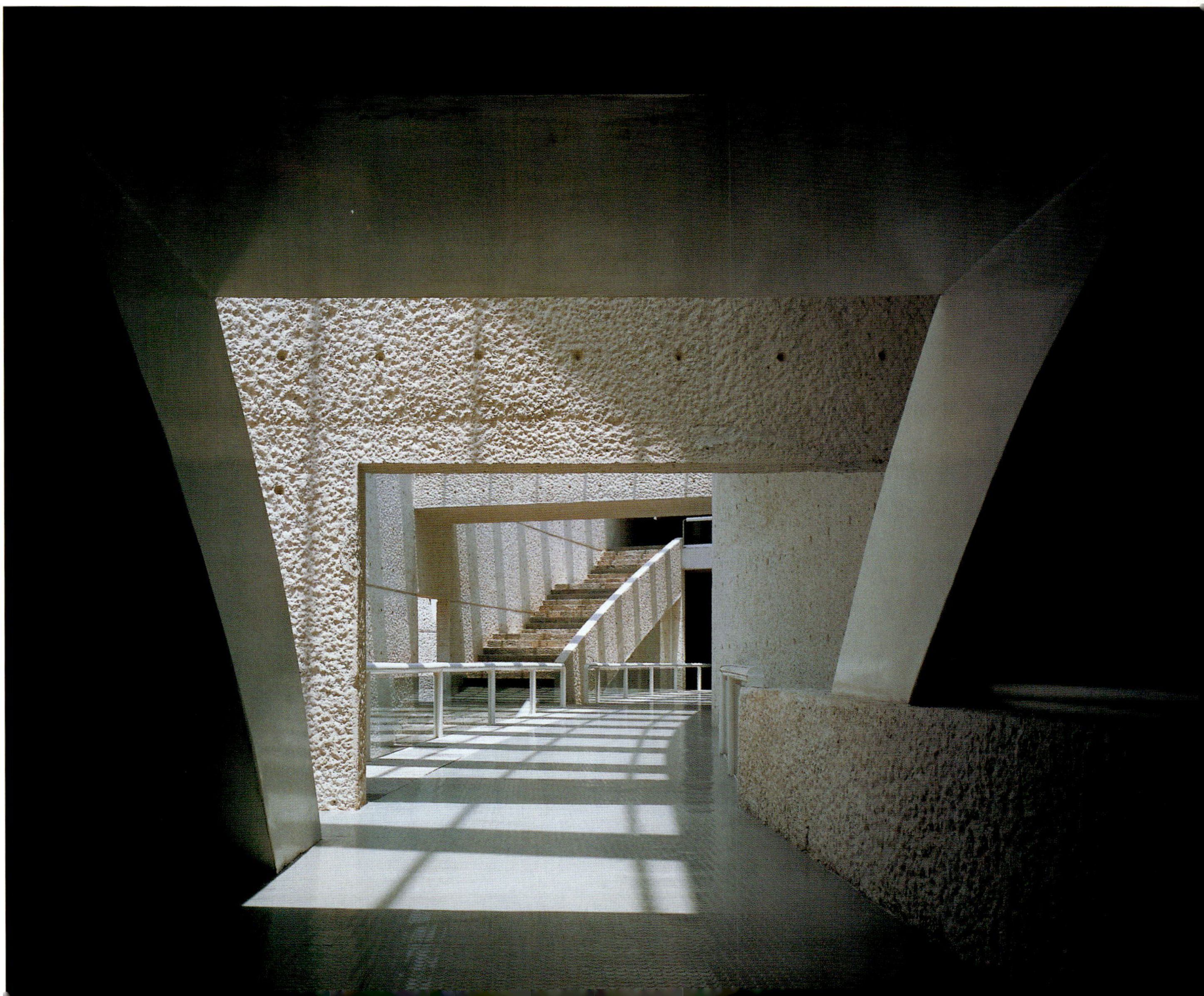

Architects **Augusto Quijano Arquitectos, S.C.P., Merida**

Award Winning Building **Rectoría de la Universidad del Mayab**

Location **Campus Universidad del Mayab, Chablekal, Yucatán, Mexico**

Design and Construction Period **1992–1994**

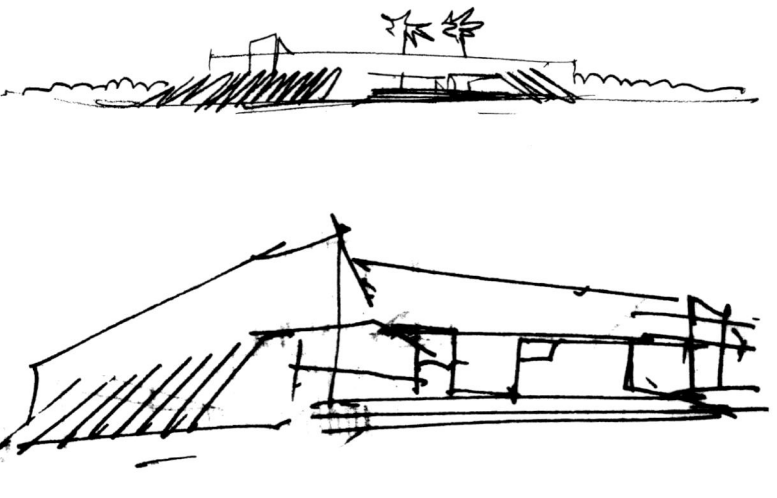

Award Award of Mexican Architecture 1996 (IV Biennale of Architecture, Silver Medal)

Given by Federación de Colegios de Arquitectos de la República Mexicana

Prize Presentation December 1996

Members of the Jury Julio de la Peña Lomelin, Mauricio Romano del Valle, Félix Sánchez Aguilar, Antonio Toca Fernández, Ramón Torres Martinez, Francisco Treviño Loustaunau, Héctor Velázquez Moreno

Design Team Augusto Quijano Axle (Principal), Ligia Quijano Axle, Enrique Cabrera Peniche, Lourdes Lara Castro, Mariano Cobá Ayala

Structural Engineering Ing. Agustín Peón de Regil

Civil Engineering Ing. Agustín Peón de Regil

Mechanical Engineering IPSA DE C.V.

Electrical Engineering LOAL, S.A. de C.V.

Air Conditioning Consultant Tecnoterma Peninsular, S.A. de C.V.

Lighting Consultant Ing. Armando Rodríguez Garza

Interior Design Augusto Quijano Arquitectos, S.C.P.

Landscape Architecture Augusto Quijano Arquitectos, S.C.P.

Approximate Cost US$ 420,000

Site Area 4,720 m²

Building Area 1,389.86 m²

Total Floor Area 1,389.86 m²

Photographer Roberto Cárdenas Cabello

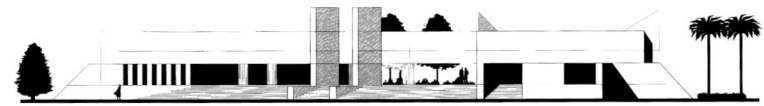

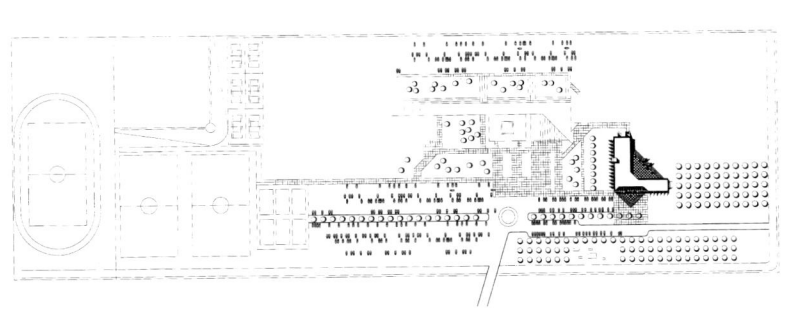

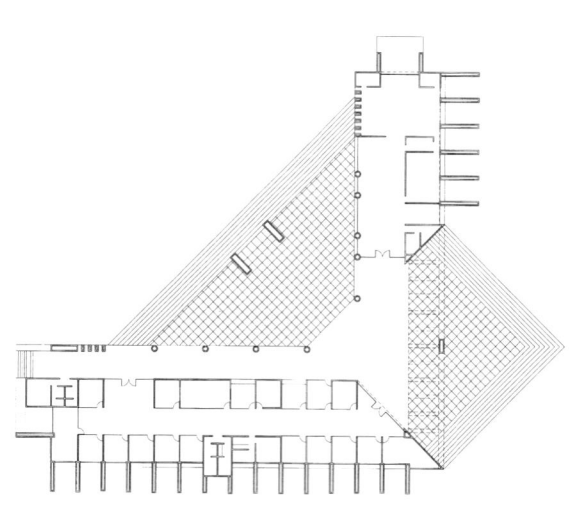

Architects **ABT Consulting Engineers, Arnhem**

Representative Building **Terminal West, Amsterdam Airport Schiphol**

Location **Amsterdam Airport Schiphol, The Netherlands**

Design and Construction Period **1989–1993**

Award BNA-Cube 1996 for the complete work of ABT Consulting Engineers

Given by BNA Bond van Nederlandse Architekten

Prize Presentation June / 28 / 1996

Members of the Jury J.M.R. Berger, J. Brouwer, K.W. Christiaanse,
   H. Kerkdijk, J.G. Kraus, J.H. Pesman

Architect Benthem Crouwel NACO

Structural Engineering ABT Consulting Engineers / DHV

Mechanical Engineering Ketel / Deerns Consulting Engineers

Electrical Engineering Ketel / Deerns Consulting Engineers

Planning and Coordination PRC Management Consultant BV

Acoustic Engineering Peutz Associates

Air Conditioning Consultant Ketel / Deerns Consulting Engineers

Bagage Handling Suystem Van der Lande Industries

Interior Design Kho Liang le Associates

Quantity Surveying Bouwkosten Management BV

General Contractor K.L.S. 2000 v.o.f.

Approximate Cost Hfl. 550,000,000

Total Floor Area 112,000 m²

Photographer Fotostudio Louk Heimans BV, Arnhem

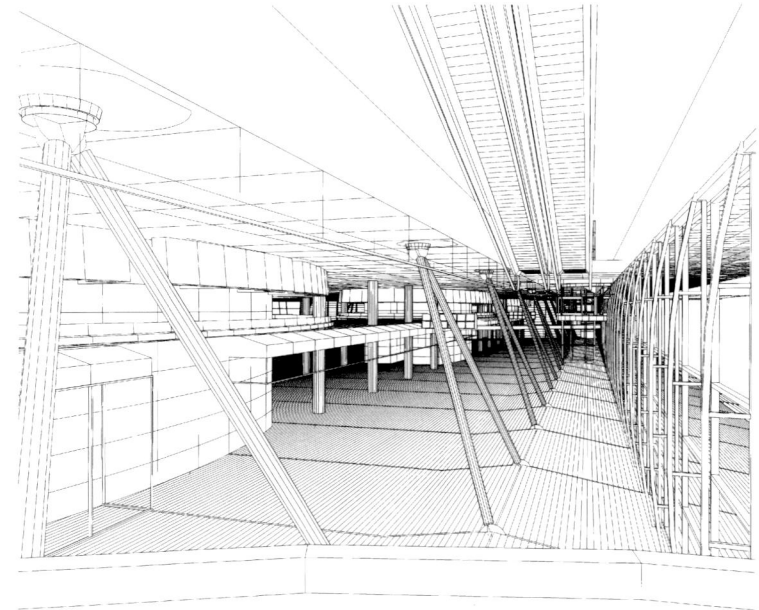

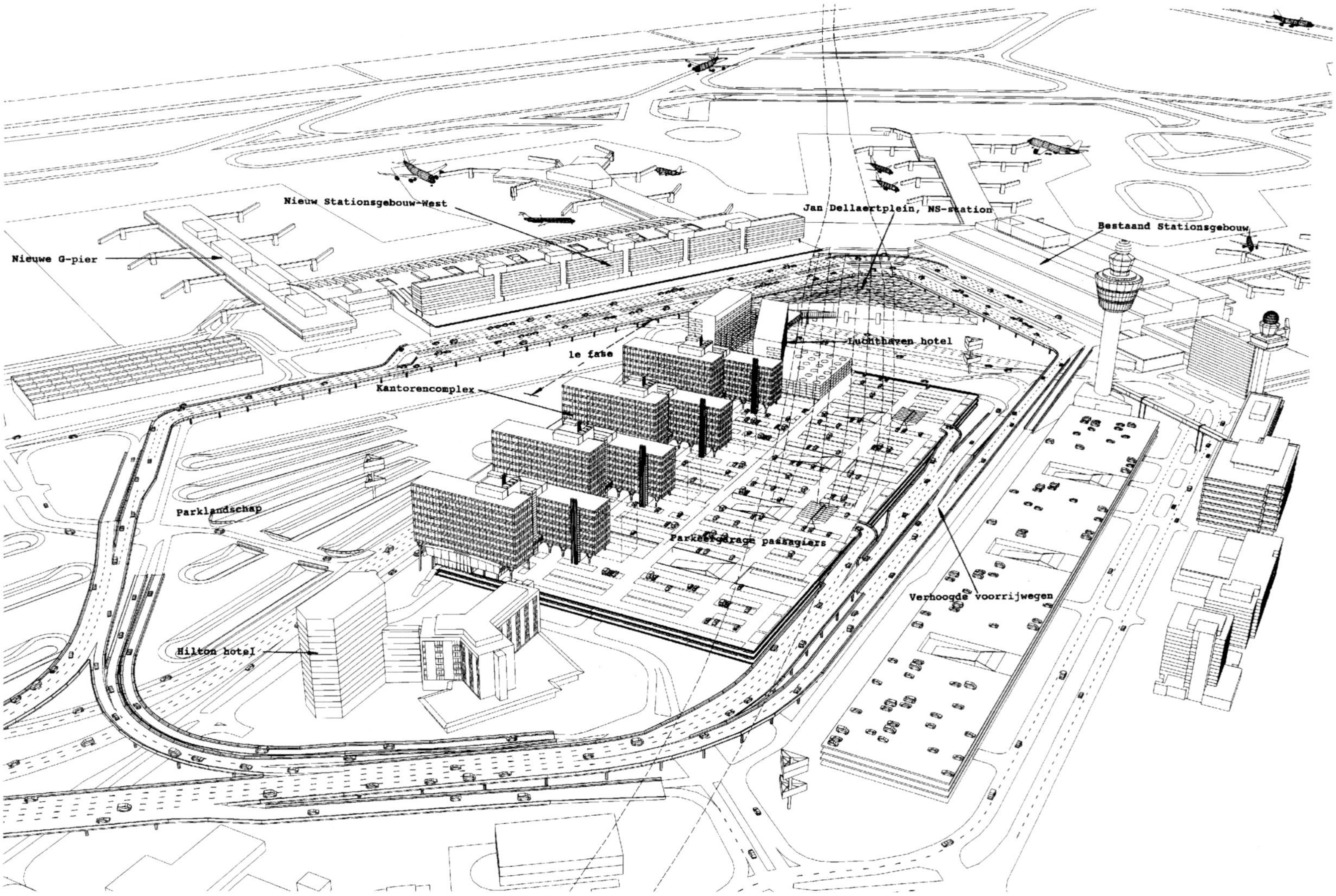

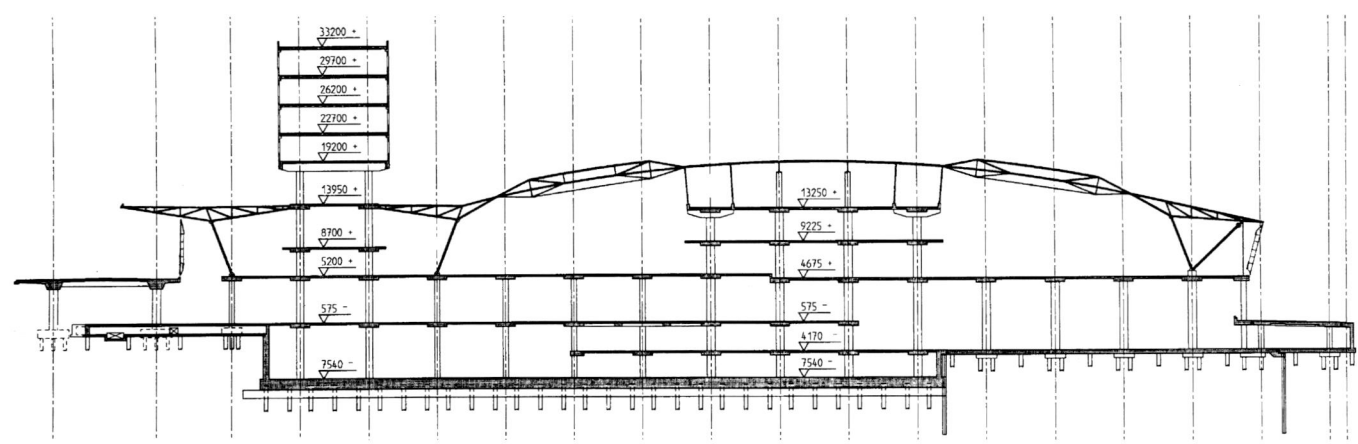

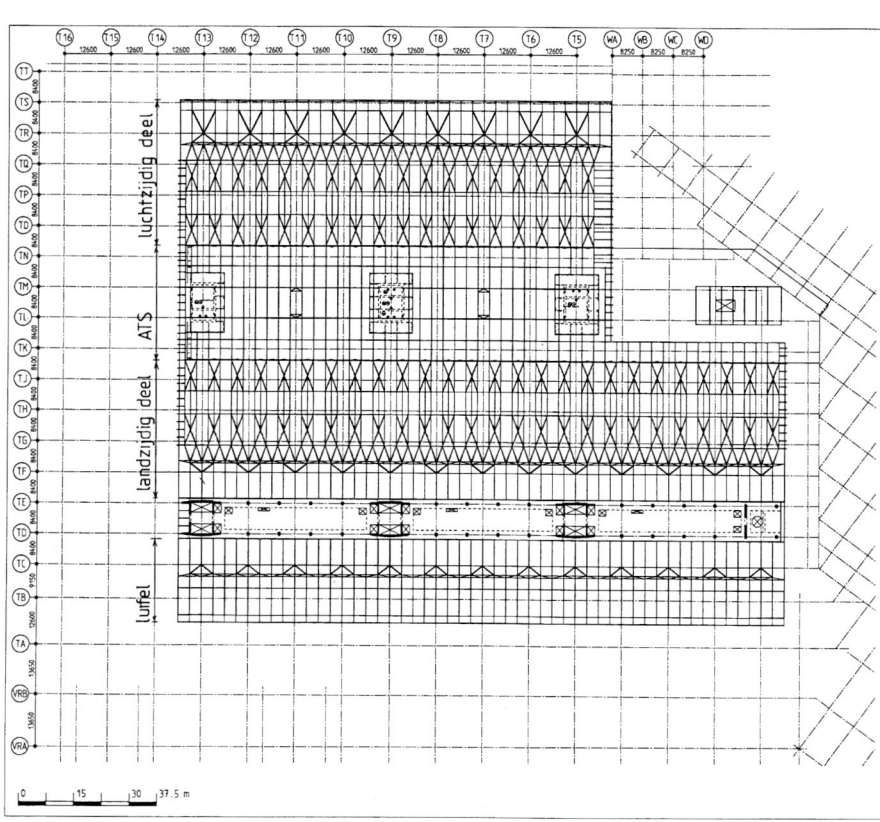

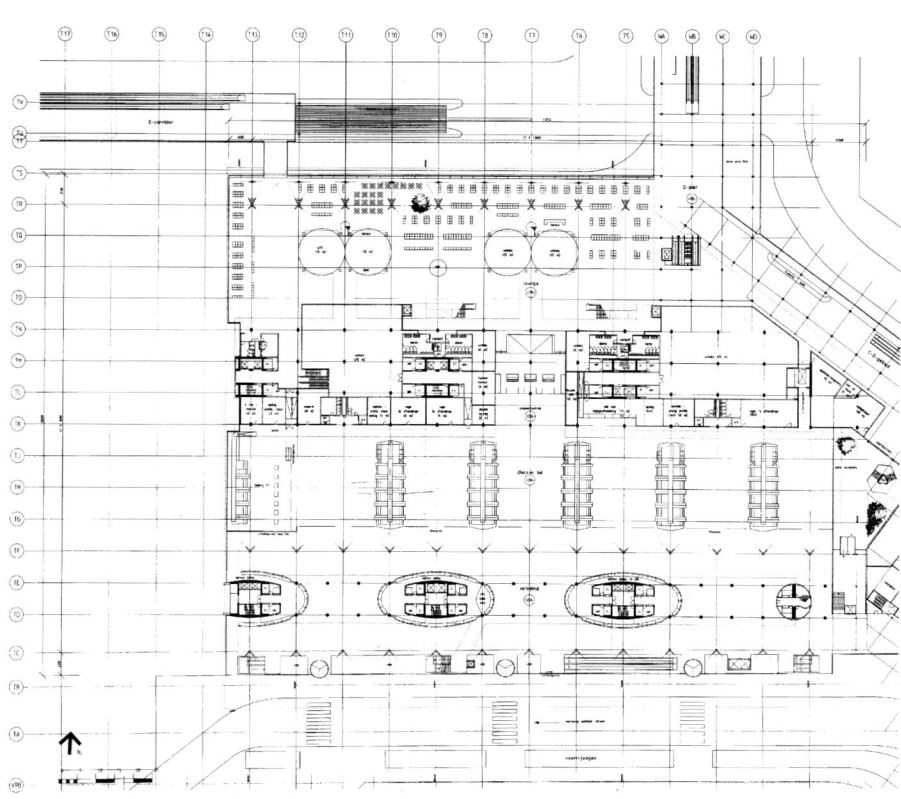

Architect **Álvaro Siza Vieira, Porto**

Award Winning Building **Castro & Melo Building**

Location **Chiado, Lisbon, Portugal**

Design and Construction Period **1991–1994**

Award Prémio Secil de Arquitectura 1996

Given by AAP Associação dos Arquitectos Portugueses and Secil

Prize Presentation January / 30 / 1997

Members of the Jury Gonçalo Byrne (President), Alexandre Brás Mimoso, João
  Luís Carrilho da Graca, Manuel Mendes, Rui Sousa Cardim, Pedro Vieira de
  Almeida, Vasco Cunha, Victor Mestre

Design Team Carlos Castanheira, Jorge Carvalho

Structural Engineering STA Segadães Tavares Associados Lda.

Civil Engineering Grade Ribeiro (STA Segadães Tavares Associados Lda.)

Mechanical Engineering Carlos Palma (STA Segadães Tavares Associados Lda.)

Electrical Engineering Vieira Pereira (STA Segadães Tavares Associados Lda.)

Life Safety Consultant Grade Ribeiro (STA Segadães Tavares Associados Lda.)

Approximate Cost US$ 400,000,000

Site Area 570 m^2

Building Area 570 m^2

Total Floor Area 3,009 m^2

Photographer José Manuel Costa Alves

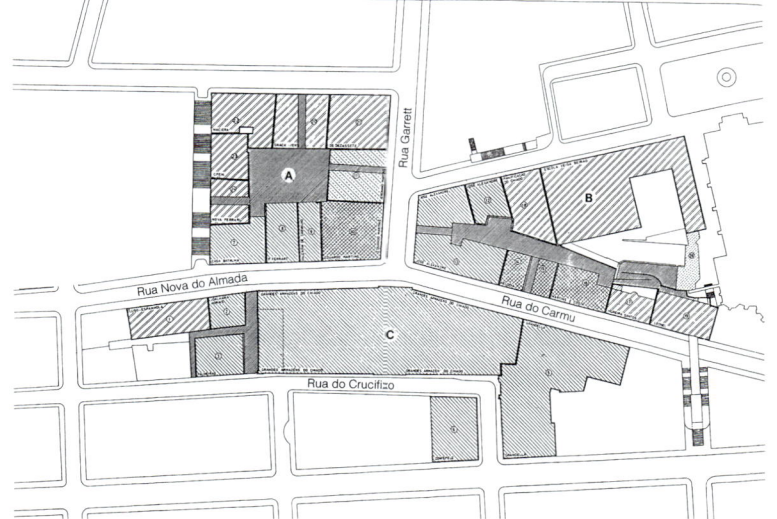

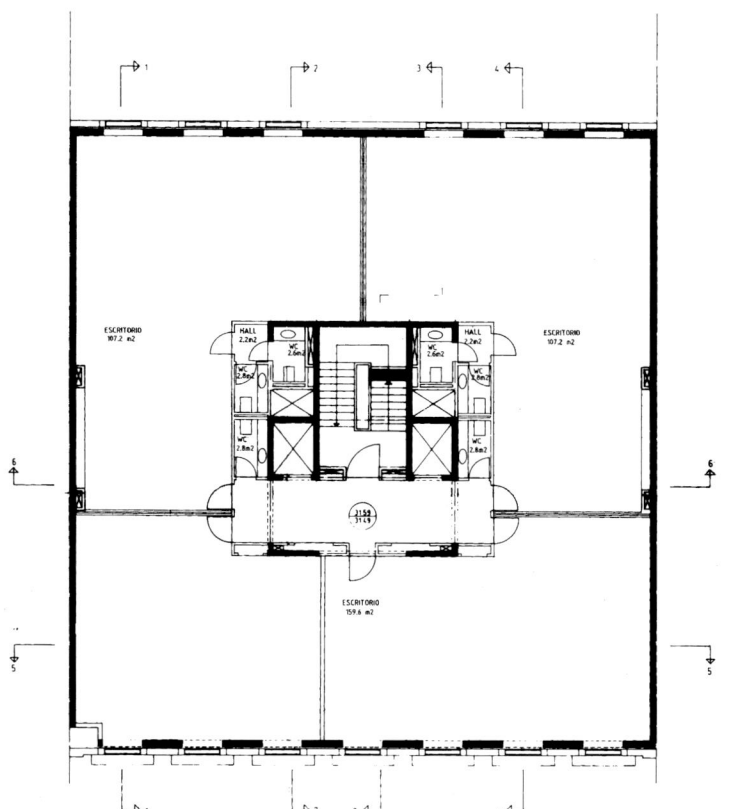

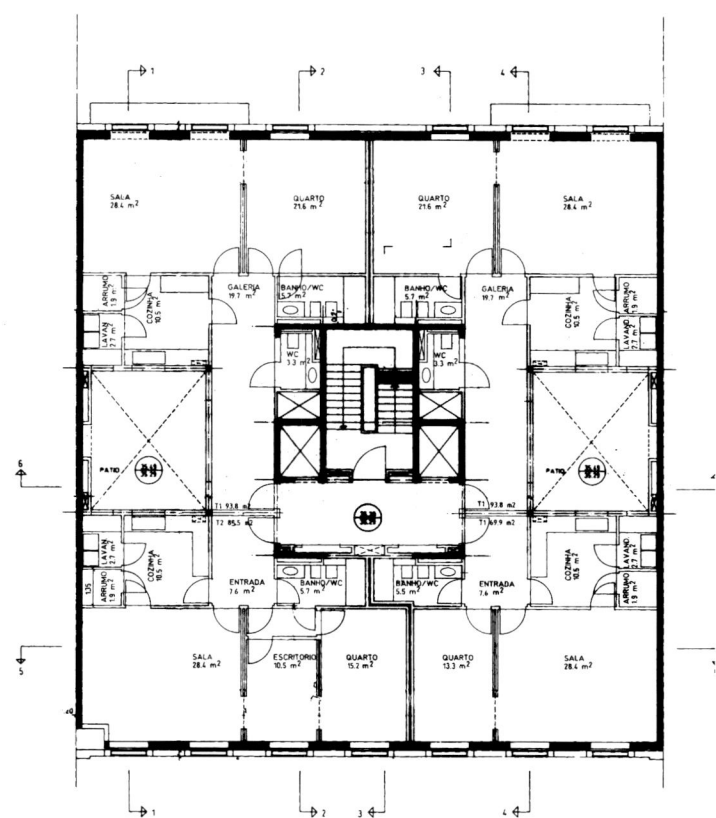

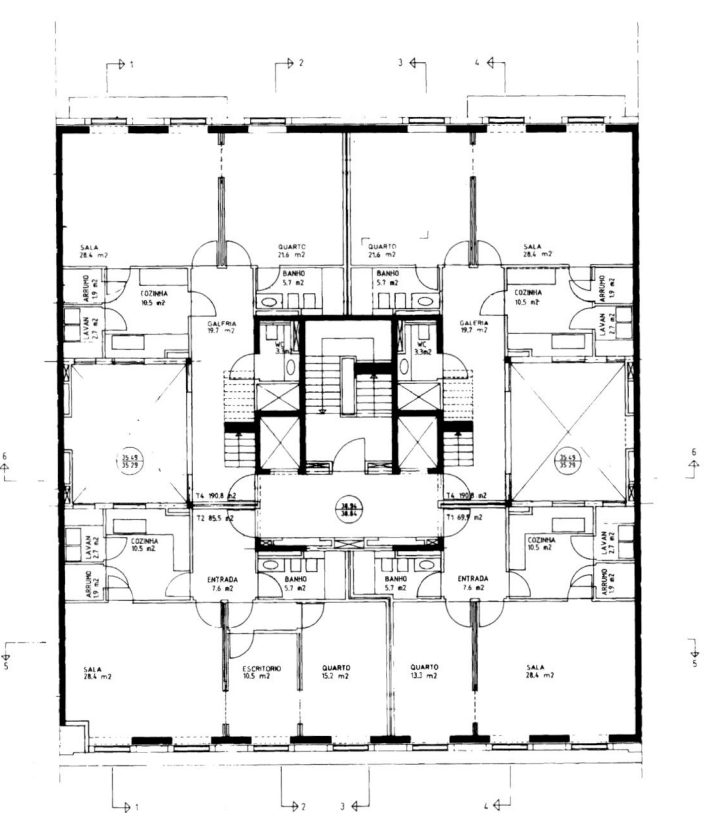

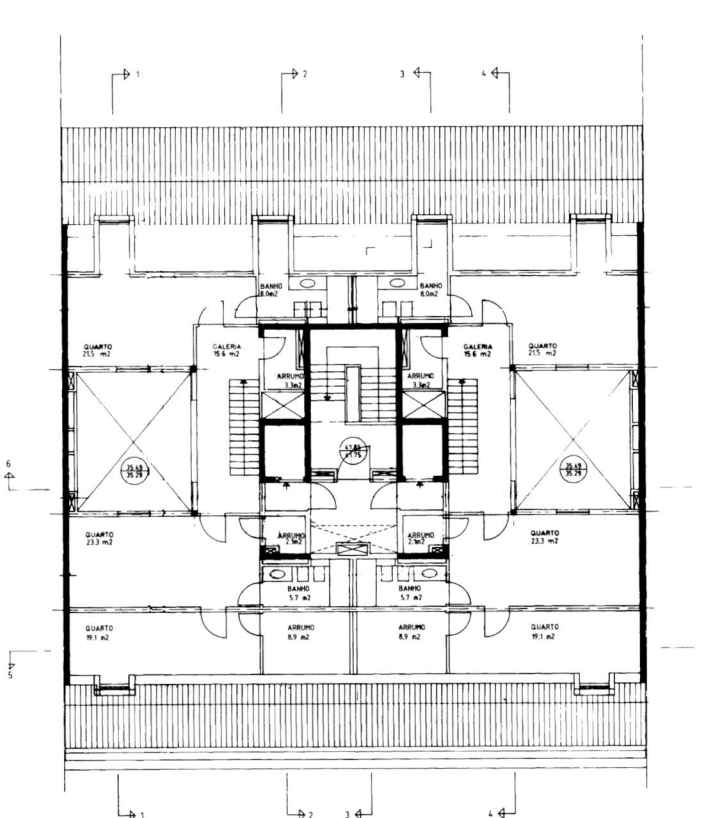

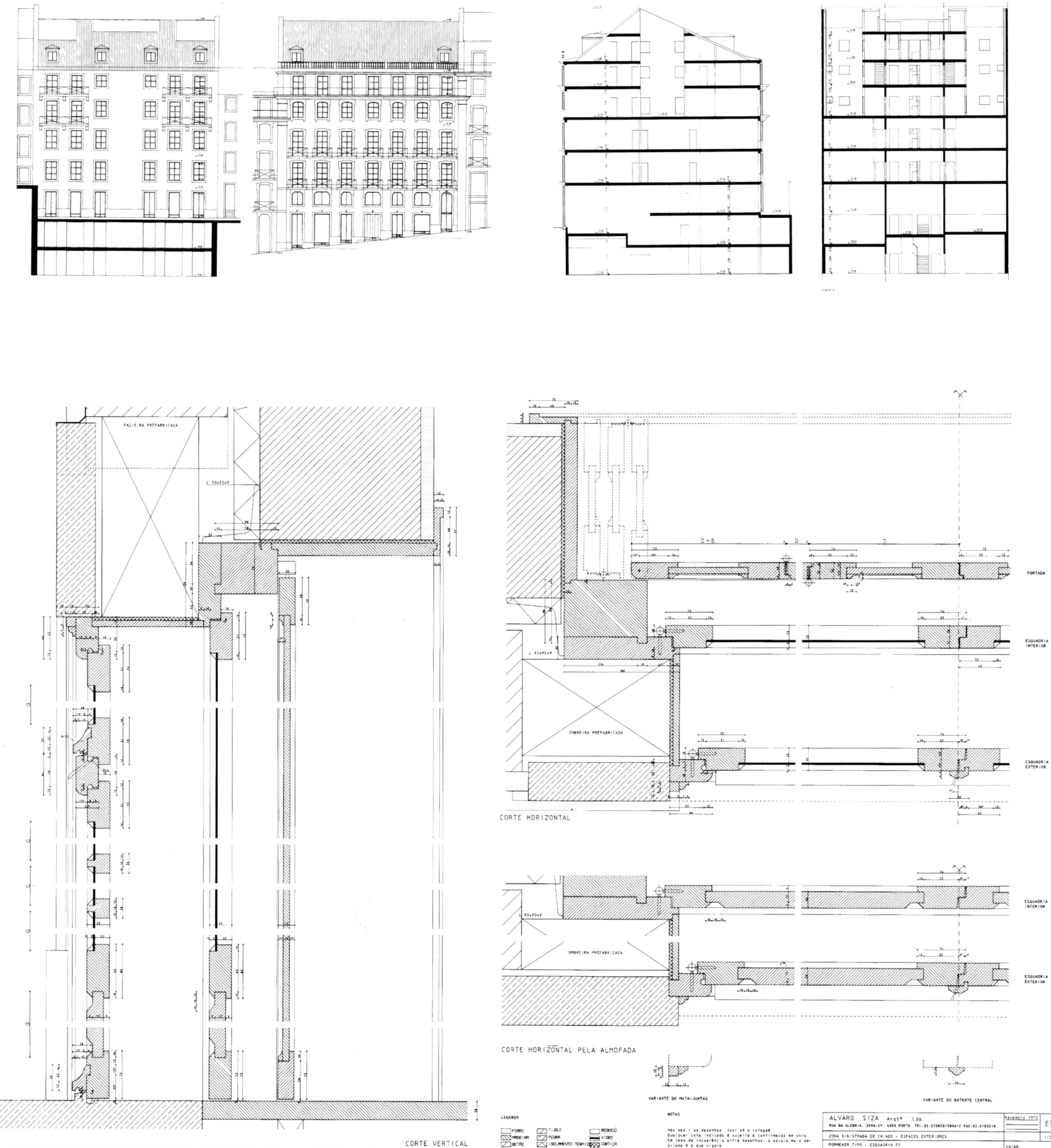

CORTE VERTICAL

CORTE HORIZONTAL

CORTE HORIZONTAL PELA ALMOFADA

VARIANTE DO MATA-JUNTAS

VARIANTE DO BATENTE CENTRAL

Architect   **Slobodan Jevdjenovic, Belgrade**
Award Winning Building   **Pedestrian Bridge with Trade Centre**
Location   **Užice, Serbia**
Design and Construction Period   **1992–1995**

Award   Prize for the Best Building in 1995
Given by   SAS Union of Architects of Serbia
Prize Presentation   February / 25 / 1996
Members of the Jury   Branislav Ihković, Branislav Mitrović, Miloš Perovi,
   Miodrag Jovanovic, Dragan Ivanović
Design Team   Slobodan Jevdjenović
Structural Engineering   Nebojša Votricević
Civil Engineering   Nebojša Votricević
Electrical Engineering   Milan Tatljak
Air Conditioning Consultant   Zorana Mileusnić-Jevdjenović
Interior Design   Slobodan Jevdjenović
Landscape Architecture   Slobodan Jevdjenović
Quantity Surveying   Dragan Djordjević
Approximate Cost   DM 500,000
Building Area   416 m^2
Total Floor Area   416 m^2
Photographer   Slobodan Jevdjenović

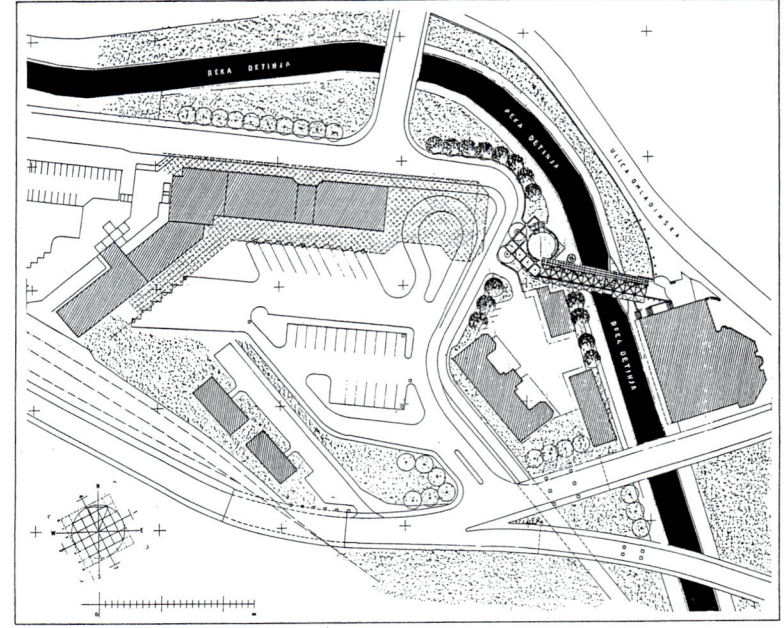

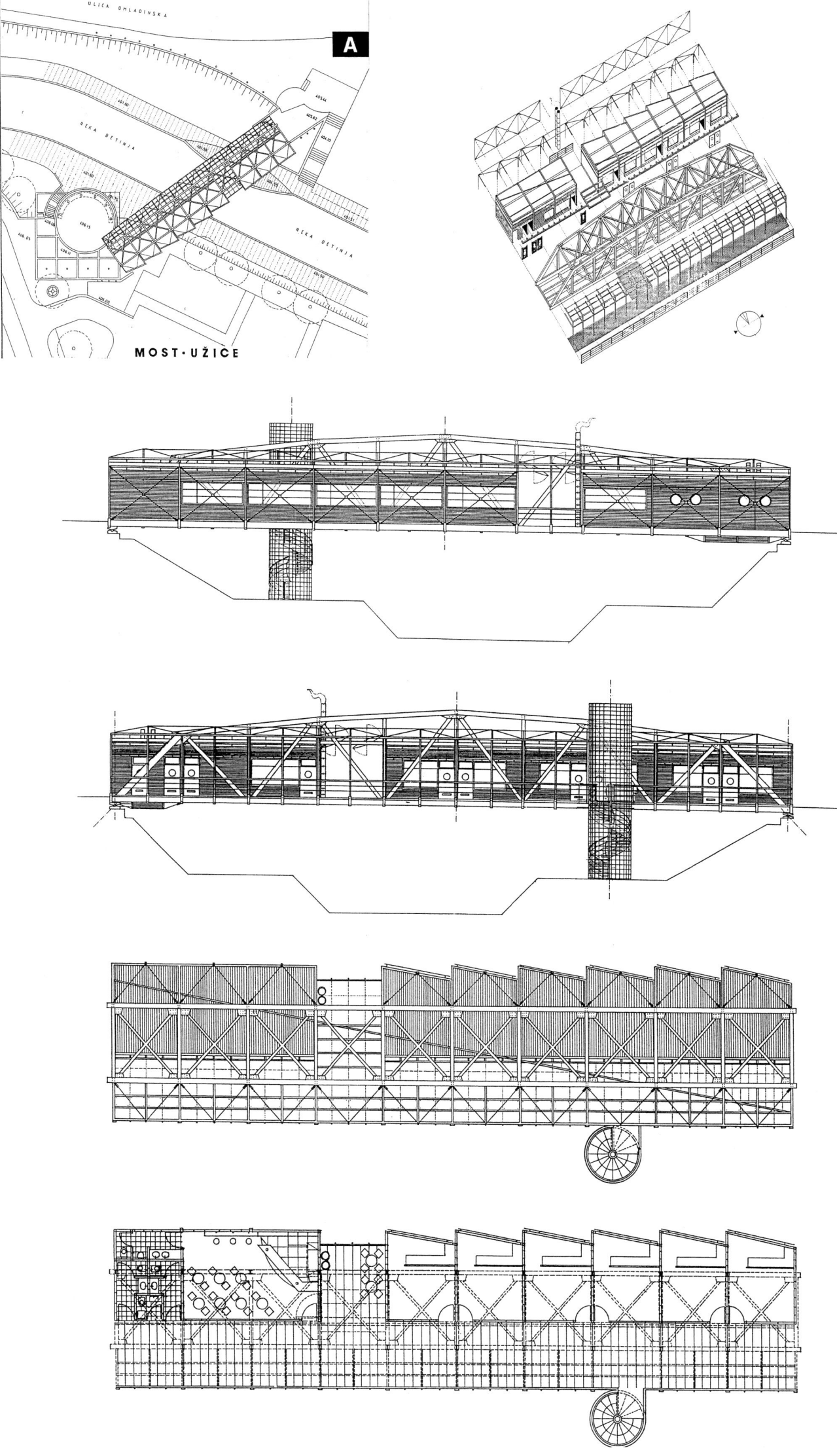

MOST·UŽICE

Architects **DP Architects Pte. Ltd., Singapore**

Award Winning Building **Bugis Junction**

Location **Singapore, Singapore**

Design and Construction Period **1990–1995**

Award 4th SIA Architectural Design Award (Honorable Mention)

Given by SIA Singapore Institute of Architects

Prize Presentation November / 27 / 1995

Members of the Jury Richard Frewer, Hijjas Bin Kasturi, Ir. Syahrul Syarif,
Eric Lye, Abdul Hussain, Goh Chong Chia

Design Team Chan Sui Him (Director), Ho Lip Shang, Catherine Chong,
Song Yew Kee, Tong Bin Sin, Liew Siong Chong

Structural Engineering Meinhardt (S) Pte Ltd

Civil Engineering Meinhardt (S) Pte Ltd

Mechanical Engineering Beca Carter Hollings & Ferner (S.E. Asia) Pte Ltd

Electrical Engineering Beca Carter Hollings & Ferner (S.E. Asia) Pte Ltd

Environmental Engineering (Environmental Graphics) Communication Arts
Incorporated (USA)

Acoustic Engineering Acviron Acoustics Consultants Pte Ltd

Air Conditioning Consultant Beca Carter Hollings & Ferner (S.E. Asia) Pte Ltd

Lighting Consultant T. Kondos Associates Incorporated (USA)

Interior Design Hotel: Rifenberg Associates (Bangkok); Retail:
Communication Arts Incorporated (USA)

Landscape Architecture Studio Land Incorporated (USA)

Quantity Surveying Rider Hunt Levitt & Bailey

Approximate Cost S$ 300,000,000

Site Area 25,986 m^2

Building Area 119,221 m^2

Total Floor Area 149,513 m^2

Photographer DP Architects Pte Ltd., Keppel Land Ltd.

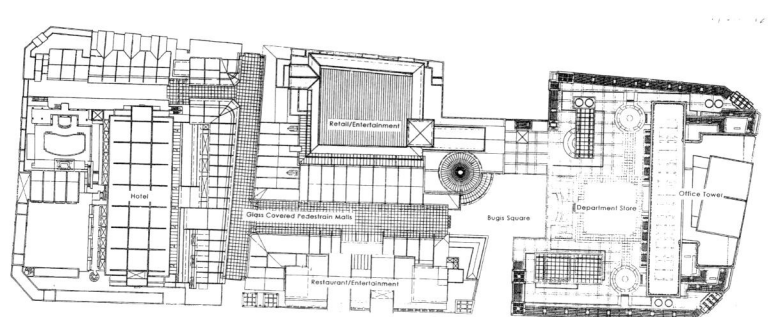

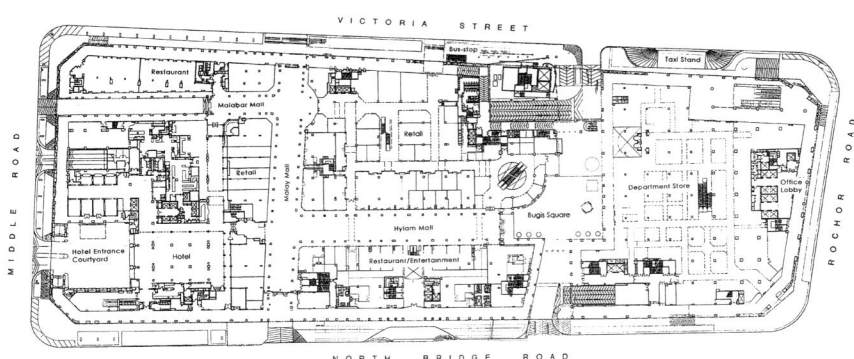

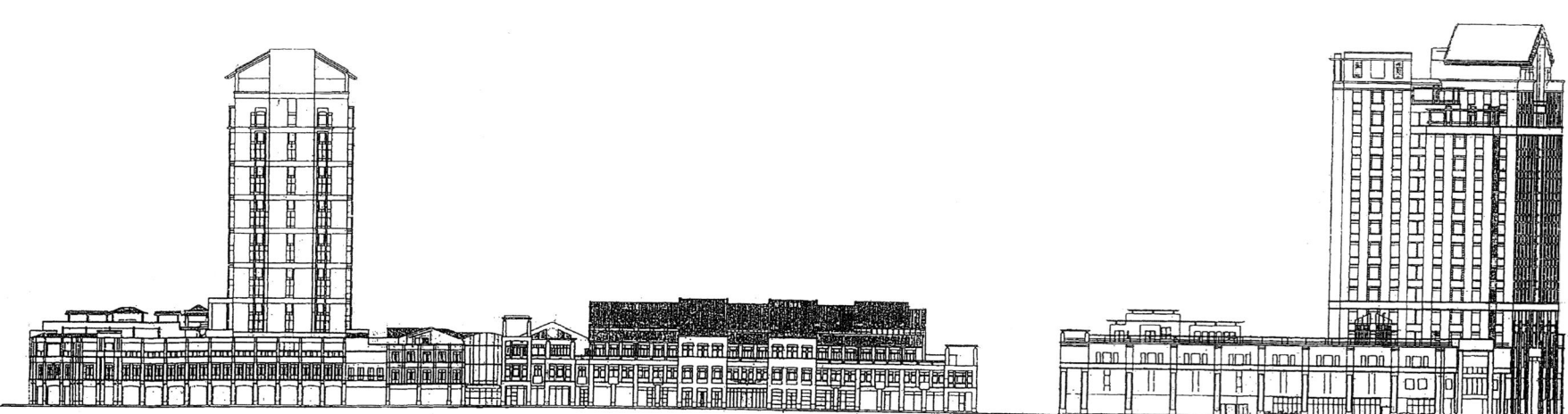

Architects **Forum Architects (Lim Cheng Kooi, Architect in Charge;**
   Ho Sweet Woon, Partner in Charge), Singapore
Award Winning Building **Semi-Detached House at 14C Sian Tuan Avenue**
Location **Bukit Timah Road, Singapore, Singapore**

Award 4th SIA Architectural Design Award (Honorable Mention; Category:
   Terrace / Semi-Detached Houses)
Given by SIA Singapore Institute of Architects
Prize Presentation November / 27 / 1995
Members of the Jury Richard Frewer, Hijias Bin Kasturi, Ir Syahrul Syarif,
   Eric Lye, Abdul Hussain, Goh Chong Chia
Design Team Forum Architects
Structural Engineering SLP Consulting Engineers
Civil Engineering SLP Consulting Engineers
Lighting Consultant Forum Architects
Landscape Architecture Ng Geok Lan
Quantity Surveying PQS Consultants
Approximate Cost S$ 500,000
Site Area 407.16 m²
Total Floor Area 272.63 m²
Photographer Xiao Photo Workshop

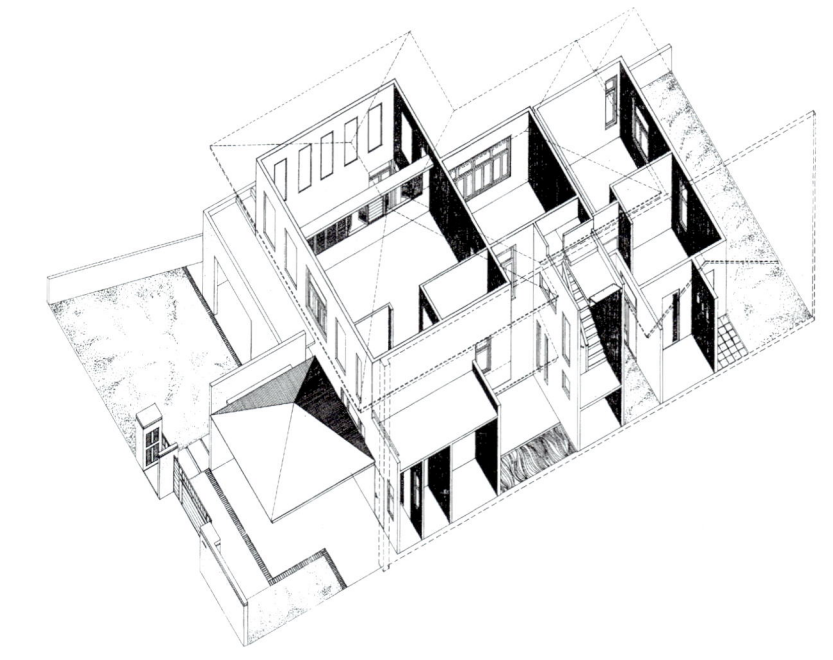

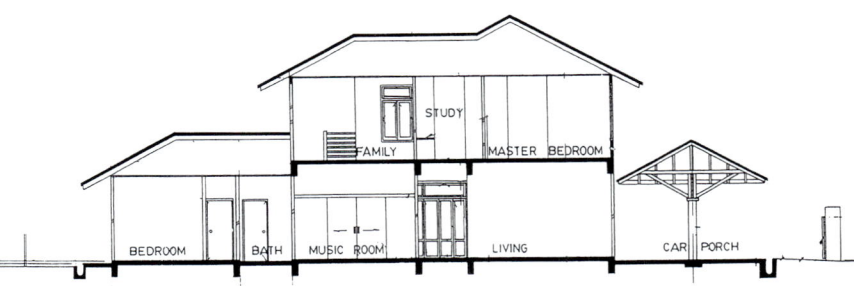

3 LIVING ROOM
4 DINING
5 MUSIC ROOM
6 BEDROOM
7 BEDROOM
8 FAMILY
9 MASTER BEDROOM
10 VOID OVER LIVING

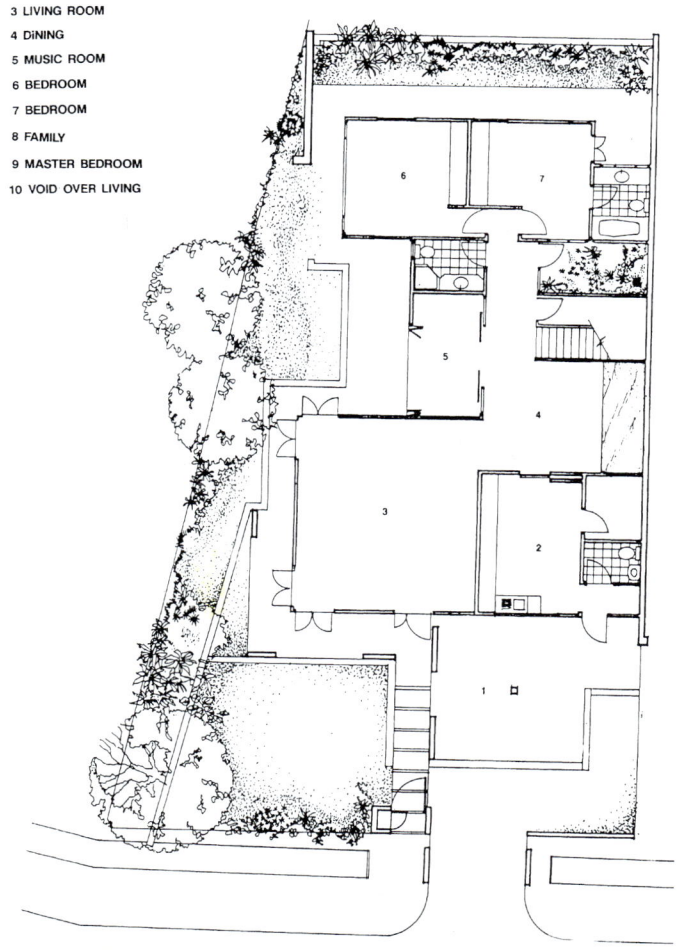

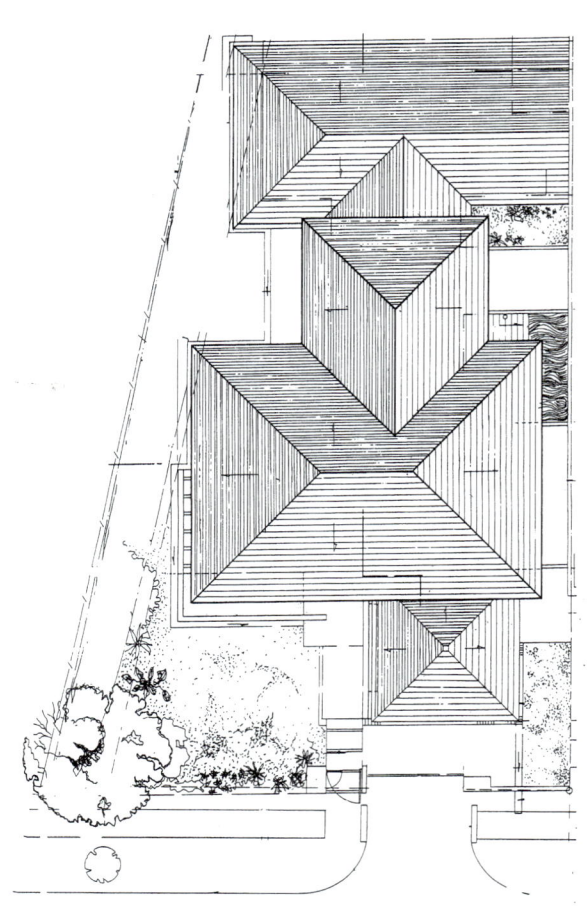

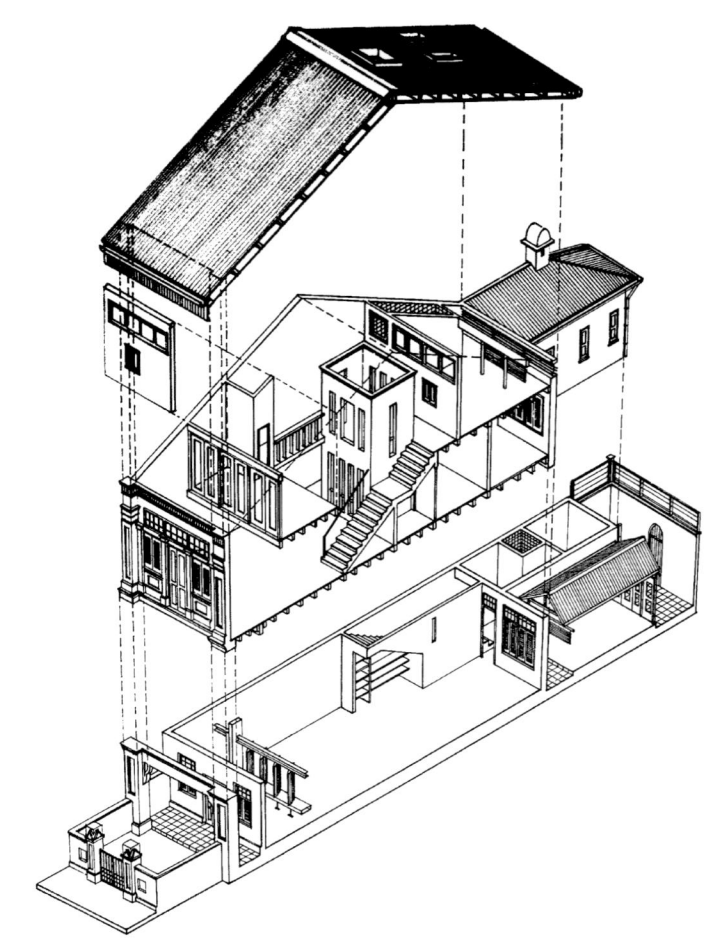

Architects **RichardHo Architects, Singapore**

Award Winning Building **No. 12 Koon Seng Road**

Location **Singapore, Singapore**

Award 4th SIA Architectural Design Award (Category: Conservation)

Given by SIA Singapore Institute of Architects

Prize Presentation November / 27 / 1995

Members of the Jury Richard Frewer, Hijias Bin Kasturi, Ir. Syahrul Syarif, Eric Lye, Abdul Hussain, Goh Chong Chia

Design Team Richard K.F. Ho, Simon Jeffries, Paul Karakusevic

Structural Engineering Tham & Wong Consulting Engineers

Approximate Cost US$ 130,000

Site Area 110 m²

Building Area 250 m²

Total Floor Area 250 m²

Photographer Albert K.S. Lim

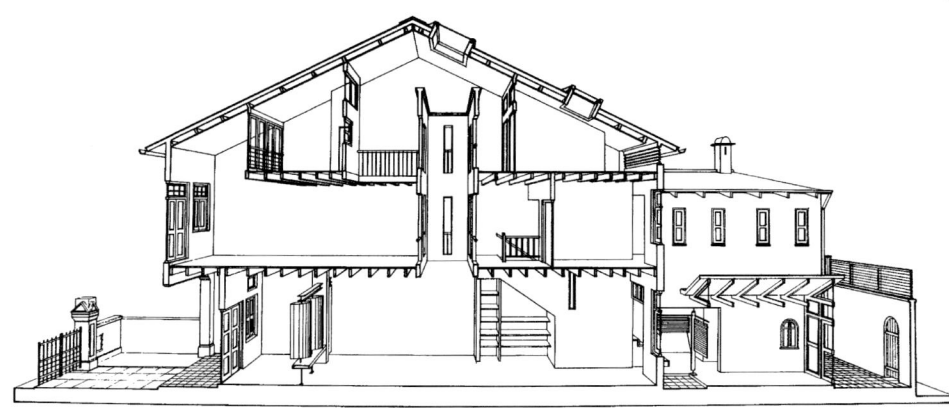

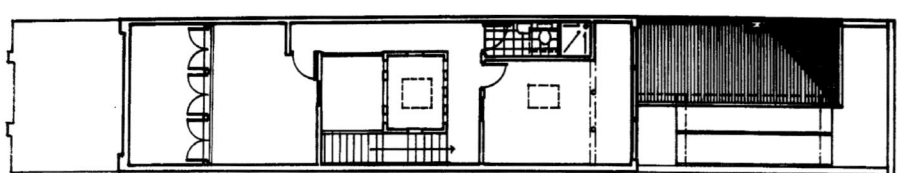

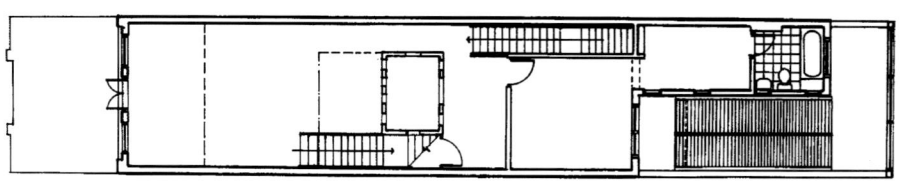

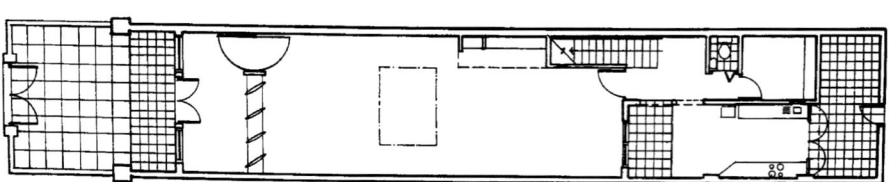

Architects **Geldenhuys & Jooste Architects, Vanderbijlpark**

Award Winning Building **Grandstand Addition to Existing Clubhouse**

Location **Vaal Triangle Technikon, Vanderbijlpark, South Africa**

Design and Construction Period **1993–1994**

Award ISAA Award of Merit 1995

Given by ISAA Institute of South African Architects

Prize Presentation November / 18 / 1995

Members of the Jury Roger Fisher, Muhammed Mayet, Lone Poulsen

Design Team Humphries Jooste (Project and Design Architect)

Structural Engineering Christo van der Merwe & Partners

Civil Engineering Christo van der Merwe & Partners

Electrical Engineering C.A. du Toit & Partners Incorporated

Quantity Surveying Bert van den Heever Partnership

Approximate Cost R 2,000,000

Site Area 10 ha

Building Area 1,150 m^2

Total Floor Area 1,350 m^2

Photographer François Swanepoel

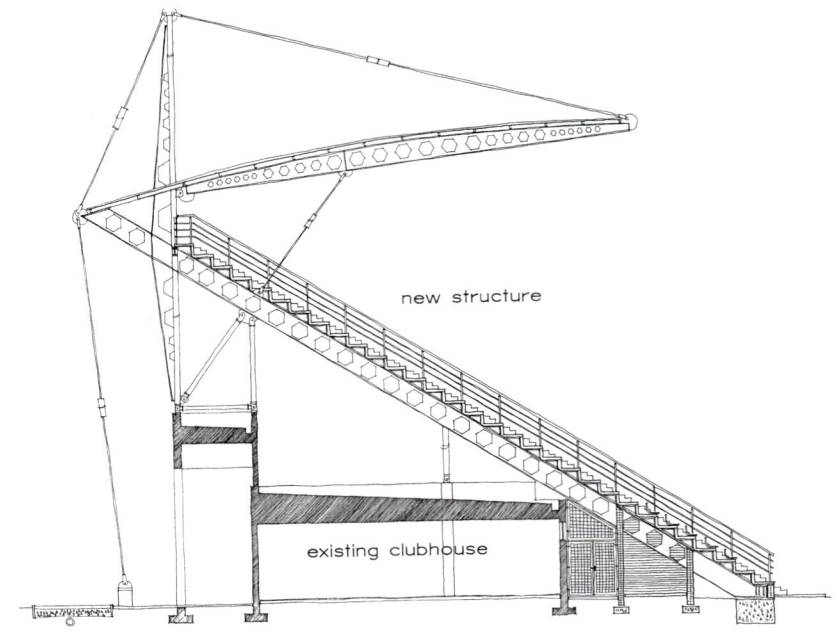

Architect **Louw Apostolellis Bergenthuin, Johannesburg**

Award Winning Building **House Van Vught**

Location **Dainfern, Johannesburg, South Africa**

Design and Construction Period **1993–1994**

Award ISAA Award of Merit 1995

Given by ISAA Institute of South African Architects

Prize Presentation 1995

Members of the Jury Roger Fisher, Muhammed Mayet, Lone Poulsen

Design Team Achilles Apostolellis

Structural Engineering Ellmer & Van Greunen Inc.

Electrical Engineering Bruwer's Electrical

Lighting Consultant Quali-Tech Lighting

Landscape Architecture Christine Cilliers

Approximate Cost R 150,000

Site Area 1,212 m²

Building Area 337 m²

Total Floor Area 436 m²

Photographer Achilles Apostolellis

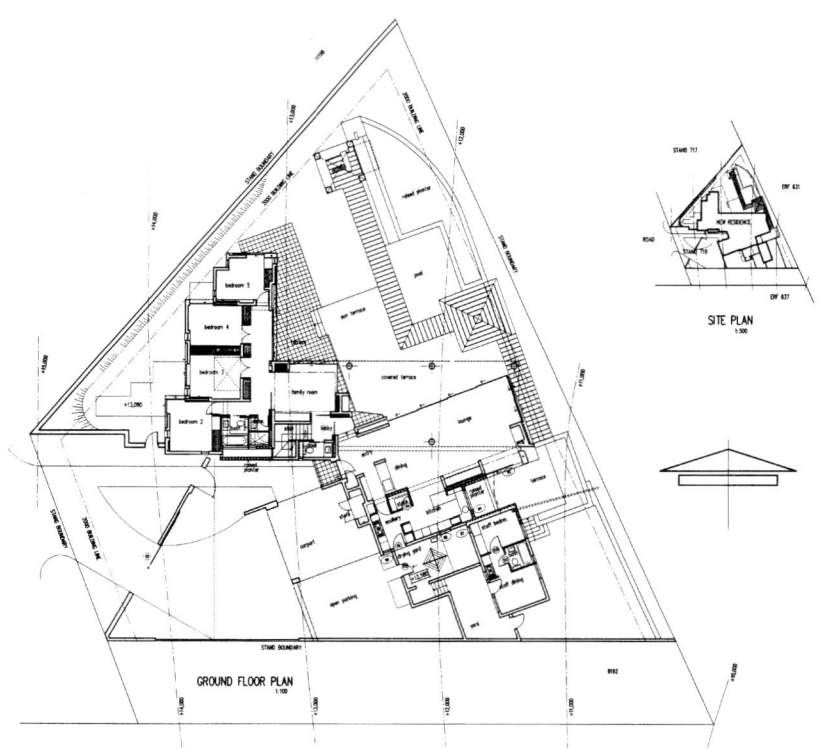

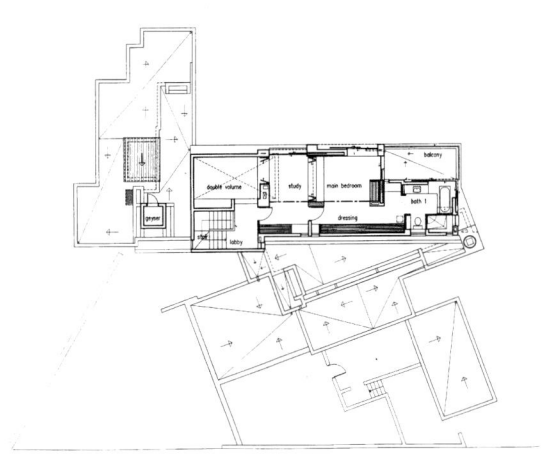

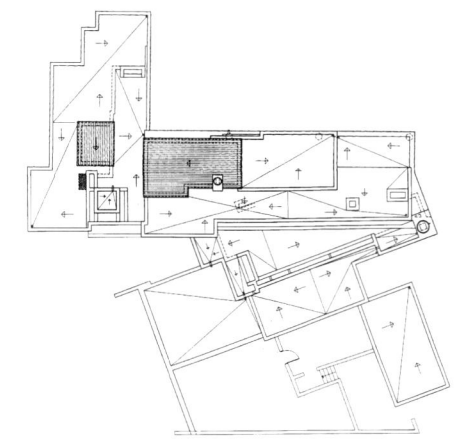

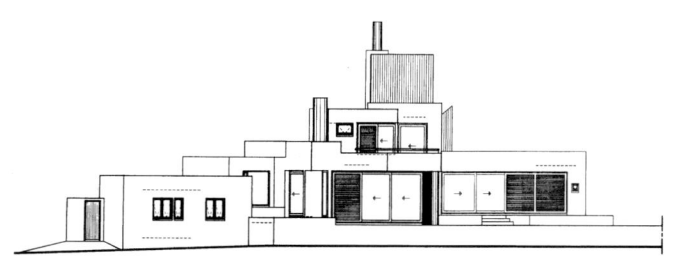

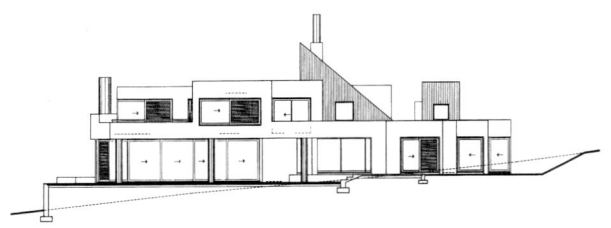

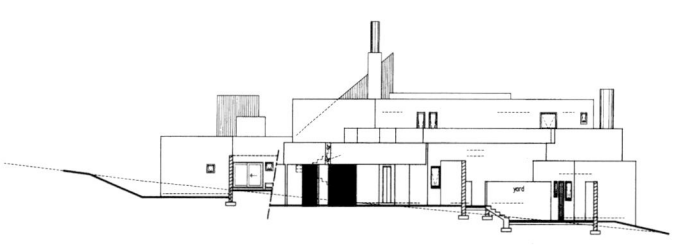

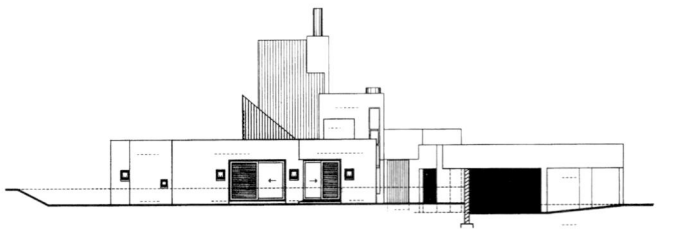

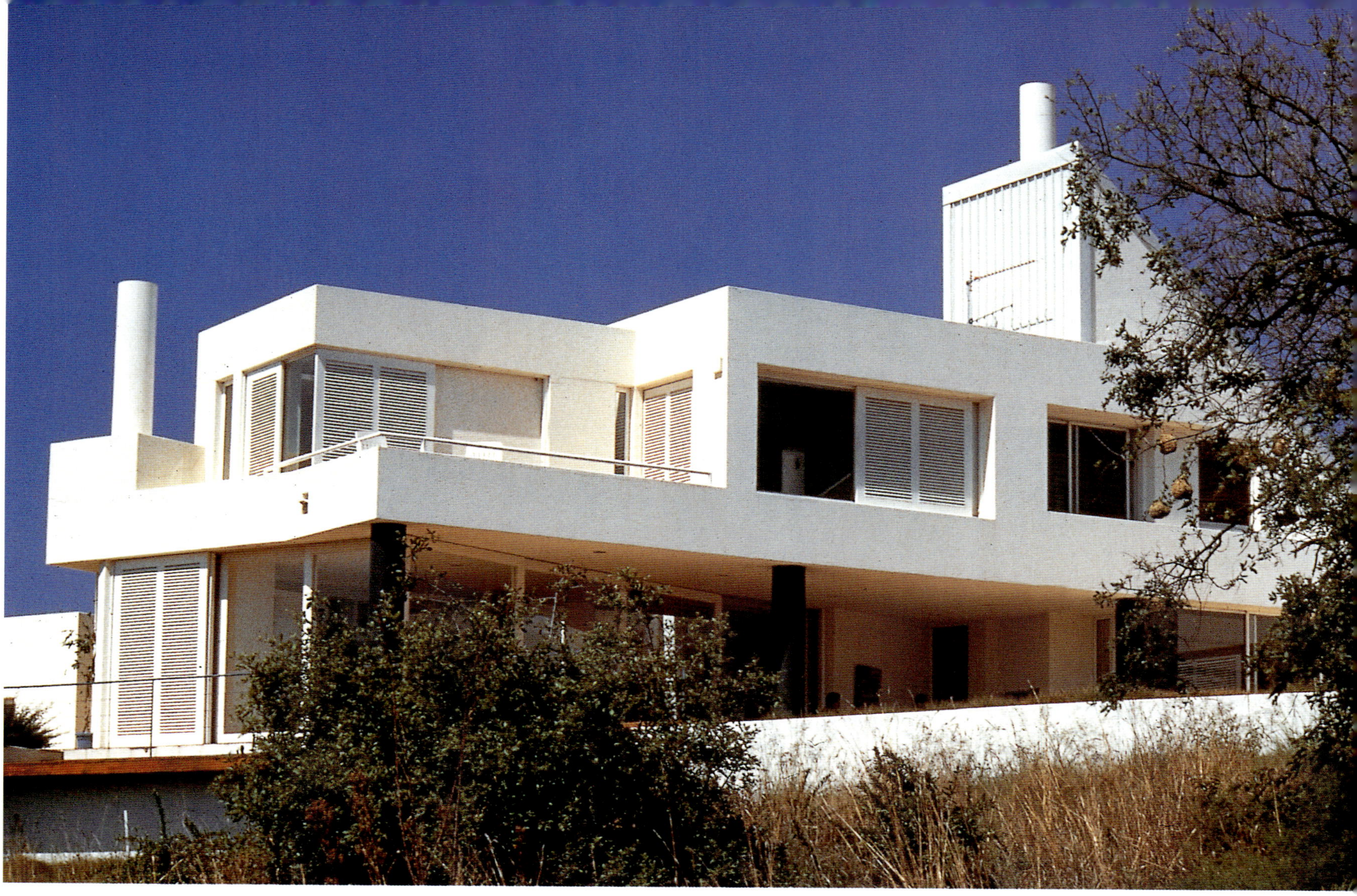

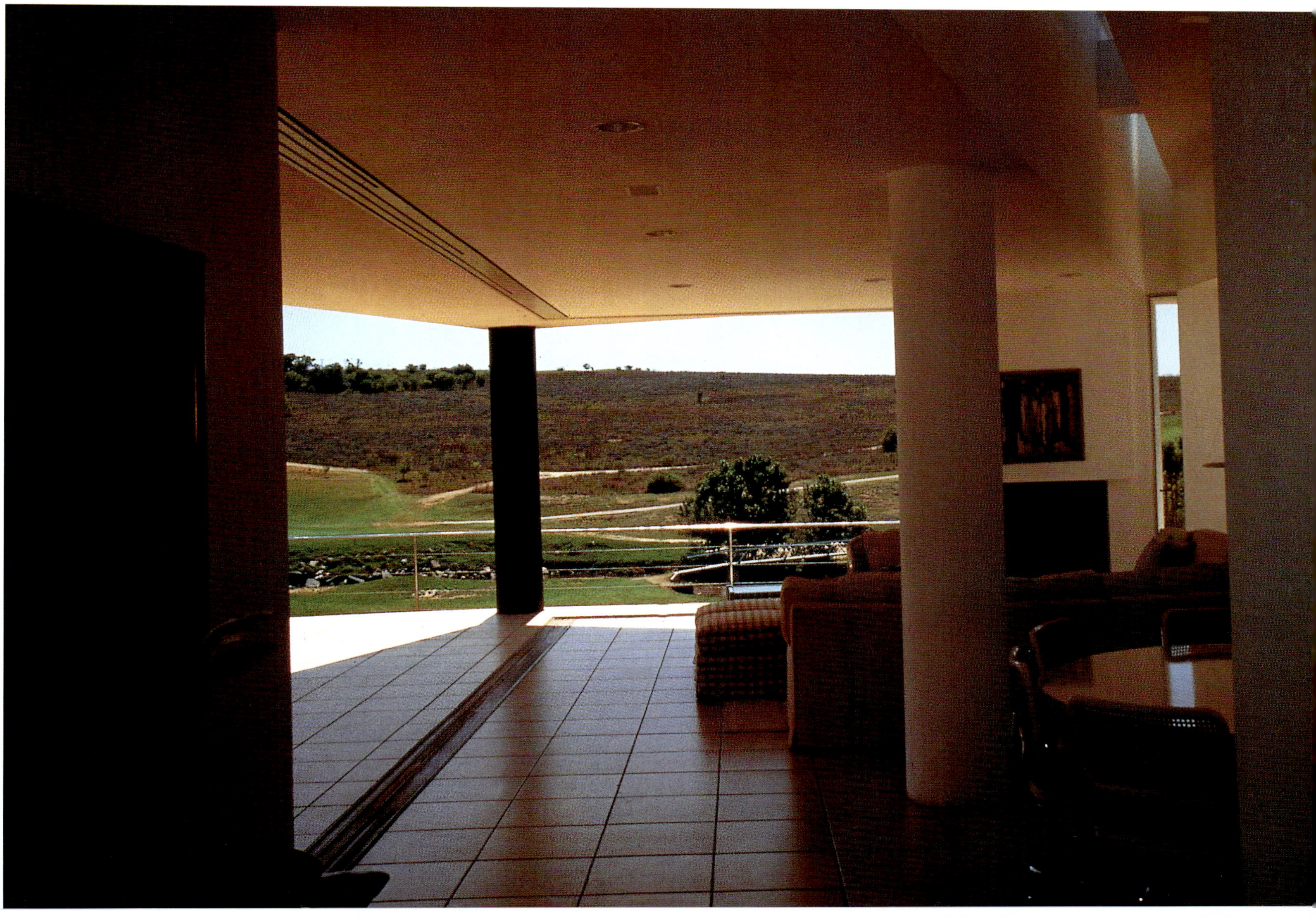

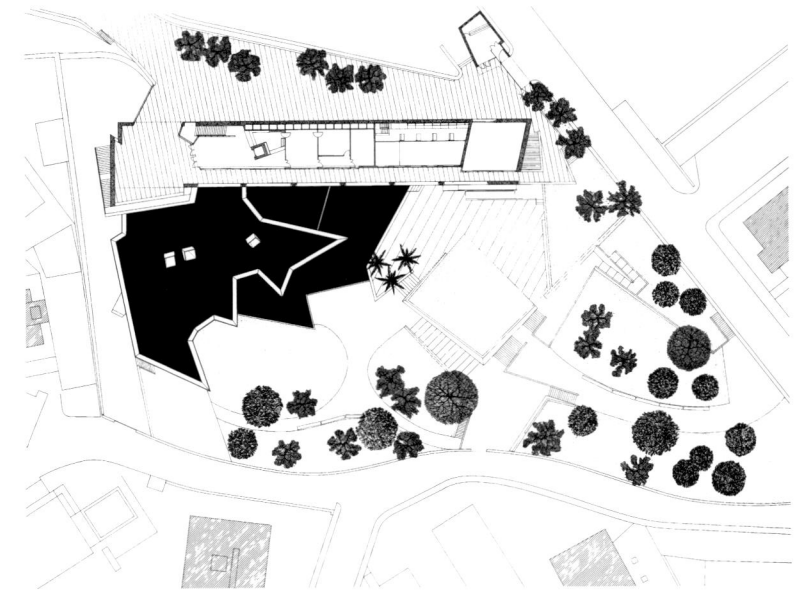

Architect **Rafael Moneo Vallés, Madrid**

Representative Building **Pilar & Joan Miró Foundation**

Location **Joan de Suridakis 29, Palma de Mallorca, Spain**

Design and Construction Period **1989–1993**

Award 1) 1996 Pritzker Architecture Prize; 2) Gold Medal of the UIA
International Union of Architects

Given by 1) The Hyatt Foundation; 2) UIA International Union of Architects

Prize Presentation 1) June / 12 / 1996; 2) July 1996

Members of the Jury 1) J. Carter Brown (Chairman), Giovanni Agnelli,
Charles Correra, Ada Louise Huxtable, Toshio Nakamura, Jorge Silvetti,
The Lord Rothschild (Juror emeritus), Bill Lacy (Executive Director)

Design Team José Rafael Moneo Vallés with Emilio Tuñon, Luis Moreno,
Luis Rojo

Structural Engineering Mariano Moreno

Civil Engineering Mariano Moreno

Mechanical Engineering Gustavo Alvarez

Installations JG Asociados

Construction Supervision Rafael Moneo (Architect), Rafael Balaguer (Architect),
Antonio Esteva (Site Supervisor)

Approximate Cost Pts 700,000,000

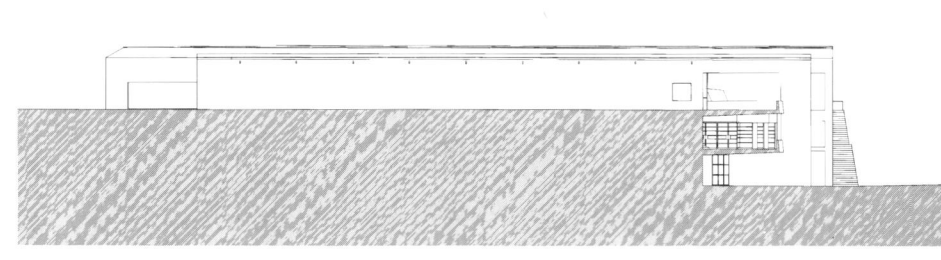

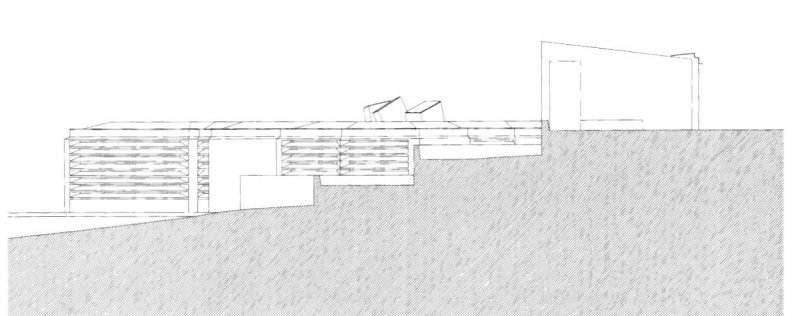

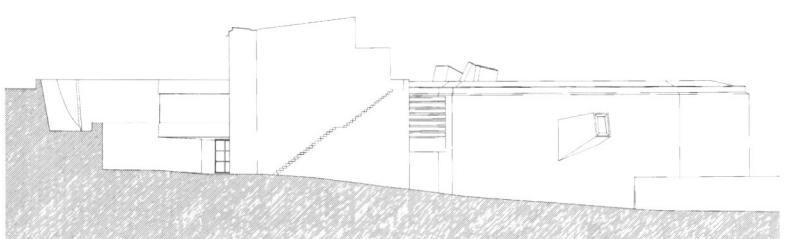

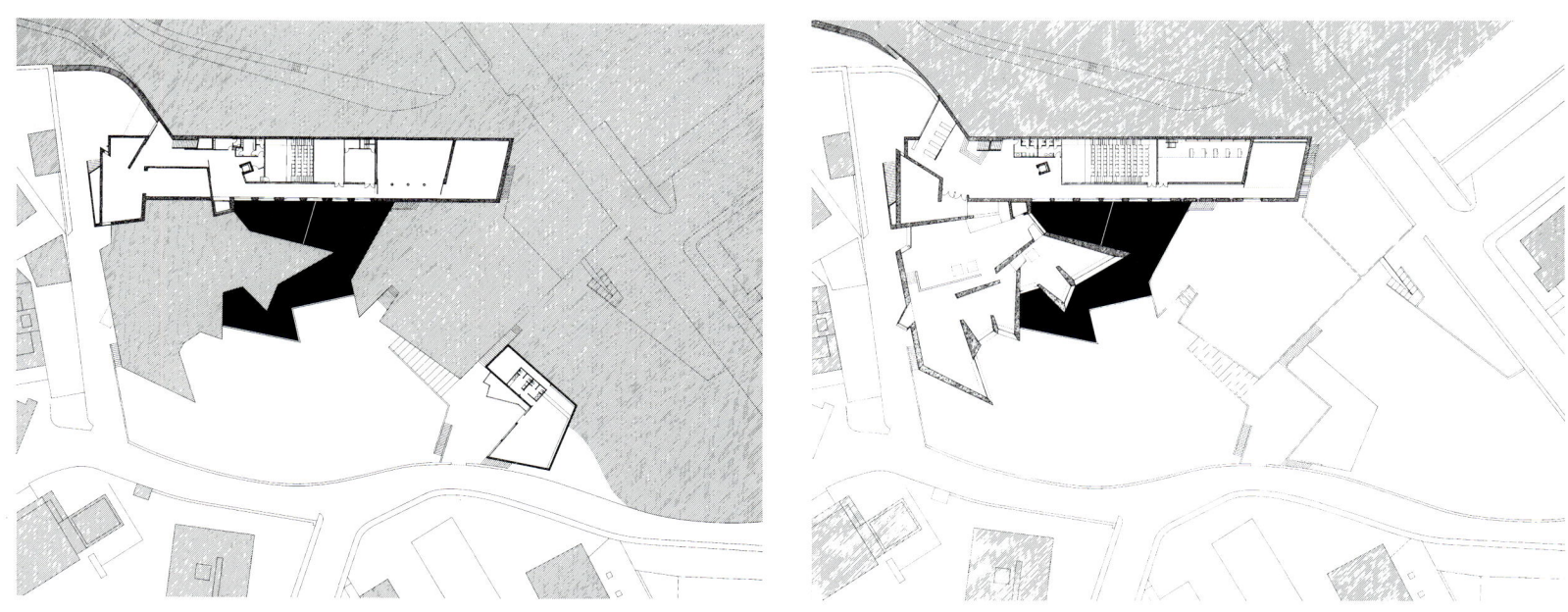

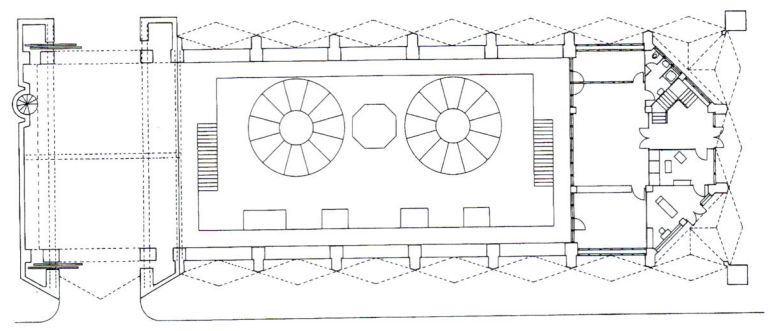

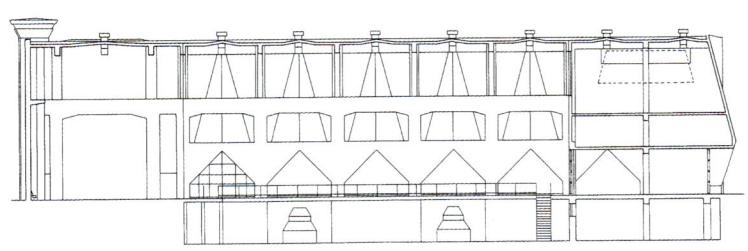

Architect **Joaquín Vaquero Palacios**

Representative Building **Central Electrica de Proaza**

Location **Proaza, Asturias, Spain**

Design and Construction Period **1964–1968**

Award Medalla de Oro de la Arquitectura

Given by Consejo Superior de los Colegios de Arquitectos de Espana

Prize Presentation September / 18 / 1996

Members of the Jury Jaime Duró, Ramon Queiro, Alberto Penin,
   Rafael de la Hoz, Carmen Pinol, José A. Fernandez Ordoñez

Design Team Vaquero & Hidroelectrica del Cantabrio, Oviedo, Spain

Structural Engineering Bymesa, Madrid / Düsseldorf

Civil Engineering Hidroelectrica del Cantabrio, Oviedo, Spain

Mechanical Engineering Hidroelectrica del Cantabrio, Oviedo, Spain

Electrical Engineering Hidroelectrica del Cantabrio, Oviedo, Spain

Air Conditioning Consultant Hidroelectrica del Cantabrio, Oviedo, Spain

Lighting Consultant Hidroelectrica del Cantabrio, Oviedo, Spain

Life Safety Consultant Hidroelectrica del Cantabrio, Oviedo, Spain

Interior Design Joaquín Vaquero Palacios (mural paintings and sculptures)

Landscape Architecture Joaquín Vaquero Palacios

Building Area 1,100 m^2

Total Floor Area 1,570 m^2

Photographer Vaquero Turcios

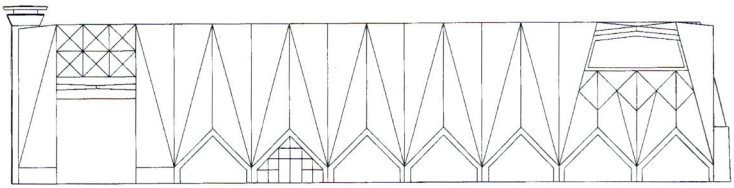

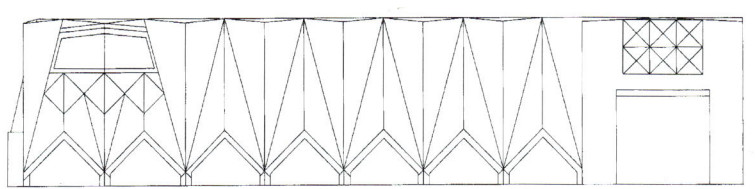

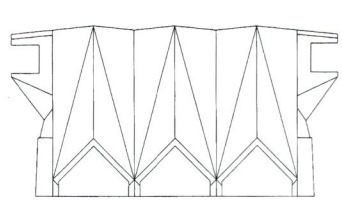

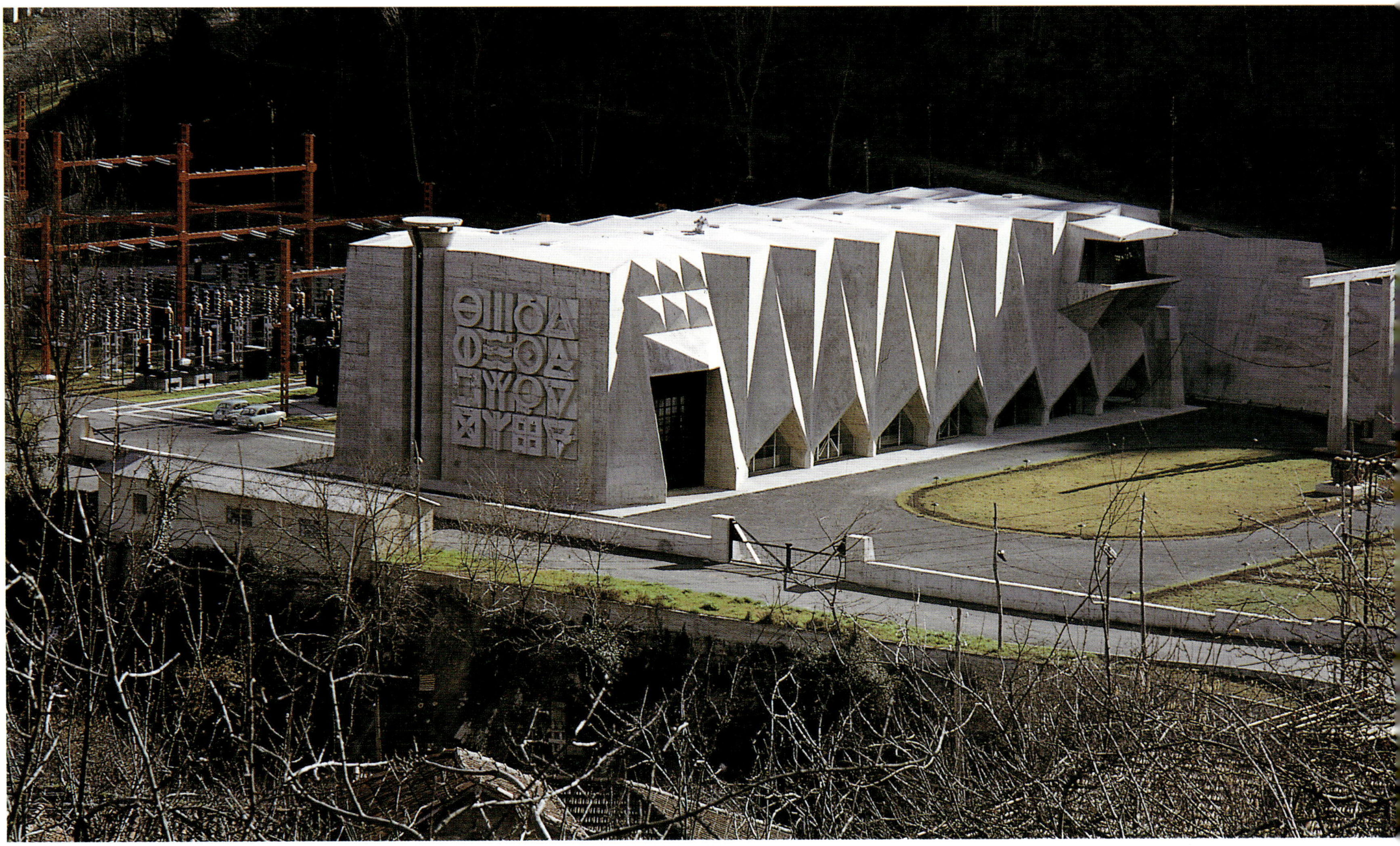

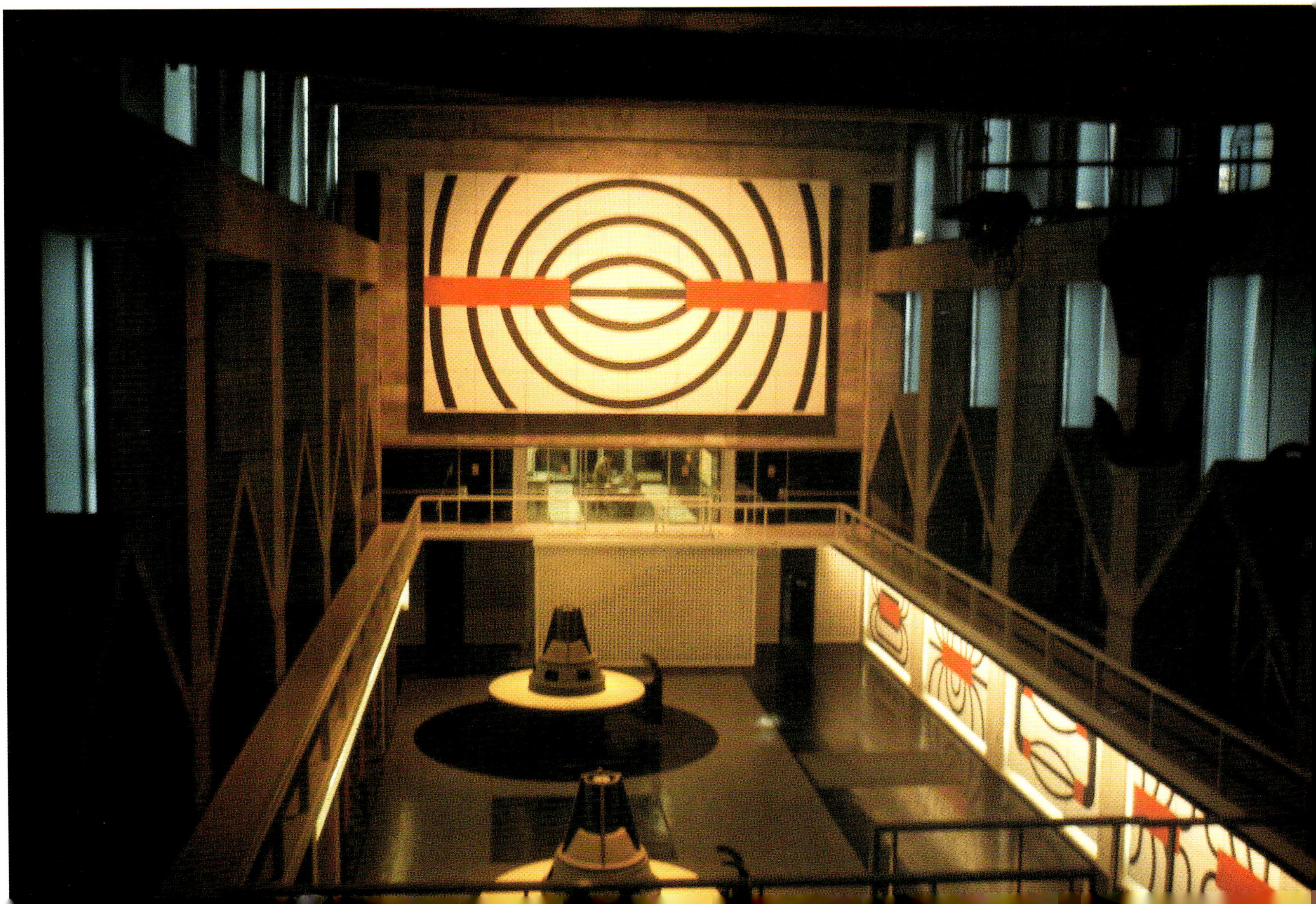

Architects **Alexandre Micheli, Geneva; BAILLIF & LOPONTE, Carouge**

Award Winning Building **Housing Complex (Coopérative de logement Emphytéhome)**

Location **Geneva, Switzerland**

Design and Construction Period **1990–1994**

Award Prix INTERASSAR

Given by INTERASSAR (Intergroupe des Associations d'Architectes)

Prize Presentation 1996

Members of the Jury C. Marteau, J. Bolliger, R. Brodbeck, M. Cavaleri, J.-L. Chilier, R. Frei, E. Galley, C. Layaz

Design Team Daniel Baillif, Alexandre Micheli, Gabriel Schaer, Stéphane Monnard

Structural Engineering Jean-Pierre Cêtre and Michel Paquet

Civil Engineering Jean-Pierre Cêtre and Michel Paquet

Artist Philippe Deléglise

Approximate Cost Sfr 4,900,000

Site Area 312 m^2

Building Area 312 m^2

Total Floor Area 2,450 m^2

Photographer François Schaer, Alexandre Micheli

 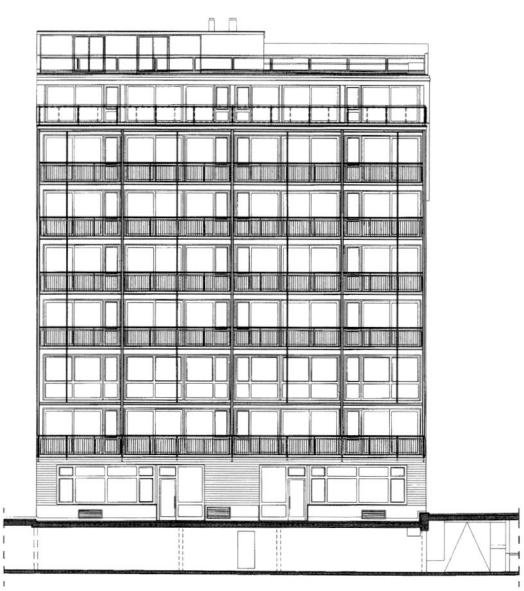 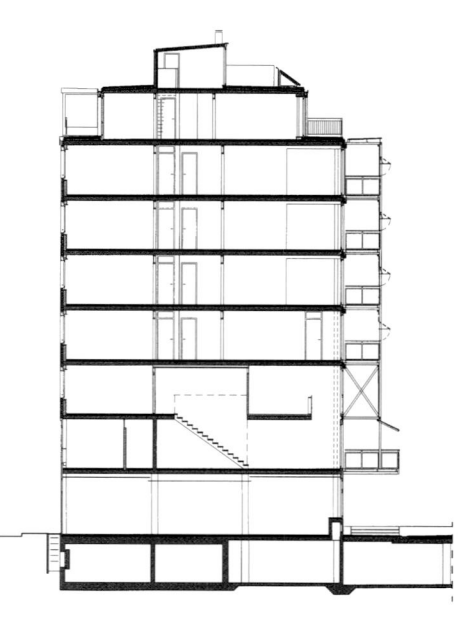

RUE DES GARES
IMMEUBLE RENCONTRE
IMMEUBLE 21 RUE DES GARES
COUR

IMMEUBLE RENCONTRE
IMMEUBLE 21 RUE DES GARES

IMMEUBLE RENCONTRE

IMMEUBLE RENCONTRE
IMMEUBLE 21 RUE DES GARES
GARAGE SOUTERRAIN

IMMEUBLE RENCONTRE
IMMEUBLE 21 RUE DES GARES

IMMEUBLE RENCONTRE

Kronenbourg

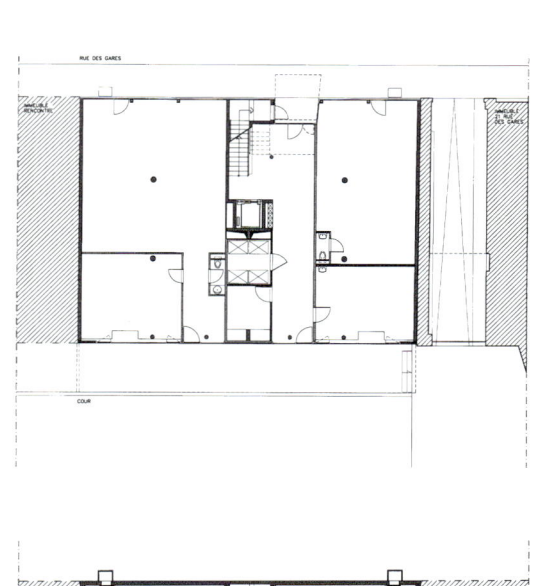

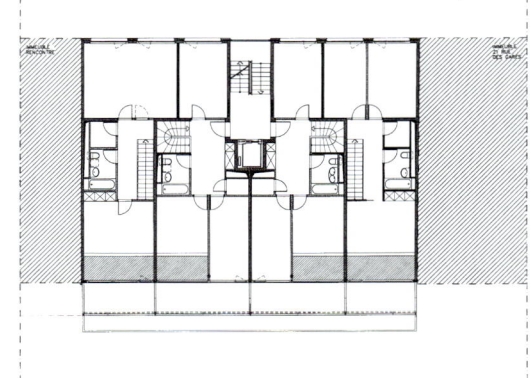

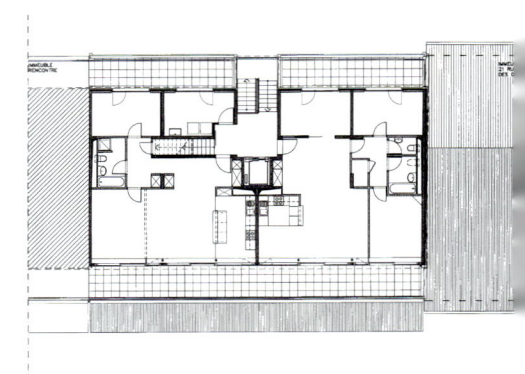

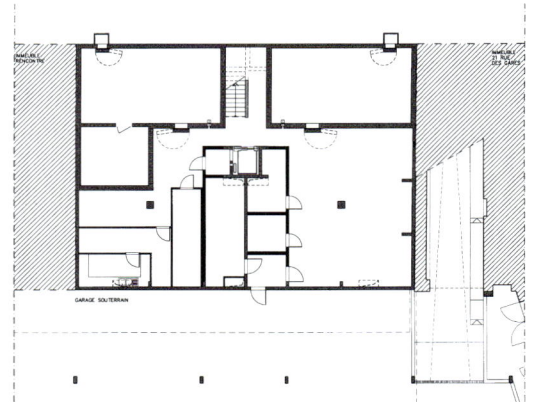

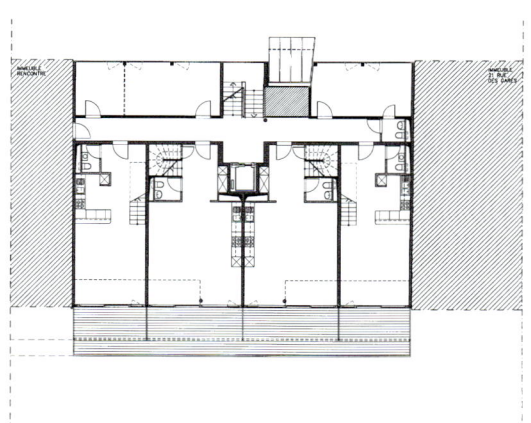

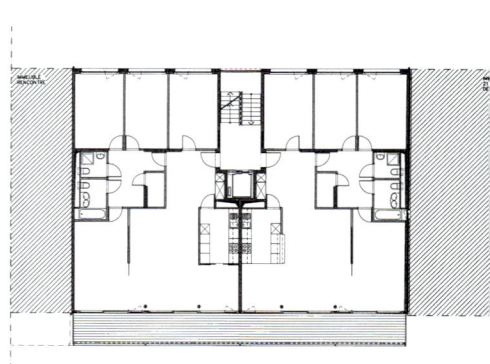

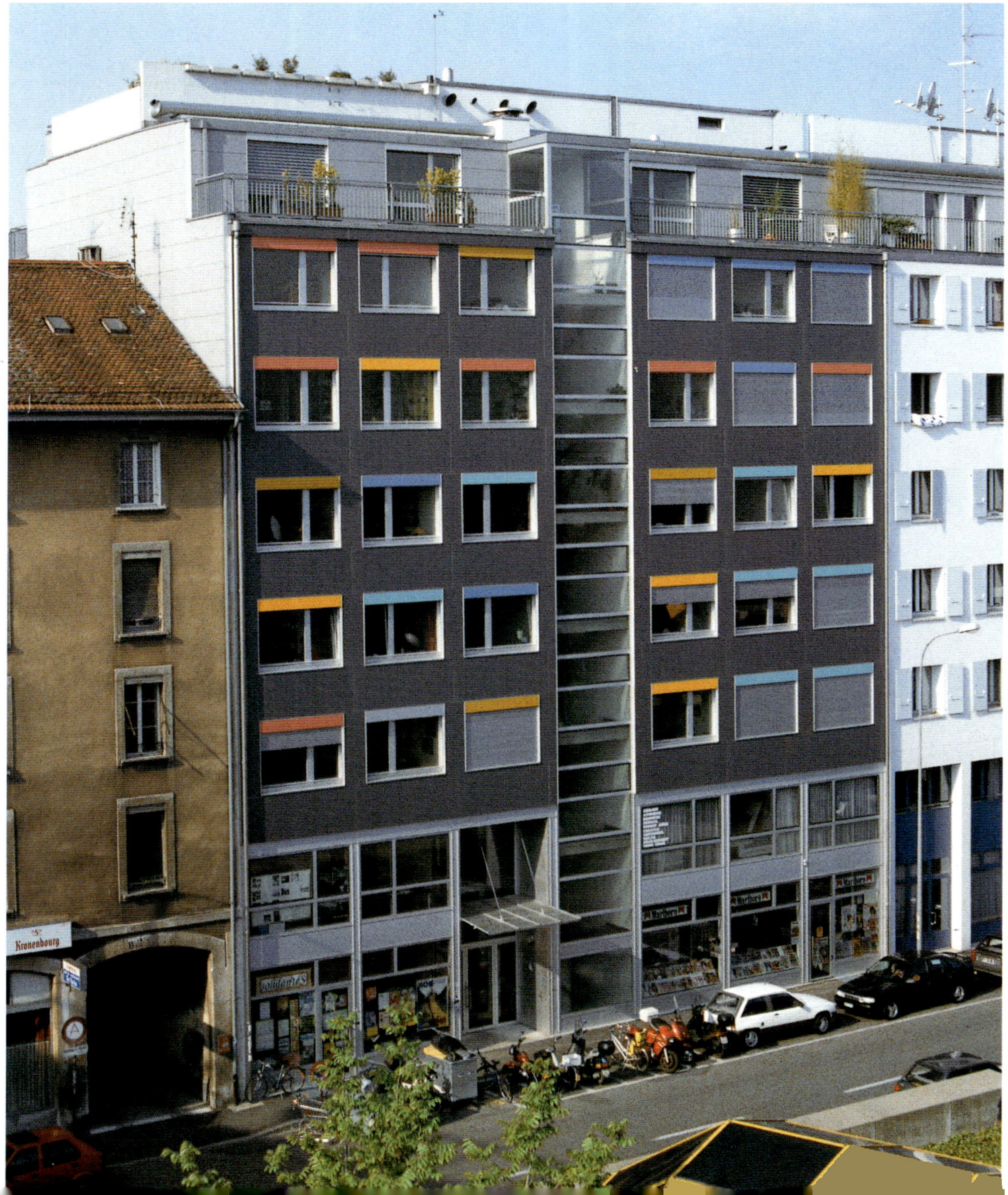

Architects **Merih Karaaslan, Nuran Ünsal, Mürşit Günday, Ankara**

Award Winning Building **Terrace Houses**

Location **Ankara, Turkey**

Design and Construction Period **1989–1992**

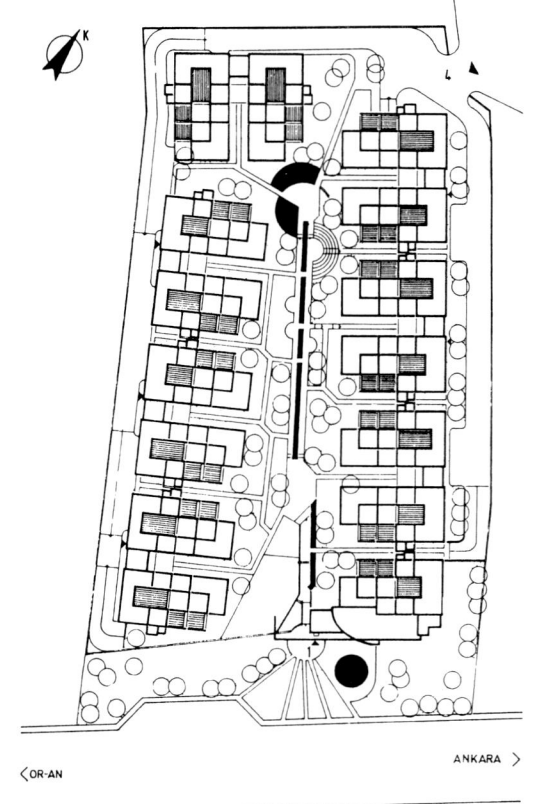

<OR-AN   ANKARA >

Award 1) National Architectural Award 1996 (Project Award);
2) Noteworthy Collaboration between Architect and Client

Given by 1) Chamber of Architects of Turkey; 2) Turkish Free-Lance
Architects Association

Prize Presentation 2) January / 20 / 1996

Members of the Jury Baran Idil, Yurdanur Sepkin, Kamutay Türkoğlu,
Mürşit Günday, Abdi Güzer

Design Team Karaaslan Architecture Design Team and Hüsnü Ceyhan

Structural Engineering Danyal Kubin, Joseph Kubin

Civil Engineering Danyal Kubin, Joseph Kubin

Mechanical Engineering Bahri Türkmen, Bülent Özgür

Constructor Sürücüler Construction Inc.

Air Conditioning Consultant Bahri Türkmen, Bülent Özgür

Lighting Consultant Ali Gündüz

Landscape Architecture Karaaslan Architecture Ltd. and Turkay Ateş
(Consultant)

Quantity Surveying Karaaslan Architecture Ltd.

Approximate Cost US$ 3,800,000

Site Area 11,919 m²

Building Area 4,360 m² (ground floor area)

Total Floor Area 18,954 m²

Photographer Merih Karaaslan

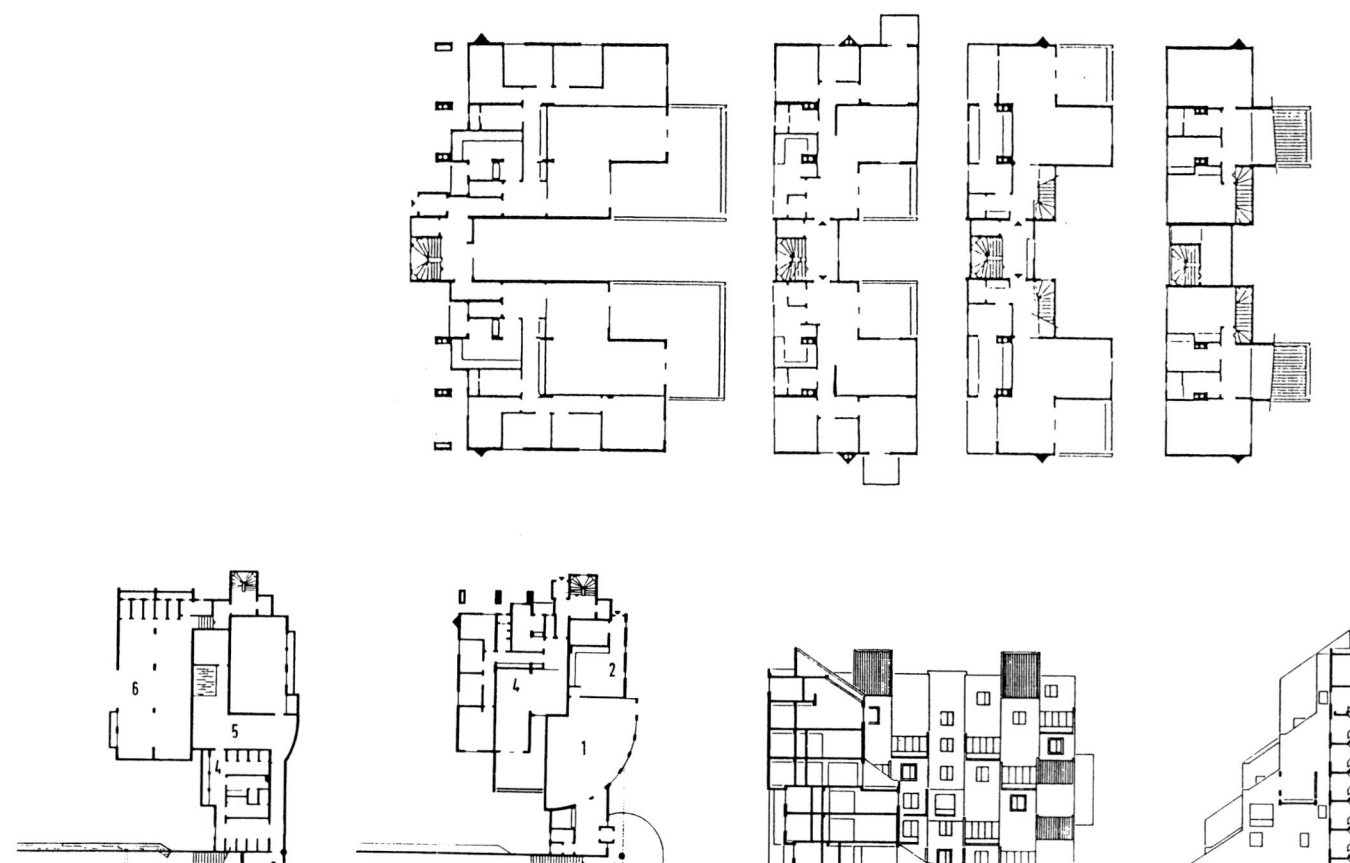

Architect **Şevki Pekin, Istanbul**

Award Winning Building **Summer House**

Location **Bodrum, Turkey**

Award National Architecture Award 1996 (Building Award)

Given by Chamber of Architects of Turkey

Prize Presentation April / 25 / 1996

Members of the Jury Orhan Sahinler, Aydan Balamir, Tamer Başbuğ, Salih Zeki Pekin

Design Team Şevki Pekin

Mechanical Engineering Şevki Pekin

Approximate Cost US$ 30,000

Site Area 1,500 m²

Building Area 37.5 m²

Total Floor Area 75 m²

Photographer Şevki Pekin

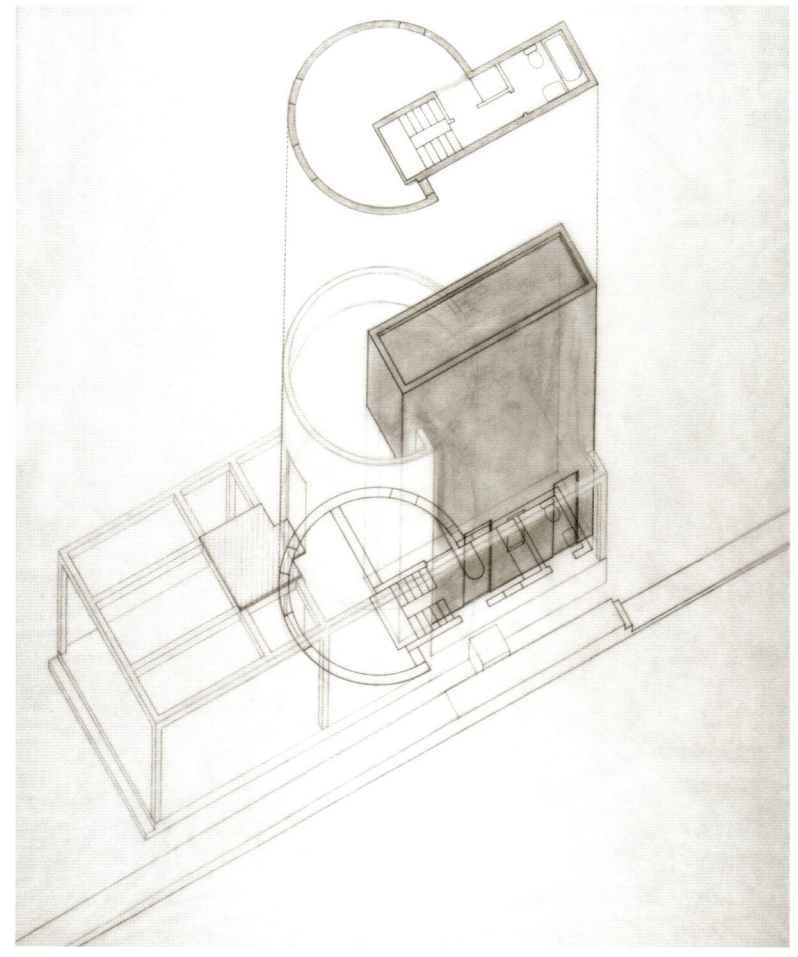

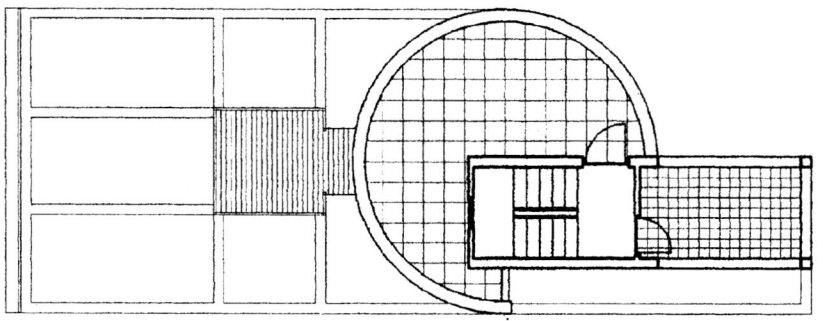

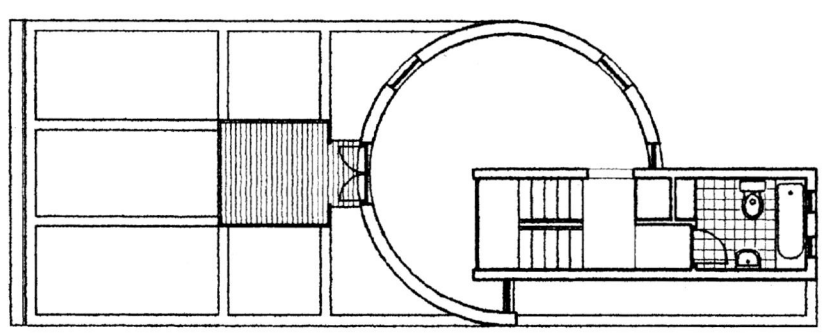

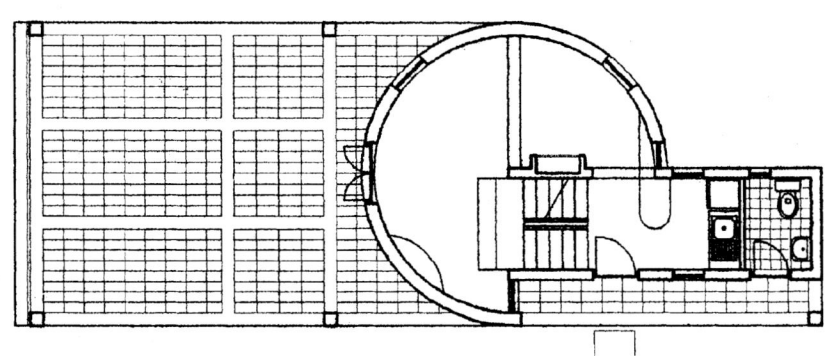

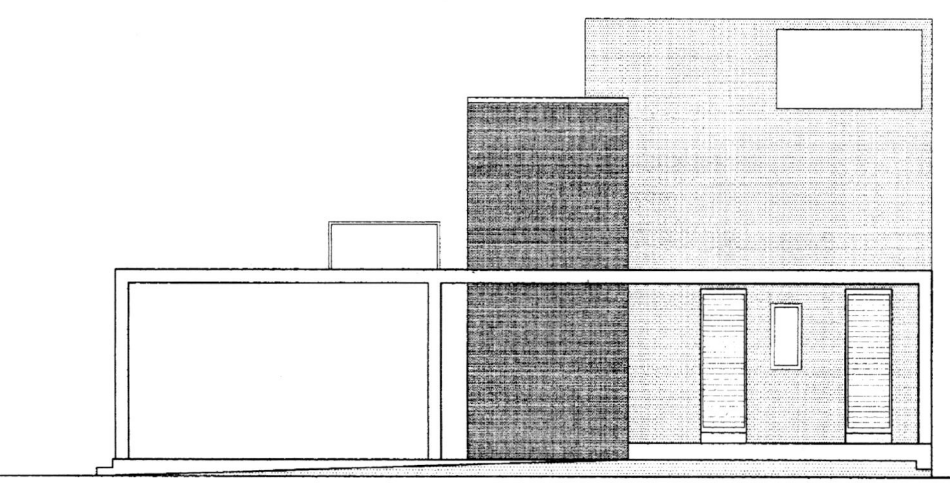

Architects **Ahrends Burton and Koralek, London**

Award Winning Building **Techniquest Science Discovery Centre**

Location **Cardiff, UK**

Design and Construction Period **1992–1995**

Award RIBA Regional Architecture Award 1996 (Wales)

Given by RIBA The Royal Institute of British Architects

Prize Presentation 1996

Design Team Ahrends Burton Koralek

Structural & Services Engineers Buro Happold

Mechanical Subcontractor Johnson & Baxter Ltd

Electrical Subcontractor Celtic Contracting Services Ltd

Lighting Installation Furse Ltd

Quantity Surveying BHQS

Approximate Cost £ 3,425,000

Photographer Peter Cook

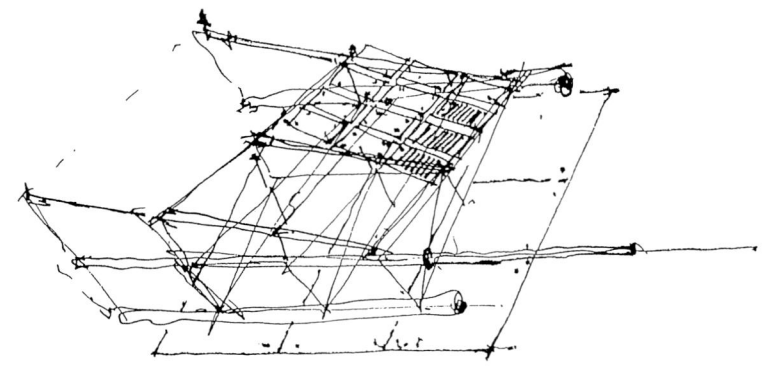

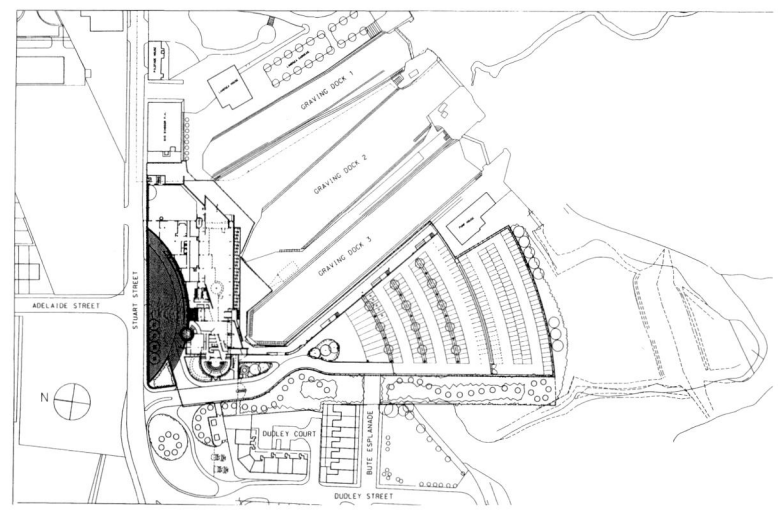

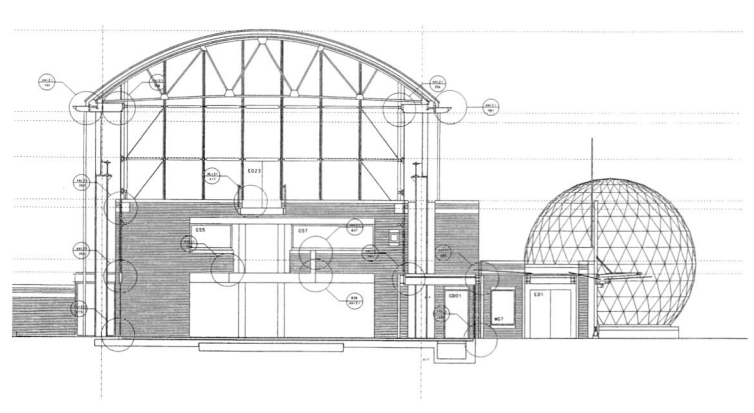

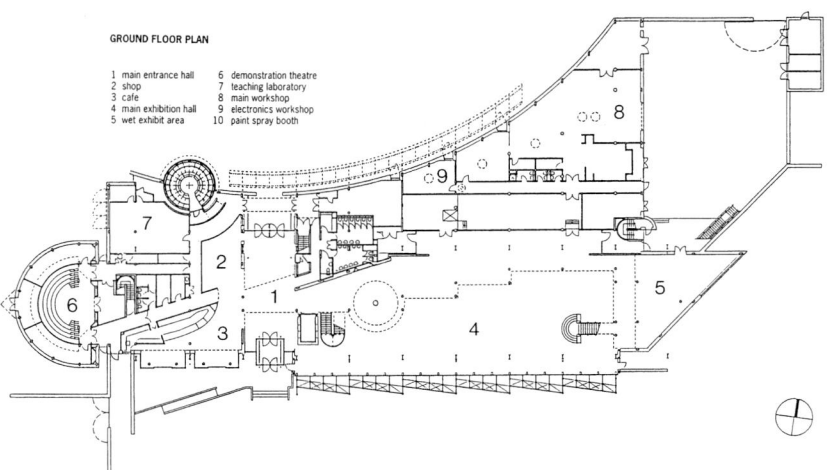

GROUND FLOOR PLAN

1 main entrance hall
2 shop
3 cafe
4 main exhibition hall
5 wet exhibit area
6 demonstration theatre
7 teaching laboratory
8 main workshop
9 electronics workshop
10 paint spray booth

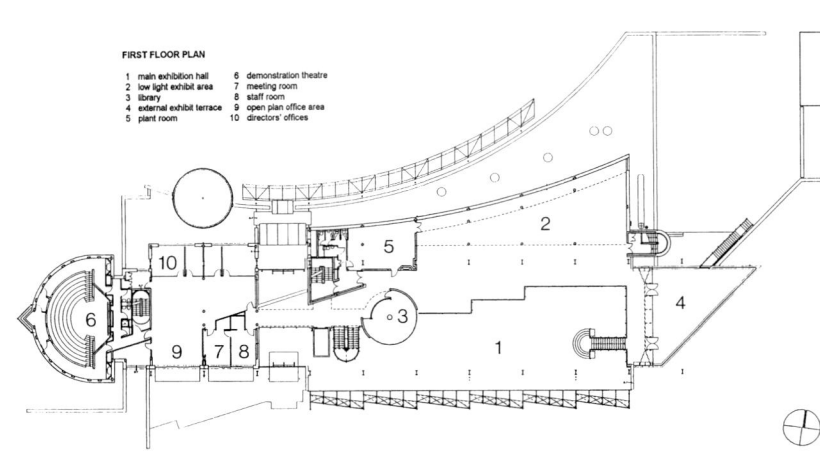

FIRST FLOOR PLAN

1 main exhibition hall
2 low light exhibit area
3 library
4 external exhibit terrace
5 plant room
6 demonstration theatre
7 meeting room
8 staff room
9 open plan office area
10 directors' offices

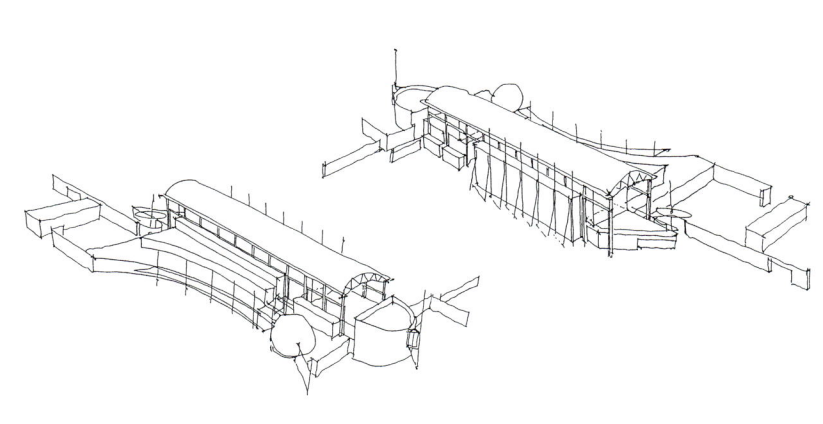

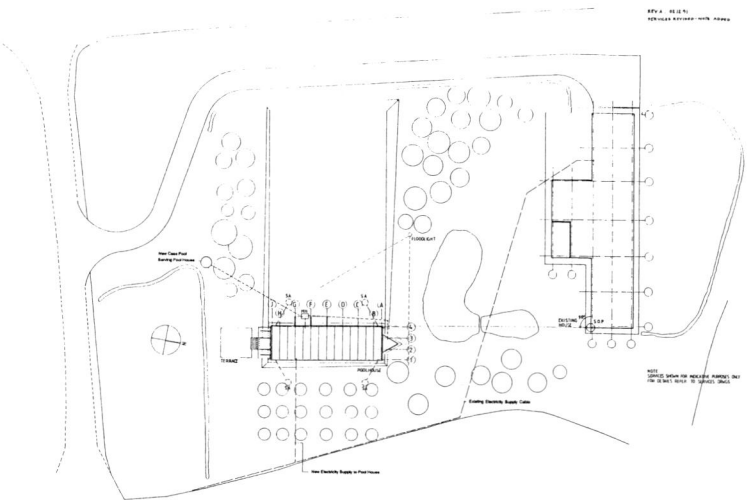

Architects **Allford Hall Monaghan Morris Architects, London**

Award Winning Building **The Poolhouse, Pewsey**

Location **Pewsey, Wiltshire, UK**

Design and Construction Period **1991–1993**

Award RIBA Regional Architecture Award 1996 (Wessex Region)

Given by RIBA The Royal Institute of British Architects

Prize Presentation November 1996

Structural Engineering The Samuely Partnership

Mechanical Engineering YRM Engineers

Electrical Engineering YRM Engineers

Environmental Engineering YRM Engineers

Quantity Surveying Appleyard & Trew

Approximate Cost £ 300,000

Site Area 3,600 m²

Building Area 90 m²

Total Floor Area 155 m²

Photographer Dennis Gilbert

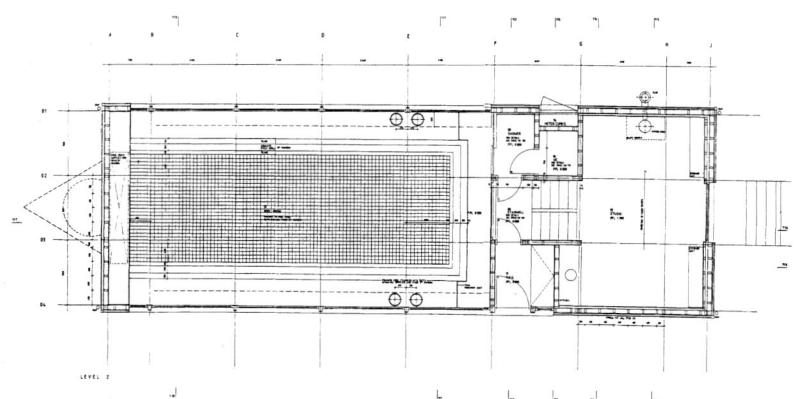

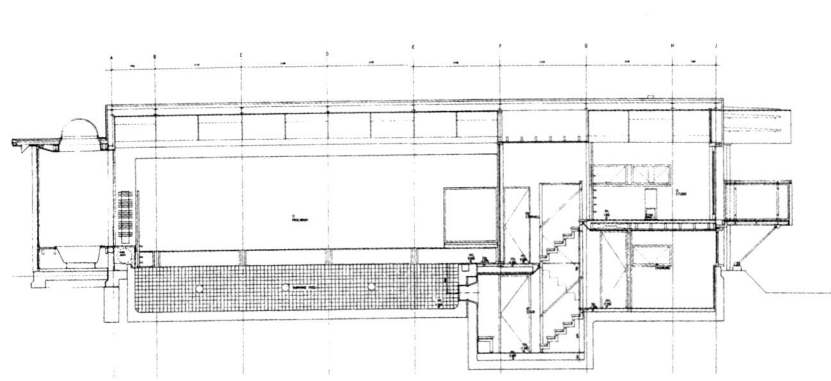

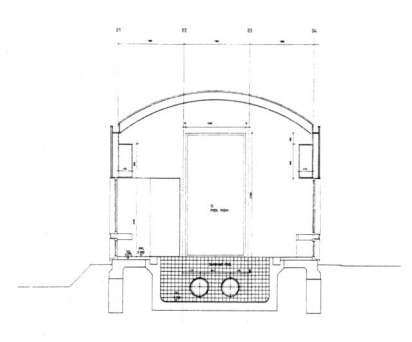

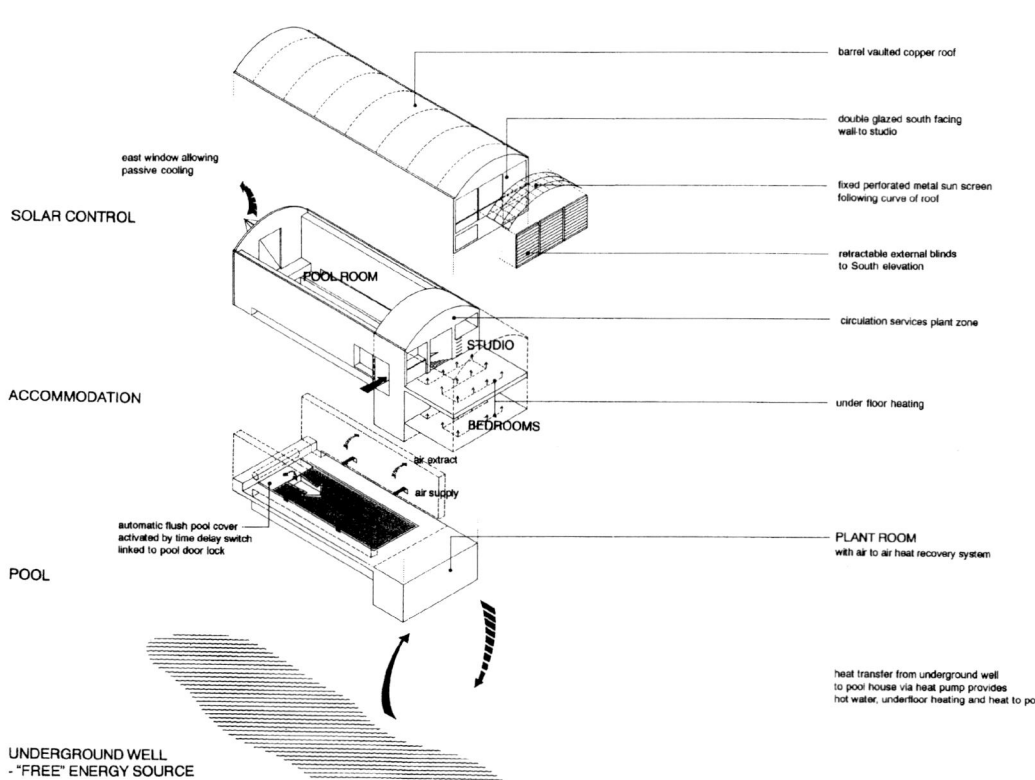

SOLAR CONTROL

east window allowing
passive cooling

ACCOMMODATION

POOL

UNDERGROUND WELL
- "FREE" ENERGY SOURCE

POOL ROOM

STUDIO

BEDROOMS

automatic flush pool cover
activated by time delay switch
linked to pool door lock

air extract

air supply

barrel vaulted copper roof

double glazed south facing
wall-to studio

fixed perforated metal sun screen
following curve of roof

retractable external blinds
to South elevation

circulation services plant zone

under floor heating

PLANT ROOM
with air to air heat recovery system

heat transfer from underground well
to pool house via heat pump provides
hot water, underfloor heating and heat to pool

Architects **Allies and Morrison, London**

Award Winning Building **Sarum Hall School**

Location **London, UK**

Design and Construction Period **1993–1995**

Award RIBA Regional Architecture Award 1996 (London Region)

Given by RIBA The Royal Institute of British Architects

Prize Presentation November / 21 / 1996

Members of the Jury appointed by RIBA but not specified

Design Team Joanna Green, Tim Makower, Laurie Hallows,
    Honor Thompson, Sarah Jackson, Terry McCarthy, Kevin Ausop

Structural Engineering Price & Myers

Mechanical Engineering Max Fordham & Partners

Electrical Engineering Max Fordham & Partners

Landscape Architecture Livingston Eyre Associates

Quantity Surveying Barrie Tankel Partnership

Approximate Cost £ 1,200,000

Site Area 600 m^2

Photographer Charlotte Wood

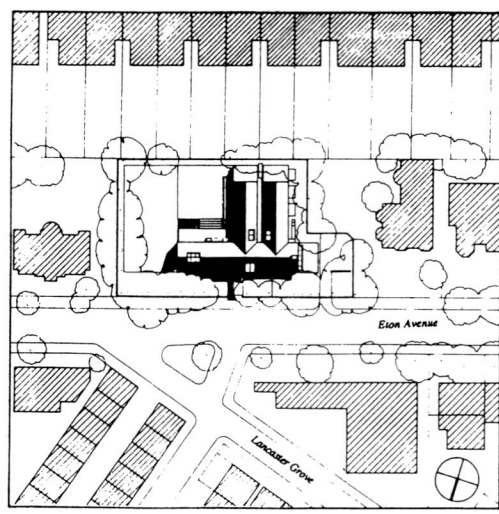

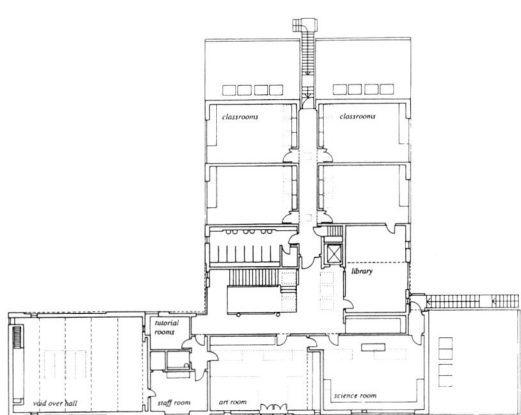

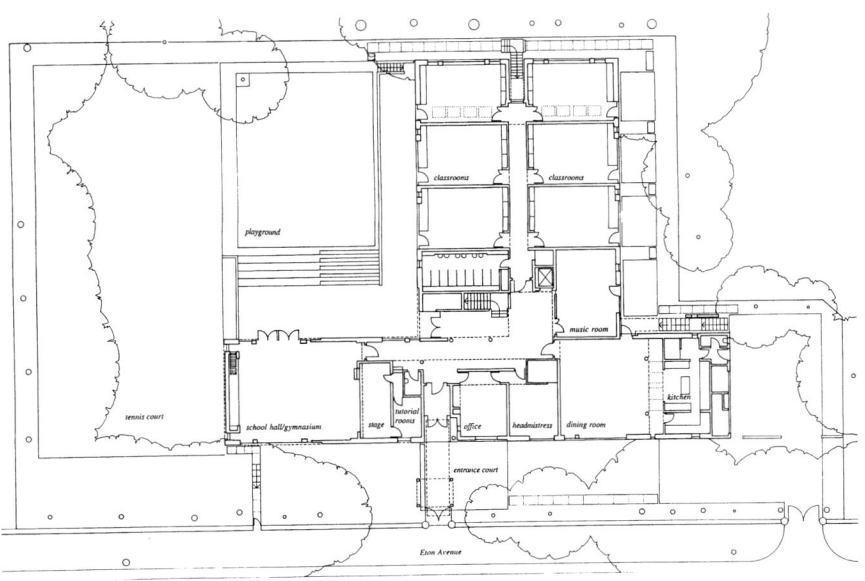

Architects **Allies and Morrison, London**

Award Winning Building **Nunnery Square, Sheffield**

Location **Sheffield, UK**

Design and Construction Period **1993–1995**

Award RIBA Regional Architecture Award 1996 (Yorkshire Region)

Given by RIBA The Royal Institute of British Architects

Prize Presentation November / 21 / 1996

Members of the Jury appointed by RIBA but not specified

Design Team Marianne Davys, Paul Appleton, Pauline Stockmans, Paul
   Summerlin, Ian Sutherland, Julian Cowie, Annette Lecuyre, Chris Procter

Structural Engineering Hunter Jennings & Titchmarsh

Mechanical Engineering Hiltons Building Services Ltd.

Electrical Engineering Hiltons Building Services Ltd.

Landscape Architecture Allies and Morrison

Quantity Surveying Rex Proctor and Partners

Approximate Cost £ 12,500,000

Building Area 13,990 m²

Photographer Peter Cook

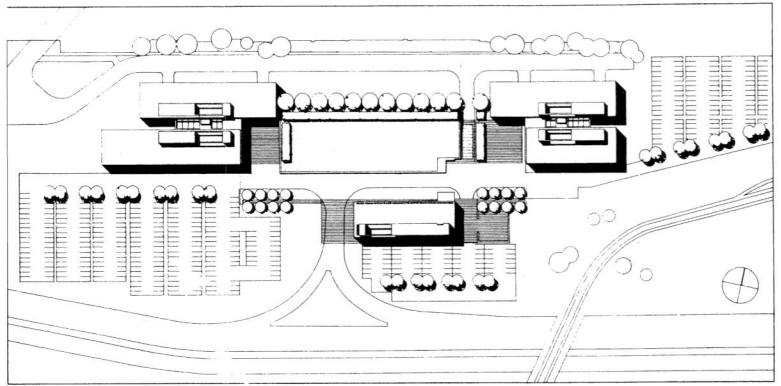

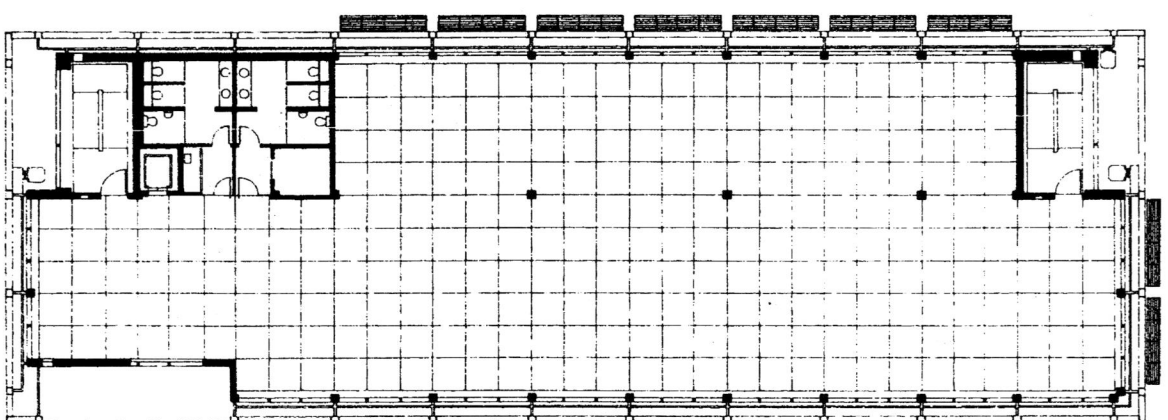

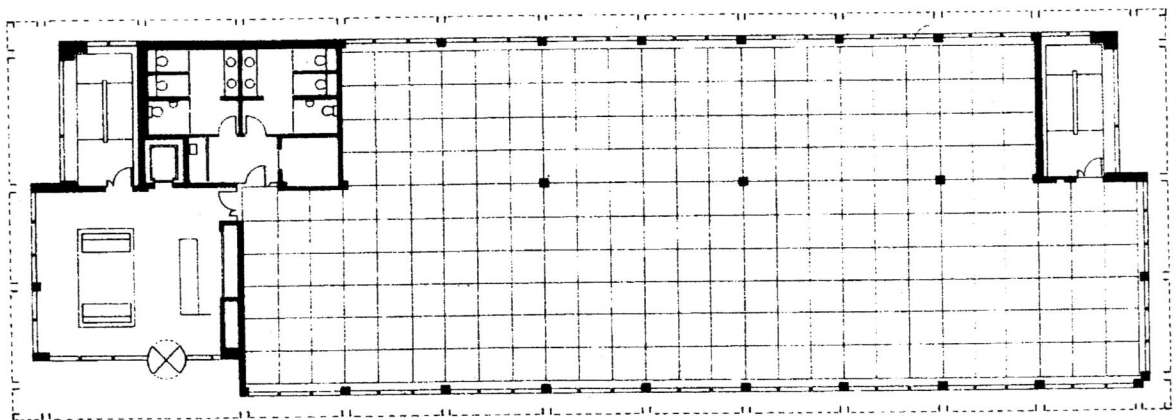

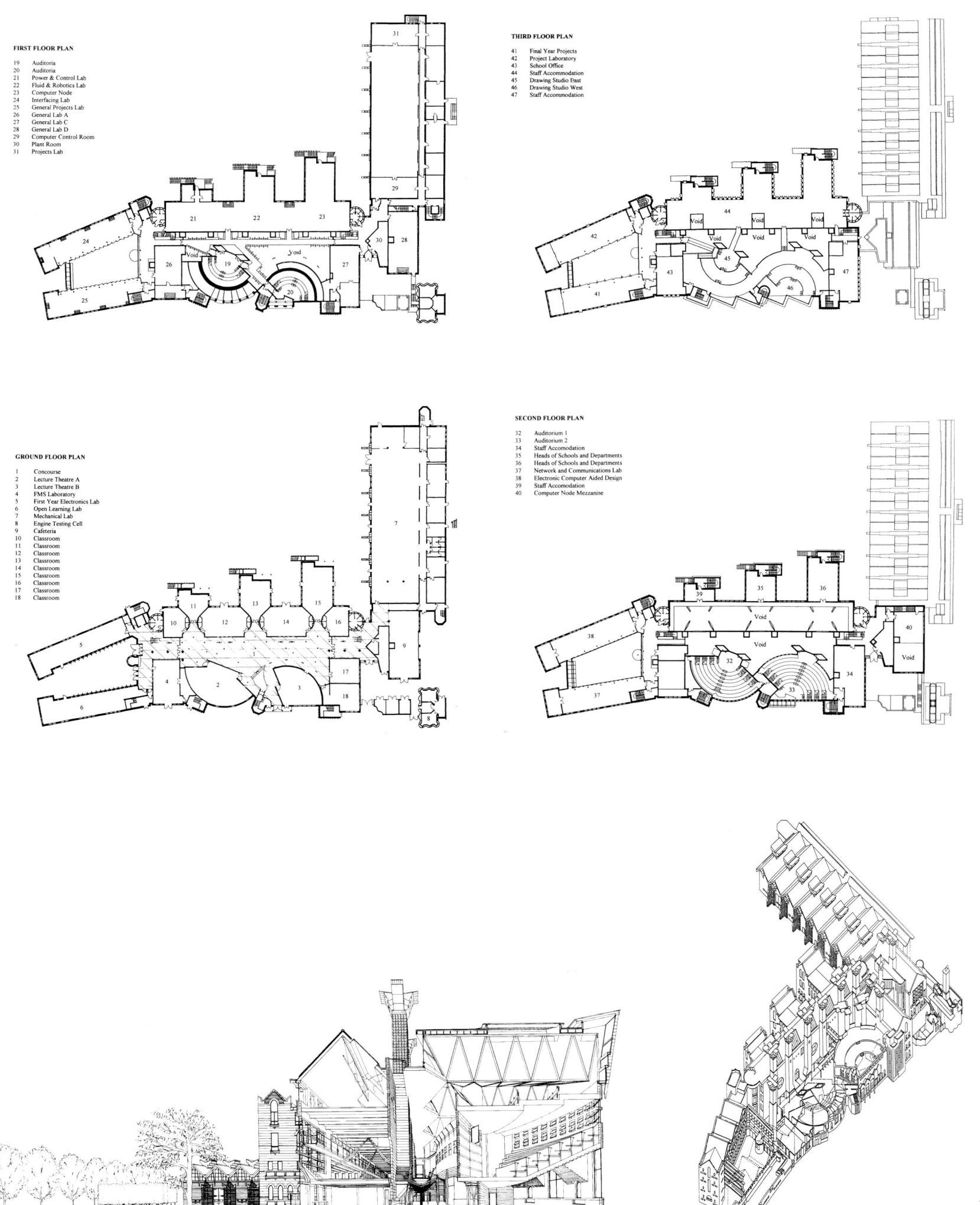

FIRST FLOOR PLAN

19 Auditoria
20 Auditoria
21 Power & Control Lab
22 Fluid & Robotics Lab
23 Computer Node
24 Interfacing Lab
25 General Projects Lab
26 General Lab A
27 General Lab C
28 General Lab D
29 Computer Control Room
30 Plant Room
31 Projects Lab

THIRD FLOOR PLAN

41 Final Year Projects
42 Project Laboratory
43 School Office
44 Staff Accommodation
45 Drawing Studio East
46 Drawing Studio West
47 Staff Accommodation

GROUND FLOOR PLAN

1 Concourse
2 Lecture Theatre A
3 Lecture Theatre B
4 FMS Laboratory
5 First Year Electronics Lab
6 Open Learning Lab
7 Mechanical Lab
8 Engine Testing Cell
9 Cafeteria
10 Classroom
11 Classroom
12 Classroom
13 Classroom
14 Classroom
15 Classroom
16 Classroom
17 Classroom
18 Classroom

SECOND FLOOR PLAN

32 Auditorium 1
33 Auditorium 2
34 Staff Accomodation
35 Heads of Schools and Departments
36 Heads of Schools and Departments
37 Network and Communications Lab
38 Electronic Computer Aided Design
39 Staff Accomodation
40 Computer Node Mezzanine

Architects   **Michael Hopkins & Partners, London**

Award Winning Building   **The Queen's Building, Emmanuel College**

Location   **Cambridge, UK**

Design and Construction Period   **1992–1995**

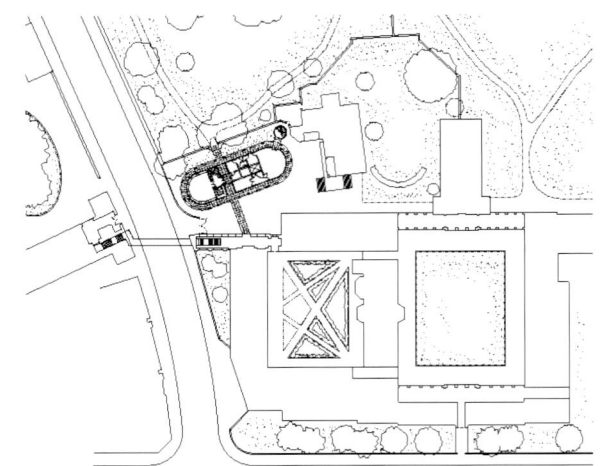

Award   1) RIBA Regional Architecture Award 1996 (Eastern Region);

　2) RIBA Architecture in Education Award 1996

Given by   RIBA The Royal Institute of British Architects

Prize Presentation   1996

Design Team   Michael Hopkins & Partners

Structural Engineering   Büro Happold, Bath

Civil Engineering   Büro Happold

Mechanical Engineering   Büro Happold

Electrical Engineering   Büro Happold

Acoustic Engineering   Arup Acoustics, London

Quantity Surveying   Davis Langdon & Everest, Oxon

Approximate Cost   £ 3,500,000

Site Area   2,500 m²

Building Area   326 m² (ground floor area including colonnade)

Total Floor Area   1,200 m²

Photographer   Dennis Gilbert

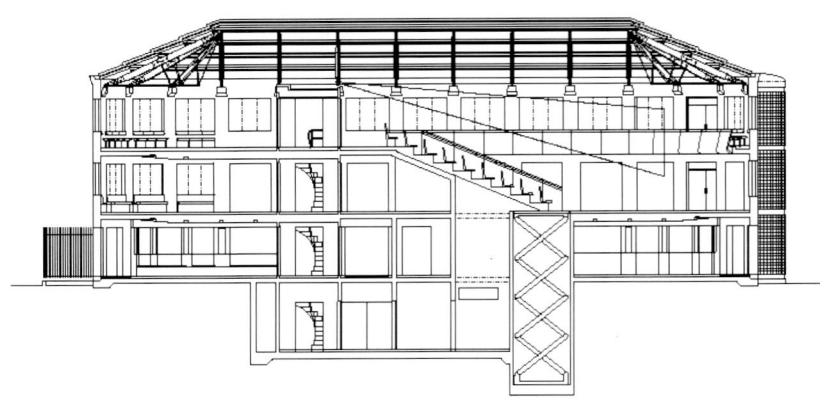

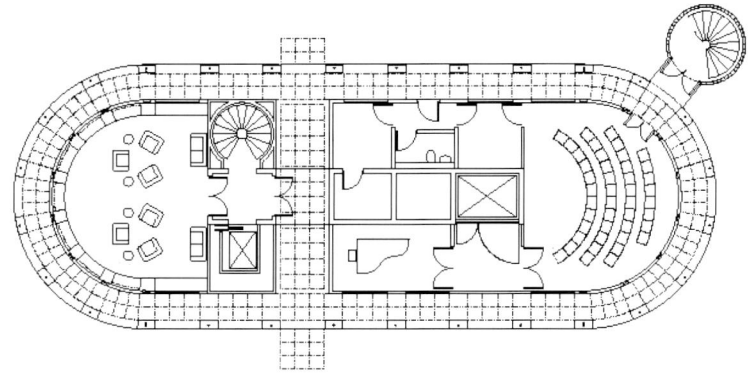

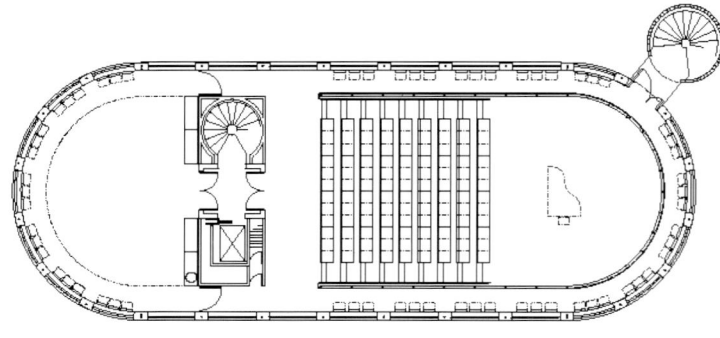

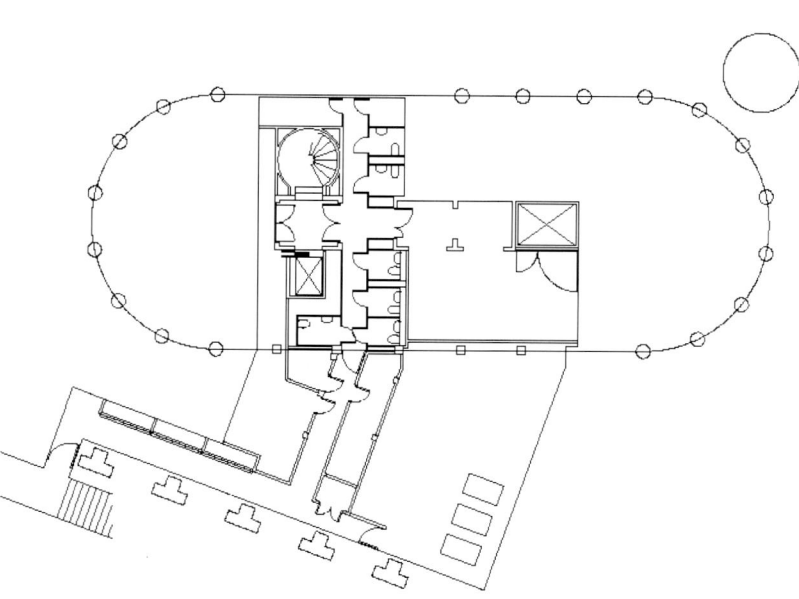

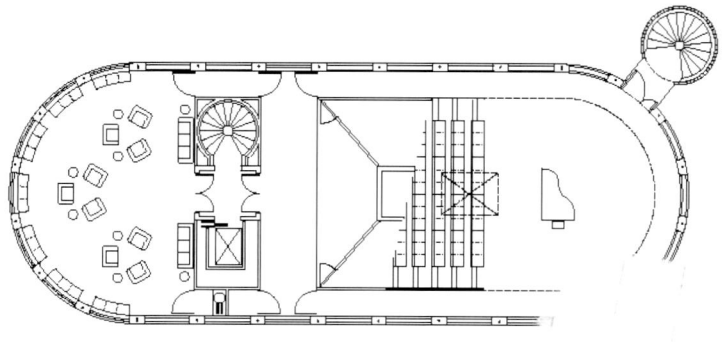

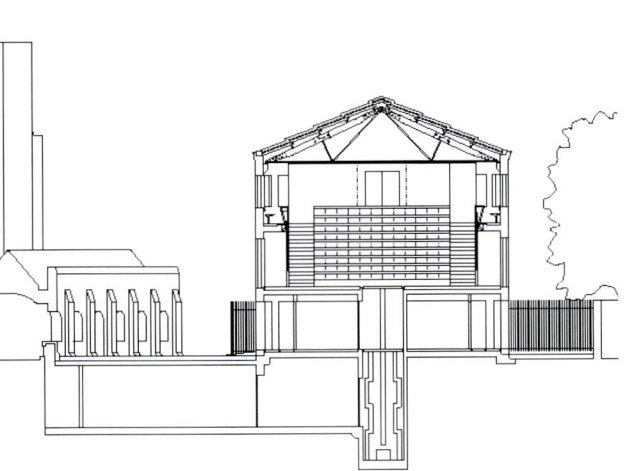

Architects **Anshen and Allen, Architects, Los Angeles**

Award Winning Building **Bourns Hall College of Engineering, University of California, Riverside**

Location **Riverside, California, USA**

Design and Construction Period **1990–1995**

Award AIA National Honor Award for Architecture 1996

Given by AIA The American Institute of Architects

Prize Presentation May / 12 / 1996

Members of the Jury Barton Myers, Laurie Becklemann, Fred Clarke III, James M. Cutler, Laurie D. Olin, Patrick Jones, Carol Shen, Alicia C. Trevino, Frank D. Welch

Design Team Anshen and Allen

Structural Engineering Ove Arup & Partners, California

Civil Engineering Albert Webb Associates

Mechanical Engineering Ove Arup & Partners, California

Electrical Engineering Ove Arup & Partners, California

Laboratory Planner Earl Walls Associates

Lighting Consultant David A. Mintz, Inc.

Life Safety Consultant Rolf Jensen & Associates, Inc.

Interior Design Carmen Nordsten Igonda Design

Landscape Architecture Pamela Burton & Company

Quantity Surveying Adamson Associates

Approximate Cost US$ 29,000,000

Site Area 15,800 m^2

Building Area 6,000 m^2

Total Floor Area 15,000 m^2

Photographer Timothy Hursley, J. Scott Smith

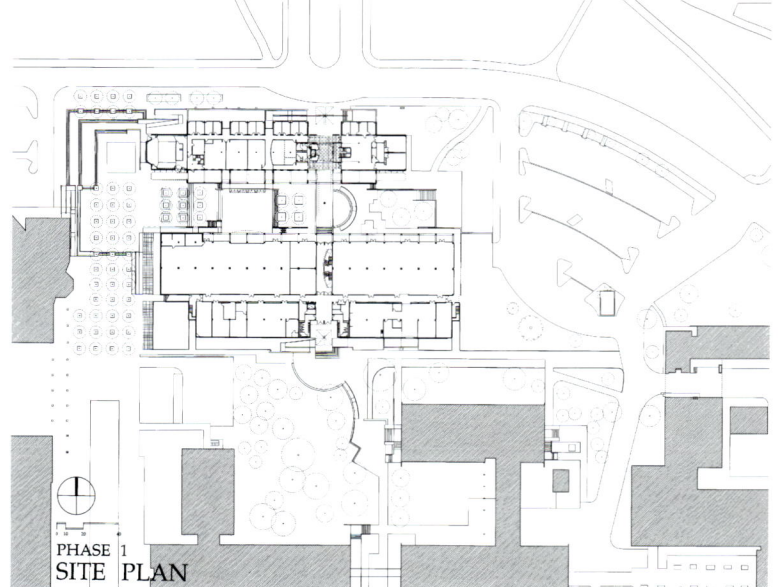

PHASE 1
SITE PLAN

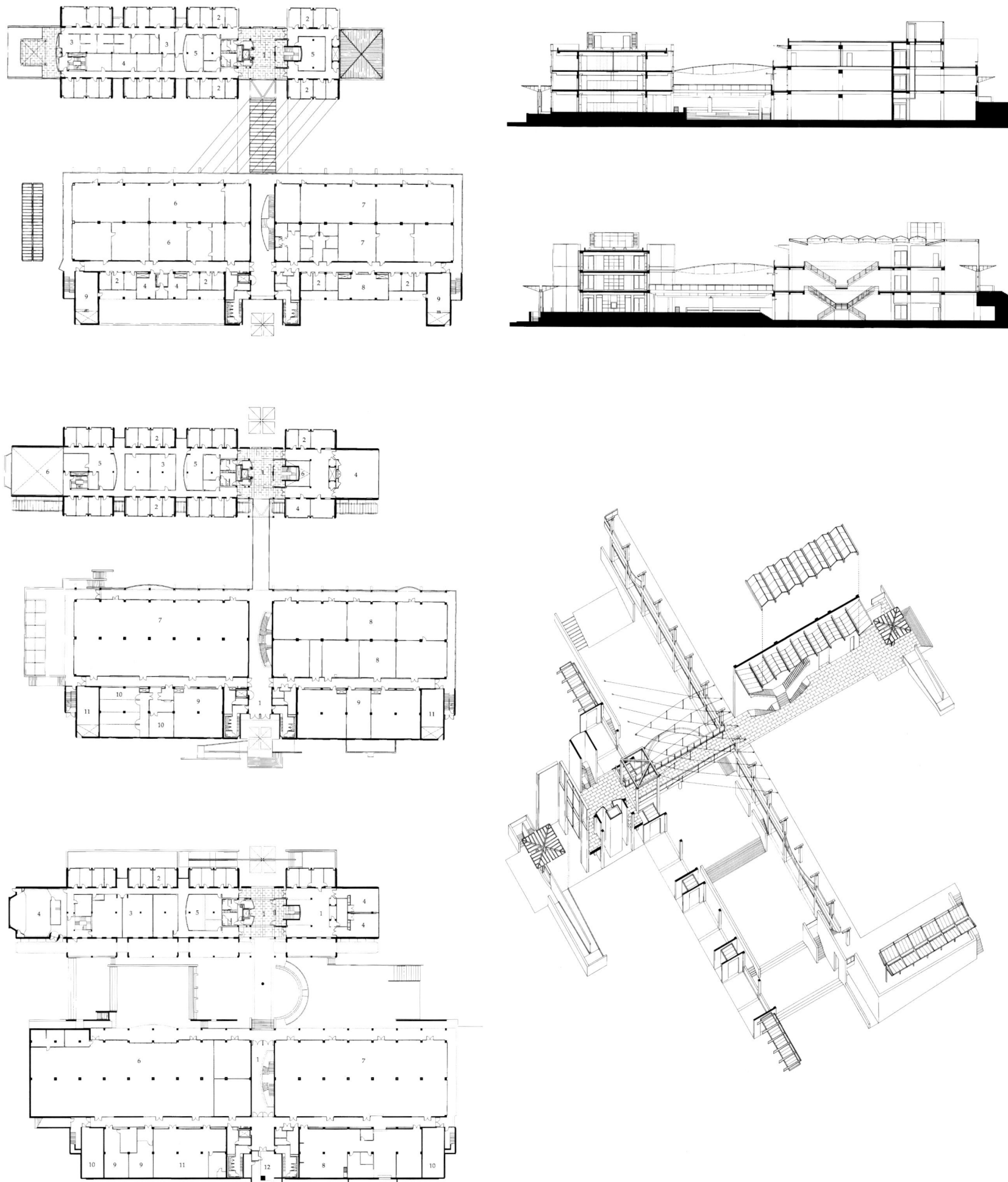

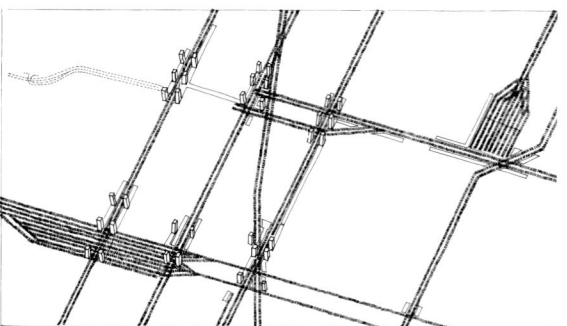

Architects **R.M. Kliment & Frances Halsband Architects, New York**

Award Winning Building **Entrance Pavilion – Long Island Rail Road, Pennsylvania Station**

Location **34th Street between Seventh and Eighth Avenues, New York City, New York, USA**

Design and Construction Period **1990–1994**

Award 1) AIA National Honor Award for Architecture 1996; 2) AIA New York City Award for Architecture; 3) AIA New York State Award of Excellence 1995

Given by AIA The American Institute of Architects

Prize Presentation 1) May / 12 / 1996; 2) 1995; 3) 1995

Members of the Jury 1) Barton Myers, Laurie Beckelmann, Fred Clark, James Cutler, Laurie Olin, Carol Shen, Alicia C. Trevino, Frank Welch; 2) Albert Pole, David Chipperfield, Paul Tesar, Pamela Babey; 3) Robert Traynham Coles, Bruno B. Freschi, O.C., David Lewis, R. Randall Vosbeck, Roberta Washington

Design Team Design Architect for Entrance Pavilion: R.M. Kliment & Frances Halsband Architects; Architects and Engineers for LIRR Penn Station

Structural Engineering TAMS Consultants, Inc.

Mechanical Engineering TAMS Consultants, Inc.

Electrical Engineering TAMS Consultants, Inc.

Lighting Consultant for Entrance Pavilion H.M. Brandston & Partners, Inc.

General Contractor A.J. Pegno Construction Corporation

Construction Manager Bechtel Corporation

Approximate Cost US$ 20,000,000 (Entrance Pavilion and Climate Control Equipment); US$ 190,000,000 (LIRR Penn Station Improvement Project)

Site Area 2,000 sq. ft.

Building Area 5,800 sq. ft.

Photographer Cervin Robinson

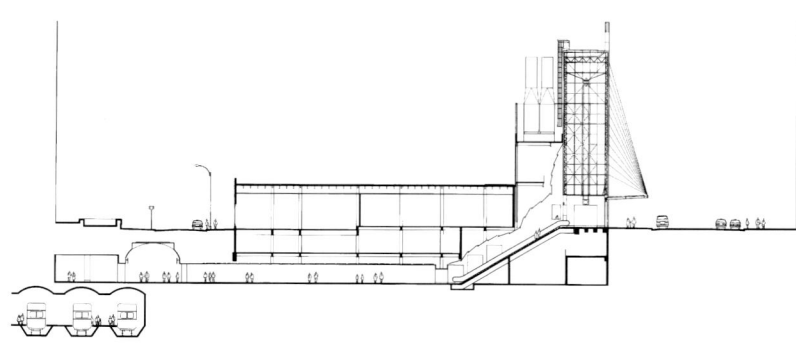

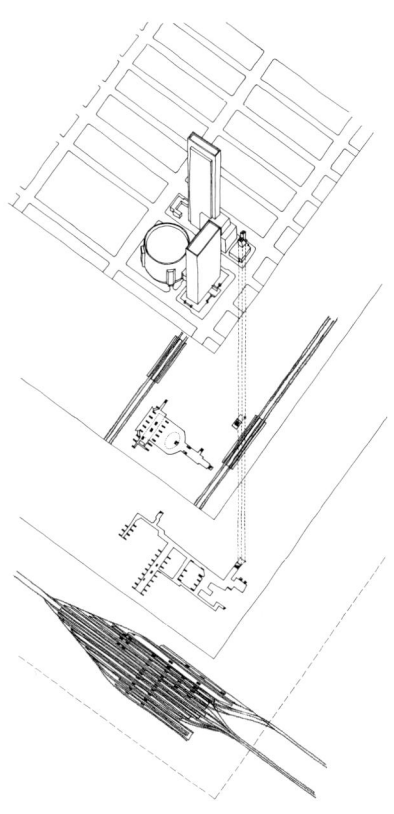

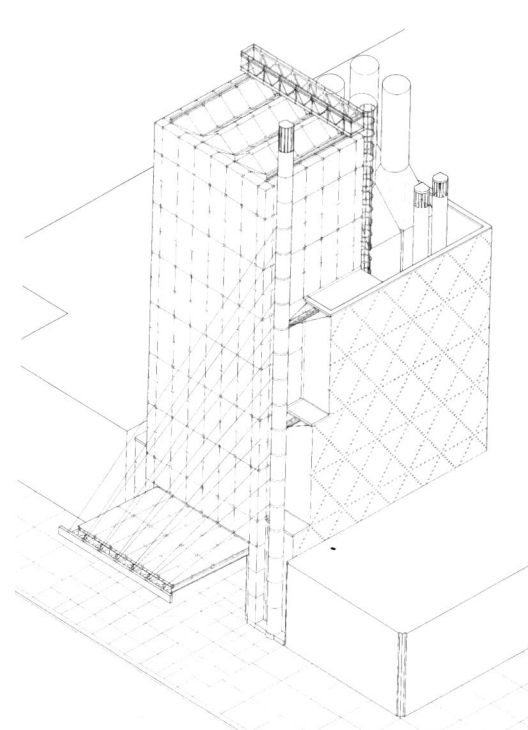

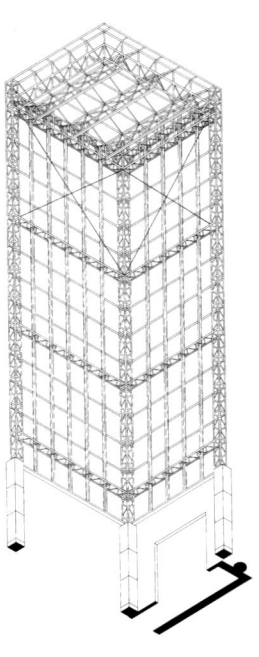

Architects **Murphy / Jahn, Chicago**

Award Winning Building **Kurfürstendamm No. 70**

Location **Kurfürstendamm, Berlin, Germany**

Design and Construction Period **1988–1994**

Award 1) AIA Chicago Chapter Award 1994; 2) AIA National Honor Award
  for Architecture 1996

Given by AIA The American Institute of Architects

Prize Presentation 1) 1994; 2) May / 12 / 1996

Design Team Helmut Jahn, Rainer Schildknecht, Steven Cook,
  Sabford Gorshow (M/J Team)

Structural Engineering Friedrich Mueller

General Contractor CogefarImpresit

Mechanical Engineering Ing. Büro Wilhelm Lutz VDI

Client EUWO Unternehmensgrupe

Façade Sub-Contractor BERTI

Site Area 60 m^2

Total Floor Area 1,142 m^2

Photographer H.G. Esch

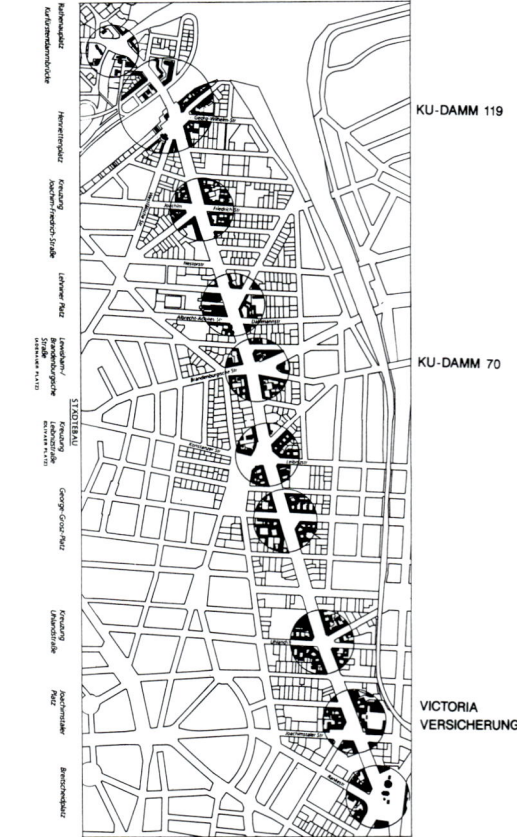

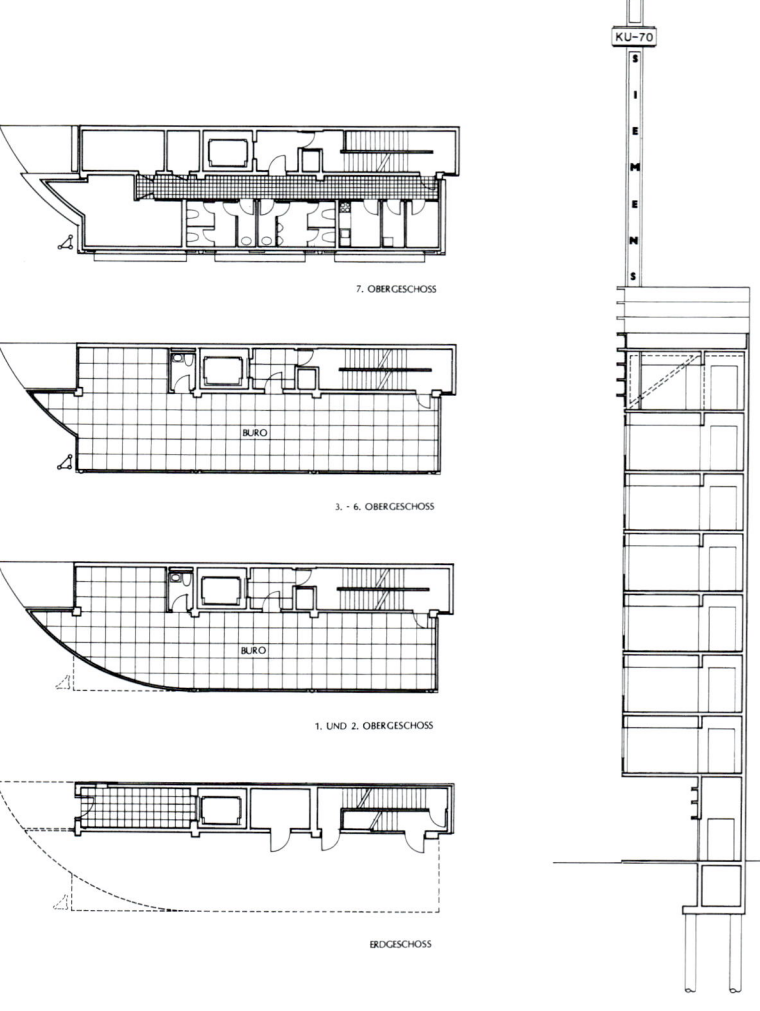

Architects **Murphy / Jahn, Chicago**

Award Winning Building **Munich Order Center – M.O.C.**

Location **Munich, Germany**

Design and Construction Period **1989–1993**

Award 1) AIA Chicago Chapter Award 1994; 2) AIA National Honor Award
for Architecture 1996

Given by AIA The American Institute of Architects

Prize Presentation 1) 1994; 2) May / 12 / 1996

Design Team Helmut Jahn, Rainer Schildknecht, Steven Cook, Mark Frisch,
Sanford Gorshow, Fritz Ludwig (M/J Team)

Client Archimedes Gewerbe – und Büro; Centrum GmbH & Co.

Structural Engineering Burggraf, Weichinger & Partner GmbH

Mechanical Engineering KLA Kuehn-Lehr Associates

Electrical Engineering KLA Kuehn-Lehr Associates

Landscape Architecture Wofgang Roth

*General Contractor – Interior, Landscape Architecture, Mechanical and Electrical
Engineering, Elevators* Bayerische Industrie und Gewerbe Bau GmbH & Co.

General Contractor – Structural Engineering, Curtainwall Glass Roof, Sun Shades
Firma Noell

Curtain Wall and Statics Ingenieurbüro Schalm

Lighting Consultant Francis Krahe & Associates

Total Floor Area 78,000 m²

Photographers Architekturfoto Engelhardt & Sellin, Images Publishing Group

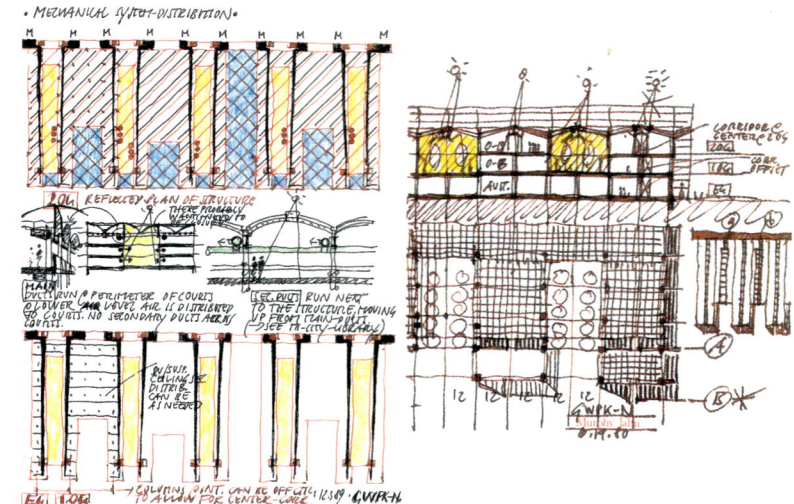

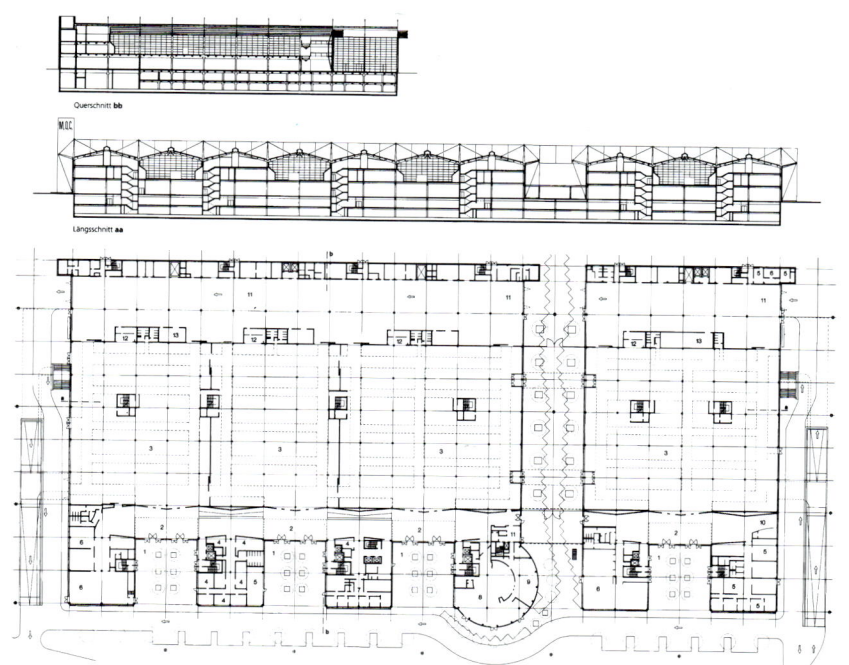

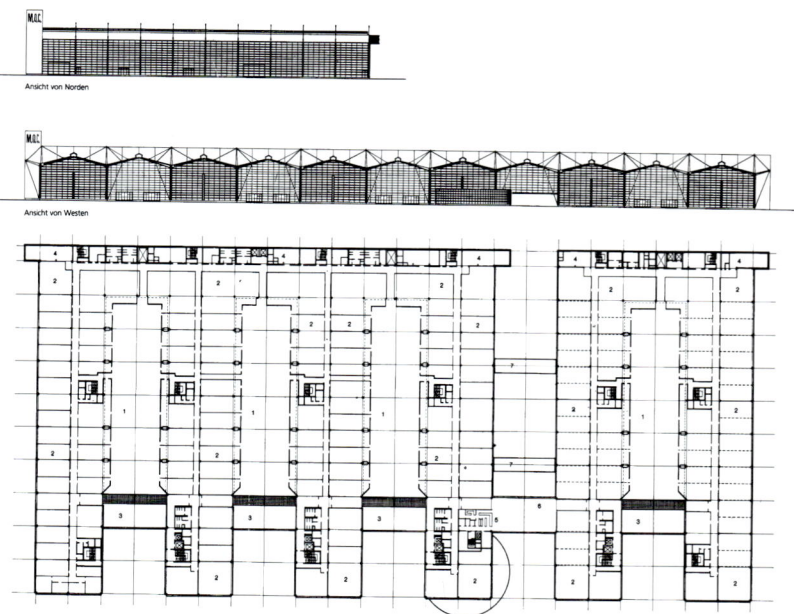

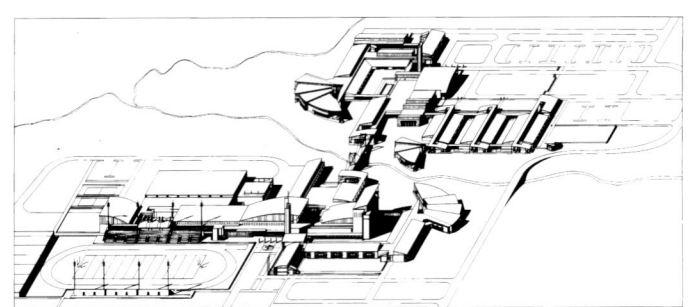

Architects **Perkins & Will, Burgess & Niple Ltd., Chicago**

Award Winning Building **Perry Community Education Village**

Location **Perry, Ohio, USA**

Design and Construction Period **1988–1993**

Award AIA National Honor Award for Architecture 1996

Given by AIA The American Institute of Architects

Prize Presentation May / 12 / 1996

Members of the Jury Barton Myers (Chair), Laurie Beckelmann, Fred Clarke III, James M. Cutler, Laurie D. Olin, Patrick Jones, Carol Shen, Alicia C. Trevino, Frank Welch

Design Team Perkins & Will: C.W. Brubaker (Principal in Charge); Ralph E. Johnson (Design Principal); Project Directors: James G. Woods, Raymond C. Bordwell, James Nowak (Senior Project Architect); Project Architects: Michael Palmer, Eric Spielman; Design Team: August Battaglia, Jerry Johnson, Greg Bennett, Celeste Robbins, Bill Schmalz, Steve Roberts, Betty Fakatselis, Anita Ambriz–Burgess & Niple, Ltd.: Team Members: Jerry Keltch (Principal), David Kalina (Principal), Ray Corby (Project Manager), Tim Clapper (Construction Supervisor), Jim Alban (Construction Project Manager)

Structural Engineering Perkins & Will, Burgess & Niple, Ltd.

Civil Engineering Burgess & Niple, Ltd.

Mechanical Engineering Burgess & Niple, Ltd.

Electrical Engineering Burgess & Niple, Ltd.

Acoustic Engineering Kirkegaard & Associates, Inc.

Interior Design Perkins & Will, Burgess & Niple, Ltd.

Landscape Architecture Perkins & Will, Burgess & Niple, Ltd.

Approximate Cost US$ 70,000,000

Site Area 80 acres

Building Area 390,000 sq. ft. (High School & Fitness Center)

Total Floor Area 390,000 sq. ft.

Photographer Hedrich/Blessing, Wayland

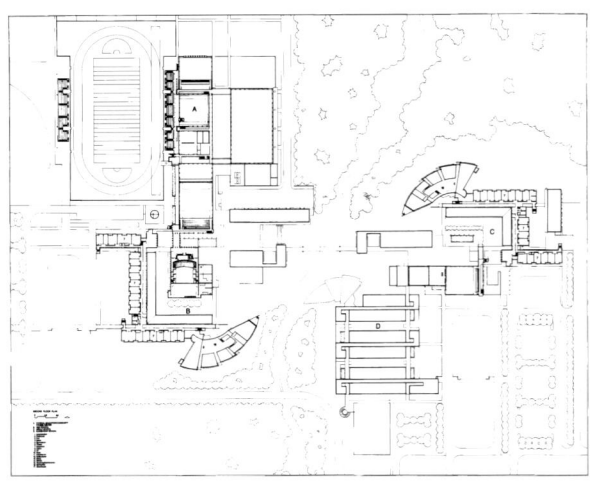

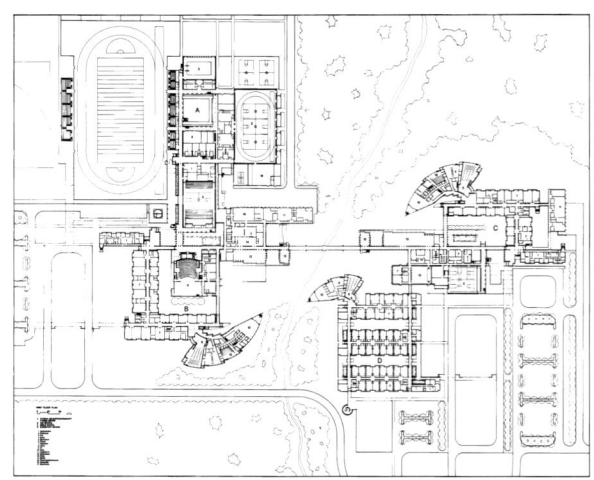

Architects **Sasaki Associates, Watertown**

Award Winning Building **Cleveland Gateway**

Location **Cleveland, Ohio, USA**

Design and Construction Period **1990–1994**

Award 1) AIA National Honor Award 1996 (Urban Design); 2) Honor Award 1994 (Planning and Urban Design)

Given by 1) AIA The American Institute of Architects; 2) American Society of Landscape Architects

Prize Presentation 1) April 1996; 2) October 1996

Members of the Jury 1) Barton Meyers, Marilyn Jordan Taylor, J. Woodson Rainey, Jr.; 2) Roger Trancik, Fritz Steiner, Ignacio Bunster-Ossa, Leslie Kerr

Master Planning and Urban Design, Landscape Architecture, Parking and Transportation Management, and Signage Sasaki Associates, Inc.

Architecture Jacobs Field – HOK Sport, Kansas City; Ground Arena–Ellerbe Becket, Kansas City; Parking Garages – van Dijk, Pace, Westlake & Partners; Service Area – Richard Fleischman Architects, Inc.

Sasaki Associates Team Alan Ward (Design Principal), David Hirzel (Managing Principal), Dennis Pieprz (Project Urban Designer), James Doolin (Project Manager), John Barry (Environmental Graphics), Robert Brooks, Edward Boiteau, Richard Galehouse, Darrell Bird, Thomas DiCicco, Elen Deming, Neil Dean, Jeanne Lukenda, Ivanna Strum, Chuck Coronis, and David Oldman

Approximate Cost US$ 10,000,000 (Site Work); US$ 425,000,000 (Total Project)

Site Area 181,150 m²

Photographers Alex MacLean / Landslides, Roger Mastroianni, Alan Ward

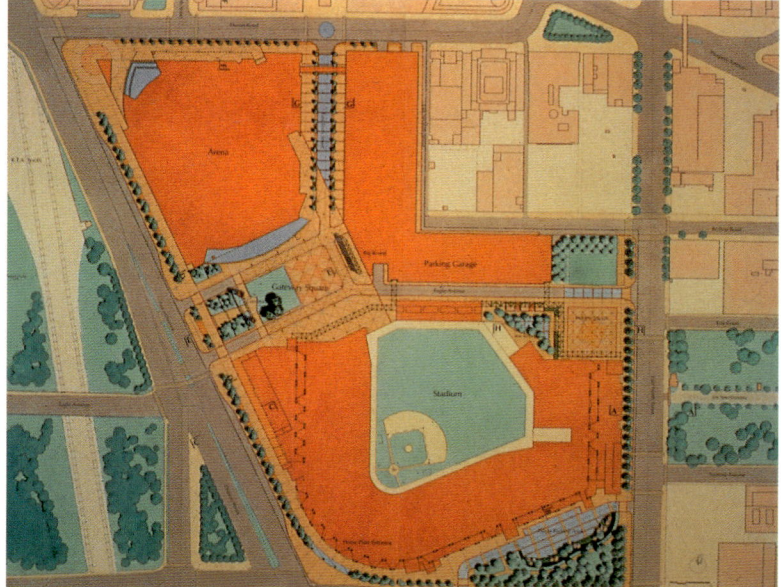

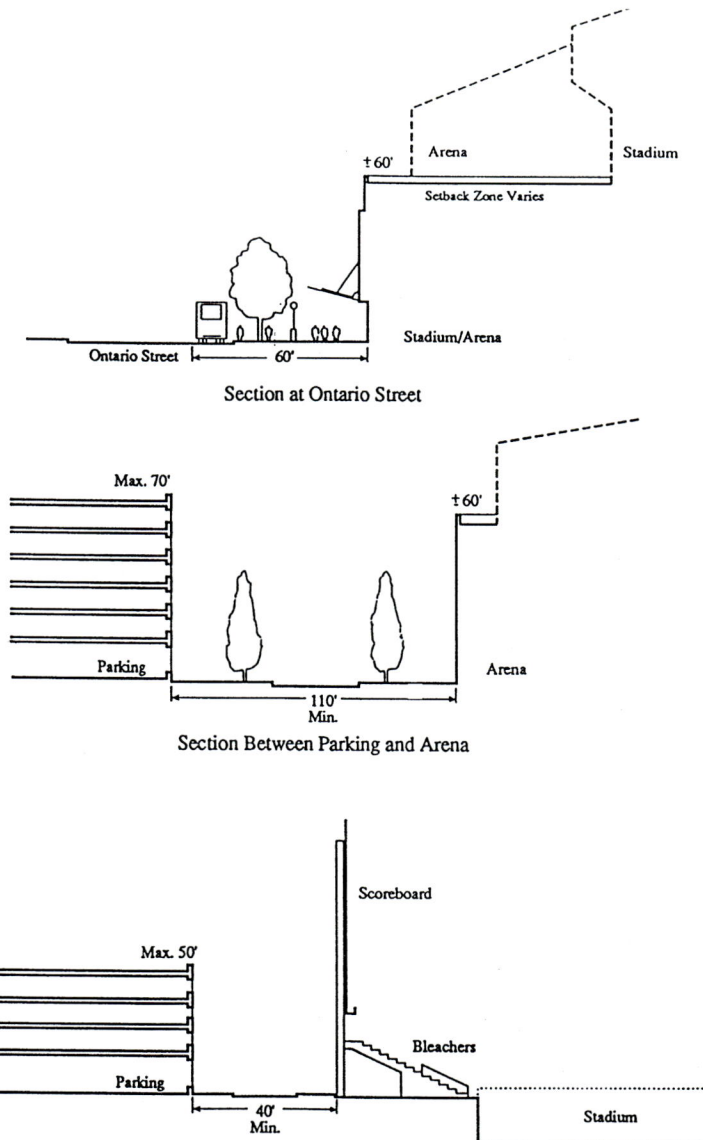

Section at Ontario Street

Section Between Parking and Arena

Section Between Parking and Outfield Bleachers

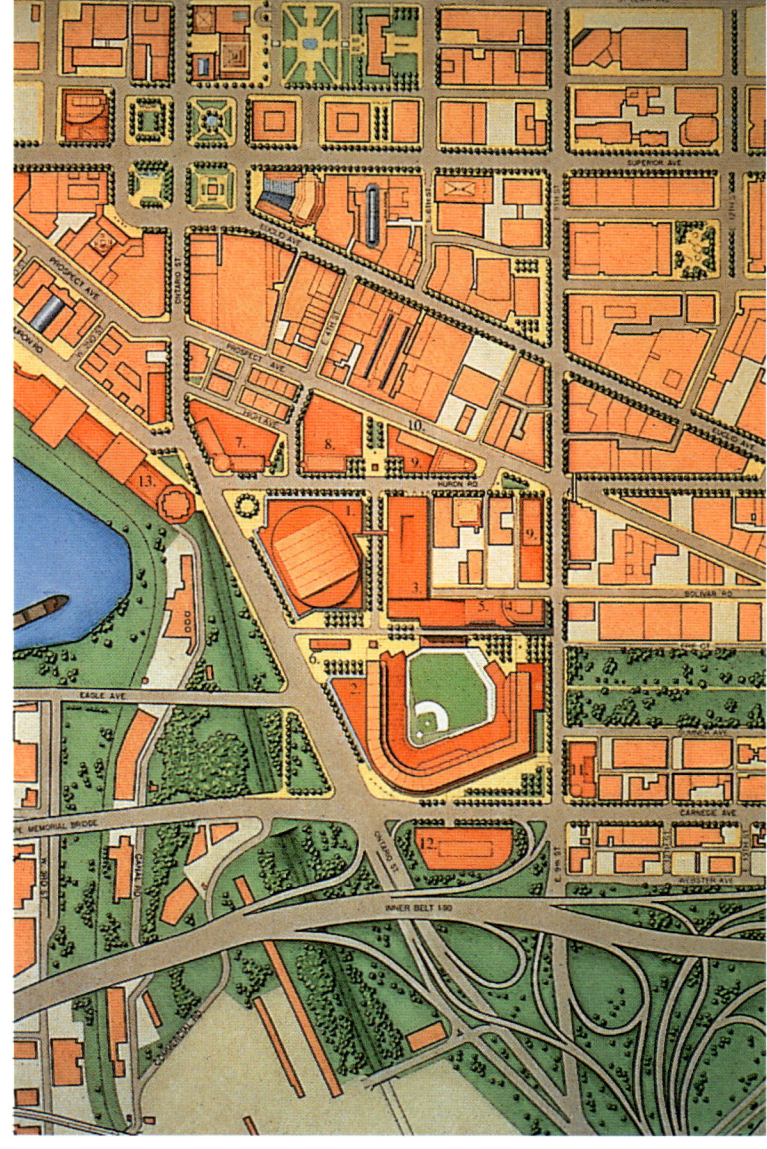

**COMPREHENSIVE LISTING
OF PROJECTS:**

AMA 1997 includes awards from national associations of architects who are members of the UIA, listed country by country in alphabetical order. Within each country, the individual architects are also listed alphabetically. A number of selected projects are documented in detail in the first section of the book, and these are only briefly outlined in the general section, with a cross reference specifying the page on which the detailed description can be found.

The awards in question are the highest accolades presented by the respective national architects' associations. Where such an association does not actually grant an award itself, an equivalent award by another institution or foundation has been included on the recommendation of the national architects' association.

Australia

Architects **Denton Corker Marshall Pty Ltd, Melbourne**
Award Winning Building **Melbourne Exhibition Centre**

Award 1) Sir Zelman Cowen Award for Public Buildings 1996; 2) RAIA Victorian Chapter Sir Osborne McCutcheon Award for Commercial Architecture; 3) RAIA Gold Medal 1996
see page 14

Austria

Architects **ATP–Achammer-Tritthart & Partner**
Award Winning Building **Siemens Microelectronic-Centre Dresden**
Location **Dresden, Germany**

Award Nominierung zum Staatspreis für Consulting 1995
Given by Bundeskammer der Architekten und Ingenieurkonsulenten
Prize Presentation January / 9 / 1996

Austria

Architects **BRUMI Architekten, Arch. Wolfgang Brunbauer, Vienna**
Award Winning Building **Arena Nova Wiener Neustadt**
Location **Vienna, Austria**

Award Nominierung zum Staatspreis für Consulting 1995
Given by Bundeskammer der Architekten und Ingenieurkonsulenten
Prize Presentation January / 9 / 1996

Austria

Architects **CPEC (Chao Phraya Engineering Consortium), Vienna**
Award Winning Building **Cambodia, Main Report**

Award Nominierung zum Staatspreis für Consulting 1996
Given by Bundeskammer der Architekten und Ingenieurkonsulenten
Prize Presentation November / 25 / 1996

Austria

Architects **DKE Wasserbauengineering & Consulting GesmbH, Vienna**
Award Winning Building **Ground Water Plant Freudenau**

Award Nominierung zum Staatspreis für Consulting 1995
Given by Bundeskammer der Architekten und Ingenieurkonsulenten
Prize Presentation January / 9 / 1996

Austria

Architects **Gruppe Wasser, Vienna**
Award Winning Building **Environmental Information System for the**
   Huangpu Area, China
Location **Huangpu, China**

Award Nominierung zum Staatspreis für Consulting 1996
Given by Bundeskammer der Architekten und Ingenieurkonsulenten
Prize Presentation November / 25 / 1996

Austria

Architect **Hans Hollein, Vienna**
Associated Architects **Atelier 4 / Philippe Tixier, Clermond-Ferrand**
Award Winning Building **Centre Européen du Volcanisme (Vulcania)**
Location **St. Ours-les-Roches, Auvergne, France**
Design and Construction Period **1994–2000**

Award Staatspreis für Consulting 1995
Given by Bundeskammer der Architekten und Ingenieurkonsulenten
Prize Presentation January / 9 / 1996
Members of the Jury Josef Stiegler (Austria), Thomas Brendel (Germany),
   Gerhart Bruckmann (Austria), Sepp Frank (Austria), Matthias Rant (Austria),
   Martin S. van Treeck (France), J. Zwaenepoel (Belgium)
Design Team Hans Hollein, Hans-Peter Wunsch (Job Captain), Atelier 4 /
   Philippe Tixier (Associated Architect), Clermont-Ferrand
Structural Engineering BET ITC, Clermont-Ferrand
Geology Consultant Geoconsult Ingenieurgemeinschaft, Vienna
Mechanical Engineering BET Choulet, Clermont-Ferrand
Electrical Engineering BET Choulet, Clermont-Ferrand
Air Conditioning Consultant BET Choulet, Clermont-Ferrand
Environmental Engineering Gilles Clement, Paris
Landscape Architecture Gilles Clement, Paris

Acoustic Engineering Capri Acoustique, Suresnes
Lighting Consultant Lichtdesign, Köln
Client Conseil Régional d'Auvergne, Président Valery Giscard d'Estaing
Scenographic Consultant Rainer Verbizh, Paris
Quantity Surveying Michel Forgue, Le Rivier d'Apprieu
Approximate Cost FF 211,000,000 (construction costs), FF 44,000,000
   (exhibition design), FF 4,500,000 (interiors)
Site Area 570,000 m^2
Total Floor Area 18,176 m^2
Photographer Arch. Baniahmad (Studio Prof. Hollein)

Austria

Architect **Wilhelm Holzbauer, Vienna**
Award Winning Building **Festival Theater Baden-Baden**
Location **Baden-Baden, Germany**
Design and Construction Period **1995–1997**

 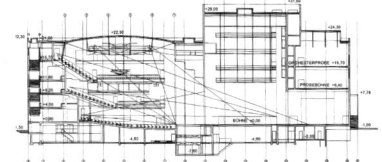

Award Nominierung zum Staatspreis für Consulting 1996
Given by Bundeskammer der Architekten und Ingenieurkonsulenten
Prize Presentation November / 25 / 1996
Design Team Irresberger, Hummer, Dukan, Rabenstein, Mayer, Stubnja, Köberl,
   Tischler, Jarda, Stoht
Structural Engineering Ingenieurgesellschaft Mayer-Vorfelder und Dinkelacker,
   Sindelfingen
Mechanical Engineering Ingenieurbüro Heinrich Wiczkowiak (IBW),
   Recklinghausen
Electrical Engineering Ingenieurpartnerschaft (IPS), Tübingen
Acoustic Engineering Müller BBM, Planegg
Air Conditioning Consultant Ingenieurpartnerschaft (IPS), Tübingen
Lighting Consultant Dieter Irresberger

Interior Design Wilhelm Holzbauer
Landscape Architecture Stadtgartenamt Baden-Baden, Weigel
Quantity Surveying 98,500 m^2
Approximate Cost DM 125,000,000
Site Area 8,400 m^2
Building Area 4,450 m^2
Total Floor Area 8,900 m^2

Austria

Architects **Kirsch-Muchitsch und Partner, Linz**
Award Winning Building **Replacement of the Superstructure of the**
  Brenner Highway "Mushroom Bridges" with no Interruption to Traffic
Location **Brenner Highway, Austria**
Design and Construction Period **1992–1995**

Award Staatspreis für Consulting 1996
Given by Bundeskammer der Architekten und Ingenieurkonsulenten
Prize Presentation 1996
Members of the Jury Josef Stiegler, Werner Konas, Thomas Brendel, Gerhart   *Civil Engineering* Büro Baumann – Obholzer
  Bruckmann, Sepp Frank, Martin S. van Treeck, Jozef Camille Zwaenepoel   *Bridge Inspections* Büro M. Wicke
Design Team Kirsch-Muchitsch und Partner

Austria

Architects **KWI Architects Engineers Consultants, St. Pölten**
Award Winning Building **Cogeneration plant for the wood processing**
  industry
Location **Carinthia, Austria**
Design and Construction Period **1995–1997**

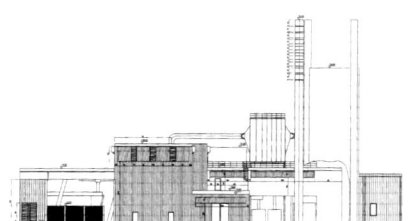

Award Nominierung zum Staatspreis für Consulting 1996
Given by Bundeskammer der Architekten und Ingenieurkonsulenten
Prize Presentation November / 25 / 1996
Members of the Jury Josef Stiegler, Werner Konas, Thomas Brendel, Gerhart
Bruckmann, Sepp Frank, Martin S. van Treeck, Jozef Camille Zwaenepoel
Design Team and Engineering KWI Architects Engineers Consultants

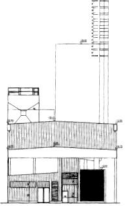
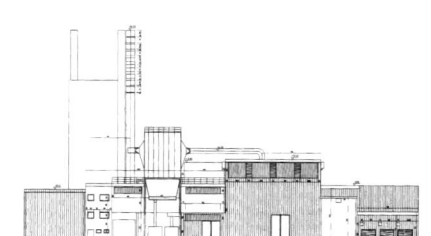

Austria

Architect **Hans Lechner, Vienna**
Award Winning Building **General Renovations Schönbrunn Zoo (first phase)**
Location **Schönbrunn, Austria**
Design and Construction Period **1991–1995**

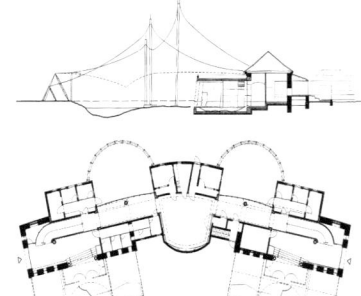

Award Nominierung zum Staatspreis für Consulting 1996
Given by Bundeskammer der Architekten und Ingenieurkonsulenten
Prize Presentation 1996
General Planner Büro Hans Lechner
Structural Engineering / Site Supervision Rainhard Weis
Mechanical Engineering Büro Ramsmaier
Electrical Engineering Büro Pruckmayer   *Building Area* 1,210 m²
Landscape Architecture Maria Auböck   *Total Floor Area* 980 m²
Approximate Cost ÖS 46,000,000   *Photographer* Studio Hans Lechner
Site Area 6,125 m² (4,100 m² outer enclosure)

Austria

Architect **Wolfgang Meixner**
Award Winning Building **Informationssystem Hofburg**

Award Nominierung zum Staatspreis für Consulting 1995
Given by Bundeskammer der Architekten und Ingenieurkonsulenten
Prize Presentation January / 9 / 1996

Austria

Architect **Matthias Rant, Vienna**
Award Winning Building **Bali Bird Park**

Award Nominierung zum Staatspreis für Consulting 1996
Given by Bundeskammer der Architekten und Ingenieurkonsulenten
Prize Presentation November / 25 / 1996

Austria

Architects **Regional Consulting – Ziviltechniker GesmbH, Vienna**
Award Winning Project **Urban Development Tirana**

Award Nominierung zum Staatspreis für Consulting 1996
Given by Bundeskammer der Architekten und Ingenieurkonsulenten
Prize Presentation November / 25 / 1996

Austria

Architects **Bengt Sprinzl und Utz Purr, Vienna**
Award Winning Building **Bank Austria, Branch Office Hirschstetten**
Location **Hirschstetten, Vienna, Austria**
Design and Construction Period **1992–1995**

Award Nominierung zum Staatspreis für Consulting 1995
Given by Bundeskammer der Architekten und Ingenieurkonsulenten
Prize Presentation January / 9 / 1996
Members of the Jury Thomas Brendel, Gerhart Bruckmann, Sepp Frank,
   Matthias Rant, Martin S. van Treeck, Jozef Camille Zwaenepoel
Design Team Bengt Sprinzl und Utz Purr
Structural Engineering Walter Pistulka
Civil Engineering / Construction Biology Walter Pistulka
Mechanical Engineering Peter Schur
Electrical Engineering José Srof
Environmental Engineering Peter Schur
Air Conditioning Consultant Peter Schur
Lighting Consultant José Srof
Interior Design Bengt Sprinzl und Utz Purr
Landscape Architecture Bengt Sprinzl and Utz Purr
Quantity Surveying Bengt Sprinzl and Utz Purr
Approximate Cost ATS 26,500
Site Area 1.266 m²

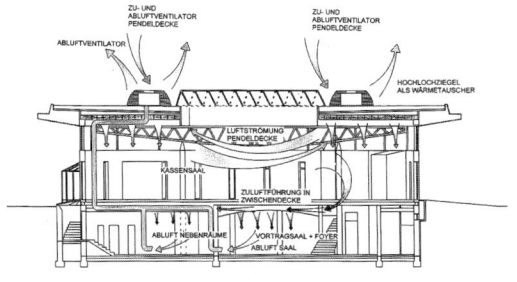

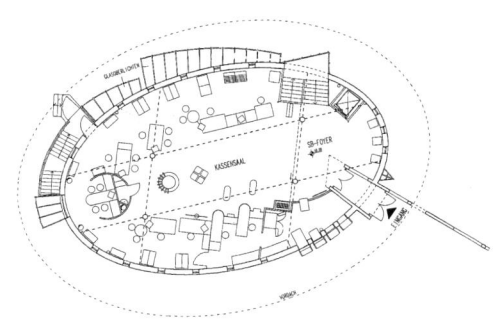

Building Area 296 m²
Total Floor Area 529 m² (net), 619 m² (gross)
Photographer Martin Schiebel

Brazil

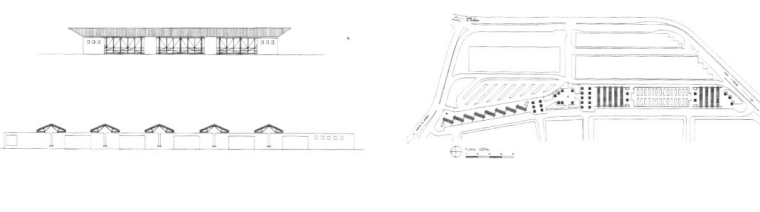

Architects **José Brandão, Ronaldo L'Amour, Recife**
Award Winning Building **Shopping Popular de Santa Rita**
Location **Recife, Brazil**
Design and Construction Period **1994–1996**

Award 1) III Bienal de Arquitectura del Rio Grande del Sul;
   2) X Bienal Panamericana de Arquitectura de Quito
Given by 1) Instituto dos Arquitetos do Brasil; 2) El Colegio de Arquitectos
   del Ecuador
Prize Presentation 1) November / 20-23 / 1996; 2) November / 11-15 / 1996
Members of the Jury 1) Raj Barrkumar (USA), Alberto Sartori (Chile),
   Carlos Fernando Pontual (Brazil), Éolo Maia (Brazil), Gregorio Repsold (Brazil),
   Juvenal Baracco (Peru); 2) José Ordoñez v. (Ecuador), José Luis Cañavate
   (Spain), Ken Martin (UK), Gonzalo Bustamante (Ecuador)
Design Team Fátima Nogueira, Kátia Araújo
Structural Engineering Clayton Gonçalves Holanda
Civil Engineering Construtora Andrade Guedes Ltda.

Electrical Engineering Maria do Socorro dos Santos
Lighting Consultant Maria do Socorro dos Santos
Landscape Architecture Beatriz Assmann
Approximate Cost US$ 1,800,000
Site Area 15,000 m²
Building Area 2,500 m²
Total Floor Area 2,500 m²

Brazil

Architects **Carlos Bratke, João Belo (collaborator), São Paulo**
Award Winning Building **House of the Architect**
Location **Av. Eng. Oscar Americano, Morumbi, São Paulo, SP, Brazil**
Design and Construction Period **1992–1994**

Award Prêmio Abcem
Given by Instituto de Arquitetos do Brasil
Prize Presentation June 1995
Design Team Carlos Bratke, João Belo (collaborator)
Structural Engineering Aluizio A.M. D'Avilla
Metallic Structure Projeto Alpha
Hydraulic and Electrical Engineering M.H.A. Engenharia
Landscape Architecture Carlos Bratke, Denise Barretto
Building Area 714 m²
Photographer Carolina Bratke, José Moscardi

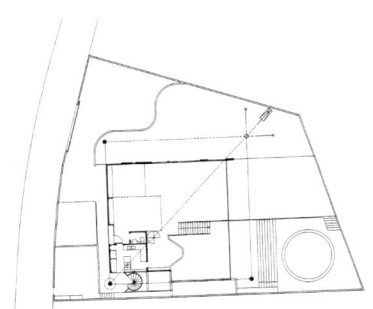

Brazil

Architect **Janer Lagarreta Paixão Coelho, Porto Alegre**
Award Winning Building **Refurbishment of Beach Cottage**
Location **Calle Egidio Michaelsen 69, Esq. Kalil Sehbe, Torres, R.G.S.,
   Brazil**
Design and Construction Period **1994–1995**

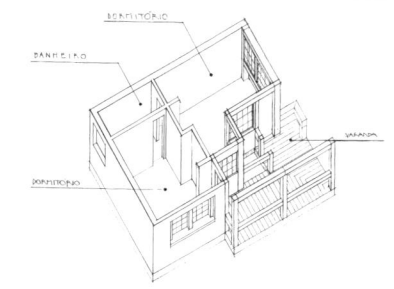

Award III Bienal de Arquitectura del Rio Grande del Sul (1st Prize in
   the Category Edificación de pequeño porte)
Given by Instituto dos Arquitetos do Brasil
Prize Presentation November 1995
Members of the Jury Carlos Reininger de A. Moura. Ester J.B. Gutierrez,
   Sergio Saffer, Silvio Belmonte de Abreu Filho, Ivan Mizoguchi
Design Team Janer Lagarreta Paixão Coelho

Approximate Cost US$ 100,000
Site Area 420 m²
Building Area 179 m²
Total Floor Area 326 m²
Photographer Fernando Brentano / Ester Meyer

Architects **Moacyr Moojen Marques, José Carlos Marques, Sérgio Moacir
Marques, Anna Paula Canez, Porto Alegre**
Award Winning Building **Centro Comercial Nova Olaria**
Location **Rua General Lima e Silva, 776 e Rua Luís Afonso, 84 e 90,
Cidade Baixa, Porto Alegre, RS, Brazil**
Design and Construction Period **1992–1994**

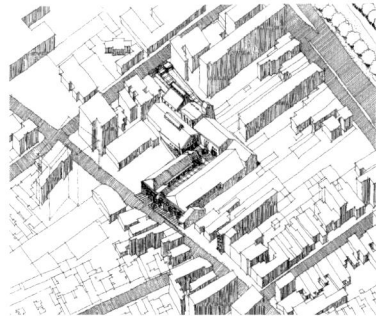 

Award III Bienal de Arquitectura del Rio Grande del Sul (Edificação de
grande porte)
Given by Instituto dos Arquitetos do Brasil
Prize Presentation November / 20 / 1995
Members of the Jury Carlos Reinigite de Azevedo Moura, Ester Judite B.
Gutierrez, Sérgio Saffer, Silvio Belmonte de Abreu Filho, Ivan Mizoguchi
Structural Engineering Concreto Armado – Fridman Azambuja cia Ltda.: Eng°.
Salomão Fridman e Eng°. Paulo Azambuja
Civil Engineering SERTEC Engenharia Ltda.
Kitchen Installations TEKINOX Ltda.
Electrical Engineering Elentel Engenharia Ltda.-Eng°. Renato Seganredo
Fireproof Design Químico Industrial Cláudio Hanssen
Hydraulic Engineering Arquitecto Antônio Joaquim Machado
Air Conditioning Consultant Eng°. João Carlos Barbosa

Lighting Consultant Moacyr Moojen Marques, José Carlos Marques,
Sérgio Moacir Marques, Anna Paula Canez
Construction Consultant Eng°. Raul Rego Faillace
Interior Design Moacyr Moojen Marques, José Carlos Marques, Sérgio Moacir
Marques, Anna Paula Canez
Landscape Architecture Moacyr Moojen Marques, José Carlos Marques,
Sérgio Moacir Marques, Anna Paula Canez
Quantity Surveying SERTEC Engenharia
Approximate Cost R$ 1,000,000
Site Area 4,920 m^2
Building Area 3,987 m^2

Architect **Fernando de Mello Franco, São Paulo**
Associated Architects **Marta Moreira, Milton Braga, São Paulo**
Award Winning Building **DPTO Propaganda & Marketing Building**

Award Best Built for Commercial Buildings
see page 16

Architect **Edgardo Victor Olaszek, São Paulo**
Award Winning Building **Punta del Este Building**
Location **Praia da Enseada, Guarujá, Brazil**
Design and Construction Period **1989–1991**

Award Edificios Residenciales (Honorable Mention)
Given by Instituto dos Arquitetos do Brasil
Prize Presentation March / 22 / 1995
Members of the Jury Joaquim Guedes, Marília S. de Almeida, Abrahão
Sanovicz, Décio Tozzi, Wilis Myasaka, Tito Livio Frascino, Gianfranco Vannucci
Design Team Luciana Rodriguez, Vinicius de Oliveira, Elena Olaszek
Structural Engineering Paulo Sérgio de Souza Campos
Civil Engineering NOVArq Empreendimentos Imobiliários Ltda.
Electrical Engineering Dicil
Interior Design Edgardo Victor Olaszek
Approximate Cost US$ 600,000.00
Site Area 330 m^2
Building Area 1,070 m^2
Total Floor Area 130 m^2

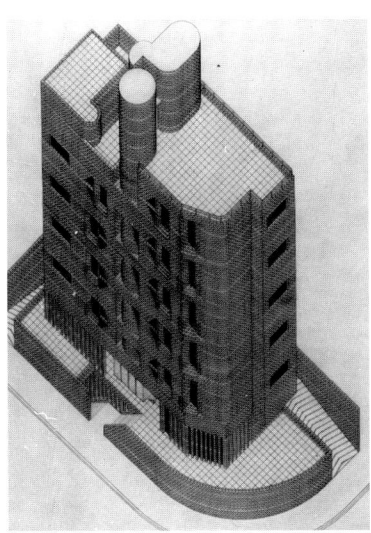

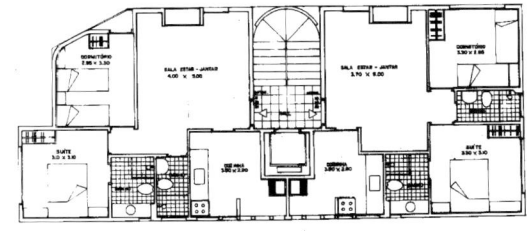

Architect **Otavio Leonídio Ribeiro, Rio de Janeiro**
Award Winning Building **Casa Pacelli**

Award Arquiteto Hélio Uchôa
see page 20

Architects **Fernando dos Santos Rocha Machado, Rovena Schumacher,**
  Evaldo Schumacher, Caxias do Sul
Award Winning Building **iT Club (Night Club)**
Location **Caxias do Sul, Rio Grande do Sul, Brazil**
Design and Construction Period **1994–1994**

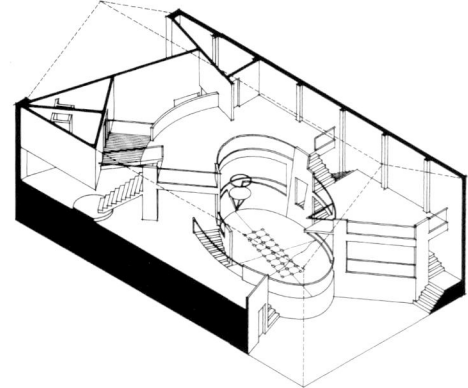

Award III Bienal de Arquitectura del Rio Grande del Sul
  (Interior Design Category)
Given by Instituto dos Arquitetos do Brasil
Prize Presentation November 1995
Members of the Jury Carlos de Azevedo Moura, Ester Judite Gutierrez,
  Sergio Saffer, Silvio Belmonte de Abreu Filho, Ivan Mizoguchi
Design Team Fernando dos Santos Rocha Machado, Rovena Schumacher,
  Evaldo Schumacher, Gisela Grazziotin, Rovena Vaccaro
Structural Engineering Eduardo Ekman
Civil Engineering Eduardo Ekman
Mechanical Engineering José O. Vianna
Electrical Engineering Bruno Nora
Acoustic Engineering Bruno Nora
Air Conditioning Consultant Paulo Reis
Lighting Consultant Bruno Nora
Life Safety Consultant José O. Vianna

Interior Design Fernando dos Santos Rocha Machado, Rovena Schumacher,
  Evaldo Schumacher
Quantity Surveying Marcelo Rech
Approximate Cost US$ 300,000
Site Area 1,250 m^2
Building Area 328.05 m^2
Total Floor Area 436.14 m^2
Photographer Joel Jordani

Architects **Les Architectes Boutros et Pratte, Montreal**
Award Winning Building **Plaza Laurier (Henri-Julien Avenue)**
Location **Montreal, Quebec, Canada**
Design and Construction Period **1990–1994**

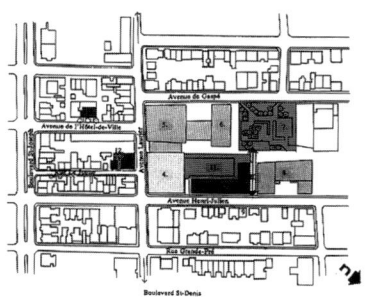
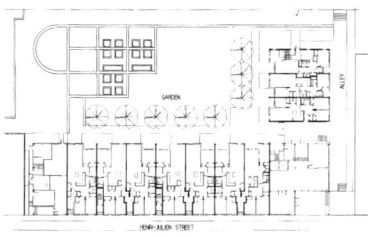

Award 1997 Governor General's Award for Architecture
Given by The Royal Architectural Institute of Canada
Prize Presentation June 1997
Project Team Raouf Boutros (Principal in Charge), Normand Pratte,
  Christine Gervais, Robert Abou, Albert De Coen, Jean-Jacques Binoux
Structural Engineering Toutant, Ladouceur & Ass.
General Contractor Construction Cogerex, Montreal
Mechanical Engineering St-Amant, Vézina, Vinet, Brassard et ass.
Electrical Engineering St-Amant, Vézina, Vinet, Brassard et ass.
Site Area 4,200 m^2
Building Area 1,525 m^2
Total Floor Area 7,600 m^2
Photographer Yves Lefebvre, Montreal

Architects **Les Architectes Boutros et Pratte, Montreal**

Award Winning Building **Plaza Laurier (Laurier Avenue)**

Award 1997 Governor General's Award for Architecture

see page 22

Architects **Les Architectes Boutros et Pratte, Montreal**

Award Winning Building **Plaza Laurier (Hotel-de-Ville Avenue)**

Location **Montreal, Quebec, Canada**

Design and Construction Period **1992–1994**

Award 1997 Governor Generals Award for Architecture

Given by The Royal Architectural Institute of Canada

Prize Presentation June 1997

Project Team Raouf Boutros (Principal in Charge), Normand Pratte, Christine Gervais, Robert Abou, Albert De Coen, Jean-Jacques Binoux

Structural Engineering Toutant, Ladouceur & Ass.

General Contractor Construction Cogerex, Montreal

Mechanical Engineering St-Amant, Vézina, Vinet, Brassard et ass.

Electrical Engineering St-Amant, Vézina, Vinet, Brassard et ass.

Site Area 565 m^2

Building Area 280 m^2

Total Floor Area 1,120 m^2

Photographer Yves Lefebvre

Architects **Busby Bridger Architects, Vancouver**

Award Winning Building **Headquarters for the A.P.E.G.B.C.**

Award 1997 Governor General's Award for Architecture

Given by The Royal Architectural Institute of Canada

Prize Presentation June 1997

Architects **Cormier, Cohen, Davies, architectes, Montreal**

Award Winning Building **Parc de l'aventure basque en Amérique**

Award 1997 Governor Generals Award for Architecture

Given by The Royal Architectural Institute of Canada

Prize Presentation June 1997

Architects **A.J. Diamond, Donald Schmitt and Company, Toronto**

Award Winning Building **York University Student Centre Corporation and York University**

Location **North York, Ontario, Canada**

Design and Construction Period **1993 (completed)**

Award 1997 Governor General's Award for Architecture

Given by The Royal Architectural Institute of Canada

Prize Presentation June 1997

Members of the Jury Douglas Cardinal, Ken Greenberg, Dan Hanganu, Phyllis Lambert, Christine Macy, Abraham Zabludovsky

Design Team A.J. Diamond, Philip Beesley, George Friedman, Michael Leckman, Marie Black, Dalibor Cizek, Stuart Feldman, Anne Marie Fleming, John Iwanski, Jarle Lovelin, Tracey Winton

Structural Engineering Jones Christofferson

Mechanical Engineering Merber Corporation

Electrical Engineering Carinci Burt Rogers Engineering

Project Management UMA Spantec Ltd.

Furnishings A.J. Diamond, Donald Schmitt and Company, Core Design Services

Model Maker Richard Sinclair

Approximate Cost CAN$ 18,000,000

Photographer Steven Evans, André Beneteau

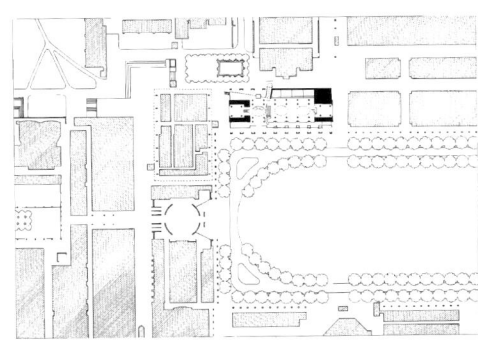

Canada

Architects **Hughes Baldwin Architects, Vancouver**
Award Winning Building **Renfrew Branch Library**
Location **Vancouver, Canada**
Design and Construction Period **1992–1994**

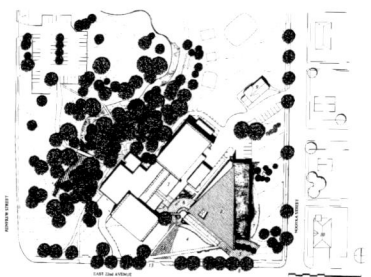

Award 1997 Governor General's Award for Architecture
Given by The Royal Architectural Institute of Canada
Prize Presentation June 1997
Members of the Jury Douglas Cardinal, Ken Greenberg, Dan Hanganu,
   Phyllis Lambert, Christine Macy, Abraham Zabludovsky
Design Team Roger Hughes (Partner in Charge), Bruce Carscadden,
   Natalka Lubiw, Ken Chui, Stan Kiericki
Structural Engineering C.Y. Loh Associates
Mechanical Engineering YONEDA & Associates
Electrical Engineering R.A. DUFF & Associates Inc.
Acoustic Engineering Brown Strachan Associates
Landscape Architecture Christopher Phillips & Associates Landscape
   Architecture Inc.

Quantity Surveying BTY Cost Consultants
Approximate Cost CAN$ 3,200,000
Site Area 15,000 m^2
Building Area Library: 1,542 m^2; Parkade: 1,622 m^2
Total Floor Area 1,542 m^2
Photographer Gary Otte

Canada

Architects **Kuwabara Payne McKenna Blumberg, Toronto**
Award Winning Buildings **Grand Valley Institution for Women, Kitchener;**
   and Joseph S. Stauffer Library at Queen's University, Kingston
Location **Ontario, Canada**

Award 1997 Governor General's Award for Architecture
Given by The Royal Architectural Institute of Canada
Prize Presentation June 1997

Canada

Architects **Brian MacKay-Lyons Architecture and Urban Design, Halifax**
Award Winning Building **House on the Nova Scotia Coast 12**
Location **Nova Scotia, Canada**
Design and Construction Period **1995–1996**

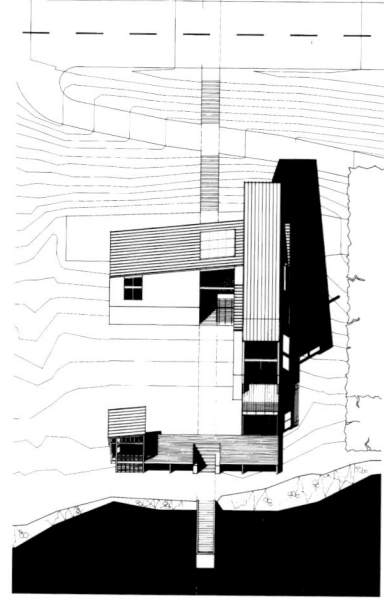
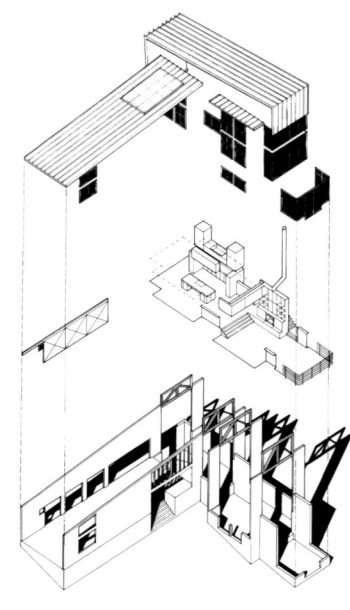

Award 1997 Governor General's Award for Architecture
Given by The Royal Architectural Institute of Canada
Prize Presentation June 1997
Members of the Jury Douglas Cardinal, Ken Greenberg, Dan Hanganu,
   Phyllis Lambert, Christine Macy, Abraham Zabludovsky
Design Team Brian MacKay-Lyons with Niall Savage, Doug Wigle, Tony Gillis,
   Hilary Backman
Structural Engineering Campbell Comcau Engineering
Civil Engineering EDM Environmental Design and Management
Builder Cyril Smith
Landscape Architecture EDM Environmental Design and Management
Photographer Jamie Steeves

Canada

Architects **Montgomery and Sisam Architects, Toronto**

Award Winning Building **The Humber River Bicycle Pedestrian Bridge**

Award 1997 Governor General's Award for Architecture

see page 24

Canada

Architects **Patkau Architects Inc., Vancouver**

Award Winning Building **Barnes House**

Award 1997 Governor General's Award for Architecture

Given by The Royal Architectural Institute of Canada

Prize Presentation June 1997

Canada

Architects **Patkau Architects Inc., Vancouver**

Award Winning Building **The Canadian Clay & Glass Gallery**

Award 1997 Governor General's Award for Architecture

Given by The Royal Architectural Institute of Canada

Prize Presentation June 1997

Canada

Architects **Saucier et Perrotte architectes, Montreal**

Award Winning Building **Usine C / Carbone 14**

Location **1345 Lalonde, Montréal, Quebec, Canada**

Design and Construction Period **1992–1995**

Award 1) Mention d'excellence 1995; 2) 1997 Governor General's Award
for Architecture

Given by 1) Ordre des Architectes du Québec; 2) The Royal Architectural
Institute of Canada

Prize Presentation 1) November 1995; 2) June 1997

Members of the Jury 1) Börkur Bergmann, Jacques Charttrand, Vittorio
Gregotti, André Ramoisy, Armand Vaillancourt; 2) Douglas Cardinal,
Ken Greenberg, Dan Hanganu, Phyllis Lambert, Christine Macy,
Abraham Zabludovsky

Design Team André Perrotte, Gilles Saucier, Adrian Blackwell, Yves Bouchard,
Martin Bouchard, Robert d'Errico, Oscar Juarros, Franck Thonon

Structural Engineering Martoni-Cyr et ass.

Mechanical Engineering Le Groupe Teknika

Electrical Engineering Le Groupe Teknika

Air Conditioning Consultant Le Groupe Teknika

Interior Design Saucier et Perrotte architectes

Landscape Architecture Saucier et Perrotte architectes

Approximate Cost CAN$ 6,100,000 (with equipment)

Site Area 2,572 m²

Building Area 1,854.5 m²

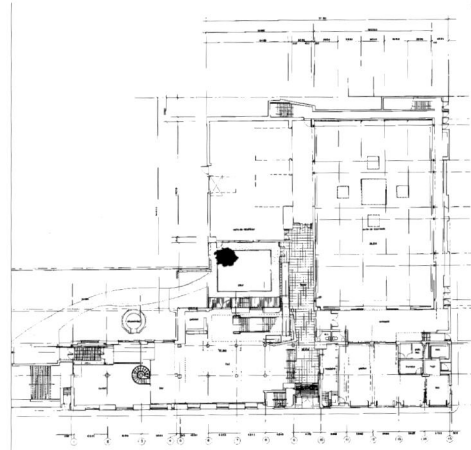

Total Floor Area 5,109.5 m²

Photographer Alain Laforest

Canada

Architects **Brigitte Shim and Howard Sutcliffe, Toronto**

Award Winning Building **Craven Road House**

Award 1997 Governor General's Award for Architecture

see page 28

Architects **Sturgess Architecture (Jeremy Sturgess, Gordon Filewych,**
Bob Horvarth); FSC Groves Hodgson Manasc Architects (Vivian Manasc,
Richard Isaac, Keith Annett), Calgary
Award Winning Building **Yukon Visitor's Reception Centre**
Location **Whitehorse, Yukon, Canada**
Completion Date **June 1992**

Award 1997 Governor General's Award for Architecture
Given by The Royal Architectural Institute of Canada
Prize Presentation June 1997
Members of the Jury Douglas Cardinal, Ken Greenberg, Dan Hanganu,
    Phyllis Lambert, Christine Macy, Abraham Zabludovsky
Design Team Sturgess Architecture
Engineering Ferguson Simek Clark (Yellowknife)
Exhibit Design D. Jensen & Associates
Model Maker Gordon Filewych
Budget CAN$ 2,300,000
Site Area 26,300 m²

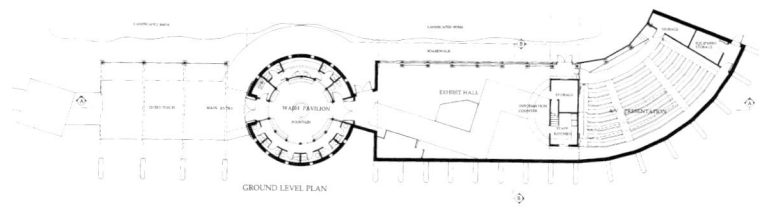

Building Area 827 m²
Total Floor Area 875 m²
Photographer Robin Armour, Chris Klein, Jeremy Sturgess

Architect **Stephen Teeple Architect Incorporated, Toronto**
Award Winning Building **Burt C. Matthews Hall Addition**
Location **University of Waterloo, Canada**
Design and Construction Period **1994–1996**

Award 1997 Governor General's Award for Architecture
Given by The Royal Architectural Institute of Canada
Prize Presentation June 1997
Design Team Stephen Teeple, Cheryl Atkinson, Helen Pak, Steven Mannell,
    Ralph Giannone, Guy D'Alesio, Bruce McLean
Structural Engineering Yolles Partnership Ltd.
Mechanical Engineering Crossey Engineering Ltd.
Electrical Engineering Crossey Engineering Ltd.
Lighting Consultant Crossey Engineering Ltd.
Interior Design Stephen Teeple Architect Incorporated
Landscape Architecture Sara Heinonen Landscape Architecture
Quantity Surveying Vermeulens Cost Consultants
Approximate Cost CAN$ 2,500,000
Site Area 3,030 m²
Building Area 1,580 m² / *Total Floor Area* 1,580 m²
Photographer Richard Johnson

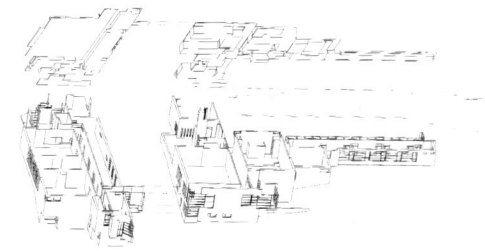

Architect **Pierre Thibault, Quebec**
Award Winning Building **Queen of Heart Theatre / Théâtre de la Dame**
    de Cœur

Award 1997 Governor General's Award for Architecture
see page 26

Architects **TRAME Groupe Conseil (architects Bart, Carrier, Gauthier /**
Fortier & Associés), Rouyn-Noranda
Award Winning Building **Quebec University at Abitibi-Témiscamingue**
Location **445 boul. de l'Université, Rouyn-Noranda, Quebec, Canada**
Design and Construction Period **1992–1996**

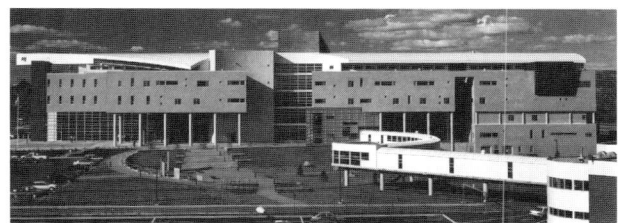

Award 1997 Governor General's Award for Architecture
Given by The Royal Architectural Institute of Canada
Prize Presentation June / 28 / 1997
Members of the Jury Douglas Cardinal (Alberta), Ken Greenberg (Ontario),
 Dan Hanganu (Quebec), Phyllis Lambert (Quebec), Christine Macy
 (Nova Scotia), Abraham Zabludovsky (Mexico)
Design Team Frédéric Carrier (Project Architect), Martine Brière, Philippe Drolet,
 Christian Noël
Structural Engineering Société d'expert-conseils Pellemon, Rouyn-Noranda
Civil Engineering Société d'expert-conseils Pellemon, Rouyn-Noranda
Mechanical Engineering Groupe Stavibel, Rouyn-Noranda
Electrical Engineering Groupe Stavibel, Rouyn-Noranda
Acoustic Engineering J.M.L.A., Montréal
Air Conditioning Consultant Groupe Stavibel, Rouyn-Noranda
Interior Design TRAME Groupe Conseil

Landscape Architecture DEVAMCO
Approximate Cost CAN$ 20,000,000
Site Area 75,000 m^2
Building Area 2,000 m^2
Total Floor Area 12,000 m^2
Photographer Alain Laforest

Architects **Zeidler Roberts Partnership Inc. Architects; Associated**
 Baltimore Architects, Toronto
Award Winning Building **Columbus Center of Marine Research and**
 Exploration
Location **Baltimore, Maryland, USA**
Design and Construction Period **1991–1995**

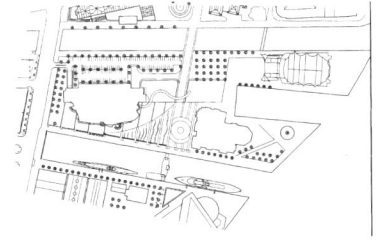

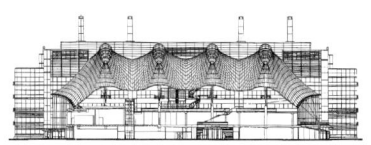

Award 1997 Governor General's Award for Architecture
Given by The Royal Architectural Institute of Canada
Prize Presentation June 1997
Members of the Jury Douglas Cardinal, Ken Greenberg, Dan Hanganu,
 Phyllis Lambert, Christine Macy, Abraham Zabludovsky
Design Team Eberhard Zeidler (Partner in Charge of Design), Peter Wakayama
 (Partner in Charge of Administration), Barbara Hopewell, Locksley Wright,
 Ian Fairlie, Dalibor Vokac, Joey Loh, Steve Carroll, Lyndon Devaney,
 Horhon Chu
Master Plan Consultant Cho Wilks Benn
Exhibit Consultant Associates & Ferren
Development Team Harbor Development Services Partnership
Construction Manager Barton Malow / Essex
Structural Engineering Delon Hampton & Associates; Peter Sheffield &
 Associates Ltd.
Civil Engineering Rummel Klepper & Kahl
Mechanical Engineering HC Yu and Associates
Electrical Engineering HC Yu and Associates
Environmental Engineering Rowan, Williams, Davies & Irwin Inc.

Acoustic Engineering Aercoustics Engineering, Polysonics Inc.
Air Conditioning Consultant HC Yu and Associates
Lighting Consultant George Sexton Associates
Life Safety Consultant Code Consultants Incorporated
Interior Design Zeidler Roberts Partnership Inc. Architects
Landscape Architecture Hargreaves Associates
Approximate Cost US$ 58,700,000 (construction cost)
Site Area 11.8 acres
Building Area 4,395 m^2
Total Floor Area 24,173 m^2
Photographer Michael Dersin

Architects **Fernando Castillo Velasco, Eduardo San Martín, Patricio Wenborne, Pedro Gastón Pascal, Santiago de Chile; Collaborators: José Asencio Peña, Jorge Benitez Castro, Emilio García Fernández, Gloria Barros, Jorge Atria**
Award Winning Building **Comunidad Andalucía**
Location **Santiago de Chile, Chile**
Design and Construction Period **1989–1991**

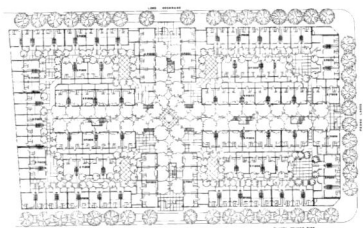

Award Gran Premio X Bienal de Arquitectura Chilena
Given by Colegio de Arquitectos de Chile
Prize Presentation July – August 1995
Members of the Jury Antoine Grumbach (France), Antonio Cruz (Spain), Félix Pozo (Spain), Mario Pérez de Arce (Premio Nacional de Arquitectura), Hélene de Garay (Venezuela), Carlos Campuzano (Columbia), Glenda Kapstein (Chile), Manuel Moreno (Director of the Jury)
Design Team Fernando Castillo Velasco, Eduardo San Martín, Patricio Wenborne, Pedro Gastón Pascal
Structural Engineering Ernesto Herbach
Civil Engineering Elias Roitburd
Mechanical Engineering Guillermo Molina, Ramón Marin
Electrical Engineering Carlos Panozo
Interior Design Fernando Castillo Velasco, Eduardo San Martin, Patricio Wenborne, Pedro Gastón Pascal
Landscape Architecture Fernando Castillo Velasco, Eduardo San Martin, Patricia Wenborne, Pedro Gastón Pascal
Quantity Surveying Cristina Silva, Enrique Sabat
Approximate Cost US$ 631,000
Site Area 8,230 m^2
Building Area 3,717 m^2
Total Floor Area 6,125 m^2
Photographer Guy Wenborne

People's Republic of China

Architects **Ling Benli, Xiang Zuquan, Zhang Xiulin, Hu Rong, Shanghai**
Award Winning Building **Shanghai Radio & TV Tower**
Location **Lujiazui Finance & Trade Development Zone, Shanghai, P.R. China**
Design and Construction Period **1988–1994**

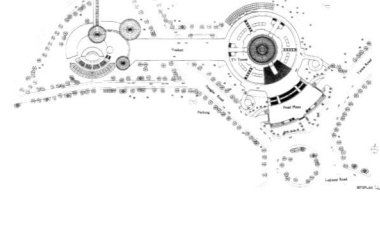

Award Prize of Architectural Design
Given by ASC The Architectural Society of China
Prize Presentation November / 25 / 1996
Members of the Jury Liu Kaiji, Guan Zhaoye, Li Dehua, Wang Guoyu, Shi Xuehai, Lu Xiaodi, Zhang Zugang, Fu Yitong, Zhou Ningcui
Structural Engineering Jiang Huancheng
Mechanical Engineering Xu Lushen, Wang Xueliang
Electrical Engineering Jiang Yuxin, Wu Wenfang
Approximate Cost US$ 100,000,000 (construction cost)
Site Area 30,600 m^2 (site A), 19,800 m^2 (site B)
Building Area 70,000 m^2
Total Floor Area 5 ha
Photographer Liu Dalong

People's Republic of China

Architects **Bai Demao, Ye Mouzhao, Liu Xiaozhong, Beijing**
Award Winning Building **Enjili Residential Quarter**
Location **Beijing, P.R. China**
Design and Construction Period **1987–1994**

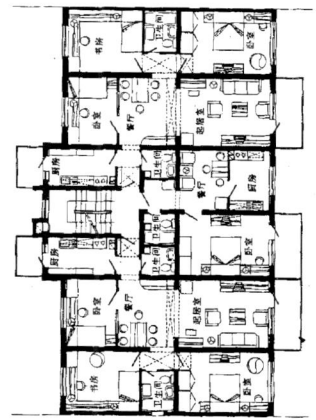

Award Prize of Architectural Design
Given by ASC The Architectural Society of China
Prize Presentation November / 25 / 1996
Members of the Jury Liu Kaiji, Guan Zhaoye, Li Dehua, Wang Guoyu,
  Shi Xuehai, Lu Xiaodi, Zhang Zugang, Fu Yitong, Zhou Ningcui
Design Team and Engineering Peking Institute of Architectural Design
  and Research
Approximate Cost RMB 219,000,000
Site Area 99,800 m^2
Building Area 26,340 m^2

Total Floor Area 140,813 m^2
Photographer Yang Chaoying

People's Republic of China

Architects **Xin Tonghe, Teng Dian, Shanghai**
Award Winning Building **Shanghai Museum**
Location **Shanghai Central Square, Shanghai, P.R. China**
Design and Construction Period **1994–1996**

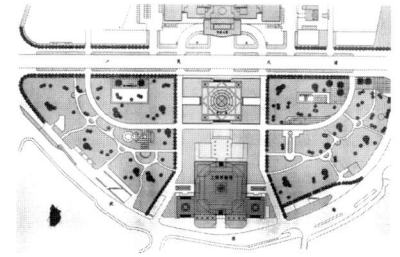

Award Prize of Architectural Design
Given by ASC The Architectural Society of China
Prize Presentation November / 25 / 1996
Members of the Jury Liu Kaiji, Guan Zhaoye, Li Dehua, Wang Guoyu,
  Shi Xuehai, Lu Xiaodi, Zhang Zugang, Fu Yitong, Zhou Ningcui
Design Unit Shanghai Institute of of Architectural Design & Research

Chief Designer Xin Tonghe, Teng Dian
Photographer Mao Jiawei, Chen Borong, Xin Tonghe

People's Republic of China

Architects **Peng Yigang, Zhang Hua, Shanghai**
Award Winning Building **Exhibition Hall of the Sino – Japanese War**
  in 1894
Location **Weihai, Shandong, P.R. China**
Design and Construction Period **1993–1996**

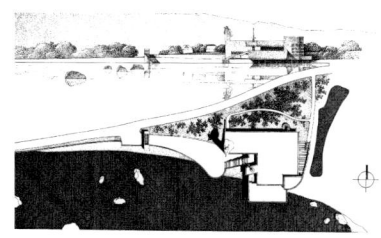

Award Prize of Architectural Design
Given by ASC The Architectural Society of China
Prize Presentation November / 25 / 1996
Members of the Jury Liu Kaiji, Guan Zhaoye, Li Dehua, Wang Guoyu,
  Shi Xuehai, Lu Xiaodi, Zhang Zugang, Fu Yitong, Zhou Ningcui
Design Team Architectural Design and Research Institute of Tianjin University
Structural Engineering Ma Kuixiang
Electrical Engineering Li Li
Environmental Engineering Shen Youyue
Air Conditioning Consultant Li Songshen
Lighting Consultant Li Li
Interior Design Peng Yigang, Zhang Hua

Landscape Architecture Sculptures: Li Yousheng
Approximate Cost RMB 30,000,000
Site Area 800 m^2
Building Area 3,000 m^2
Total Floor Area 5,700 m^2
Photographer Xiu Tingfa

Architects **Liang Yingtian, Zhou Lin, Liang Peichen, Wu Xin, Beijing**
Award Winning Building **Office Building of the Chinese People's Political Consultative Conference National Committee**
Location **Beijing, P.R. China**
Design and Construction Period **1993–1995**

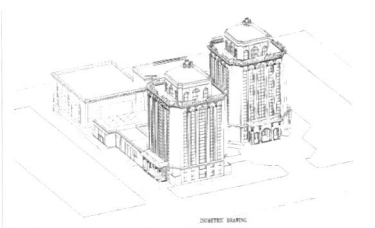

Award Prize of Architectural Design
Given by ASC The Architectural Society of China
Prize Presentation November / 25 / 1996
Members of the Jury Liu Kaiji, Guan Zhaoye, Li Dehua, Wang Guoyu,
   Shi Xuehai, Lu Xiaodi, Zhang Zugang, Fu Yitong, Zhou Ningcui
Design Team Building Design Institute of the Ministry of Construction
Structural Engineering Fan Zhong
Electrical Engineering Dong Shouzhen
Environmental Engineering Jin Xiaohong, Fang Xuesong
Acoustic Engineering Cao Xiaozhen
Air Conditioning Consultant Ding Gao

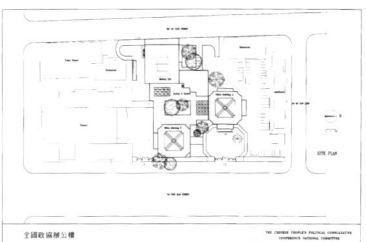

Lighting Consultant Dong Shouzhen
Interior Design Huang Deling
Quantity Surveying Cui Li, Shen
   Wenzhong
Approximate Cost US$ 30,000,000
Site Area 12,380 m^2
Building Area 5,080 m^2
Total Floor Area 42,000 m^2
Photographer Zhang Guangyuan

Colombia

Architects **Alejandro Echeverri R. & Juan Bernardo Echeverri C., Medellin**
Award Winning Building **Casa Posada**
Location **Antioquia, Colombia**
Design and Construction Period **1994–1995**

Award 1) XV Bienal Colombiana de Arquitectura; 2) X Bienal Panamericana
   de Arquitectura de Quito .
Given by 1) Sociedad Colombiana de Arquitectos; 2) El Colegio de
   Arquitectos del Ecuador
Prize Presentation 1) October / 30 / 1996; 2) November / 15 / 1996
Members of the Jury 1) Antonio Cruz V. (Spain), Carlos Jiménez C. (Costa Rica),
   German Samper G. (Columbia), Rodrigo Tascón B (Colombia), Juan Felipe
Gómez T. (Colombia); 2) Luis Oleas (Ecuador), Milton Barragan (Ecuador), Pedro
Belaunde (Perú), Antonio González (España), Pedro Ramírez Vásquez (Mexico),
   Mark Mulligan (USA)
Design Team Alejandro Echeverri R., Juan Bernardo Echeverri C.,
   Luis Fernando Morales (Colaborador)
Structural Engineering Luis Bernardo González

Civil Engineering Luis Fernando Tobzá
Mechanical Engineering Ricardo Aguilar
Electrical Engineering Juan Gonzalo Ríos
Landscape Architecture Alejandro Echeverri R., Juan Bernardo Echeverri C.
Approximate Cost US$ 180,000
Site Area 6,100m^2
Building Area 425 m^2
Total Floor Area 348 m^2 (primer nivel), 77 m^2 (nivel inferior)
Photographer Alejandro Echeverri R., Juan Felipe Gómez

Colombia

Architects **Katia González, Francisco González, Carlos Hernandez, Eduardo Samper Martinez, Bogota**
Award Winning Building **Customs Hall at Barranquilla**
Location **Barranquilla, Colombia**
Award Premio Carlos Arbelaez Camacho

Given by Sociedad Colombiana de Arquitectos
Prize Presentation October / 30 / 1996

Colombia

Architects **Jiménez & Cortes Boshell, Bogota**
Award Winning Building **Edificio Av. 82**

Award XV Bienal Colombiana de Arquitectura
see page 32

Costa Rica

Architect **Rolando Barahona Sotela, San José**
Award Winning Building **Hotel Europa–Zurquí, Costa Rica**
Location **San José, Costa Rica**
Design and Construction Period **1991–1994**

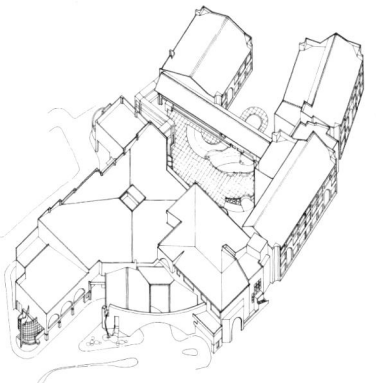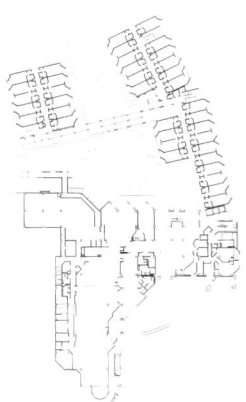

Award Premio Mejor Proyecto Nacional de Arquitectura
Given by Colegio de Arquitectos de Costa Rica
Prize Presentation June 1996
Members of the Jury Charles Johnson (USA), Bart Prince (USA),
  Theodore Brown (USA), Mario Paredes (Chile), Mario Azofeifa (Costa Rica),
  Juan Bernal Ponce (Chile / Costa Rica)
Design Team Rolando Barahona Sotela
Structural Engineering Luis Rojas y Asoc. S.A.
Civil Engineering Luis Rojas y Asoc. S.A.
Mechanical Engineering William Bolaños S.A.
Electrical Engineering Cañas y Sequeira S.A.
Environmental Engineering Rolando Barahona
Acoustic Engineering William Bolaños S.A.
Air Conditioning Consultant William Bolaños S.A.
Lighting Consultant Cañas y Sequeira S.A.
Life Safety Consultant Instituto Nacional de Seguros
Interior Design Rolando Barahona Sotela Arch.

Landscape Architecture Rolando Barahona Sotela Arch.
Quantity Surveying Sr. Mauricio Ventura
Approximate Cost $ 14,000,000.00
Site Area 16,000 m^2
Building Area 15,000 m^2
Total Floor Area 4,700 m^2
Photographer Rolando Barahona Sotela

Costa Rica

Architect **William Monge Quesada, San José**
Award Winning Building **Remodelling of the Juan Mora Fernandez Plaza**
Location **Ciudad de San José, Costa Rica**
Design and Construction Period **1994–1995**

Award Premio Mejor Proyecto Nacional de Arquitectura (Honorable Mention)
Given by Colegio de Arquitectos de Costa Rica
Prize Presentation June 1996
Members of the Jury Charles Johnson (USA), Bart Prince (USA), Theodore

Brown (USA), Mario Paredes (Chile), Mario Azofeifa (Costa Rica), Juan Bernal
  Ponce (Chile / Costa Rica)
Design Team Departamento de Restauración del Teatro Nacional
Mechanical Engineering Compañia Durman Esquirel
Electrical Engineering Carlos Sanchez
Landscape Architecture William Monge Quesada
Approximate Cost $ 200,000
Site Area 2,250 m^2
Photographer William Monge Quesada

Costa Rica

Architect **Jaime Ravillón Oviedo, San José**
Award Winning Building **Hotel**
Location **Costa Rica**

Award Premio Mejor Proyecto Nacional de Arquitectura
Given by Colegio de Arquitectos de Costa Rica
Prize Presentation June 1996
Members of the Jury Charles Johnson (USA), Bart Prince (USA),
  Theodore Brown (USA), Mario Paredes (Chile), Mario Azofeifa (Costa Rica),
  Juan Bernal Ponce (Chile/Costa Rica)

Architect **Jaime Ravillón Oviedo, San José**

Award Winning Building **Estudios Conte**

Location **Costa Rica**

Award Premio Mejor Proyecto Nacional de Arquitectura

Given by Colegio de Arquitectos de Costa Rica

Prize Presentation June 1996

Members of the Jury Charles Johnson (USA), Bart Prince (USA), Theodore Brown (USA), Mario Paredes (Chile), Mario Azofeifa (Costa Rica), Juan Bernal Ponce (Chile / Costa Rica)

Architect **Bruno Stagno, San José**

Award Winning Building **FORD Showroom – Banco de San José**

Location **San José, Costa Rica**

Design and Construction Period **1994–1995**

Award Premio Mejor Proyecto Nacional de Arquitectura

Given by Colegio de Arquitectos de Costa Rica

Prize Presentation June 1996

Members of the Jury Charles Johnson (USA), Bart Prince (USA), Theodore Brown (USA), Mario Paredes (Chile), Mario Azofeifa (Costa Rica), Juan Bernal Ponce (Chile / Costa Rica)

Design Team Bruno Stagno, Carlos Araya

Structural Engineering Luis Zamora

Civil Engineering Ramón Ramirez

Mechanical Engineering Francisco Quesada

Electrical Engineering Carlos Brenes

Air Conditioning Consultant Max Acosta

Interior Design Bruno Stagno

Landscape Architecture Bruno Stagno

Approximate Cost US$ 800,000.00

Site Area 10,000 m^2

Building Area 1,530 m^2

Total Floor Area 1,530 m^2

Architects **Percy Zamora Ulloa, Juan Carlos Garro León, San José**

Award Winning Building **Centro Costarricense de la Ciencia y la Cultura**

Location **San José, Costa Rica**

Design and Construction Period **1990–1993**

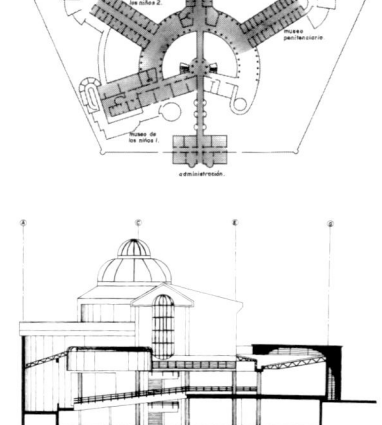

Award Premio Mejor Proyecto Nacional de Arquitectura (Honorable Mention)

Given by Colegio de Arquitectos de Costa Rica

Prize Presentation June / 3 / 1996

Members of the Jury Charles Johnson (USA), Bart Prince (USA), Theodore Brown (USA), Mario Paredes (Chile), Mario Azofeifa (Costa Rica), Juan Bernal Ponce (Chile / Costa Rica)

Civil Engineering Guillermo Hidalgo

Mechanical Engineering Felipe Terán

Electrical Engineering Alfredo Povedano

Approximate Cost CAN$ 1,750,000

Site Area 95,000 m^2

Building Area 12,565 m^2

Photographer Percy Zamora Ulloa

Croatia

Architects **Tomislav Ćurković & Zoran Zidarić, Zagreb**

Award Winning Building **Zrišport (shop for sport equipment)**

Location **Zagreb, Croatia**

Design and Construction Period **1994–1995**

Award Bernardo Bernardi Award for the best interior design

Given by Croatian Architects Association

Prize Presentation April / 24 / 1996

Members of the Jury Stijepo Butijer, Marija Cacić, Sanja Filer, Zlatko Hanzek,
   Berislav Iskra, Nenad Kondza, Vesna Mikic Brodnjak, Milan Mitevcki, Veljko
   Oloic, Vinko Penezić, Robert Plejić, Sasa Randić, Kresimir Rogina, Dragomir
   Sutlar, Miroslav Skugor, Emil Spirić, Darovan Iuslk, Vesna Vinski, Velimir
   Neidhardt, Ivan Crnković, Tomislav Premerl

Design Team Tomislav Ćurković, Zoran Zidarić, Dragana Milenković,
   Saša Paris (concept collaboration)

Interior Design Tomislav Ćurković & Zoran Zidarić

Approximate Cost Kuna 140,000

Building Area 38,3 m²

Photographer Darko Bavoljak

Croatia

Architect **Stanko Fabris, Zagreb**

Award Winning Building **Lifetime achievement**

Award Viktor Kovačić Award for the architectural lifetime achievement

Given by Croatian Architects Association

Prize Presentation April / 24 / 1996

Croatia

Architect **Ante Kuzmanić, Split**

Award Winning Building **Convent of Servants of Mercy – Split**

Location **Ciril – Metodova 4, Split, Croatia**

Design and Construction Period **1991–1994**

Award Viktor Kovačić Award 1995 for the best new building

Given by Croatian Architects Association

Prize Presentation April / 24 / 1996

Design Team Ana Marija Madunić, Ivan Bebić, Ankica Bilandić, Antonija Vidak

Structural Engineering Darko Fadić, Nikola Hrnjak

Civil Engineering Anta Runjić

Acoustic Engineering Goran Šimić

Air Conditioning Consultant Romana Bradašić

Lighting Consultant Lena Grgić

Life Safety Consultant Ivan Bebić

Interior Design Ante Kuzmanić

Landscape Architecture Ivan Bebić

Approximate Cost DEM 8,000,000

Total Floor Area 6,720 m²

Photographer Damir Fabijanić, Branko Ostojić

Ecuador

Architects **Arquitectura X., Quito**
Award Winning Building **Casa Samaniego**
Location **Ecuador**

Award X Bienal Panamericana de Arquitectura de Quito
Given by El Colegio de Arquitectos del Ecuador

Prize Presentation November / 12 / 1996
Members of the Jury Luis Oleas (Ecuador), Milton Barragán (Ecuador), Pedro Belaunde (Peru), Antonio González (Spain), Pedro Ramirez Vásquez (Mexico), Mark Mulligan (USA)

Ecuador

Architects **Fausto Banderas, Marcelo Banderas, Quito**
Award Winning Building **Hostel for Street-Children**
Location **Ecuador**

Award X Bienal Panamericana de Arquitectura de Quito
Given by El Colegio de Arquitectos del Ecuador

Prize Presentation November / 12 / 1996
Members of the Jury Luis Oleas (Ecuador), Milton Barragán (Ecuador), Pedro Belaunde (Peru), Antonio González (Spain), Pedro Ramirez Vásquez (Mexico), Mark Mulligan (USA)

Ecuador

Architects **José Brandão, Ronaldo L'Amour, Recife**
Award Winning Building **Calçadão dos Mascates (Camelódromo)**
Location **Recife, Brazil**
Design and Construction Period **1993–1994**

 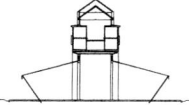 

Award X Bienal Panamericana de Arquitectura de Quito
Given by El Colegio de Arquitectos del Ecuador
Prize Presentation November / 12 / 1996
Members of the Jury José Ordoñez v. (Ecuador), José Luis Cañavate (Spain), Ken Martin (UK), Gonzalo Bustamante
Design Team Antônio Amaral, Maria de Lourdes Nóbrega
Structural Engineering Engest Engenharia Estrutural Ltda.
Civil Engineering Construtora Celi Ltda. y Pernambuco Construtora Ltda.
Electrical Engineering Maria do Socorro dos Santos
Lighting Consultant Maria do Socorro dos Santos
Interior Design Laboratório de Diseño Industrial de la Universidade Federal de Pernambuco

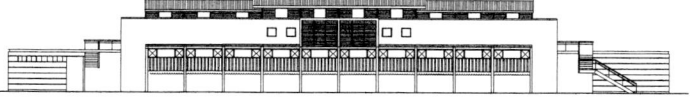

Landscape Architecture Beatriz Assmann
Approximate Cost US$ 2,500,000
Site Area 12,000 m²
Building Area 6,770 m²
Total Floor Area 5,300 m²

Ecuador

Architects **José Brandão, Ronaldo L'Amour, Recife**
Award Winning Building **Market (Mercado das Flores)**
Location **Recife, Brazil**
Design and Construction Period **1994–1996**

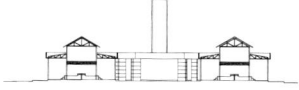 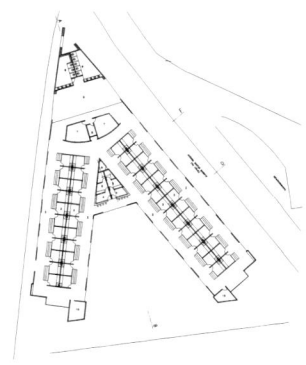

Award X Bienal Panamericana de Arquitectura de Quito
Given by El Colegio de Arquitectos del Ecuador
Prize Presentation November / 12 / 1996
Members of the Jury José Ordoñez v. (Ecuador), José Luis Cañavate (Spain), Ken Martin (UK), Gonzalo Bustamante
Design Team Milton Botler, Luís Moriel, Isaac Azoubel
Structural Engineering Engest–Engenharia Estrutural Ltda.
Civil Engineering Valengue Construtora Ltda.
Electrical Engineering Maria do Socorro dos Santos
Lighting Consultant Maria do Socorro dos Santos

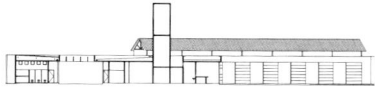

Interior Design José Brandão, Ronaldo L'Amour
Landscape Architecture Beatriz Assmann
Approximate Cost US$ 400,000
Site Area 1,800 m² / *Building Area* 1,200 m² / *Total Floor Area* 1,200 m

Ecuador

Architects **David Calvache y Hernan León, Quito**
Award Winning Building **Remodelling of the former Eloy Alfaro School**
Location **Ecuador**

Award X Bienal Panamericana de Arquitectura de Quito
Given by El Colegio de Arquitectos del Ecuador
Prize Presentation November / 12 / 1996

Ecuador

Architects **Carlos Campuzano & Gustavo Duque, Bogota**
Award Winning Building **Bibliotéca de la Capilla, Los Andes University**
Location **School of Architecture, Bogota, Colombia**
Design and Construction Period **1995–1996**

 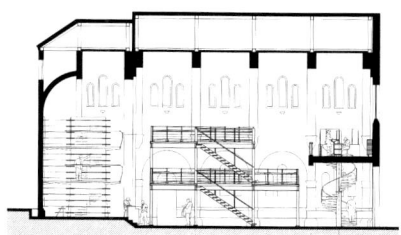

Award X Bienal Panamericana de Arquitectura de Quito
Given by El Colegio de Arquitectos del Ecuador
Prize Presentation November / 12 / 1996
Members of the Jury Miguel Centellas (Spain), Emilio Randazzo (Italy),
   Alfonso Ortiz (Ecuador)
Design Team Gustavo Duque, Carlos Campuzano
Structural Engineering Carlos Castro
Civil Engineering Marcelo Menza, Horacio Hermida
Environmental Engineering Humberto Coronel
Acoustic Engineering Gonzalo Duran
Air Conditioning Consultant Homayoon Kharaghani

Lighting Consultant I.D. José Luis Mendoza
Interior Design Carlos Campuzano, Gustavo Duque
Quantity Surveying Marcelo Menza
Approximate Cost US$ 200,000.00
Site Area Los Andes University Campus
Building Area 325 m^2
Total Floor Area 170 m^2
Photographer Carlos Campuzano, Mauricio Hernandez

Ecuador

Architects **Rafael Fontes, Gustavo Medeiros, Bolivia**
Award Winning Building **Rehabilitación del Ingenio San Marcos para**
   Museo Café
Location **Bolivia**

Award X Bienal Panamericana de Arquitectura de Quito
Given by El Colegio de Arquitectos del Ecuador
Prize Presentation November / 12 / 1996
Members of the Jury Miguel Centellas (Spain), Emilio Randazzo (Italy),
   Alfonso Ortiz (Ecuador)

Ecuador

Architect **Gregorio Repsold, Vitório**
Award Winning Building **Administration Building Águia Branca**
Location **BR 262, Cariacica, E.S., Brazil**
Design and Construction Period **1993–1995**

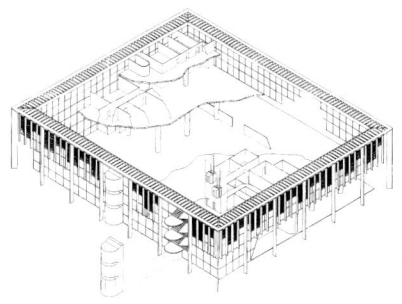

Award X Bienal Panamericana de Arquitectura de Quito
Given by El Colegio de Arquitectos del Ecuador
Prize Presentation November / 12 / 1996
Members of the Jury Luis Oleas, Milton Barragán, Pedro Belaunde,
   Antonio González, Pedro Ramirez Vásquez, Mark Mulligan
Design Team Gregorio Repsold
Structural Engineering MCA Tecnologia
Civil Engineering Nilton Chieppe
Mechanical Engineering Nilton Chieppe
Electrical Engineering Nilton Chieppe
Environmental Engineering Grupo Águia Branca
Air Conditioning Consultant Vititioning Consultantr

Lighting Consultant GV Dias
Interior Design Olimpia Repsold
Landscape Architecture Gregorio Repsold, Olimpia Repsold
Approximate Cost US$ 2,750,000
Site Area 11,827 m^2
Building Area 5,500 m^2
Total Floor Area 1,100 m^2
Photographer Olimpia Repsold

Ecuador

Architects **Juan Carlos Ruiz, Mary Betty Boland and Franklin Subirana, Santa Cruz de la Sierra**

Award Winning Building **Plaza Samaipata**

Location **Santa Cruz de la Sierra, Bolivia**

Award X Bienal Panamericana de Arquitectura de Quito

Given by El Colegio de Arquitectos del Ecuador

Prize Presentation November / 12 / 1996

Members of the Jury José Luís Cañavate (Spain), Ken Martin (UK), Gonzalo Bustamante (Ecuador)

Ecuador

Architects **Javier Vera – Arquitectos, Medellin**

Award Winning Building **Biblioteca Universidad Pontificia Bolivariana**

Location **Medellin, Colombia**

Design and Construction Period **1993–1995**

 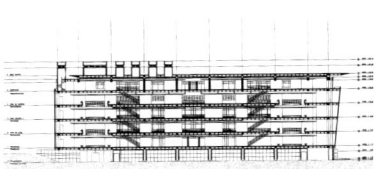

Award X Bienal Panamericana de Arquitectura de Quito

Given by El Colegio de Arquitectos del Ecuador

Prize Presentation November / 12 / 1996

Members of the Jury Luis Oleas (Ecuador), Milton Barragán (Ecuador), Pedro Belaunde (Peru), Antonio González (Spain), Pedro Ramirez Vásquez (Mexico), Mark Mulligan (USA)

Design Team Javier Vera Londoño, Alejandro Velasquez M.

Structural Engineering Jaime Muñoz Duque y Cia

Civil Engineering Convel S.A.

Electrical Engineering Zugom y Cia. Ltda.

Life Safety Consultant Convel S.A.

Interior Design Javier Vera – Arquitectos, Industrial Design Team Carlos Vera, Natalia Santos

Landscape Architecture Monica Gomez

Approximate Cost US$ 2,800,000

Site Area 2,500 m²

Building Area 7,032 m²

Total Floor Area 1,507 m²

Photographer Juan Felipe Gomez

France

Architects **Roland Castro, Sophie Denissof, Paris**

Award Winning Building **Remodelling of 480 Apartments, Quai de Rohan, Lorient**

Location **Quai de Rohan, Lorient, France**

Design and Construction Period **1991–1996**

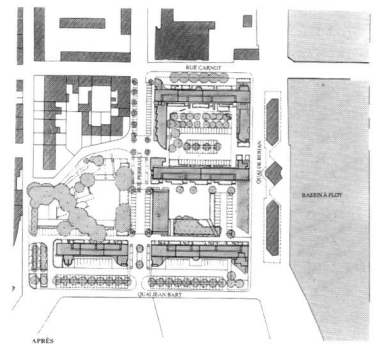

Award 1) Mention à l'Equerre d'Argent; 2) Prix Architecture Bretagne 1996

Given by 1) Le Moniteur; 2) Maison de l'Architecture de Bretagne

Prize Presentation 1) January / 29 / 1997; 2) November / 9 / 1996

Members of the Jury 1) Marc-Noël Vigier, Francis Ampe, Christian De Portzamparc, Bernard Tschumi, Jeremy Dixon, Manuel Gausa, Geert Bekaert, Jacques Lucan, Bertrand Lemoine; 2) Jean Pierre Le Dantec

Design Team Roland Castro, Sophie Denissof (Architect in Charge); Aura Nantes, Christophe Gautier (Associated Architects); Rita Ceccherini, Bernard Cuomo (Assistants)

Structural Engineering AUA Structures

Mechanical Engineering Ethis

Accompagnement Social Serge Brunet (TETRA), Paris; Brigitte Maltet, Antenne DSQ puis Contrat de Ville á Lorient

Life Safety Consultant SOCOTEC

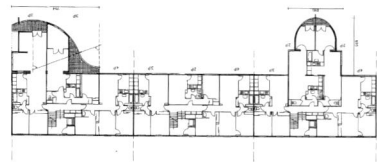

Landscape Architecture Ronan Desormeaux

Approximate Cost FF 111,000,000

Total Floor Area 38,000 m²

Photographer Nicolas Borel

France

Architect **Jean Dubuisson, Paris**

Award 1996 Grand Prix National d'Architecture (Hommmage)

Given by French Ministry of Culture (Region Nord, Pas-de-Calais)

Prize Presentation 1996

France

Architects **Fabrice Dusapin & François Leclercq, Paris**
Award Winning Building **CNP Service Centre and Public Garden**

Award Prix Special du Jury
see page 42

France

Architects **Pierre-Louis Faloci, Bénédicte d'Albas, Paris**
Award Winning Building **Musée de la Civilisation Celtique du Mont-Beuvray**
Location **France**

Award Equerre d'Argent

Given by Le Moniteur
Prize Presentation January / 1 / 1997
Members of the Jury Marc-Noël Vigier (President), Christian De Portzamparc, Bernard Tschumi, Jacques Lucan, Jeremy Dixon, Manuel Gausa, Geert Bekaert, Bertrand Lemoine, Francis Ampe

France

Architects **Thierry Lacoste, Antoinette Robain, Paris**
Award Winning Building **Extension and Refurbishment of the Overseas Archives Centre (CAOM)**
Location **Chemin du Moulin de Testas, Aix-en-Provence, France**
Design and Construction Period **1993–1996**

 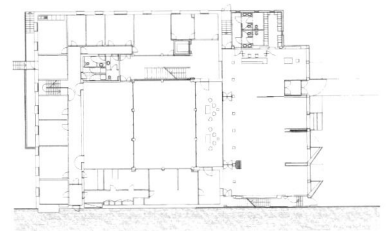

Award Prix de la première œuvre (first built work)
Given by Le Moniteur
Prize Presentation January 1997
Members of the Jury Marc-Noël Vigier (President), Christian De Portzamparc, Bernard Tschumi, Jacques Lucan and Jeremy Dixon, Manuel Gausa, Geert Bekaert, Bertrand Lemoine, Professional: Francis Ampe
Design Team Thierry Lacoste, Antoinette Robain, Claire Guieysse
Structural Engineering Batiserf
Civil and Hydraulic Engineering Louis Choulet
Acoustic Engineering Capri acoustique
Air Conditioning Consultant Louis Choulet
Natural Lighting Engineer Observatoire 1
Security Standards Control Véritas

Interior Design Thierry Lacoste, Antoinette Robain, Claire Guieysse
Site Pilot Domisis
Landscape Architecture David Besson
Quantity Surveying Michel Forgue
Approximate Cost FF 11,000,000 (October 1994)
Building Area 653 m^2 (new); 1.590 m^2 (refurbished)
Photographer Jean Marie Monthiers

France

Architect **Bernard Tschumi, Paris**
Award Winning Building **Le Fresnoy, National Studio for Contemporary Arts, Le Fresnoy**

Award 1996 Grand Prix National d'Architecture
see page 44

Georgia

Architect **Vakhtang Davitaia, Tbilisi**
Award Winning Building **Exhibition Hall of the Georgian Foundation of Culture**
Location **Tbilisi, Georgia**

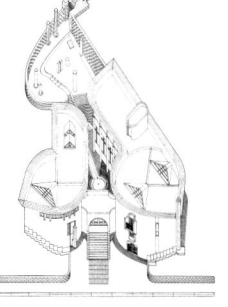 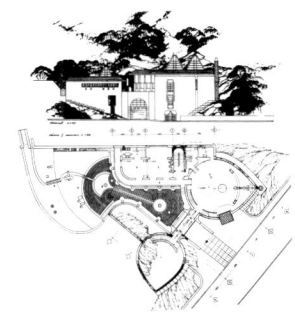

Award Rustaveli Award in Literature, Art and Architecture
Given by Rustaveli Award Committee
Prize Presentation June 1996
Members of the Jury Murman Lebanidze, Tariel Chanturia, Guram Fandjikidze, Guram Mirianashvili, Irakli Tsitsishvili, Levan Bokeria, Nodar Mgaloblishvili, etc.
Design / Engineering Design Bureau of the Georgian Technical University
Interior Design Vakhtang Davitaia

Landscape Architecture Vakhtang Davitaia
Approximate Cost US$ 650,000
Site Area 800 m^2 / *Building Area* 390 m^2 / *Total Floor Area* 750 m^2

Germany

Architect **Heinz Bienefeld †, Swisttal-Ollheim**
Representative Building Kindergarten

Award Der Große BDA Preis for the complete work of Heinz Bienefeld
see page 46

Germany

Architects **Jürgen Böge und Ingeborg Lindner-Böge, Hamburg**
Award Winning Building **Office Building Heidenkampsweg**

Award BDA Hamburg Architekturpreis 1996
see page 50

Germany

Architects **Rebecca E. Chestnutt, Robert Niess, Berlin**
Award Winning Building **Luisenbad Library**

Award BDA Berlin Architekturpreis 1996 (Honorable Mention)
see page 54

Germany

Architects **Deubzer und König, Berlin**
Award Winning Building **Virchow Hospital**
Location **Berlin-Wedding, Germany**

Award BDA Berlin Architekturpreis 1996 (Honorable Mention)
Given by BDA Bund Deutscher Architekten Berlin
Prize Presentation November / 7 / 1996
Members of the Jury Julia Bolles-Wilson, Kees Christiaanse, Manfred Eichel, Falk Jaeger, Otto Steidle

Germany

Architects **Engel und Zillich, Berlin**
Award Winning Building **Housing Estate Spruch**
Location **Kalksteinweg 17a, 12349 Berlin, Germany**
Design and Construction Period **1993–1995**

Award BDA Berlin Architekturpreis 1996 (1. Prize)
Given by BDA Bund Deutscher Architekten Berlin
Prize Presentation November / 7 / 1996
Members of the Jury Julia Bolles-Wilson, Kees Christiaanse, Manfred Eichel, Falk Jaeger, Otto Steidle
Design Team Engel und Zillich: Fausto Machicao, Burkhard Niehaus (Partner in Charge), Christian Bauß, Jason Coleman, Britta Heidepriem, Angelika Scheib, Joana Thomas
Structural Engineering Rabe und Frankenbach

Site Supervision IBR Ingenieurbüro Ruths
Colour Concept Oskar Putz
Landscape Architecture Werner und Andreas Bos
Site Area 83,000 m²
Building Area 54,000 m²
Photographer Uwe Rau

Germany

Architects **von Gerkan, Marg und Partner – Meinhard von Gerkan, Klaus Staratzke with Karsten Brauer, Hamburg**
Award Winning Building **Jumbo Shed for Lufthansa**
Location **Airport Hamburg-Fuhlsbüttel, Germany**
Design and Construction Period **1986–1992**

Award BDA Hamburg Architekturpreis 1996 (1. Preisrang)
Given by BDA Bund Deutscher Architekten Hamburg
Prize Presentation November / 14 / 1996
Members of the Jury Dietmar Eberle (Austria), Charlotte Frank (Germany), Hilde Léon (Chair, Germany), Carsten Lorenzen (Denmark), Manfred Sack (Germany)

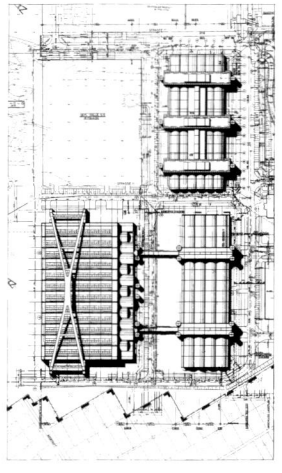

Design Team Meinhard von Gerkan with Karsten Brauer, Klaus Staratzke,
Manfred Stanek, Reinhold Niehoff (Partner in Charge), Michael Engel,
Claudius Schönherr, Dagmar Winter, Winfried Gust, Sabine Oehme,
Gunter Maaß, Peter Klein (Staff)
Structural Engineering Ing.-Büro Assmann

Civil Engineering Ing.-Büro Schmidt Reuter
Air Conditioning Consultant Ing.-Büro Schmidt Reuter
Approximate Cost DM 110,000,000
Total Floor Area 18,000 m²
Photographer Klaus Frahm

Germany

Architects **Gössler und Schnittger Architekten (Bernhard and
Daniel Gössler, Knut Schnittger), Hamburg**
Award Winning Building **Office Building Katharinenhof**
Location **Hamburg, Germany**
Design and Construction Period **1991–1993**

Award BDA Hamburg Architekturpreis 1996 (1. Preisrang)
Given by BDA Bund Deutscher Architekten Hamburg
Prize Presentation November / 14 / 1996
Members of the Jury Dietmar Eberle (Austria), Charlotte Frank (Germany),
Hilde Léon (Chair, Germany), Carsten Lorenzen (Denmark), Manfred Sack
(Germany)
Design Team Daniel Gössler, Kerstin Döring
Civil Engineering Büro Binnewies, Hamburg
Site Area 715 m²

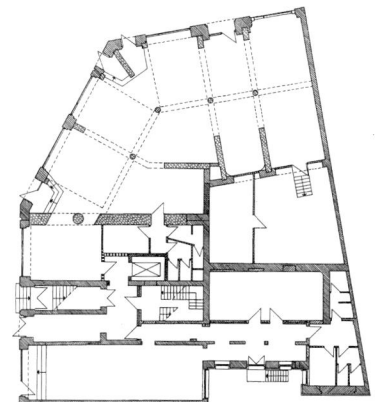

Total Floor Area 690.60 m²
Photographer Daniel Gössler, Arno Declair, Monika Ruberg

Germany

Architects **Architekten Grüntuch / Ernst, Berlin**
Award Winning Building **Canopy and Lobby Hotel Consul**
Location **Knesebeckstraße 8-9, Berlin, Germany**
Design and Construction Period **1992–1994**

Award Hans-Schaefers-Preis 1996
Given by BDA Bund Deutscher Architekten Berlin
Prize Presentation November / 7 / 1996
Design Team A. Grüntuch, A. Grüntuch-Ernst, B. Haller, H. Heyer, O. Menk
Structural Engineering R. Wagner, Stuttgart und Leonhardt, Andrä und Partner,
Berlin
Approximate Cost DM 300,000

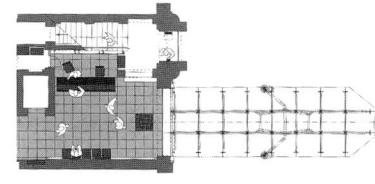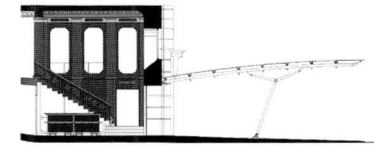

Building Area 250 m²
Total Floor Area 250 m²
Photographer Jörg Hempel

Germany

Architects **Hermann & Valentiny, Remerschen, Luxembourg**
Award Winning Building **Hotel and Service Centre**

Award Architekturpreis des Landes Sachsen-Anhalt 1995
see page 56

Germany

Architect **Thomas Herzog, Munich**
Representative Building **Wilkhahn Production Hall and Energy Plant**

Award Auguste-Perret-Prize 1996 for the complete work of Thomas Herzog
see page 58

Architects **Höhne & Rapp Architekten, Berlin/Amsterdam**
Award Winning Building **Apartment Complex Achillesstraße 34**
Location **Berlin-Weißensee, Karow, Germany**
Design and Construction Period **1993–1996**

 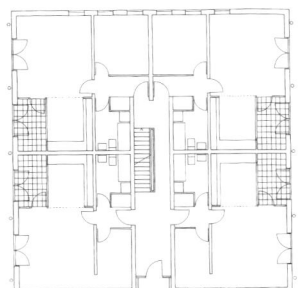

Award Hans-Schaefer-Preis 1996
Given by BDA Bund Deutscher Architekten Berlin
Prize Presentation November / 7 / 1996
Members of the Jury Julia Bolles-Wilson, Kees Christiaanse, Manfred Eichel,
   Falk Jaeger, Otto Steidle
Design Team Peter Baumgärtner, Al Laufeld, Stefan Rolli
Structural Engineering Pape, Berlin
Mechanical Engineering Wegmann und Partner, Berlin
Electrical Engineering Ingenieurbüro Harry Unruh, Berlin
Landscape Architecture Thomanek & Duquesnoy, Berlin

Quantity Surveying Wilfried Panke, Berlin
Building Area 324 m²
Total Floor Area 962.05 m²
Photographer Ivan Nemec, Frankfurt/M. / Berlin

Germany

Architects **Kahlfeldt Architekten, Berlin**
Award Winning Building **Engelhardt Hof**

Award BDA Berlin Architekturpreis 1996 (Honorable Mention)
see page 62

Germany

Architect **Marc-Olivier Mathez, Hamburg**
Award Winning Building **Rehrstieg Housing Complex at Hamburg-
   Neuwiedenthal (renewal and addition)**

Award BDA Hamburg Architekturpreis 1996 (1. Preisrang)
see page 66

Germany

Architects **Rausch und Willems, Berlin**
Award Winning Building **Housing Complex Emsthaler Platz, Berlin-Tegel**
Location **Berlin-Tegel, Germany**

Award BDA Berlin Architekturpreis 1996 (Honorable Mention)
Given by BDA Bund Deutscher Architekten Berlin
Prize Presentation November / 7 / 1996
Members of the Jury Julia Bolles-Wilson, Kees Christiaanse, Manfred Eichel,
   Falk Jaeger, Otto Steidle

Germany

Architects **Carsten Roth Architekten, Hamburg**
Award Winning Building **Remodelling of a Car Factory and
   Construction of a Studio-Flat**
Location **Hamburg Rotherbaum, Germany**

Award BDA Hamburg Architekturpreis 1996 (1. Preisrang)
Given by BDA Bund Deutscher Architekten Hamburg
Prize Presentation November / 14 / 1996
Members of the Jury Dietmar Eberle, Charlotte Frank, Hilde Léon,
   Carsten Lorenzen, Manfred Sack

Germany

Architects **Schneider und Schumacher, Frankfurt am Main**
Award Winning Building **Info-Box**

Award BDA Berlin Architekturpreis 1996 (Honorable Mention)
see page 70

Germany

Architects **Schneider und Schumacher, Frankfurt am Main**
Award Winning Building **Office Building for Thompson Advertising Agency**

Award 1) BDA Berlin Architekturpreis 1996 (Honorable Mention);
   2) Honorable Mention for Excellent Building in Hessen
see page 72

Architects **Architectural Service Department, Hong Kong**
Award Winning Building **Chan Nam Chong Memorial School**

Award President's Prize

Given by HKIA The Hong Kong Institute of Architects
Prize Presentation March / 8 / 1996
Members of the Jury Joseph Ho, Lo Kin Leung, Lo King Man, Anthony Ng, Stephen Poon

---

Hong Kong

Architects **Simon Kwan & Associates Ltd., Hong Kong**
Award Winning Building **Hong Kong Industrial Technology Centre**
Location **72, Tat Chee Avenue, Kowloon Tong, Hong Kong**

 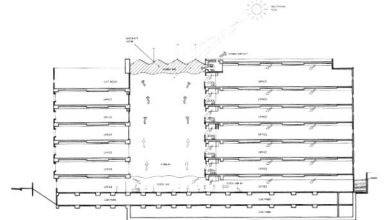

Award Certificate of Merit
Given by HKIA The Hong Kong Institute of Architects
Prize Presentation March / 11 / 1996
Members of the Jury Joseph Ho, Lo Kin Leung, Lo King Man, Anthony Ng, Stephen Poon
Structural Engineering Ove Arup and Partners (HK) Ltd.
Civil Engineering Ove Arup and Partners (HK) Ltd.
Interior Design Simon Kwan & Associates Ltd.
Landscape Architecture Peter Tan and Associates Ltd.

Quantity Surveying Davis Langdon & Seah (HK) Ltd.
Approximate Cost US$ 26,000,000
Site Area 5,700 m^2 / *Building Area* 3,880 m^2 / *Total Floor Area* 22,000 m^2
Photographer Keran Yip

Hong Kong

Architects **P & T Architects & Engineers Ltd., Hong Kong**
Award Winning Building **Singapore International School**
Location **Hong Kong**
Design and Construction Period **1993–1995**

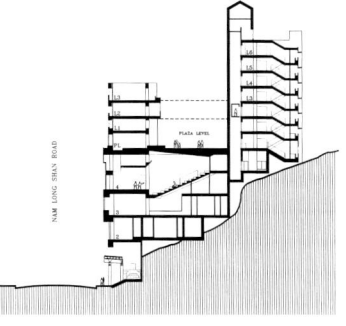 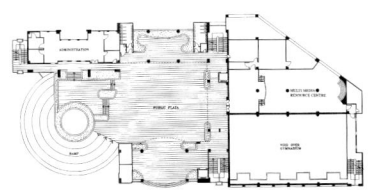

Award Certificate of Merit
Given by HKIA The Hong Kong Institute of Architects
Prize Presentation June / 30 / 1995
Members of the Jury Joseph Ho, Lo Kin Leung, Lo King Man, Anthony Ng, Stephen Poon
Design Team P & T Architects and Engineers Ltd.
Project Director Bernard Lim
Structural Engineering OAP Partners
Civil Engineering OAP Partners
Mechanical Engineering Meinhardt
Electrical Engineering Meinhardt

Environmental Engineering Meinhardt
Landscape Architecture Earthasia
Quantity Surveying MDA (HK) Ltd.
Approximate Cost HKD 103,000,000
Total Floor Area 12,000 m^2
Photographer Bobby K. C. Sum

Hong Kong

Architects **Rocco Design Limited, Hong Kong**
Award Winning Building **Peninsula Hotel Extension**
Location **Salisbury Road, Kowloon, Hong Kong**

Award Silver Medal
Given by HKIA The Hong Kong Institute of Architects
Prize Presentation March / 8 / 1996
Members of the Jury Joseph Ho, Lo Kin Leung, Lo Kin Man, Anthony Ng, Stephen Poon
Design Team Rocco Design Limited
Structural Engineering Mitchell, McFarlane, Brentnall & Partners

Mechanical Engineering J. Roger Preston & Partners
Electrical Engineering J. Roger Preston & Partners
Acoustic Engineering Campbell & Shillinglaw
Air Conditioning Consultant J. Roger Preston & Partners
Lighting Consultant Isometrix; Light Directions Ltd.
Interior Design Denton Corker Marshall Interiors Ltd., Orlando Diaz-Azcuy Designs, Philippe Starck, Richmond International
Landscape Architecture Earthasia Ltd.
Quantity Surveying C S Toh & Sons & Associates
Approximate Cost US$ 110,000,000
Site Area 5,923 m^2 / *Building Area* 72,241 m^2 / *Total Floor Area* 61,571 m^2

Hong Kong

Architects **TAOHO Design Architects Ltd., Hong Kong**
Award Winning Building **Ho Sin-Hang Engineering Building, Chinese University of Hong Kong**
Location **Shatin, New Territories, Hong Kong**
Design and Construction Period **1991–1994**

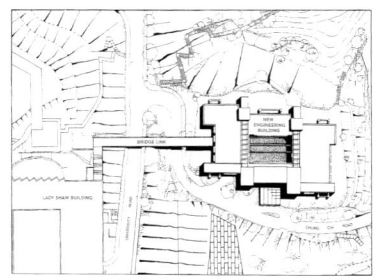

Award Certificate of Merit
Given by HKIA The Hong Kong Institute of Architects
Prize Presentation March / 8 / 1996
Members of the Jury Joseph Ho, Lo Kin Leung, Lo Kin Man, Anthony Ng, Stephen Poon
Design Team TAOHO Design Architects Ltd
Structural Engineering Ove Arup & Partners
Civil Engineering (Geotechnical) John Connell & Associates, Ltd
Mechanical Engineering Ove Arup & Partners
Electrical Engineering Ove Arup & Partners
Air Conditioning Consultant Krueger Engineering (Asia) Ltd

Life Safety Consultant (Fire Services) General Engineering Co.
Interior Design TAOHO Design Architects Ltd
Quantity Surveying Davis Langdon & Seah
Approximate Cost US$ 15,250,000
Site Area 3,600 m^2
Building Area 1,993m^2
Total Floor Area 19,150 m^2
Photographer Tao Ho

Hungary

Architects **Zs. Csomay, M. Heppes, Budapest**
Award Winning Building **Hotel 'ART'**
Location **12. Királyi Pál st., Budapest, Hungary**
Design and Construction Period **1992–1994**

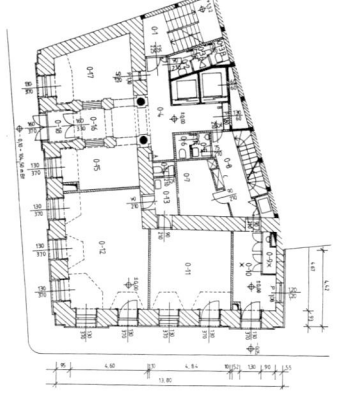

Award Pro Architectura Prize
Given by Ministry of Environment and Regional Policy
Members of the Jury Péter Szabó, Imre Kovács, Csaba Masznyik, Ferenc Ábrahám, Horváthné Judit Tóth, Gábor Winkler, Imre Körmendy, Annamaria Péter
Structural Engineering Z. Újváry-Menyhért, K. Lendvay
Mechanical Engineering E. Bajor
Electrical Engineering P. Gáspár
Interior Design Zs. Csomay, M. Heppes
Site Area 235 m^2

Building Area 235 m^2
Total Floor Area 1,847 m^2
Photographers L. Lelkes, M. Heppes

Hungary

Architects **Annamária Erdöss & László Bordács, Budapest**
Award Winning Building **St. George Hospital**
Location **Székesfehérvár, Hungary**
Design and Construction Period **1982–1995**

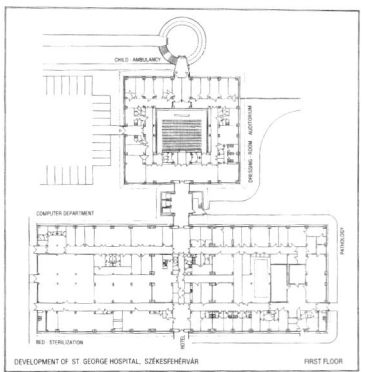

Award YBL Prize
Given by Ministry for Environment and Regional Policy
Prize Presentation March / 14 / 1996
Design Team Közti Architectural and Engineering Co.
Structural Engineering János Parditka
Mechanical Engineering Zsolt Gyulai, András Hámori, Tamás Lukács
Electrical Engineering Endre Máté
Interior Design Judit Láng
Landscape Architecture Péter Csontos
Approximate Cost HUF 7,000,000,000

Site Area 4,2 ha
Building Area 7,000 m^2
Total Floor Area 42,000 m^2
Photographer Annamária Erdöss

Hungary

Architect **Tamás Guzsik, Budapest**

Award YBL Miklós Prize
Given by Ministry of Environment and Regional Policy
Prize Presentation March / 15 / 1996

Hungary

Architect **Miklós Kapsza, Budapest**

Award YBL Miklós Prize
Given by Ministry of Environment and Regional Policy
Prize Presentation March / 15 / 1996

Hungary

Architect **József Kocsis, Szentendre**
Award Winning Building **Bank**
Location **Esztergom, Hungary**
Design and Construction Period **1992–1994**

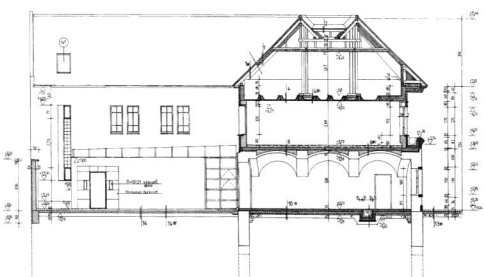

Award YBL Miklós Prize
Given by Ministry of Environment and Regional Policy
Prize Presentation March / 15 / 1996
Members of the Jury Ferenc Bán, János Böhönyei, Lajos Zalaváry
Design Team J. Kocsis, Gy. Alföldi, M. Ágajos Zalaváryy
Structural Engineering Lászó Mózes
Civil Engineering József Vajda
Mechanical Engineering András Eperjessy
Electrical Engineering János Udvary
Air Conditioning Consultant Zsolt Lengyel
Lighting Consultant János Udvary
Interior Design Jozsef Kocsis, György Alföldi
Quantity Surveying Ákos Gajdos

Approximate Cost HUF 100,000,000
Site Area 384 m^2
Building Area 305 m^2
Total Floor Area 661 m^2
Photographer Gábor Medvigy

Hungary

Architect **József Koller, Pécs**
Award Winning Building **Kocsagvar, House of Ferto-Hansag National Park**
Location **Sarrod, Hungary**
Design and Construction Period **1991–1994**

Award Pro Architectura Prize
Given by Ministry of Environment and Regional Policy
Prize Presentation June / 30 / 1995
Members of the Jury Péter Szabó, Imre Kovács, Csaba Masznyik,
    Ferenc Ábrahám, Horváthné Judit Tóth, Gábor Winkler, Imre Körmendy,
    Annamaria Péter
Design Team Jozsef Koller, Terezia Zambo (Implementation), Laszlo Ferenczy
    (Processing Colleague)
Structural Engineering Jeno Dulanszky
Civil Engineering Peter Koch
Mechanical Engineering Zsolt Eordogh
Electrical Engineering Bela Hegyi

Lighting Consultant Karoly Zsamboki
Landscape Architecture Peter Koch
Quantity Surveying Gyula Parkanyi
Approximate Cost HUF 120,000,000
Site Area 15,000 m^2
Building Area 1,205 m^2
Total Floor Area 1,652 m^2
Photographer Antal Kiss

India

Architect **Jayant Dharap, Pune**
Award Winning Building **The Meadows Resort at Aurangabad**
Location **Aurangabad, India**

Award JIIA Journal of Indian Institute of Architects (Interior)
Given by The Indian Institute of Architects
Prize Presentation July 1996

India

Architects **Anupama Kohli & Rajeev Agarwal, New Delhi**
Award Winning Interior Architecture **Oxford Cut (Accessories Shop & Barber Shop)**
Location **Vasant Vihar, New Delhi, India**
Design and Construction Period **1994–1995**

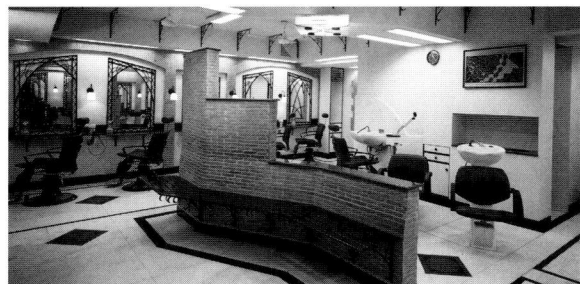

Award JIIA Journal of Indian Institute of Architects (Interior)
Given by The Indian Institute of Architects
Prize Presentation July / 1 / 1996
Members of the Jury P.G. Patki, Kulbhushan Jain, Porus Master, Vasant Ranade, Anil Nagrath
Design Team Anupama Kohli & Rajeev Agarwal
Approximate Cost US$ 22,000
Site Area 120 m^2

Building Area 120 m^2
Total Floor Area 120 m^2
Photographer Aditya Arya, New Delhi

Ireland

Architects **Architectural Service of the Office of Public Works, Dublin**
Award Winning Building **Chapel Royal, Dublin Castle**
Location **Dublin, Ireland**

Award RIAI Triennial Gold Medal 1989 - 1990 - 1991
Given by The Royal Institute of Architects of Ireland

Ireland

Architects **De Blacam & Meagher, Dublin**
Award Winning Building **Chapel of Reconciliation, Knock, Co. Mayo**
Location **Ireland**

Award RIAI Triennial Gold Medal 1989-1990-1991
Given by The Royal Institute of Architects of Ireland

Ireland

Architects **Burke Kennedy Doyle & Partners; Dublin**
Award Winning Building **Housing at Failte Park, Bray, Co. Wicklow**
Location **Ireland**

Award RIAI Triennial Gold Medal 1989 - 1990 - 1991
Given by The Royal Institute of Architects of Ireland

Ireland

Architects **Dunphy, O'Connor, Baird Architects, Dublin**
Award Winning Building **The Swiss Cottage**
Location **Cahir, Co. Tipperary, Ireland**
Design and Construction Period **1986–1989**

Award The Restoration Medal
Given by The Royal Institute of Architects of Ireland
Prize Presentation September 1996
Design Team T. Austin Dunphy, John R. Redmill
Mechanical Engineering The Engineering Section, Office of Public Works
Electrical Engineering The Engineering Section, Office of Public Works
Lighting Consultant Dunphy, O'Connor, Baird Architects

Life Safety Consultant Dunphy, O'Connor, Baird Architects
Interior Design Dunphy, O'Connor, Baird Architects
Landscape Architecture The Parks Department (Office of Public Works)
Quantity Surveying Aidan Quinn ARICS (Office of Public Works)
Approximate Cost IR£ 500,000

Site Area 10,000 m²
Building Area 88.5 m²
Total Floor Area 202.27 m²
Photographer Con Brogan (Office of Public Works)

Ireland

Architect **Neil Hegarty, Cork**
Award Winning Building **Social Housing for families and elderly people in Inner Cork City**
Location **Grattan St., Peters St., Coach St., Broad St., Cork, Ireland**
Design and Construction Period **1987–1988**

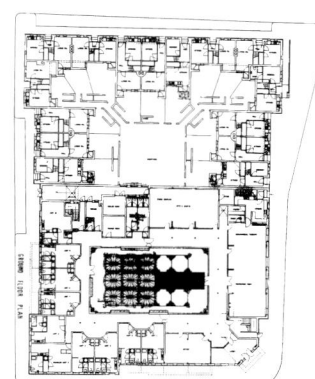

Award Housing Silver Medal
Given by The Royal Institute of Architects of Ireland
Prize Presentation April / 25 / 1996
Members of the Jury David Thompson, Derek Jago, Paul Quilligan
Design Team Neil Hegarty
Structural Engineering Ove Arup & Partners
Civil Engineering Ove Arup & Partners
Mechanical Engineering Peter Kerins & Partners
Electrical Engineering Peter Kerins & Partners
Environmental Engineering Neil Hegarty
Acoustic Engineering Neil Hegarty
Air Conditioning Consultant Neil Hegarty
Lighting Consultant Neil Hegarty
Life Safety Consultant Neil Hegarty

Interior Design Neil Hegarty
Landscape Architecture Neil Hegarty
Quantity Surveying James P. McGrath & Associates
Approximate Cost IR£ 2,100,000
Site Area 3,343 m²
Building Area 1,622 m²
Total Floor Area 3,753 m²
Photographers Finbarr O'Connell, Tony O'Connell

Ireland

Architects **Murray O'Laoire Associates, Limerick**
Award Winning Building **Tourist Information Office and Civic Park**
Location **Arthur's Quay Park, Limerick, Ireland**

Award RIAI Triennial Gold Medal 1989-1990-1991
Given by The Royal Institute of Architects of Ireland

Ireland

Architect **Scott Tallon Walker, Dublin**
Award Winning Building **School of Engineering (phase 1), University College Dublin**

Location **Belfield, Dublin, Ireland**
Award RIAI Triennial Gold Medal 1989 - 1990 - 1991
Given by The Royal Institute of Architects of Ireland

Israel

Architects **Chyutin Bracha and Chyutin Michael, Jerusalem**
Award Winning Building **Givatayim Theater and Esslingen Youth Hostel**
Location **Givatayim, Israel**
Design and Construction Period **1991–1996**

Award The Zeev Rechter Prize
Given by Association of Architects and City Planners in Israel
Prize Presentation November / 27 / 1996
Members of the Jury Ulrik Plesner (Chairman), Haim Dotan,
   Gabriella Nussbaum
Structural Engineering Israel David Engineers Ltd.
Civil Engineering Israel David Engineers Ltd.

Mechanical Engineering L. Lustig Engineers
Electrical Engineering G. B. Engineers
Acoustic Engineering S. Mashiah Consultant

Air Conditioning Consultant M. Doron–I. Shahar Consulting Eng. Ltd.

Lighting Consultant Sean McAlister, Theater Cons. & Lighting Cons.

Life Safety Consultant Idan Safety Consultant

Interior Design Chyutin Architects Ltd.

Landscape Architecture Gabinet Baroch Architect

Quantity Surveying Baltsan–Epstein Engineers

Approximate Cost US$ 4,500,000

Site Area 4,000 m²

Building Area 1,500 m²

Total Floor Area 3,500 m²

Photographer Chyutin Michael

Israel

Architects **D. Reznik Architects, Jerusalem and Fowler, Ferguson, Kingston, Ruben Architects, Salt Lake City, USA**

Award Winning Building **The Jerusalem Centre for Near Eastern Studies (Mormon University in Jerusalem)**

Award The Zeev Rechter Prize

see page 74

Italy

Architects **Pasquale Culotta, Giuseppe Leone, Palermo**

Award Winning Building **Refurbishment and Remodelling of the Cefalú Town Hall (Palermo)**

Location **Cefalú, Palermo, Italy**

Award Premio Speciale della Giuria fuori concorso per la migliore architettura realizzata in Italia nel Biennio 1994–1995

Given by CLEAN Cooperativa Libraria Editrice Architettura Napoli

Prize Presentation May 1995

Members of the Jury Gianni Cosenza, Francesco dal Co, Nicola di Battista, Alberto Ferlenga, Benedetto Gravagnuolo, Vittorio Magnago Lampugnani, Francesco Venezia

Italy

Architect **Fabio Pitoni, Labro**

Award Winning Building **Theatre at Labro**

Location **Labro, Italy**

Award Premio Nazionale di Architettura Luigi Cosenza 1996, Miglior Progetto Realizzato

Given by CLEAN Cooperativa Libraria Editrice Architettura Napoli

Prize Presentation May 1995

Members of the Jury Gianni Cosenza, Francesco dal Co, Nicola di Battista, Alberto Ferlenga, Benedetto Gravagnuolo, Vittorio Magnago Lampugnani, Francesco Venezia

Jamaica

Architect **Harold Morrison Associates, Kingston**

Award Winning Building **Sunshine Village / Singles Negril**

Location **Negril, Jamaica**

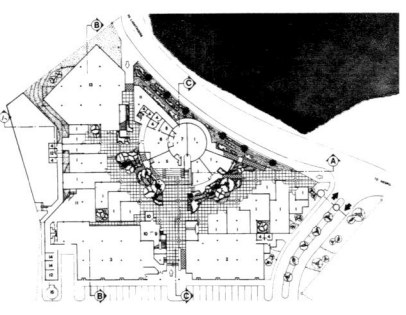

Award Governor General's Award for Excellence in Architecture

Given by The Jamaican Institute of Architects

Prize Presentation November / 7 / 1992

Members of the Jury Rasem J. Badvan, Juan Marques Meva, Gene R. Summers

Design Team Harold Morrison Associates

Structural Engineering Jentech Consultants

Civil Engineering Jentech Consultants

Mechanical Engineering L.W. Hardie & Associates

Electrical Engineering L.W. Hardie & Associates

Environmental Engineering L.W. Hardie & Associates

Air Conditioning Consultant L.W. Hardie & Associates

Life Safety Consultant L.W. Hardie & Associates

Interior Design Harold Morrison Associates Interiors Ltd.

Landscape Architecture Mary-Anne Rickham

Quantity Surveying Stoppi Cairney Bloomfield

Approximate Cost J$ 57,000,000 (US$ 1,628,571.00)

Site Area 4046.7 m²

Building Area 5574 m²

Total Floor Area 55,000 sq. ft.

Photographers R.V. Woodstock & N. Hylton

Architect **Furuichi & Associates, Tokyo**
Award Winning Building **Saikai Sea Pearl Centre and Annex**
Location **Sasebo, Nagasaki, Japan**
Design and Construction Period **1991–1994**

Award 1) JIA Award for the Best Young Architects of the Year 1995;
  2) 1996 Selected Architectural Designs of the AIJ
Given by 1) JIA The Japan Institute of Architects; 2) AIJ Architects
  Institute of Japan
Prize Presentation 1) October / 26 / 1995; 2) September 1995
Members of the Jury Atsushi Kitagawara, Takefumi Aida, Yoshiro Ikehara
Design Team Furuichi & Associates
Structural Engineering Hoshino Architect & Engineer, Inc.
Civil Engineering Tokyo Landscape Architects, Inc.
Mechanical Engineering Watanabe Mechanical Engineering Office
Electrical Engineering Misuzu Electrical Engineering Office
Environmental Engineering Tokyo Landscape Architects Inc.
Acoustic Engineering Nagata Acoustics Inc.
Air Conditioning Consultant Watanabe Mechanical Engineering Office

Lighting Consultant Misuzu Electrical Engineering Office
Interior Design Furuichi & Associates
Landscape Architecture Tokyo Landscape Architects Inc.
Quantity Surveying Mune Planning Office
Approximate Cost ¥ 3,034,000,000 (Sea Pearl Centre), ¥ 431,670,000 (Annex)
Site Area 10.5 ha
Building Area 3,308.78 m^2 (Sea Pearl Centre), 1,590.42 m^2 (Annex)
Total Floor Area 5,721.74 m^2 (Sea Pearl Centre), 1,733.08 m^2 (Annex)
Photographer Furudate K.

Japan

Architect **Toshiaki Ishida, Tokyo**
Award Winning Building **NOS-h, a second house for an artisan**

Award JIA Award for the Best Young Architects of the Year 1996
see page 78

Japan

Architects **Kazutoshi Katayama Architects & Associates, Tokyo**
Award Winning Building **Sainokuni Chichibu Forest Lodge and Study Centre**

Award JIA Award for the Best Young Architects of the Year 1995
see page 82

Japan

Architect **Takasaki Masaharu, Tokyo**
Award Winning Building **Kihoku Astronomical Museum**

Award JIA Award for the Best Young Architects of the Year 1996
see page 76

Japan

Architect **Dan Norihiko, Tokyo**
Award Winning Building **Hachijo Atelier**
Location **Hachijo Island, Tokyo, Japan**
Design and Construction Period **1991–1993**

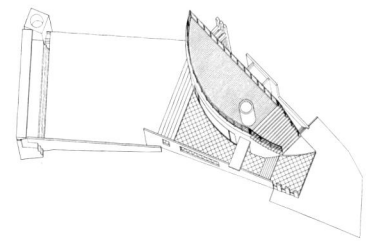 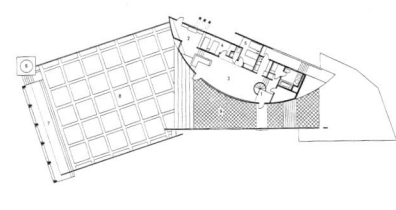

Award JIA Award for the Best Young Architects of the Year 1995
Given by JIA The Japan Institute of Architects
Prize Presentation October / 26 / 1995
Members of the Jury Atsushi Kitagawara, Yoshiro Ikehara, Takefumi Aida
Design Team Norihiko Dan and Associates
Structural Engineering Yutaka Aoki
Mechanical Engineering Nobuaki Yamada
Electrical Engineering Nobuaki Yamada

Air Conditioning Consultant Nobuaki Yamada
Site Area 1,476.14 m^2
Building Area 160.18m^2
Total Floor Area 155.76 m^2
Photographers Fujitsuka Mitsumasa, Shinkenchiku-Sha

Kazakhstan

Architect **Ualikhanov, Chotä, Almaty**
Award Winning Building **Série du Domaine Symbolique: Armoires d' État du Kazakstan, Étendard du Président, Emblèmes d'Almaty et d'Académie des Sciences**

Award Gold Medal 1996
Given by Kazakhstan Union of Architects
Prize Presentation July / 1 / 1996
Members of the Jury Kayarbaev A., Rustambekov A., Jaksalykov F., Baïrov S., Tokhaev N.

South Korea

Architect **Beak, Moon-Ki, Seoul**
Award Winning Building **Shiwa Building**
Location **1008-26 Daechi-dong, Kangnam gu, Seoul, South Korea**

Award 17th Korean Institute of Architects Prize 1995
Given by Korean Institute of Architects
Prize Presentation October / 13 / 1995

South Korea

Architects **Byun, Young and Kim, Seok-Ju, Seoul**
Award Winning Building **The Chosun Ilbo Pyungchon Building**
Location **1591-8 Gwanyangdong Anyangsi, Gyeonggido, South Korea**
Design and Construction Period **1992–1994**

 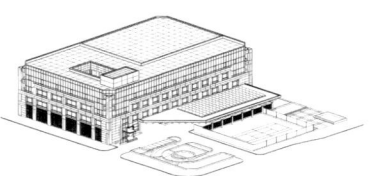

Award 17th Korean Institute of Architects Prize 1995
Given by Korean Institute of Architects
Prize Presentation November 1995
Design Team Wondoshi Architects Group, Ltd.
Structural Engineering Seoul Structural Engineers Associates
Mechanical Engineering Hanil Mechanical Engineering Consultant
Electrical Engineering Moon, Y., H., Electrical Design Co, Ltd.
Air Conditioning Consultant Hanil Mechanical Engineering Consultant
Lighting Consultant Moon, Y., H., Electrical Design Co, Ltd.

Interior Design Wondoshi Architects Group, Ltd.
Approximate Cost US$ 25,000,000
Site Area 9,916 m^2
Building Area 5,236 m^2
Total Floor Area 28,455 m^2

South Korea

Architect **Cha, Woon-Ki, Seoul**
Award Winning Building **Teak-Hyung's House**
Location **Tosoo-ri, Toichon.myun, Kwangju-kun, Kyongki-do, South Korea**

Award 17th Korean Institute of Architects Prize 1995
Given by Korean Institute of Architects
Prize Presentation October / 13 / 1995

South Korea

Architects **Kang, Ki-Se, P.E. and Park, Young-Kern, Seoul**
Award Winning Building **Pundang Olympic Sports Centre**
Location **Sohyun-dong, Pundang-gu, Sungnam-shi, Kyungki-do, South Korea**
Design and Construction Period **1991–1994**

Award 17th Korean Institute of Architects Prize 1995
Given by Korean Institute of Architects
Prize Presentation November / 28 / 1995
Members of the Jury Kim, Sung Kuk; Kim, Jung Sik; Kim, Chang Su; Lee, Sang Heon; Choi, Young Jip
Design Team Won, Hyung Joon; Park, Hyung Il; Park, Jong Seok; Park, Byung Tai; Kim, Chang Hyun
Structural Engineering Jeon & Associates Co., Ltd.
Civil Engineering Samsan Engineering
Mechanical Engineering Hanil Mech, Eng, Consultants Co., Ltd.

Electrical Engineering Hanyang Electrical Engineers Co., Ltd.
Air Conditioning Consultant Hanil Mech, Eng, Consultants Co., Ltd.

Lighting Consultant Hanyang Electrical Engineers Co., Ltd.

Life Safety Consultant Hanil M.E.C. and Hanyang E.E.

Interior Design BAUM Architects, Engineers & Consultants Co., Ltd.

Landscape Architecture BAUM Architects, Engineers & Consultants Co., Ltd.

Approximate Cost W 22,000,000,000 (US$ 27,500,000)

Site Area 4,558 m^2

Building Area 2,209.55 m^2

Total Floor Area 19,995 m^2

Photographer Yoon, Chang Jin

South Korea

Architects **Kim, Jung-Chul and Lee, Hyoung-Jae, Seoul**

Award Winning Building **Ye – Darm Presbyterian Church**

Location **134-1, 4, Dongsomoon – dong, Sumgbook – Gu, Seoul, South Korea**

Design and Construction Period **1992–1994**

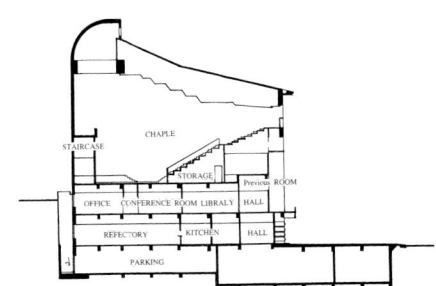

Award 1) 17th Korean Institute of Architects Award 1995;
2) Design Award, Annual SEOUL CITY Architecture Design Award Program 1995; 3) Design Award, Annual K.I.R.A. Design Award Program 1994

Given by 1) Korean Institute of Architects; 2) Seoul City; 3) Korean Institute of Registered Architects

Prize Presentation 1) 1995; 2) 1995; 3) 1994

Members of the Jury Kang Suk-Won, Ahn Young-Bae, Lee-Myung-Ho

Design Team Kim, Jung-Chul and Lee, Hyoung-Jae

Structural Engineering Shin, Soon-Ho / Wooram Structure

Mechanical Engineering Sam Joo Engineering

Interior Design ADIF Design

Landscape Architecture Lee Soo-Sung

Approximate Cost W 1,350,494,000 (US$ 1,588,817)

Site Area 2,026.7 m^2

Building Area 890.64 m^2

Total Floor Area 4,394.2 m^2

Photographer Kim, Tae-Oh

South Korea

Architects **Seok Chul Kim & Associates, ARCHIBAN, Seoul**

Award Winning Building **Myung bo Plaza**

Location **18-5, Cho-Dong, Jung-Gu, Seoul, South Korea**

Design and Construction Period **1992–1994**

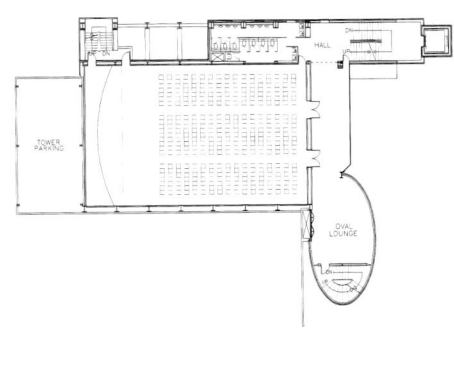

Award 17th Korean Institute of Architects Prize 1995

Given by Korean Institute of Architects

Prize Presentation October / 13 / 1995

Design Team ARCHIBAN

Structural Engineering Byung-sik Kang

Civil Engineering CHUN – IL Engineering

Mechanical Engineering YOO – SUNG Mechanical Engineering

Electrical Engineering MOO – LIM Electrical Engineering

Environmental Engineering ARCHIBAN

Acoustic Engineering ARCHIBAN

Air Conditioning Consultant YOO – SUNG Mechanical Engineering

Lighting Consultant Lito Lighting

Life Safety Consultant ARCHIBAN

Interior Design Min – International

Landscape Architecture Go Un Landscaping Co. Ltd.

Approximate Cost US$ 10,000,000

Site Area 1,272.4 m^2

Building Area 725.8 m^2

Total Floor Area 6,076.36 m^2

Photographer Hee Woong Jeong, ARCHIBAN

South Korea

Architect **Kim, Woo-Sung, Seoul**

Award Winning Building **Hanhwa Group Research & Engineers Centre**

Location **Taeduk Science Town, Yoosung gu, TaeJeun, South Korea**

Award 17th Korean Institute of Architects Prize 1995

Given by Korean Institute of Architects

Prize Presentation October / 13 / 1995

Latvia

Architects **Aigars Andersons, Ingrida Andersone, Saldus**
Award Winning Building **Saldus St. Gregors Christian Ministry Training Centre**
Location **Saldus, Latvia**
Design and Construction Period **1993–1995**

 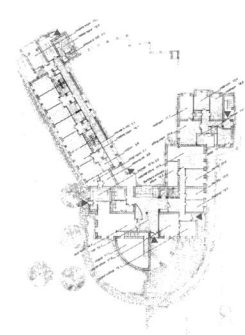

Award The Best New Structure of 1995 in Latvia
Given by The Latvia Association of Architects
Prize Presentation December / 28 / 1995
Members of the Jury Andrejs Holcmanis, Aigars Sparāns, Juris Poga, Gunta Lukstiņa, Obgerts Krauklis, Gunārs Melbergs, Sergejs Ņikiforovs
Design Team Aigars Andersons, Ingrida Andersone
Structural Engineering Aigars Andersons, Ingrida Andersone
Electrical Engineering Andris Sudmalis
Environmental Engineering Jānis Janson

Interior Design Ingrida Andersone
Approximate Cost US$ 586,000
Site Area 6,225 m² / *Building Area* 859 m² / *Total Floor Area* 2,206 m²
Photographer Aleksandrs Hehlovskis

Lithuania

Architect **Algirdas Žebrauskas, Telsiai**
Award Winning Building **Rainai Victim's Chapel**
Location **Rainai, Telšai Region, Lithuania**
Design and Construction Period **1990–1991**

 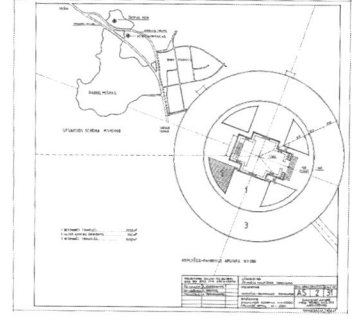

Award Lithuanian National Award for Culture and Art
Given by Lithuanian National Award for Culture and Art Committee
Prize Presentation December / 14 / 1994
Members of the Jury M. Martinaitis (Chief), V. Nasvytis, A. Steponavičius, R. Gaštas
Design Team Jonas Virakas, Algirdas Žebrauskas
Structural Engineering Algis Bružas
Interior Design Algirdas Žebrauskas, Remigijus Midvikis, Antanas Kmieliauskas, Algirdas Dovydenas

Landscape Architecture Algirdas Žebrauskas
Approximate Cost US$ 50,000
Site Area 15,000 m² / *Building Area* 97 m² / *Total Floor Area* 148 m²
Photographers Zenonas Nekrošius, Jonas Danauskas

Luxembourg

Architects **Christian Bauer Architectes, Bridel**
Award Winning Building **House Bauer**

Award 1995 Prix Luxembourgeois d'Architecture (Honorable Mention)
see page 86

Luxembourg

Architects **Atélier d'Architecture BENG (Marco Bidaine, Nico Engel, Yves Noury, Albert Goedert), Esch-sur-Alzette**
Award Winning Building **Résidence Grobirchen**
Location **Esch-sur-Alzette, Luxembourg**
Design and Construction Period **1991–1992**

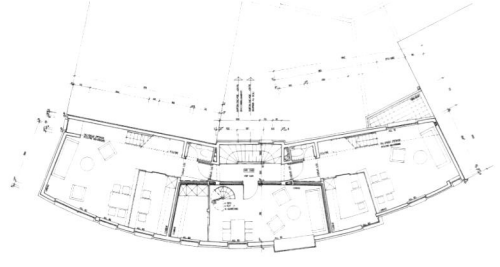

Award 1995 Prix Luxembourgeois d'Architecture (Honorable Mention)
Given by Fondation de l'Architecture et de l'Ingénierie
Prize Presentation 1995
Members of the Jury Dominique Perrault, Stephane Beel, Jean Flammang, Enrico Lunghi, Bohdan Paczowski
Design Team Atélier d'Architecture BENG
Structural Engineering Tr. Engineering

Interior Design Atélier d'Architecture BENG
Approximate Cost F.lux 22,000,000
Site Area 1.6 ares / *Building Area* 1.4 ares / *Total Floor Area* 450 m²
Photographer Christof Weber

Luxembourg

Architect **Stanislaw Berbec, Luxembourg**
Award Winning Project **A typological approach to rural architecture**
  in the Grand Duchy of Luxembourg
Location **Luxembourg, Luxembourg**
Design and Construction Period **1992**

Award 1995 Prix Luxembourgeois d'Architecture
Given by Fondation de l'Architecture et de l'Ingénierie
Prize Presentation November / 10 / 1995
Members of the Jury Stéphane Beel, Jean Flammang, Enrico Lunghi,
  Bohdan Paczowski, Dominique Perrault
Design Team Stanislaw Berbec with Anna Bienkowska-Bogdan, Christine
  Mormont-Berbec, Bernard Isfort, Christophe Bogdan

Luxembourg

Architects **Leon Glodt, Regina Pizzinini, Bridel**
Award Winning Building **Villa Petite**

Award 1995 Prix Luxembourgois d'Architecture
see page 90

Luxembourg

Architect **Nico Steinmetz, Luxembourg**
Award Winning Building **House & Workshop Malakoff**

Award 1) 1995 Prix Luxembourgeois d'Architecture (Lauréat);
  2) Distinguished Finalist Benedictus–Du Pont Award
see page 88

Macedonia

Architects **Ljiljana and Miodrag Mitrović, Skopje**
Award Winning Building **House Mario**
Location **Metrika, Skopje, Macedonia**
Design and Construction Period **1993–1995**

Award Grand Prix of AAM for 1995
Given by AAM Association of Architects of Macedonia
Prize Presentation December / 26 / 1995
Design Team Ljiljana and Miodrag Mitrović
Structural Engineering Ljubomir Troschanovski
Site Supervisory GP Granit, Skopje

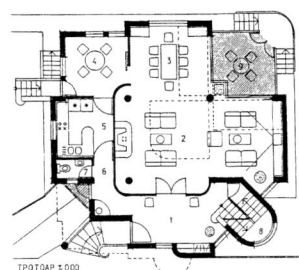

Landscape Architecture Ljiljana and Miodrag Mitrović
Building Area 296 m²

Malaysia

Architects **Architecture Bureau, Kuala Lumpur**
Award Winning Building **Taiko – Regional Headquarter and Storage**
  Warehouse
Location **No 2 Jalan UI / 15, Seksyen UI, Hicom Glenmarie Industrial Park,**
  40000 Shah Alam, Malaysia

Award PAM Architecture Award 1995 (Industrial Buildings Category)
Given by PAM Pertubuhan Akitek Malaysia
Prize Presentation September / 15 / 1996
Members of the Jury Dato Haji Esa Bin Mohamed (President PAM),
  Tay Kheng Soon, Dato Ibrahim Hussein
Design Team Architecture Bureau, Joseph Khoo
Structural Engineering M/S Kemasepakat Sdn. Bhd.
Civil Engineering M/S Kemasepakat Sdn. Bhd.
Mechanical and Electrical Engineering M/S Enmac Sekutu (M) Sdn. Bhd.
Interior Design M/S Architecture Bureau
Landscape Architecture M/S Architecture Bureau
Quantity Surveying M/S TAQ-Surveyors

Approximate Cost US$ 600,600
Site Area 3,549 m²
Building Area 1,832.48 m²
Total Floor Area 1,593.5 m²
Photographer M/S Architecture Bureau

Malaysia

Architects **Daya Bina Sdn. Bhd.**

Award Winning Building **Hotel Instana**

Award PAM Architecture Award 1995 (Commercial Buildings Category)

Given by PAM Pertubuhan Akitek Malaysia

Prize Presentation September / 15 / 1995

Members of the Jury Dato Haji Esa Bin Mohamed (President PAM), Tay Kheng Soon, Dato Ibrahim Hussein

Malaysia

Architect **Design Nexus Architect, Kuala Lumpur**

Award Winning Building **Maxis HQ**

Award PAM Architecture Award 1995 (Interior Design Category)

Given by PAM Pertubuhan Akitek Malaysia

Prize Presentation September / 15 / 1995

Members of the Jury Dato Haji Esa Bin Mohamed (President PAM), Tay Kheng Soon, Dato Ibrahim Hussein

Malaysia

Architect **Akitek Gayasari**

Award Winning Building **Dalat Sports Complex**

Award PAM Architecture Award 1995 (Institutional Buildings Category)

Given by PAM Pertubuhan Akitek Malaysia

Prize Presentation September / 15 / 1995

Members of the Jury Dato Haji Esa Bin Mohamed (President PAM), Tay Kheng Soon, Dato Ibrahim Hussein

Malaysia

Architects **GDP Architects Sdn. Bhd., Kuala Lumpur**

Award Winning Building **Yong's House**

Award PAM Architecture Award 1995 (Single Residential Category)

Given by PAM Pertubuhan Akitek Malaysia

Prize Presentation September / 15 / 1995

Members of the Jury Dato Haji Esa Bin Mohamed (President PAM), Tay Kheng Soon, Dato Ibrahim Hussein

Malaysia

Architects **T.R. Hamzah & Yeang Sdn. Bhd.**

Award Winning Building **Tai Pan Crest**

Award PAM Architecture Award 1995 (Commercial Buildings Category)

Given by PAM Pertubuhan Akitek Malaysia

Prize Presentation September / 15 / 1995

Members of the Jury Dato Haji Esa Bin Mohamed (President PAM), Tay Kheng Soon, Dato Ibrahim Hussein

Malaysia

Architects **Architect Ikhtisas Sdn. Bhd.**

Award Winning Building **Yayasan Sabah Community College**

Award PAM Architecture Award 1995 (Institutional Buildings Category)

Given by PAM Pertubuhan Akitek Malaysia

Prize Presentation September / 15 / 1995

Members of the Jury Dato Haji Esa Bin Mohamed (President PAM), Tay Kheng Soon, Dato Ibrahim Hussein

Malaysia

Architects **Lee Architectural Consultancy**

Award Winning Building **Factory for Otis Manufacturing Co.**

Award PAM Architecture Award 1995 (Industrial Buildings Category)

Given by PAM Pertubuhan Akitek Malaysia

Prize Presentation September / 15 / 1995

Members of the Jury Dato Haji Esa Bin Mohamed (President PAM), Tay Kheng Soon, Dato Ibrahim Hussein

Malaysia

Architect **Laurence Loh Akitek, Penang**
Award Winning Building **18 units 6 storeys Aurora Court Apartments**
Location **Perak Road, Penang, Malaysia**
Design and Construction Period **1990–1993**

Award PAM Architecture Award 1993
   (Repetitive Residential Building Category)
Given by PAM Pertubuhan Akitek Malaysia
Prize Presentation 1993
Members of the Jury Jimmy Lim (President PAM)
Design Team Laurence Loh Akitek
Structural Engineering Peter Leow & Associates
Civil Engineering Peter Leow & Associates
Mechanical and Electrical Engineering Pintar Juara
   Engineering Konsultan

Interior Design Laurence Loh Akitek
Landscape Architecture Laurence Loh
Akitek
Approximate Cost RM 1,400,000
Site Area 1,330 m²
Building Area 360 m²
Total Floor Area 1,670 m²

Malaysia

Architect **Ong Keng Poh Architect**
Award Winning Building **Disted Kolej Yeap Chor Ee Campus**

Award PAM Architecture Award 1995 (Conservation & Adaptive Reuse
   Buildings Category)

Given by PAM Pertubuhan Akitek Malaysia
Prize Presentation September / 15 / 1995
Members of the Jury Dato Haji Esa Bin Mohamed (President PAM),
   Tay Kheng Soon, Dato Ibrahim Hussein

Malaysia

Architect **Lee Robin Architect**
Award Winning Building **Cheras Leisuremall**

Award PAM Architecture Award 1995 (Commercial Buildings Category)

Given by PAM Pertubuhan Akitek Malaysia
Prize Presentation September / 15 / 1995
Members of the Jury Dato Haji Esa Bin Mohamed (President PAM),
   Tay Kheng Soon, Dato Ibrahim Hussein

Malaysia

Architects **Akitek Urbanisma Sdn. Bhd., Kuala Lumpur**
Award Winning Building **Salehuddin A. Wahid´s Residence**

Award PAM Architecture Award 1995 (Single Residential Category)
Given by PAM Pertubuhan Akitek Malaysia

Prize Presentation September / 15 / 1995
Members of the Jury Dato Haji Esa Bin Mohamed (President PAM),
   Tay Kheng Soon, Dato Ibrahim Hussein

Mexico

Architect **Jorge Agostoni, Mexico City**
Award Winning Building **Museo de las Culturas del Norte**
Location **Chihuahua, Chihuahua, Mexico**

Award Award of Mexican Architecture 1996 (IV Biennial of Architecture,
   Silver Medal)
Given by Federación de Colegios de Arquitectos de la República Mexicana
Prize Presentation 1996

Mexico

Architects **Alvares – Bulnes Arquitectos, Mexico City**
Award Winning Building **Museo del Espacio Histórico Mexicano**
Location **Monterrey, Nueva León, Mexico**

Award Award of Mexican Architecture 1996 (IV Biennial of Architecture,
   Silver Medal)
Given by Federación de Colegios de Arquitectos de la República Mexicana
Prize Presentation 1996

Mexico

Architects **Alvarez Augusto H. Arquitectos, Mexico City**
Award Winning Building **Casa Alvarez-Fuentes**
Location **Merida, Yucatán, Mexico**

Award Award of Mexican Architecture 1996 (IV Biennial of Architecture, Silver Medal)
Given by Federación de Colegios de Arquitectos de la República Mexicana
Prize Presentation 1996

Mexico

Architects **Moises Becker Kabachnik, Mexico City**
Award Winning Building **Taller de Arquitectura Becker Arquitectos**

Award Award of Mexican Architecture 1996 (IV Biennial of Architecture, Honorable Mention)
see page 92

Mexico

Architect **Teodoro González de León, Mexico**
Award Winning Building **Conservatorio Nacional de Música de la Ciudad de las Artes**

Award Award of Mexican Architecture 1996 (IV Biennial of Architecture, Honorable Mention)
see page 94

Mexico

Architect **Teodoro González de León, Mexico**
Award Winning Building **Colegio Nacional (renewal)**
Location **Mexico City, Mexico**
Design and Construction Period **1993–1994**

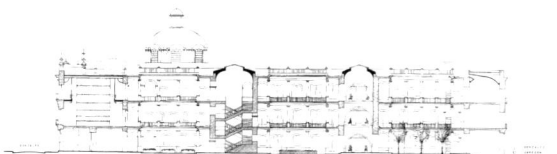

Award Award of Mexican Architecture 1996 (IV Biennial of Architecture, Silver Medal)
Given by Federación de Colegios de Arquitectos de la República Mexicana
Prize Presentation November 1996
Members of the Jury Julio de la Peña Lomelín, Mauricio Romano del Valle, Félix Sánchez Aguilar, Antonio Toca Fernández, Rámon Torres Martinéz, Francisco Treviño Loustaunau, Héctor Velasquez Moreno, José Luis Cortez Delgado, Rutilo Malacara de Léon
Collaborator Architect Miguel Barbachano Osorio
Structural Engineering Colinas de Buen, S.A.
Hydraulics and Sanitary Engineering GHA y Asociados, S.A.
Electrical Engineering COESA INGENIERIA, S.A.
Audio Video Consultant Architect Agustín García Garibay
Air Conditioning Consultant DYPRO
Lighting Consultant STARCO

Interior Design Architect Luis A. de Regil
Site Area 7,400 m² / *Building Area* 2,460 m²
Photographer Pedro Hiriart

Mexico

Architects **Grupo LBC Arquitectos, Mexico City**
Award Winning Building **Private House**
Location **Celaya, Guanajuato, Mexico**

Award Award of Mexican Architecture 1996 (IV Biennial of Architecture, Silver Medal)
Given by Federación de Colegios de Arquitectos de la República Mexicana
Prize Presentation 1996

Mexico

Architect **Felipe Leal Fernandez, Mexico City**
Award Winning Building **Office of the Painter Vicente Rojo**
Location **Mexico City, Mexico**

Award Award of Mexican Architecture 1996 (IV Biennial of Architecture, Silver Medal)
Given by Federación de Colegios de Arquitectos de la República Mexicana
Prize Presentation 1996

Mexico

Architects **Luis Méndez Jiménez Izquierdo, César Pérez Becerril, Enrique Ruiz Gutierrez Topete, Mexico City**
Award Winning Building **Lumen Industrial Warehouse and Offices**
Location **Buena Suerte No. 51, Tlahuac, Mexico City, Mexico**
Design and Construction Period **1993–1995**

Award Award of Mexican Architecture 1996 (IV Biennial of Architecture, Gold Medal)
Given by Federación de Colegios de Arquitectos de la República Mexicana
Prize Presentation December / 6 / 1996
Members of the Jury Julio de la Peña Lomelín, Mauricio Romano del Valle, Félix Sánchez Aguilar, Antonio Toca Fernández, Rámon Torres Martinéz, Francisco Treviño Loustaunau, Héctor Velasquez Moreno, José Luis Cortez

Delgado, Rutilo Malacara de Léon
Design Team Enrique Peña Mendoza, Gustavo Frias Fuentes
Structural Engineering Ingeniero Heriberto Izquierdo
Civil Engineering Ingeniero Heriberto Izquierdo
Electrical Engineering INAKEN S.A.
Environmental Engineering INAKEN S.A.
Approximate Cost US$ 2,500,000
Site Area 10,171 m^2
Building Area 6,900 m^2 (warehouse), 1,550 m^2 (office buildings), 8,450 m^2 (total)
Total Floor Area 7,714 m^2
Photographer Alberto Moreno Guzman

Mexico

Architects **Augusto Quijano Arquitectos, S. C. P., Merida**
Award Winning Building **Rectoría de la Universidad del Mayab**

Award Award of Mexican Architecture 1996 (IV Biennial of Architecture, Silver Medal)
see page 100

Mexico

Architects **Francisco Serrano, Susana Garcia Fuertes, Mexico City**
Award Winning Building **Office Building Complex in the City Centre**
Location **Mexico City, Mexico**

Award Award of Mexican Architecture 1996 (IV Biennial of Architecture, Silver Medal)
Given by Federación de Colegios de Arquitectos de la República Mexicana
Prize Presentation 1996

Mexico

Architects **Ten Arquitectos (Enrique Norten), Mexico City**
Award Winning Building **Televisa Service Building**
Location **Mexico City, Mexico**

Award Award of Mexican Architecture 1996 (IV Biennial of Architecture, Silver Medal)
Given by Federación de Colegios de Arquitectos de la República Mexicana
Prize Presentation 1996

Morocco

Architects **Abdelkader Chekkouri, Rabat**
Award Winning Building **Oum Rabia**

Award Prix de l'Ordre National des Architèctes du Maroc (ERAC)
Given by Ordre National des Architèctes du Maroc
Prize Presentation 1996

Morocco

Architects **Rachid Haloui, Najib Bensouda, Serghini Slitini, Taoufik N'Fifi, Rabat**
Award Winning Building **An Nassim**

Award Prix de l'Ordre National des Architèctes du Maroc (ERAC Centre Nord)
Given by Ordre National des Architèctes du Maroc
Prize Presentation 1996

Morocco

Architects **Taoufik El Kadiri, Rabat**
Award Winning Building **Marmoucha**

Award Prix de l'Ordre National des Architèctes du Maroc (ERAC Centre)
Given by Ordre National des Architèctes du Maroc
Prize Presentation 1996

Morocco

Architects **Abdellatif Loutati, Mme Soumya Laraki, Rabat**
Award Winning Building **El Houda**

Award Prix de l'Ordre National des Architèctes du Maroc (ERAC Sud)
Given by Ordre National des Architèctes du Maroc
Prize Presentation 1996

Morocco

Architects **Abdelilah Slimani, Jamal Guessous, Ahmed Kharim, Rabat**
Award Winning Building **El Wifaq**

Award Prix de l'Ordre National des Architèctes du Maroc (ERAC Sud)
Given by Ordre National des Architèctes du Maroc
Prize Presentation 1996

The Netherlands

Award Winner **ABT Consulting Engineers, Arnhem**
Representative Building **Terminal West, Amsterdam Airport Schiphol**

Award BNA-Cube 1996 for the complete work of ABT Consulting Engineers
see page 102

Norway

Architect **Knut Hjeltnes, Oslo**
Award Winning Building **Semi-detached house for two families;**
   Andersen and Austenå / Løvdal
Location **Tonsenveien 25, Oslo, Norway**
Design and Construction Period **1991–1994**

Award Sundts Premie 1995
Given by Norske Arkitekters Landsforbund
Prize Presentation 1995
Members of the Jury Torstein Ramberg (Chairman), Morten Finnby,
   Marius Wormdahl, Evelyne Anderson
Design Team Knut Hjeltnes
Structural Engineering Terje Orlien
Approximate Cost NOK 1,600,000

Site Area 1,041 m^2
Building Area old house : 155.2 m^2 (rehabilitated; gross area); new extension:
   98.4 m^2 (gross area)

Norway

Architect **Hoem Kloster Schjelderup Tonning Sivilarkitekter, Stavanger**
Award Winning Building **Stavanger Aftenblad Office Building**
Location **Bryne, Norway**
Design and Construction Period **1991–1992**

Award Statens Byggeskikkpris 1995
Given by Norske Arkitekters Landsforbund
Prize Presentation October / 10 / 1995
Members of the Jury Ellen S. De Vibe, Einar Dahle, Per Christian Quale
Design Team Knut Hoem, Ole Tonning
Structural Engineering Taugbøll og Øverland A/S
Civil Engineering Taugbøll og Øverland A/S
Mechanical Engineering Taugbøll og Øverland A/S
Electrical Engineering El Plan A/S
Air Conditioning Consultant Stabel A/S
Interior Design Hoem Kloster Schjelderup Tonning Sivilarkitekter
Landscape Architecture Hoem Kloster Schjelderup Tonning Sivilarkitekter
Quantity Surveying Hoem Kloster Schjelderup Tonning Sivilarkitekter
Approximate Cost NOK 4,700,000

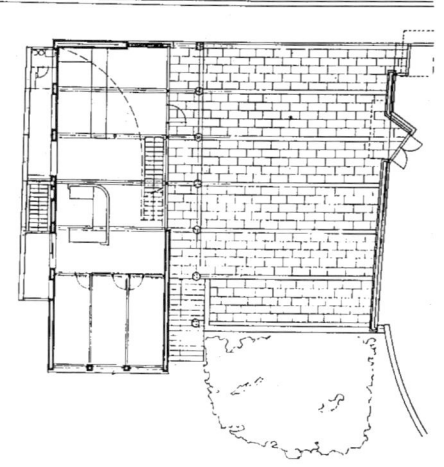

Site Area 180 m^2
Building Area 360 m^2
Total Floor Area 360 m^2

Paraguay

Architects **José Inssran, Luís Elgue, Christian Andersen, Asunción**
Award Winning Building **Asunción University (Sede de la Universidad Autónoma de Asunción)**
Location **Asunción, Paraguay**

Award Concurso del Edificio 1996
Given by Asociación Paraguaya de Arquitectos
Prize Presentation December / 30 / 1996

Peru

Architect **Javier Artadi Loyaza, Lima**
Award Winning Building **Factory (Fabrica Etiquetas Peruanas)**
Location **Peru**
Design and Construction Period **1989–1990**

Award VIII Biennial of Architecture (Honorable Mention)
Given by Colegio de Arquitectos del Peru
Prize Presentation November 1992
Design Team Javier Artadi Loyaza
Building Area 780 m^2

 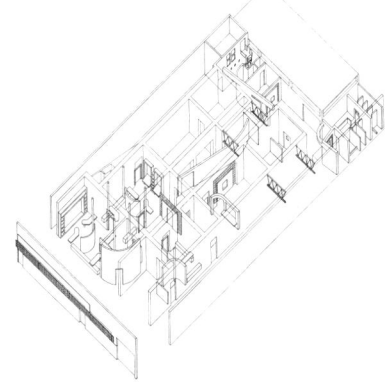

The Philippines

Architects **GF Partners, Makati City**
Award Winning Building **St. James the Greater Church**

Award Design Award of Excellence
Given by United Architects of the Philippines
Prize Presentation April / 12 / 1996
Members of the Jury United Architects of the Philippines Awards Committee

The Philippines

Architects **Francisco T. Manosa & Partners, Passig City**
Award Winning Building **Amanpulo Resort**

Award Design Award of Excellence
Given by United Architects of the Philippines
Prize Presentation April / 12 / 1996
Members of the Jury United Architects of the Philippines Awards Committee

The Philippines

Architect **Yolanda D. Reyes, Manila**
Award Winning Building **Caleruega Retreat Village**

Award Design Award in Architecture
Given by United Architects of the Philippines
Prize Presentation April / 12 / 1996
Members of the Jury United Architects of the Philippines Awards Committee

Poland

Architect **Stanislaw Niemczyk, Tychy**

Award SARP Honorary Award 1996
Given by SARP Stowarzyszenie Architektów Polkich

Prize Presentation December / 6 / 1995
Members of the Jury Krzysztof Chwalibóg, Romuald Loegler, Jacek Lenart, Andrzej Jagodzinski, Konrad Kucza Kuozynski

Portugal

Architect **Álvaro Siza Vieira, Porto**
Award Winning Building **Castro & Melo Building**

Award Prémio Secil de Arquitectura 1996
see page 106

Russia

Architects **G. Astafiev, B. Klimov, I. Vinogradsky, Moscow**
Award Winning Building **State Tretyakov Gallery**
Location **Moskow, Lavrushinsky Pereulok, Russia**
Design and Construction Period **1981–1994**

Award 1) "Architecture-95"– 3rd Russian Festival (Winner);
  2) State Prize of the Russian Federation
Given by 1) Union of Architects of Russia; 2) Commission of the President
  of the Russian Federation
Prize Presentation 1) September / 12-13 / 1995; 2) August 1996
Members of the Jury 1) V.S. Yegerev, V.P. Davidenko, V.N. Bogdanov,
  N.F. Gunenkov, V. M. Kibirev, M.O. Kondiain, V.D. Krassilnikov, M.V. Krishtal,
  N.N. Nikonov, P.I. Yushkanzev; 2) L. Vavakin, U. Gnedovsky, V. Davidenko,
  A. Ikonnikov, V. Krasilnikov, V. Orehov, V. Popov, A. Stepanov
Design Team I. Stoletov, A. Cheskidov
Structural Engineering M. Berklaid
Civil Engineering A. Beliaev, V. Glazunovsky
Mechanical Engineering R. Murashkin

Electrical Engineering V. Grigorichev
Acoustic Engineering J. Furman
Air Conditioning Consultant A. Volkov,
  N. Grozovskaja
Lighting Consultant E. Ikoeva
Life Safety Consultant T. Ershova
Interior Design G. Astafiev,
  A. Dzershkovich, B. Klimov
Landscape Architecture E. Semenova-
  Prozorovskaja
Quantity Surveying G. Astafiev,
  B. Klimov
Site Area 25,000 m²
Building Area 13,200 m²
Total Floor Area 9,000 m²
  (exhibition area)
Photographer V. Svetashkov

Russia

Architects **A.Ye. Kharitonov, Yu.P. Ossin, Ye.N. Pestov, M.V. Filyushkin,
  S.G. Popov, Nizhni Novgorod**
Award Winning Building **Administration and Bank Building**
Location **Gorky Street, Nizhni Novgorod, Russia**

Award "Architecture-95"– 3rd Russian Festival (Diploma 2nd degree)
Given by Union of Architects of Russia
Prize Presentation September / 12-13 / 1995
Members of the Jury V.S. Yegerev, V.P. Davidenko, V.N. Bogdanov,
  N.F. Gunenkov, V.M. Kibirev, M.O. Kondiain, V.D. Krassilnikov, M.V. Krishtal,
  N.N. Nikonov, P.I. Yushkanzev

Serbia

Architect **Slobodan Jevdjenović, Belgrade**
Award Winning Building **Pedestrian Bridge with Trade Centre**

Award Prize for Best Building in 1995
see page 112

Serbia

Architects **PBA Architects, Arkansas, USA**
Award Winning Building **Springdale Town Hall, Police and Courts**
Location **Springdale, Arkansas, USA**
Design and Construction Period **1993–1995**

Award Special Recognition for Project Executed Abroad
Given by SAS Union of Architects of Serbia
Prize Presentation February / 25 / 1996
Members of the Jury Branislav Ivković, Branislav Mitrović, Miodrag Jovanović,
  Milos Perović, Dragan Ivanović
Design Team Perry L. Butcher (Principal/Project Architect), Stanko Gaković
  (Design Architect), James Mayer (Project Manager), Delvin Nation (Program
  Manager), David Franks, Eva Kultermann, Tim Kwasney, Audy Lack, Eliot Neel,
  Clayton Spears, David Wilgus (Project Team)
Consultant Roth / Sheppard, Denver
Structural Engineering Joseph Looney, Springdale
Civil Engineering Neal Albright, Fayetteville

Mechanical Engineering PBA: R.D. Henard
Electrical Engineering Al Davis Engineering, Little Rock
Lighting Consultant Al Davis Engineering, Little Rock
Quantity Surveying PBA (James Trimble)
Approximate Cost US$ 3,225,000
Site Area 1.4 ha / Building Area 2,500 m²
Total Floor Area 4,300 m²
Photographer Eliot Neel

Serbia

Architects **Bogdan Slavica, Svetislav Martinović, Belgrade**
Award Winning Building **Hotel Samotlor**
Location **Russia**

Award Special Prize
Given by SAS Union of Architects of Serbia
Prize Presentation February / 23 / 1996
Members of the Jury Branislav Mitrović (president of SAS), Milos Perović,
  Miodrag Jovanović (president DANS)

Singapore

Architects **Architects 61 Pte. Ltd., Singapore**
Award Winning Building **Lippo Centre**
Location **Singapore, Singapore**

Award 4th SIA Architectural Design Award (Honorable Mention; Category:
  Office Buildings)

Given by SIA Singapore Institute of Architects
Prize Presentation November / 27 / 1995
Members of the Jury Richard Frewer, Hijias Bin Kasturi, Syahrul Syarif,
  Eric Lye, Abdul Hussain, Goh Chong Chia

Singapore

Architects **Design Environment Group, Singapore**
Award Winning Building **Radio Broadcasting Facility**
Location **Singapore, Singapore**

Award 4th SIA Architectural Design Award (Honorable Mention; Category:
  Office Buildings)

Given by SIA Singapore Institute of Architects
Prize Presentation November / 27 / 1995
Members of the Jury Richard Frewer, Hijias Bin Kasturi, Ir Syahrul Syarif,
  Eric Lye, Abdul Hussain, Goh Chong Chia

Singapore

Architects **DP Architects Pte Ltd, Singapore**
Award Winning Building **Bugis Junction**

Award 4th SIA Architectural Design Award (Honorable Mention)
see page 114

Singapore

Architects **Forum Architects (Lim Cheng Kooi, Architect in Charge;
  Ho Sweet Woon, Partner in Charge), Singapore**
Award Winning Building **Semi-Detached House at 14C Sian Tuan Avenue**

Award SIA 4th Architectural Design Award (Honorable Mention; Category:
  Terrace / Semi-Detached Houses)
see page 116

Singapore

Architects **T. R. Hamzah & Yeang Sdn. Bhd., Singapore**
Award Winning Building **Selangor Turf Club**
Location **Selangor**

Award 4th SIA Architectural Design Award (Honorable Mention; Category:
  Overseas Project)

Given by SIA Singapore Institute of Architects
Prize Presentation November / 27 / 1995
Members of the Jury Richard Frewer, Hijias Bin Kasturi, Syahrul Syarif,
  Eric Lye, Abdul Hussain, Goh Chong Chia

Singapore

Architects **Kerry Hill Architects, Singapore**
Award Winning Building **The Datai, Langkawi**
Location **Langkawi, Indonesia**

Award 4th SIA Architectural Design Award (Honorable Mention; Category:
  Overseas Projects)

Given by SIA Singapore Institute of Architects
Prize Presentation November / 27 / 1995
Members of the Jury Richard Frewer, Hijias Bin Kasturi, Syahrul Syarif,
  Eric Lye, Abdul Hussain, Goh Chong Chia

Architects **Kerry Hill Architects, Singapore**

Award Winning Building **Chedi Bandung, Indonesia**

Location **Bandung, Indonesia**

Award 4th SIA Architectural Design Award (Honorable Mention; Category: Overseas Project)

Given by SIA Singapore Institute of Architects

Prize Presentation November / 27 / 1995

Members of the Jury Richard Frewer, Hijias Bin Kasturi, Ir Syahrul Syarif, Eric Lye, Abdul Hussain, Goh Chong Chia

---

Singapore

Architects **KenLou Architects, Singapore**

Award Winning Building **Semi-Detached House**

Location **115 Dunbar Walk, Singapore 459423, Singapore**

Design and Construction Period **February–December 1994**

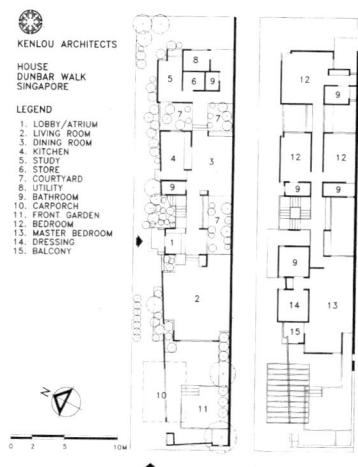

Award 4th SIA Architectural Design Award (Category: Terrace / Semi-Detached Houses)

Given by SIA Singapore Institute of Architects

Prize Presentation November / 27 / 1995

Members of the Jury Richard Frewer, Hijias Bin Kasturi, Syahrul Syarif, Eric Lye, Abdul Hussain, Goh Chong Chia

Design Team Ken Lou, Michael Lam, Leo Agus, Amy Lew

Structural Engineering MTech Consultants

Civil Engineering MTech Consultants

Interior Design KenLou Architects

Landscape Architecture Kern Teck Design Pte. Ltd.

Quantity Surveying RJ Consultants Pte. Ltd.

Approximate Cost S$ 650,000

Site Area 369 m²

Building Area 145 m²

Total Floor Area 309 m²

Photographer Ace Commercial Pte. Ltd.

Singapore

Architects **KNTA Architects, Singapore**

Award Winning Building **No. 2 Cluny Park (Checks House)**

Location **Singapore, Singapore**

Design and Construction Period **1992–1993**

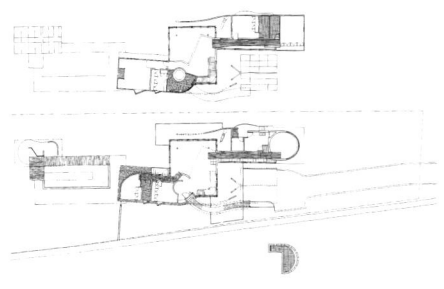

Award 4th SIA Architectural Design Award (Honorable Mention; Category: Individual Houses)

Given by SIA Singapore Institute of Architects

Prize Presentation November / 27 / 1995

Members of the Jury Abdul Hussain, Eric Lye, Hijjas Bin Kasturi, Richard Frewer, Syahrul Syarif, Goh Chong Chia

Design Team Kay Ngee Tan (Principal in Charge), Teck Kiam Tan (Principal), Choo Hin Yin, Michael Chorney, Finbarr Finn, Look Chee Meng, Bruce Ngam, Ben Smart, Yap Mong Lin, Jack Yeo

Structural Engineering Joseph Huang, OAP Singapore

Civil Engineering OAP Singapore

Interior Design KNTA Architects

Quantity Surveying CCL Chartered Surveyors

Approximate Cost S$ 1,500,000

Site Area 1,664.9 m²

Building Area 337.82 m²

Total Floor Area 545.08 m²

Photographer Dennis Gilbert

Singapore

Architects **OD Architects, Meng Ta Cheang, Singapore**
Award Winning Building **Hua Zhong Chinese High School**
Location **Bukit Timah Road, Singapore**

Award 4th SIA Architectural Design Award
Given by SIA Singapore Institute of Architects
Prize Presentation November / 27 / 1995
Members of the Jury Richard Frewer, Hijias Bin Kasturi, Syahrul Syarif,
  Eric Lye, Abdul Hussain, Goh Chong Chia
Structural Engineering TY Lin (Southeast Asia) Pte. Ltd.
Civil Engineering TY Lin (Southeast Asia) Pte. Ltd.
Mechanical Engineering Parson Brickerhoff Consultants Pte. Ltd.
Electrical Engineering Parson Brickerhoff Consultants Pte. Ltd.
Landscape Architecture Keikan Sekkei (S) Pte. Ltd.
Quantity Surveying Rider Hunt Levett and Bailey
Approximate Cost S$ 30,000,000

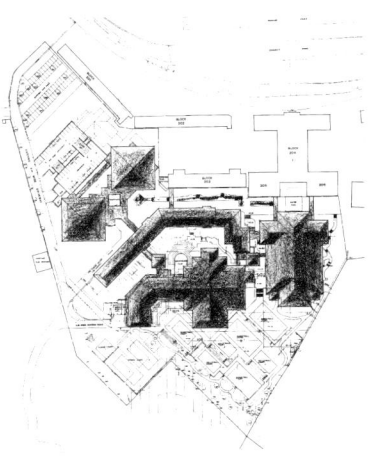

Site Area 137,600 m^2 / *Building Area* 22,000 m^2
Photographer Liew S. Shoon

Singapore

Architects **P & T Consultants Pte. Ltd. (Architects), Singapore**
Award Winning Building **American International Assurance (AIA) Tower**
Location **Robinson Road, Singapore**
Design and Construction Period **1990–1993**

Award 4th SIA Architectural Design Award (Honorable Mention; Category:
  Office Buildings)
Given by SIA Singapore Institute of Architects
Prize Presentation November / 27 / 1995
Members of the Jury Goh Hup Chor, Philip Ng
Design Team Alan Low K G, Thomas Ho, Max Ho
Structural Engineering P & T Consultants Pte. Ltd.
Civil Engineering P & T Consultants Pte. Ltd.
Mechanical Engineering Rust JRP Pte. Ltd.
Electrical Engineering Rust JRP Pte. Ltd.

Acoustic Engineering CCW Acoustic
  Pte. Ltd.
Air Conditioning Consultant Rust
  JRP Pte. Ltd.
Lighting Consultant Tino Kwan
  Lighting Consultants
Interior Design P & T Consultants
  Pte. Ltd.
Quantity Surveying PIBS Pte. Ltd.
Approximate Cost S$ 53,000,000
Site Area 1,131.9 m^2
Building Area 1,030 m^2
Total Floor Area 10,250 m^2

Singapore

Architects **P & T Consultants Pte. Ltd. (Architects), Singapore**
Award Winning Building **Tampines New Town Public Housing**
Location **Tampines, Street 45, Singapore**

Award 4th SIA Architectural Design Award (Honorable Mention; Category:
  Public Housing)
Given by SIA Singapore Institute of Architects
Prize Presentation November / 27 / 1995
Members of the Jury Richard Frewer, Hijias Bin Kasturi, Syahrul Syarif,
  Eric Lye, Abdul Hussain, Goh Chong Chia
Design Team Alan Low K G, Choy Meng Yew, Max Ho
Structural Engineering P & T Consultants Pte. Ltd.
Mechanical Engineering P & T Consultants Pte. Ltd.
Landscape Architecture Keikan Sekkei (S) Pte. Ltd.
Quantity Surveying KPK Quantity Surveyors

Approximate Cost S$ 70,000,000
Site Area 51,230 m^2
Building Area 103,681.35 m^2
Total Floor Area 103,681.35 m^2
Photographer Mr Amir

Singapore

Architects **RDC Architects Pte. Ltd., Singapore**
Award Winning Building **La Meyer Condominium Housing Development**
Location **Singapore, Singapore**

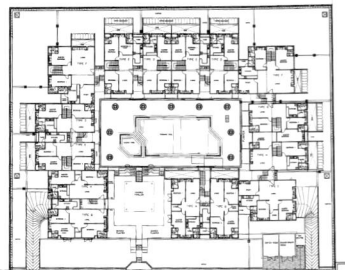

Award 4th SIA Architectural Design Award (Category: Apartments /
  Condominiums, Low Rise)
Given by SIA Singapore Institute of Architects
Prize Presentation November / 27 / 1995
Members of the Jury Richard Frewer, Hijias Bin Kasturi, Syahrul Syarif,
  Eric Lye, Abdul Hussain, Goh Chong Chia
Design Team Chan Fook Pong, James Leow Ban Hwa
Structural Engineering B&T Consultants
Civil Engineering B&T Consultants
Mechanical Engineering Design & Management Services
Electrical Engineering Design & Management Services
Landscape Architecture Peridin Asia Pte. Ltd.

Quantity Surveying Construction
  Technology Pte. Ltd.
Approximate Cost S$ 7,250,000
Site Area 4,771.4 m²
Total Floor Area 5,221.7 m²

Singapore

Architects **RDC Architects Pte. Ltd., Singapore**
Award Winning Building **NTU Halls of Residence**
Location **Singapore, Singapore**

Award 4th SIA Architectural Design Award (Honorable Mention; Category:
  Hostels & Dormitories)
Given by SIA Singapore Institute of Architects
Prize Presentation November / 27 / 1995
Members of the Jury Abdul Hussain, Eric Lye, Hijjas Bin Kasturi,
  Richard Frewer, Syahrul Syarif, Goh Chong Chia
Design Team Kenneth Chen Koon Lap, Kenneth Loh Kai Teck, Rita Soh
  Siow Lan, Philip Bay Joo Hwa
Structural Engineering Tan Ee Ping & Partners
Civil Engineering Tan Ee Ping & Partners
Mechanical Engineering Design & Management Services

Electrical Engineering Design & Management Services
Quantity Surveying Building Cost & Management Consultants
Approximate Cost S$ 70,000,000
Site Area 106,970 m²
Building Area 56,707.15 m²
Total Floor Area 58,163.13 m²

Singapore

Architects **RichardHo Architects, Singapore**
Award Winning Building **No. 12 Koon Seng Road**

Award 4th SIA Architectural Design Award (Category: Conservation)
see page 118

Singapore

Architects **Andrew Tan Architects Pte., Singapore**
Award Winning Building **Punggol Community Club**
Location **Hougang Avenue 6, Singapore**
Design and Construction Period **1989–1992**

Award 4th SIA Architectural Design Award (Honorable Mention)
Given by SIA Singapore Institute of Architects
Prize Presentation November / 27 / 1995
Members of the Jury Richard Frewer, Hijias Bin Kasturi, Syahrul Syarif,
  Eric Lye, Abdul Hussain, Goh Chong Chia
Design Team Andrew Tan Chye Hee & Siew Man Kok

Structural Engineering Oscar Faber Consultants Pte. Ltd.
Civil Engineering Oscar Faber Consultants Pte. Ltd.
Mechanical Engineering Y.P. Chee & Associates

Electrical Engineering Y.P. Chee & Associates
Air Conditioning Consultant Kian Gwan Engineering Pte. Ltd.
Lighting Consultant Lightcraft Pte. Ltd.
Fire Safety Consultant Nil-Burns System Pte. Ltd.
Landscape Architecture Nyee Phoe Flower Garden Pte. Ltd.

Approximate Cost S$ 5,200,000
Site Area 4,000 m²
Building Area 3,683.238 m²
Total Floor Area 3,869.998 m²

Singapore

Architect **Tang Guan Bee, Singapore**
Award Winning Building **Abelia**
Location **2A Ardmore Park, Singapore**
Design and Construction Period **1990–1992**

 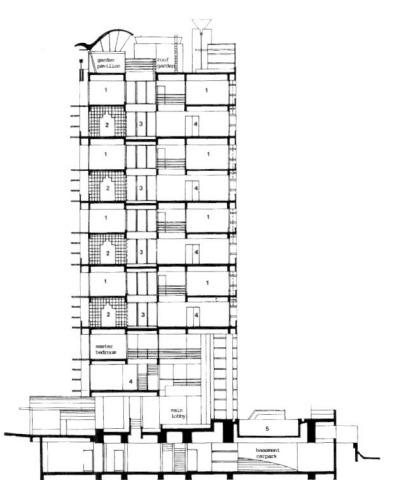

Award 4th SIA Architectural Design Award (Category: Apartments /
　Condominiums, High Rise)
Given by SIA Singapore Institute of Architects
Prize Presentation November / 27 / 1995
Members of the Jury Richard Frewer, Hijias Bin Kasturi, Syahrul Syarif, Eric Lye,
　Abdul Hussain, Goh Chong Chia
Design Team Tangguanbee Architects
Structural Engineering HCE Engineers Partnership
Mechanical Engineering Servitech Consultants
Electrical Engineering Servitech Consultants
Landscape Architecture PDAA Design
Quantity Surveying OTN Building Cost Consultants
Approximate Cost S$ 6,000,000
Site Area 1,289.3 m²

Building Area 1,220.50 m²
Total Floor Area 983.83 m²
Photographer Dennis Gilbert

Singapore

Architect **Tang Guan Bee, Singapore**
Award Winning Building **The Market Place**
Location **348 Bedok Road, Singapore**
Design and Construction Period **1993–1994**

 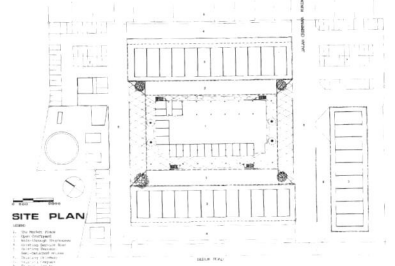

Award 4th SIA Architectural Design Award (Category: Community Buildings)
Given by SIA Singapore Institute of Architects
Prize Presentation November / 27 / 1995
Members of the Jury Richard Frewer, Hijias Bin Kasturi, Syahrul Syarif,
　Eric Lye, Abdul Hussain, Goh Chong Chia
Design Team Tangguanbee Architects
Structural Engineering Sim Bee Teck Associates
Mechanical Engineering United Project Consultants Pte. Ltd.
Electrical Engineering United Project Consultants Pte. Ltd.
Quantity Surveying Perspective Engineering Management Consultants Pte. Ltd.
Approximate Cost S$ 3,300,000

Site Area 4,264 m²
Building Area 5,826 m²
Total Floor Area 4,855 m²
Photographer Dennis Gilbert

Singapore

Architects **Timur Designs, Singapore**
Award Winning Building **No. 2 Makepeace Road**
Location **Singapore, Singapore**

Award 4th SIA Architectural Design Award (Honorable Mention; Category:
　Residential Houses)
Given by SIA Singapore Institute of Architects
Prize Presentation November / 27 / 1995
Members of the Jury Richard Frewer, Hijias Bin Kasturi, Syahrul Syarif,
　Eric Lye, Abdul Hussain, Goh Chong Chia

Singapore

Architects **Alfred Wong Partnership Pte. Ltd.; Planning & Design Department Engineering Division, Port of Singapore Authority**
Award Winning Building **Keppel Distripark**
Location **Singapore, Singapore**

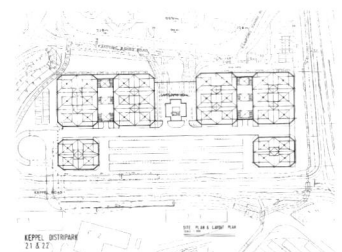

Award 4th SIA Architectural Design Award (Honorable Mention; Category: Industrial Buildings)
Given by SIA Singapore Institute of Architects
Prize Presentation November / 27 / 1995
Members of the Jury Richard Frewer, Hijias Bin Kasturi, Syahrul Syarif, Eric Lye, Abdul Hussain, Goh Chong Chia
Design Team Planning & Design Department Engineering Division, Port of Singapore Authority; Alfred Wong Partnership Pte. Ltd.
Engineering Planning & Design Department Engineering Division, Port of Singapore Authority; Alfred Wong Partnership Pte. Ltd.
Interior Design Planning & Design Department Engineering Division, Port of Singapore Authority; Alfred Wong Partnership Pte. Ltd.

Landscape Architecture Alfred Wong Partnership Pte. Ltd.
Quantity Surveying Planning & Design Department Engineering Division, Port of Singapore Authority; Alfred Wong Partnership Pte. Ltd.
Approximate Cost US$ 142,700,000
Site Area 23 ha
Building Area 140,391 m^2
Total Floor Area 125,638 m^2
Photographer Ang Choon Kiat, Alfred Wong Partnership Pte. Ltd.

Singapore

Architects **Alfred Wong Partnership Pte. Ltd. (Alfred H.K. Wong and Goh Peng Thong, Architects-in-Charge), Singapore**
Award Winning Building **United Overseas Bank Building in Xiamen**
Location **Hu Bin North Road, Xiamen, Fujian, China**

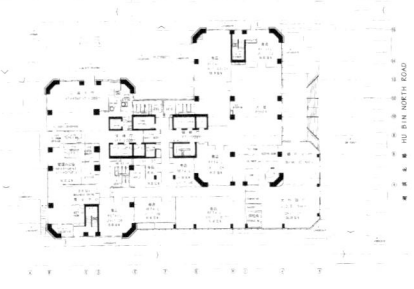

Award 1) Xiamen City Top Ten Best Building Award; 2) Best Quality Building Award
Given by 1) Xiamen City Municipal Governmental Technical Departments and Xiamen Media; 2) Xiamen Quality Control Department
Prize Presentation 1) December 1996; 2) September / 10 / 1996
Members of the Jury 1) Xiamen City Municipal, Government Technical Departments, Xiamen Media and voted by all the residents of Xiamen City; 2) Xiamen Quality Control Department
Design Team Alfred Wong Partnership Pte. Ltd. (Alfred H.K. Wong and Goh Peng Thong, Architects-in-Charge)
Structural Engineering T.Y. Lin South East Asia Pte. Ltd. with Fujian Design Institute
Civil Engineering T.Y. Lin South East Asia Pte. Ltd. and Fujian Design Institute
Mechanical Engineering Parsons Brinkerhoff Consultants Pte. Ltd. and Fujian Design Institute

Electrical Engineering Parsons Brinkerhoff Consultants Pte. Ltd. and Fujian Design Institute
Interior Design Total Integrated Design Pte. Ltd.
Landscape Architecture Alfred Wong Partnership Pte. Ltd.
Quantity Surveying BEC Consultants
Approximate Cost Rmb 250,000,000 (US$ 40,000,000)
Site Area 8,700 m^2
Building Area 38,875 m^2
Total Floor Area 38,875 m^2

Slovakia

Architect **Ladislav Foltyn, Bratislava**

Award Prize of Emil Bellus / Cena Emila Bellusa
Given by SAS Spolok Architektov Slovenska

Prize Presentation July / 1 / 1996
Members of the Jury Ivan Gurtler (President of SAS) and Members of the Presidium

Slovakia

Architects **CD-Team (Victória Cvengrosová, Virgil Droppa), Bratislava**

Award Prize of Dusan Jurkovic / Cena D. Jurkovica

Given by Spolok Architektov Slovenska
Prize Presentation December 1996
Members of the Jury Il'ja Skocek, Dana Borutová

South Africa

Architects **Stefan Antoni Architects, Cape Town**
Award Winning Building **House Santer**
Location **Bantry Bay, Cape Town, South Africa**
Design and Construction Period **1994–1995**

Award ISAA Award of Merit 1995
Given by ISAA Institute of South African Architects
Prize Presentation November/December 1995
Members of the Jury Gavin Pike, Debbie Preller, Anya van der Merwe-
  Miszweski, Gawie Fagan, Graham Jacobs
Design Team Stefan Antoni, G. Wright, H. Ellis & C. Bush
Structural Engineering T. Philotheou

Interior Design Stefan Antoni Architects
Approximate Cost R 600,000
Building Area 250 m²
Photographers J. de Villiers, Stefan Antoni

South Africa

Architects **Henri Comrie with Taljaard Carter Architects, Pretoria**
Award Winning Building **The PFG Glass Centre**
Location **Midrand, Transvaal, South Africa**
Design and Construction Period **1993–1994**

 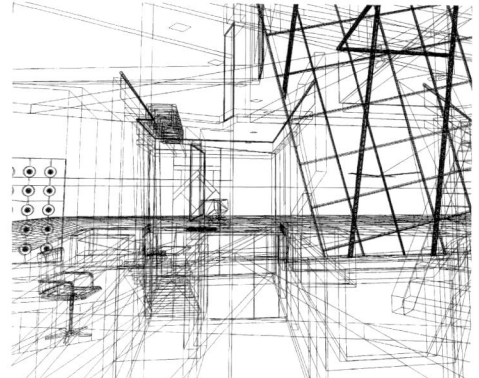

Award ISAA Award of Merit 1995
Given by ISAA Institute of South African Architects
Prize Presentation October 1995
Members of the Jury Roger Fisher, Muhammed Mayet, Lone Poulsen
Design Team Henri Comrie, Anton Comrie
Structural Engineering Ove Arup (Johannesburg)
Mechanical Engineering Spoormaker & Partners
Electrical Engineering Chorn, Goldman, Wilkin
Interior Design Dieter Üllrich
Landscape Architecture Green Inc. / John Drummond
Quantity Surveying Taljaard Meyer Storm

Approximate Cost R 3,300,000
Site Area 4,000 m² / *Building Area* 600 m² / *Total Floor Area* 1,020 m²
Photographers David Reid, Cornel van der Westhuizen

South Africa

Architects **Erasmus, Rushmere, Reid Architects, Johannesburg**
Associated Architects **Flint & Lear Architects, Johannesburg**
Award Winning Building **House Pearson**
Location **South Africa**

Award ISAA Award of Merit 1995
Given by ISAA Institute of South African Architects
Prize Presentation November 1995
Members of the Jury Jo Noero, Danie Theron, Stephanie Volpe

South Africa

Architects **GAPP Architects and Urban Designers, Cape Town
  and Johannesburg**
Associated Architects **Floris Smith and Meyer Pienaar, Johannesburg**
Award Winning Building **Sandton Library and Art Gallery**
Location **Sandton, Johannesburg, South Africa**
Design and Construction Period **1989–1994**

Award ISAA Award of Merit 1995
Given by ISAA Institute of South African Architects
Prize Presentation 1995
Members of the Jury Roger Fisher, Muhammed Mayet, Lone Poulsen
Design Team Pedro Roos, Glen Gallagher, Sylvio Rech, Karen Wygers,

Award ISAA Award of Merit 1995
Given by ISAA Institute of South African Architects
Prize Presentation 1995
Members of the Jury Roger Fisher, Muhammed Mayet, Lone Poulsen
Design Team Pedro Roos, Glen Gallagher, Sylvio Rech, Karen Wygers,
  Therese Christofidis, John Downie, Adrian Davids, Cheryl Durham,
  Nina Cohen

South Africa

Architects **Jo Noero Architects, Parkview**
Award Winning Building **Funda Community College – Soweto**
Location **Soweto, South Africa**

Award ISAA Award of Merit 1995
Given by ISAA Institute of South African Architects
Prize Presentation November 1995
Members of the Jury Roger Fisher, Lone Poulsen, Muhammed Mayet

South Africa

Architects **Jo Noero Architects, Parkview**
Associated Architects **Meirelles Lawson Architects, Parkview**
Award Winning Building **Guguletu Multisport Complex**

Award ISAA Award of Merit 1995
Given by ISAA Institute of South African Architects
Prize Presentation November 1995
Members of the Jury Gavin Pike, Debbie Preller, Anya van der Merwe-
    Miszweski, Gawie Fagan, Graham Jacobs

South Africa

Architects **Kate Otten Architects, Johannesburg**
Award Winning Building **House Staude**
Location **Melville, Johannesburg, South Africa**
Design and Construction Period **1993–1995**

Award ISAA Award of Merit 1995
Given by ISAA Institute of South African Architects
Prize Presentation November 1995
Members of the Jury Roger Fisher, Muhammed Mayet, Lone Poulsen,
Design Team Kate Otten
Structural Engineering Resnovanu Associates
Interior Design Kate Otten
Landscape Architecture Kate Otten
Approximate Cost R 500,000
Site Area 709 m²
Building Area 252 m²

Total Floor Area 330 m² (all floors and garage included)
Photographer Kate Otten

South Africa

Architects **Graham Parker, GAP, with John Blair, Johannesburg**
Award Winning Building **St. George's Pavilion**
Location **South Africa**

Award ISAA Award of Merit 1995
Given by ISAA Institute of South African Architects
Prize Presentation November 1995
Members of the Jury Jo Noero, Danie Theron, Stephanie Volpe

South Africa

Architects **Meyer Pienaar Architects, Johannesburg**
Award Winning Building **Ricardo Mulder Library**
Location **Edenvale, South Africa**
Design and Construction Period **1991–1994**

Award ISAA Award of Merit 1995
Given by ISAA Institute of South African Architects
Prize Presentation November 1995
Members of the Jury Roger Fisher, Muhammed Mayet, Lone Poulsen
Design Team Patrick McInerney (Principal Designer), Marcela Reynoso
Structural Engineering Van Heerden Calitz & Hayes
Civil Engineering Van Heerden Calitz & Hayes

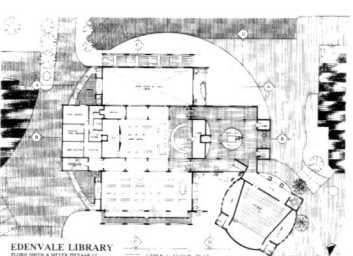

Mechanical Engineering Everitt & Germishuizen
Electrical Engineering Bell Page & Pilling
Air Conditioning Consultant Everitt & Germishuizen

Lighting Consultant   Bell Page & Pilling

Interior Design   Meyer Pienaar Architects

Quantity Surveying   Schoombie Hartmann Inc.

Contractor   Abcon

Approximate Cost   R 7,000,000

Site Area   4,000 m²

Building Area   1,500 m²

Total Floor Area   4,000 m²

Photographers   François Pienaar, Paul Gordon

South Africa

Architect   **Johann C. Slee, Johannesburg**

Award Winning Building   **Glen Towy Holiday Cottage**

Location   **Underberg Natal Midlands, South Africa**

Award   ISAA Award of Merit 1995

Given by   ISAA Institute of South African Architects

Prize Presentation   October / 6 / 1995

Members of the Jury   David Yuill, Ismail Cassimjee, Walter Peters,
   Janina Masojoda, Dean Jay, Michael Lewis

Design Team   Johann C. Slee

Structural Engineering   Owner

Lighting Consultant   Owner

Interior Design   Owner

Landscape Architecture   Owner

Approximate Cost   R 800,000

Building Area   430 m²

Total Floor Area   350 m²

Photographer   Johann C. Slee

South Africa

Architects   **Stafford Associate Architects with Dirksen Blumenfeld &
   Krause, Durban**

Award Winning Building   **Metlife, 391 Smith Street, Durban**

Location   **Durban, South Africa**

Award   ISAA Award of Merit 1995

Given by   ISAA Institute of South African Architects

Prize Presentation   November 1995

Members of the Jury   David Yuill, Ismail Caffimjee, Walter Peters,
   Janina Masojoda, Dean Jay, Michael Lewis

Spain

Architect   **Rafael Moneo Vallés, Madrid**

Representative Building   **Construction of the new Town Hall of Murcia,
   Plaza del Cardenal Belluga**

Award   1) 1996 Pritzker Architecture Prize; 2) Gold Medal of the UIA
   International Union of Architects

see page 126

Spain

Architect   **Rafael Moneo Vallés, Madrid**

Representative Building   **Pilar & Joan Miró Foundation, Palma de Mallorca**

Award   1) 1996 Pritzker Architecture Prize; 2) Gold Medal of the UIA
   International Union of Architects

see page 128

Spain

Architect   **Joaquín Vaquero Palacios**

Representative Building   **Central Electrica de Proaza**

Award   Medalla de Oro de la Arquitectura

see page 130

Sri Lanka

Architects **Nela de Zoysa Design Corporation (Pvt.) Ltd., Colombo**
Award Winning Building **Seylan Bank – Mt. Lavinia**
Location **Mt. Lavinia, Sri Lanka**
Design and Construction Period **1994–1995**

Award SLIA Design Award 1996 (Category:
Renovations–Additions–Conversions)
Given by SLIA Sri Lanka Institute of Architects
Prize Presentation February / 15 / 1996
Members of the Jury Justin Samarasekera, Geoffrey Bawa, Panini Tennakoon,
    Channa Daswatte, G.K. de Zoysa, Jayantha Perera
Design Team Nela de Zoysa Design Corporation (Pvt.) Ltd.
Structural Engineering Milroy Perera
Civil Engineering Milroy Perera
Mechanical Engineering Electro Serv (Pvt.) Ltd.
Electrical Engineering Electro Serv (Pvt.) Ltd.
Air Conditioning Consultant Electro Serv (Pvt.) Ltd.

Interior Design Nela de Zoysa Design Corporation (Pvt.) Ltd.
Landscape Architecture Nela de Zoysa Design Corporation (Pvt.) Ltd.
Quantity Surveying Nela de Zoysa Design Corporation (Pvt.) Ltd.
Approximate Cost Sri Lankan Rupees 10,000,000
Site Area 910 m²
Building Area 450 m²
Total Floor Area 650 m²

Sri Lanka

Architects **Nela de Zoysa Design Corporation (Pvt.) Ltd., Colombo**
Award Winning Building **Refurbishment of the Bank of Ceylon Auditorium**
Location **Bank of Ceylon-Head Quarters, Fort, Colombo, Sri Lanka**
Design and Construction Period **1994–1995**

Award Creative Use of Colour in Buildings
Given by SLIA Sri Lanka Institute of Architects with CIC Paints
Prize Presentation February 1996
Members of the Jury Justin Samarasekera, Geoffrey Bawa, Panini Tennakoon,
    Channa Daswatte, G.K. de Zoysa, Jayantha Perera
Design Team Nela de Zoysa Design Corporation (Pvt.) Ltd.
Interior Design Nela de Zoysa Design Corporation (Pvt.) Ltd.

Approximate Cost Sri Lankan Rupees 5,000,000
Total Floor Area 375 m²

Sri Lanka

Architect **Lochi Gunaratna, Colombo**
Award Winning Building **Laboratories for the Tea Research Institute**
Location **Talawakele, Sri Lanka**
Design and Construction Period **1969–1973**

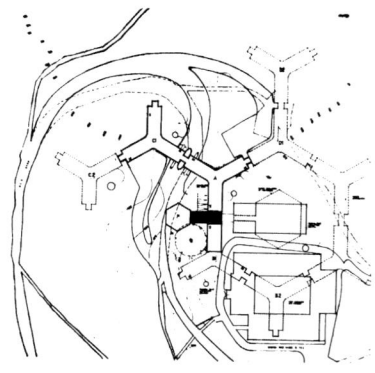 

Award SLIA Design Award 1996 (Category: Building in Non-Urban Context)
Given by SLIA Sri Lanka Institute of Architects
Prize Presentation February / 15 / 1996
Members of the Jury Justin Samarasekera, Geoffrey M. Bawa
Design Team Lochi Gunartana, V.N.C. Gunasekera (Design Assistant)
Structural Engineering State Engineering Corporation of Sri Lanka
Civil Engineering State Engineering Corporation of Sri Lanka
Mechanical Engineering State Engineering Corporation of Sri Lanka
Electrical Engineering State Engineering Corporation of Sri Lanka
Environmental Engineering State Engineering Corporation of Sri Lanka

Quantity Surveying State Engineering Corporation of Sri Lanka
Total Floor Area 4,000 m² (stage 1)
Photographers D.L. Coonghe, K.C. Perera

Sri Lanka

Architect **Vinod A. Jayasinghe, Colombo**

Award Winning Building **Jetwing House (Office Interior)**

Location **46 / 26, Nawm Mawatha, Colombo – 02, Sri Lanka**

Design and Construction Period **1995–1996**

 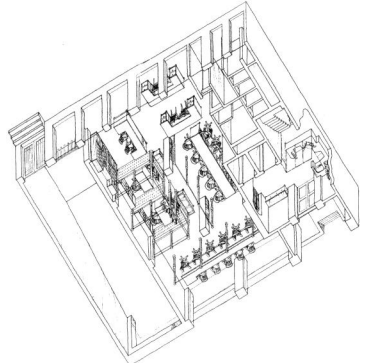

Award SLIA Design Award 1996 (Category: Interior Design)

Given by SLIA Sri Lanka Institute of Architects

Prize Presentation February / 15 / 1996

Members of the Jury Geoffrey Bawa, K.L. Gunaratne, Justin Samarasekara,
Ghanna Daswatte, S.W. Molligoda

Design Team Vinod A. Jayasinghe

Engineering Architects & Engineers for the Building Mihindu Keerthirathna
Associates Ltd.

Interior Design Vinod A. Jayasinghe

Quantity Surveying Environmental Studios

Approximate Cost US$ 100,000

Photographer Vajira Dharmaratne

Sri Lanka

Architect **Vinod A. Jayasinghe, Colombo**

Award Winning Building **Tropical Villas Hotel**

Location **Galle Road, Moragalla, Beruwala, Sri Lanka**

Design and Construction Period **1993–1995**

Award SLIA Design Award 1996 (Open Category)

Given by SLIA Sri Lanka Institute of Architects

Prize Presentation February / 15 / 1996

Members of the Jury Geoffrey Bawa, K.L. Gunaratne, Justin Samarasekara,
Ghanna Daswatte, S.W. Molligoda

Design Team Vinod A. Jayasinghe

Structural Engineering Environmental Studios

Civil Engineering Environmental Studios

Mechanical Engineering Tissa Gunasena

Electrical Engineering Tissa Gunasena

Air Conditioning Consultant Tissa Gunasena

Interior Design Vinod A. Jayasinghe

Landscape Architecture Vinod A. Jayasinghe / Dooland de Silva

Quantity Surveying Environmental Studios

Approximate Cost US$ 1,000,000

Site Area 9,793 m^2 / *Building Area* 2,386.76 m^2 / *Total Floor Area* 3,409.56 m^2

Photographer Vajira Dharmaratne

Sweden

Architects **Erséus, Frenning & Sjögren Arkitekter AB, Göteborg**

Award Winning Building **The School of Economics, Göteborg
(Handelshögskolan)**

Location **Vasagatan 1, Göteborg, Sweden**

Design and Construction Period **1989–1995**

Award Kaspar-Salin-Priset

Given by Svenska Arkitekters Riksförbund

Prize Presentation November / 28 / 1995

Members of the Jury Mats Edblom, Stefan Alenius, Pietro Raffone,
Gert Wingårdh

Design Team Peter Erséus (Chief Architect), Pelle Frenning, Ove Nilsson,
Roger Johansson, Anja Jensen, Monica Strandäng, Sven Magnus Sjögren

Structural Engineering KM Bygg AB

Electrical Engineering Gösta Sjölander AB

Acoustic Engineering Jordan Akustik

Air Conditioning Consultant Bengt Dahlgren AB

Interior Design Erséus, Frenning & Sjögren Arkitekter AB

Landscape Architecture Landskapsgruppen AB

Approximate Cost Skr 220,000

Site Area 8,650 m^2 / *Building Area* 4,800 m^2 / *Total Floor Area* 24,000 m^2

Photographer Åke Lindman, Bert Leandersson

Switzerland

Architects **Alexandre Micheli, Geneva; BAILLIF & LOPONTE, Carouge**

Award Winning Building **Housing Complex**

Award Prix INTERASSAR

see page 132

Trinidad & Tobago (West Indies)

Architect **Anthony C. Lewis, Port of Spain**
Representative Building **Parkinson / Higgins House**
Location **Pt. Galera, Trinidad & Tobago (West Indies)**
Design and Construction Period **1961**

Award Gold Medal for Excellence in Architecture
Given by Trinidad & Tobago Institute of Architects
Prize Presentation 1994
Design Team Anthony C. Lewis
Structural Engineering Elton Millet

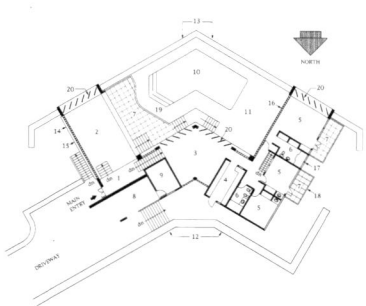

Interior Design Anthony C. Lewis
Landscape Architecture Peter Richards
Photographer Noel Norton

Trinidad & Tobago (West Indies)

Architects **Gary Turton (Turton Architects), Port of Spain**

Award **Low-Income Housing in Trinidad (1. Prize)**
Given by Trinidad & Tobago Institute of Architects

Prize Presentation November / 25 / 1996
Members of the Jury Asad Mohammed (Trinidad & Tobago), Roberto Caballero
Garcia (Cuba), Mervyn Awon (Barbados, West Indies)

Turkey

Architects **Hasan Çalişlar, Kerem Erginoğlu, Istanbul**
Award Winning Building **Tuncel Residence**
Location **Anadolu Hisari, Istanbul, Turkey**
Design and Construction Period **1994–1995**

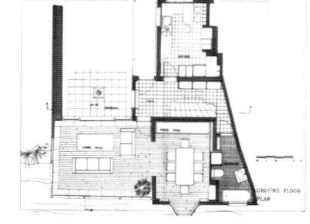

Award National Architectural Award 1996
Given by Chamber of Architects of Turkey
Prize Presentation May 1996
Members of the Jury Orhan Şahinler (Chairman), Aydan Balamir, Tamer Başbuğ,
Salih Zeki Pekin
Design Team Elvan Çalişkan, Emin Balkiş, Hasan Türkkahramani,
Mehmet Ermiyagil

Mechanical Engineering Ümit Özkan
Approximate Cost US$ 40,000
Site Area 250 m² / *Building Area* 75 m² / *Total Floor Area* 220 m²
Photographer Vasken Değirmehtaş

Turkey

Architect **Abdurahman Hanci, Istanbul**

Award National Architectural Award 1996
Given by Chamber of Architects of Turkey

Prize Presentation 1996
Members of the Jury Orhan Šahinler, Aydan Balamir, Tamer Başbuğ,
Salih Zeki Pekin

Turkey

Architects **Merih Karaaslan, Nuran Ünsal, Mürşit Günday, Ankara**
Award Winning Building **Terrace Houses**

Award 1) National Architectural Award 1996 (Project Award);
2) Noteworthy Collaboration between Architect and Client
see page 136

Turkey

Architects **Merih Karaaslan, Nuran Ünsal, Ankara**
Award Winning Building **The Peritower Hotel**
Location **Nevşehir-Cappadocia, Turkey**
Design and Construction Period **1989–1995**

Award National Architectural Award 1996 (Building Award)
Given by Chamber of Architects of Turkey
Prize Presentation 1996
Members of the Jury Orhan Şahinler (Chairman), Aydan Balamir,
Tamer Başbuğ, Salih Zeki Pekin

Design Team Ilker Aksu, Ševki Findik, Fulya Sert
Structural Engineering Danyal Kubin, Joseph Kubin
Civil Engineering Danyal Kubin, Joseph Kubin
Mechanical Engineering Bülent Özgür, Bahri Türkmen
Electrical Engineering Ali Gündüz
Air Conditioning Consultant Bülent Özgür, Bahri Türkmen
Interior Design Merih Karaaslan
Landscape Architecture Karaaslan Architecture Ltd.
Quantity Surveying Karaaslan Architecture Ltd.
Approximate Cost US$ 4,000,000
Site Area 11,760 m²
Building Area 2,590 m² (ground floor area)
Total Floor Area 11,770 m²
Photographer Merih Karaaslan

Turkey

Architect **Ševki Pekin, Istanbul**
Award Winning Building **Summer House**

Award National Architectural Award 1996 (Building Award)
see page 138

Turkey

Architect **Ševki Pekin, Istanbul**
Award Winning Building **Project for a multipurpose commercial building of the Vakko Corporation**
Location **Merter, Istanbul, Turkey**

Award National Architectural Award 1996
Given by Chamber of Architects of Turkey
Prize Presentation April / 25 / 1996
Members of the Jury Orhan Šahiler, Aydan Balamir, Tamer Başbuğ, Zeki Pekin
Design Team Ševki Pekin
Approximate Cost US$ 9,000,000
Site Area 12,000 m²
Building Area 10,000 m²

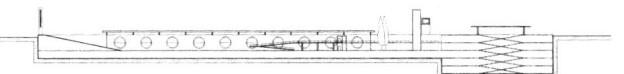

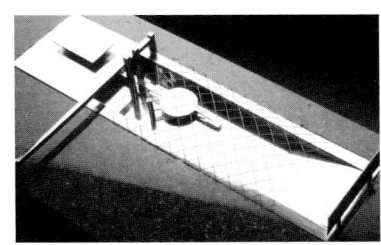

Total Floor Area 17,000 m²
Photographer Paul McMillen

Turkey

Architects **Erkut Šahinbaş, Ilhan Kural, Ankara**
Award Winning Building **Bilkent University Main Library Annex Building**
Location **Ankara, Turkey**
Design and Construction Period **1993–1995**

Award National Architectural Award 1996
Given by Chamber of Architects of Turkey
Prize Presentation April / 25 / 1996
Members of the Jury Orhan Šahinler (Chairman), Aydan Balamir, Tamer Başbuğ, Salih Zeki Pekin
Design Team Erkut Šahinbas, Ilhan Kural, Oya Caymaz
Structural Engineering Mehmet Šapci
Civil Engineering Mehmet Šapci
Mechanical Engineering Celal Okutan Co. Ltd.
Electrical Engineering Nihat Akay

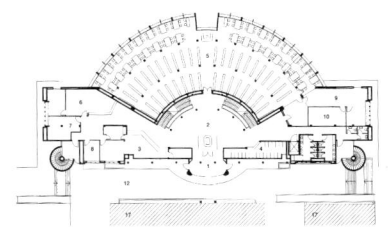

Air Conditioning Consultant Celal Okutan
Interior Design Erkut Šahinbas, Ilhan Kural
Approximate Cost US$ 3,000,000
Site Area 4,700 m²
Building Area 5,913 m²
Total Floor Area 1,464 m² (ground floor area)
Photographer Ilhan Kural, Murat Gürzumar

Turkey

Architect **Nevzat Sayin, Istanbul**

Award Winning Building **Gön II**

Location **Gaziosmanpasa, Istanbul, Turkey**

Design and Construction Period **1994–1995**

Award National Architectural Award 1996

Given by Chamber of Architects of Turkey

Prize Presentation September / 28 / 1996

Members of the Jury Orhan Sahinler (Chairman), Aydan Balamir,
Tamer Başbuğ, Salih Zeki Pekin

Design Team Nevzat Sayin, Tülay Atabey

Structural Engineering UNITERMAK – Tuncay Ayhan

Project Management PMP – Adem Bulut

Approximate Cost US\$ 2,000,000 (TL 93,000,000,000)

Site Area 6,000 m²

Building Area 2,500 m²

Total Floor Area 10,000 m²

Photographer Nevzat Sayin, Aramis Kalay

Ukraine

Architects **L. Alinauskene, V. Shvets, Lviv**

Award Winning Building **Restoration of the John the Christener Temple**

Location **Lviv, Ukraine**

Award State Architecture Award of Ukraine 1996

Given by Union of Architects of Ukraine

Prize Presentation July / 20 / 1996

Members of the Jury I. Shpara, V. Jezhov, V. Zhezherin, T. Ustenko,
G. Khorkhot, V. Prisyazhyuk, A. Ekonomov, L. Mulyar

Ukraine

Architects **V. Buryak, I. Kaspert, E. Cosinsky, Kyiv**

Award Winning Building **Main Building of the Central Medical Institution
in Slavutich Town**

Location **Slavutich Town, Ukraine**

Design and Construction Period **1986–1994**

Award State Architecture Award of Ukraine 1996

Given by Union of Architects of Ukraine and the State Committee of Ukraine
on Urban Development

Prize Presentation June / 20 / 1996

Members of the Jury V. Gusakov (Chair), A. Gorbatovsky, V. Prysyadgnyk,
A. Aconov, A. Krishyk, I. Shpara, Y. Hudyakov, Y. Belokon, N. Dyomin,
V. Yedgov, V. Gegerin, I. Ievchuk, T. Ustenko, Y. Chorchot, A. Tsvetkov,
V. Shtolko

Building Constructions E. Cosinsky

Medical Technology V. Vychegdganin

Electrical Engineering D. Shmelkin

Engineering Technology E. Mosienco

Air Conditioning G. Svetnicov

Water Supply, Sewerage L. Gorohovskaya

Communications and Signaling S. Koshmak

Automation V. Grabovsky

Decorative Picture V. Lesvinsky

Working out Organization Joint-Stock Company, Medinvestproject

Approximate Cost / Floor Area US\$ 15,000,000

Site Area 12.7 ha

Building Area 6,260 m²

Total Floor Area 32,000 m²

Photographer I. Kaspert

Ukraine

Architect **Alexander Kalugin, Kharkiv**

Award Winning Building **Administrative Centre of the Village Mikhailovka**

Location **Poltava, Mikhailovka, Ukraine**

Design and Construction Period **1986–1990**

Award State Architecture Award of Ukraine 1996

Given by Union of Architects of Ukraine

Prize Presentation 1996

Design Team Alexander Kalugin

Structural Engineering Alexander Kalugin

Mechanical Engineering Svetlana Adrianova

Electrical Engineering Natalia Olenik

Interior Design Alexander Kalugin

Landscape Architecture Alexander Kalugin

Site Area 0.8 ha / *Building Area* 850 m² / *Total Floor Area* 1,315m²

United Kingdom

Architects **Ahrends Burton and Koralek, London**
Award Winning Building **Mezzanine Sculpture Court, Whitworth Gallery,**
  University of Manchester
Location **Manchester, UK**

Award RIBA Regional Architecture Award 1996 (North West Region)
Given by RIBA The Royal Institute of British Architects
Prize Presentation 1996

United Kingdom

Architects **Ahrends Burton and Koralek, London**
Award Winning Building **Techniquest Science Discovery Centre**

Award RIBA Regional Architecture Award 1996 (Wales)
see page 140

United Kingdom

Architects **Allford Hall Monaghan Morris Architects, London**
Award Winning Building **The Poolhouse**

Award RIBA Regional Architecture Award 1996 (Wessex Region)
see page 142

United Kingdom

Architects **Allies and Morrison, London**
Award Winning Building **Newnham College**
Location **Cambridge, UK**
Design and Construction Period **1993–1995**

Award RIBA Regional Architecture Award 1996 (Eastern Region)
Given by RIBA The Royal Institute of British Architects
Prize Presentation November / 21 / 1996
Design Team Joanna Green, Julian Cowie, Annette Leanyre, Ian Sutherland,
  Deborah Miller, Sarah Jackson
Structural Engineering Whitby & Bird
Mechanical Engineering G Armstrong and Partners
Electrical Engineering G Armstrong and Partners
Interior Design Allies and Morrison

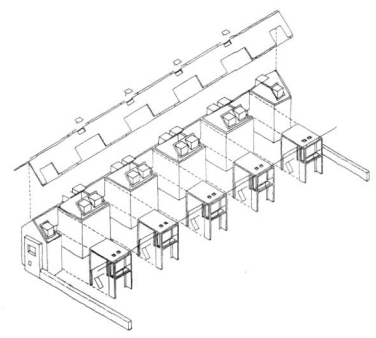 

Quantity Surveying Daniel B Connal & Partners
Approximate Cost £ 1,700,000
Site Area 1,000 m^2
Photographer Peter Cook

United Kingdom

Architects **Allies and Morrison, London**
Award Winning Building **Sarum Hall School**

Award RIBA Regional Architecture Award 1996 (London Region)
see page 144

United Kingdom

Architects **Allies and Morrison, London**
Award Winning Building **Nunnery Square, Sheffield**

Award RIBA Regional Architecture Award 1996 (Yorkshire Region)
see page 146

United Kingdom

Architects **AMEC Design and Management, Stratford-upon-Avon**
Award Winning Building **Boots D 10 Building**
Location **Nottingham, UK**
Design and Construction Period **1990–1994**

Award 1) RIBA Regional Architecture Award 1996 (East Midlands);
  2) Dulux Heritage Colours Conservation Award
Given by RIBA The Royal Institute of British Architects

Prize Presentation   1) November / 22 / 1996

Design Team   AMEC, Colin Davidson (Project Manager), Jan Sosna
  (Chief Architect), Keith Edgell (Design Leader), Peter Martin (Project Architect)

Structural Engineering   AMEC, David Walker

Civil Engineering   AMEC

Mechanical Engineering   AMEC, Tony Chadwick

Electrical Engineering   AMEC, Peter Edmunds

Commercial Manager   David Webb

Project Quantity Surveyor   Craig Seal

Construction Manager   Barry Rawson

Environmental Engineering   AMEC

Acoustic Engineering   AMEC

Air Conditioning Consultant   AMEC

Lighting Consultant   AMEC

Life Safety Consultant   AMEC

Interior Design   AMEC

Landscape Architecture   AMEC

Quantity Surveying   Gleeds, Nottingham

Approximate Cost   £ 20,000,000

Site Area   153 ha

Building Area   4,476 m^2

Total Floor Area   8,719 m^2

Photographer   Martine Hamilton-Knight

United Kingdom

Architects   **Associated Architects, Birmingham**

Award Winning Building   **The School of Art**

Location   **Margaret Street, Birmingham, UK**

Award   RIBA Regional Architecture Award 1996 (West Midlands Region)

Given by   RIBA The Royal Institute of British Architects

Prize Presentation   1996

United Kingdom

Architects   **Aukett Associates, London**

Award Winning Building   **Procter & Gamble (Health & Beauty Care) Ltd.**

Location   **Weybridge, UK**

Award   1) RIBA Regional Architecture Award 1996 (South East Region);
  2) RIBA Commercial Architecture Award

Given by   RIBA The Royal Institute of British Architects

United Kingdom

Architects   **Lord Austin-Smith, Warrington**

Award Winning Building   **The Law Courts**

Location   **London, UK**

Award   RIBA Regional Architecture Award 1996 (North West Region)

Given by   RIBA The Royal Institute of British Architects

Prize Presentation   November / 22 / 1996

United Kingdom

Architects   **Bennetts Associates, London**

Award Winning Building   **PowerGen Headquarters**

Award   RIBA Regional Architecture Award 1996 (West Midlands)

see page 148

United Kingdom

Architect   **Peter Bernamont Architects, London**

Award Winning Building   **Lemmeleg Building – Offices**

Location   **3 West Parade, Wakefield, UK**

Design and Construction Period   **1994–1995**

Award   1) City of Wakefield Design Award 1995;
  2) RIBA Architecture Award 1996

Given by   1) RIBA, Civic Trust, Royal Town Planning Institute, Landscape
  Institute, Wakefield District Council; 2) RIBA The Royal Institute of British
  Architects

Members of the Jury   1) Representatives of RIBA, Civic Trust, Royal Town
  Planning Institute, Landscape Institute, Wakefield District Council;
  2) Representatives from President of RIBA, RIBA Region, and one lay person
  appointed by RIBA

Design Team   Peter Bernamont

Structural Engineering   MJMC Ltd., Wakefield, England

Civil Engineering   Main Contractor: Lemmeleg Building and Contracting Ltd

Mechanical Engineering   Main Contractor: Lemmeleg Building and
    Contracting Ltd
Electrical Engineering   Main Contractor: Lemmeleg Building and Contracting Ltd
Client   Ptarmigan Properties and Securities Ltd
Lighting Consultant   Peter Bernamont Architects and Client
Interior Design   Peter Bernamont Architects and Client

Landscape Architecture   Peter Bernamont Architects and Client
Approximate Cost   £ 150,000 (excluding interior fit-out)
Site Area   160 m^2
Building Area   75 m^2
Total Floor Area   210 m^2
Photographers   Martine Hamilton-Knight; Peter Bernamont

United Kingdom

Architects   **Building Design Partnership, Glasgow**
Award Winning Building   **Centre 1, Inland Revenue**
Location   **East Kilbride, Scotland, UK**
Design and Construction Period   **1992–1994**

Award   RIBA Regional Architecture Award 1996 (Scotland)
Given by   RIBA The Royal Institute of British Architects
Prize Presentation   November / 22 / 1996
Design Team   Building Design Partnership
Structural Engineering   Thorburn Colquhoun
Civil Engineering   Thorburn Colquhoun
Mechanical Engineering   Cundall Johnston & Partners
Electrical Engineering   Cundall Johnston & Partners
Acoustic Engineering   Building Design Partnership
Lighting Consultant   Cundall Johnston & Partners
Interior Design   Building Design Partnership

Landscape Architecture   Building Design Partnership
Quantity Surveying   Robinson Low Francis
Approximate Cost   £ 23,800,000
Site Area   70,000 m^2
Total Floor Area   24,200 m^2 (gross internal)
Photographer   Martine Hamilton-Knight

United Kingdom

Architects   **Buttress Fuller Alsop Williams, Manchester**
Award Winning Building   **Chapel of St. Augustine of Canterbury at
    Tonbridge School**
Location   **Tonbridge, UK**

Award   RIBA Regional Architecture Award 1996 (South East Region)
Given by   RIBA The Royal Institute of British Architects

United Kingdom

Architects   **David Chipperfield Architects, London**
Award Winning Building   **First Church of Christ Scientist**
Location   **Richmond, UK**

Award   RIBA Regional Architecture Award 1996 (South East Region)
Given by   RIBA The Royal Institute of British Architects

United Kingdom

Architects   **Jane Darbyshire & David Kendall Ltd., Newcastle-upon-Tyne**
Award Winning Building   **The Former Rose Line Building, Wylam Wharf**
Location   **Sunderland, UK**

Award   RIBA Regional Architecture Award 1996 (Northern Region)
Given by   RIBA The Royal Institute of British Architects
Prize Presentation   1996

United Kingdom

Architects   **Department of Architecture & Property Services,
    Buckinghamshire County Council, Aylesbury**
Award Winning Building   **County Museum**
Location   **Church Street, Aylesbury, UK**

Award   RIBA Regional Architecture Award 1996 (Southern Region)
Given by   RIBA The Royal Institute of British Architects
Prize Presentation   January / 9 / 1997

United Kingdom

Architects **Department of Technical Services, Penrith**
Award Winning Building **Appleby War Memorial Swimming Pool**
Location **The Butts, Chapel Street, Appleby, UK**

Award RIBA Regional Architecture Award 1996 (Northern Region)
Given by RIBA The Royal Institute of British Architects
Prize Presentation 1996

United Kingdom

Architects **Nick Derbyshire Design Associates Ltd., London**
Award Winning Building **Ashford International Terminal**
Location **Ashford, UK**

Award RIBA Regional Architecture Award 1996 (South East Region)
Given by RIBA The Royal Institute of British Architects

United Kingdom

Architects **Design Shed, Liverpool**
Award Winning Building **Concert Square Buildings**
Location **Concert Square, Liverpool, UK**
Design and Construction Period **1993–1996**

Award RIBA Regional Architecture Award 1996 (North West Region)
Given by RIBA The Royal Institute of British Architects
Prize Presentation November / 22 / 1996
Members of the Jury Joanna van Heyningen, Ben Johnson, Robert Tarbuck
Design Team Jonathan Falkingham, Fiona Woodward, Emma King, Alex Morris
Structural Engineering Steve Morley Engineering
Interior Design Design Shed
Landscape Architecture Design Shed
Quantity Surveying Shenstone Associates
Approximate Cost £ 1,200,000
Site Area 1,977 m^2

 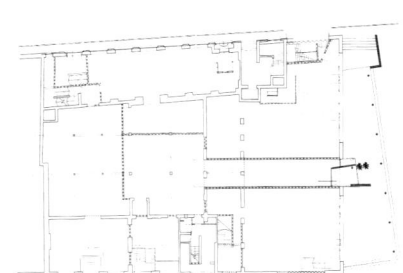

Building Area 1,335 m^2
Total Floor Area 2,103 m^2
Photographer Jonathan Keenan

United Kingdom

Architects **Design Shed, Liverpool**
Award Winning Building **Schoolhouse**
Location **Trafford Park, Manchester, UK**
Design and Construction Period **1994–1996**

Award RIBA Regional Architecture Award 1996 (North West Region)
Given by RIBA The Royal Institute of British Architects
Prize Presentation November / 22 / 1996
Members of the Jury Joanna van Heyningen, Ben Johnson, Robert Tarbuck
Design Team Jonathan Falkingham, Fiona Woodward, Emma King, Chris Moor,
   Satwinder Samra, Dana Haqjoo
Structural Engineering Eric Bassett Associates
Interior Design Design Shed
Landscape Architecture Design Shed
Quantity Surveying Simon Fenton Partnership

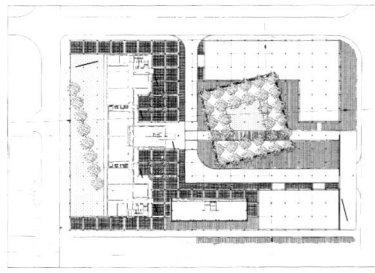 

Approximate Cost £ 1,500,000
Site Area 9,336 m^2
Building Area 279 m^2
Total Floor Area 948 m^2
Photographer Jonathan Keenan

United Kingdom

Architect **Peter Dowsett, Bournemouth**
Award Winning Building **New House**
Location **Bournemouth, UK**
Design and Construction Period **1994**

Award RIBA Regional Architecture Award 1996 (Wessex Region)
Given by RIBA The Royal Institute of British Architects
Prize Presentation November 1996
Members of the Jury RIBA, Robert Adam (Chairman)
Structural Engineering Harvey & Snowdon
Landscape Architecture R. Critchley & Associates
Approximate Cost £ 160,000
Site Area 600 m²

Building Area 190 m²
Total Floor Area 230 m²
Photographer Nigel Rigdon

United Kingdom

Architects **Philip England and Fiona Gilje, Richmond upon Thames**
Award Winning Building **Pepsi Max Big One Station**
Location **Blackpool Pleasure Beach, UK**
Design and Construction Period **1992–1993**

Lighting Consultant Phillips Lighting
Interior Design Fiona Gilje
Approximate Cost £ 1,200,000
Site Area 1,500 m²
Building Area 300 m²
Total Floor Area 260 m²
Photographer Peter Owen

Award RIBA Regional Architecture Award 1996 (North West Region)
Given by RIBA The Royal Institute of British Architects
Prize Presentation November / 7 / 1996
Members of the Jury North West Region RIBA
Design Team Philip England and Fiona Gilje
Structural Engineering W. Hare, Lancashire
Civil Engineering Shepherds, Manchester
Mechanical Engineering Blackpool Pleasure Beach
Electrical Engineering Blackpool Pleasure Beach

United Kingdom

Architects **Evans & Shalev Architects, London**
Award Winning Building **Quincentenary Library, Jesus College**
Location **Cambridge, UK**

Award RIBA Regional Architecture Award 1996 (Eastern Region)
Given by RIBA The Royal Institute of British Architects
Prize Presentation November 1996

United Kingdom

Architects **Terry Farrell & Partners, London**
Award Winning Building **Edinburgh International Conference Centre**
Location **Edinburgh, Scotland, UK**
Design and Construction Period **1989–1995**

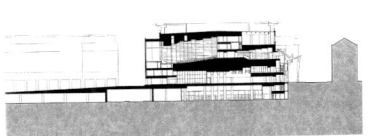

Award RIBA Regional Architecture Award 1996 (Scotland)
Given by RIBA The Royal Institute of British Architects
Design Team Terry Farrell, Derek Nolan, Duncan Whatmore, Alexandra Stevens
Structural Engineering Ove Arup & Partners, West Lothian
Mechanical Engineering Ove Arup & Partners, West Lothian
Electrical Engineering Ove Arup & Partners, West Lothian
Acoustic Engineering Sandy Brown Associates, London
Quantity Surveying Gleeds, Edinburgh

Approximate Cost £ 38,000,000
Building Area 133,000 sq. ft.
Photographer Keith Hunter, Nigel Young

United Kingdom

Architects **Feilden Clegg Architects, Bath**
Award Winning Building **Kingswood Day Preparatory School**
Location **Bath, UK**

Award RIBA Regional Architecture Award 1996 (Wessex Region)
Given by RIBA The Royal Institute of British Architects
Prize Presentation November 1996

United Kingdom

Architects **Ferguson Mann Architects, Bristol**
Award Winning Building **Dance Studio, Bristol Old Vic Theatre School**
Location **Bristol, UK**

Award RIBA Regional Architecture Award 1996 (Wessex Region)
Given by RIBA The Royal Institute of British Architects
Prize Presentation November 1996

United Kingdom

Architects **Goddard Manton Partnership, London**
Award Winning Building **Tadcaster Community Swimming Pool**
Location **Tadcaster, North Yorkshire, UK**
Design and Construction Period **1993–1995**

Award RIBA Regional Architecture Award 1996 (Yorkshire Region)
Given by RIBA The Royal Institute of British Architects
Prize Presentation November 1996
Design Team Don Manton, Chris Hearn
Structural Engineering Blackburn Wigglesworth
Civil Engineering Blackburn Wigglesworth
Mechanical Engineering John Troughear Associates
Electrical Engineering John Troughear Associates
Environmental Engineering John Troughear Associates
Lighting Consultant John Troughear Associates
Interior Design Goddard Manton Partnership
Landscape Architecture Goddard Manton Partnership

Quantity Surveying Castons Hanby Associates
Approximate Cost £ 2,000,000
Building Area 1,525 m^2
Total Floor Area 1,675 m^2
Photographer K.L. Photographers

United Kingdom

Architects **Hodder Associates, Manchester**
Award Winning Building **City Road Surgery**
Location **City Road, Hulme, Manchester, UK**
Design and Construction Period **1995–1996**

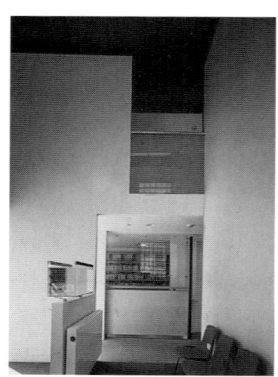

Award RIBA Regional Architecture Award 1996 (North West Region)
Given by RIBA The Royal Institute of British Architects
Prize Presentation November 1996
Members of the Jury Members of the RIBA and lay assessors
Design Team Hodder Associates (Stephen Hodder, Keith Andrews)
Structural Engineering Les Postawa
Civil Engineering Les Postawa
Mechanical Engineering Miller Walmsley Partnership, Manchester
Electrical Engineering Miller Walmsley Partnership, Manchester
Environmental Engineering Miller Walmsley Partnership, Manchester
Interior Design Hodder Associates
Landscape Architecture Hodder Associates

Quantity Surveying Thomas Sands, Manchester
Approximate Cost £ 240,000
Building Area 120 m^2
Total Floor Area 219 m^2
Photographer Dennis Gilbert

United Kingdom

Architects **Hodder Associates, Manchester**
Award Winning Building **Centenary Building, University of Salford**
Location **Peru Street, Salford, M6 6PU, UK**
Design and Construction Period **1993–1995**

Award 1) RIBA Regional Architecture Award 1996 (North West Region);
 2) RIBA Architecture in Education Award
Given by RIBA The Royal Institute of British Architects
Prize Presentation November 1996
Members of the Jury Owen Luder (President RIBA), Sir Anthony Caro,
 Hugh Pearman
Design Team Hodder Associates – Stephen Hodder, Robert Evans,
 Richard Blackwell, Vetus Lau
Structural Engineering Stephen Morley Partnership, Manchester
Civil Engineering Stephen Morley Partnership, Manchester
Mechanical Engineering Miller Walmsley Partnership

Electrical Engineering Miller Walmsley Partnership
Environmental Engineering Miller Walmsley Partnership
Interior Design Hodder Associates
Landscape Architecture Hodder Associates
Quantity Surveying Appleyard & Trew, Manchester
Approximate Cost £ 3,500,000
Building Area 1,316 m²
Total Floor Area 4,092 m²
Photographer Dennis Gilbert

United Kingdom

Architects **Haworth Tompkins Architects, London**
Associated Architects **Sursham Tompkins and Partners (Project Managers)**
Award Winning Building **Cobbs Lane (phases 1 and 3)**
Location **Wollaston, Northamptonshire, UK**
Design and Construction Period **1993–1995**

Award 1) Structural Steel Design Awards Commendation (phase1); 2) RIBA
 Regional Architecture Award 1996 (East Midlands) (phases 1 and 3)
Given by 1) British Steel / The British Constructional Steelwork Association Ltd.
 / The Steel Construction Inst., 2) RIBA The Royal Institute of British Architects
Prize Presentation 1) November / 5 / 1996, 2) November / 21 / 1996
Members of the Jury 1) Alan Watson, Jamie Troughtom; 2) RIBA Judging
 Committee
Design Team Thomas Emerson, Graham Haworth, Michael Pawlyn,
 Steve Tompkins
Structural Engineering Price and Myers (Paul Batty, Sam Price)

Civil Engineering Price and Myers (Paul Batty, Sam Price)
Mechanical and Electrical Engineering Rolton Service Consultants
 (Chris Evans, Gordon Fenwick, Helda Lira, Peter Rolton)
Quantity Surveying Tompkins Robinson Surveyors
Approximate Cost £ 2,400,000
Site Area 4,840 m²
Building Area 950 m²
Total Floor Area 1,100 m²
Photographer Andy Chopping

United Kingdom

Architects **Hodder Associates, Manchester**
Award Winning Building **Oswald Medical Practice**
Location **Chorlton, Manchester, UK**
Design and Construction Period **1993–1994**

Award RIBA Regional Architecture Award 1994 (North West Region)
Given by RIBA The Royal Institute of British Architects
Design Team Hodder Associates (Stephen R. Hodder)
Structural Engineering Eric Bassett Associates, Sale
Service Engineering Eric Bassett Associates, Sale
Main Contractor Warden Builders, Preston
Quantity Surveying Thomas Sands & Partners, Manchester
Approximate Cost £ 137,000/m²
Total Floor Area 187 m²
Photographer Chris Gascoigne

United Kingdom

Architects **Holder Mathias Alcock plc., Cardiff**
Award Winning Building **The NCM Building**
Location **Capital Waterside, Cardiff, UK**

Award RIBA Regional Architecture Award 1996 (Wales)
Given by RIBA The Royal Institute of British Architects
Prize Presentation 1996

United Kingdom

Architects **Michael Hopkins & Partners, London**
Award Winning Building **The Queen's Building, Emmanuel College**

Award 1) RIBA Regional Architecture Award 1996 (Eastern Region);
see page 158

United Kingdom

Architect **Graeme Jones, Abingdon**
Award Winning Building **The Granary**
Location **Manor Farm, Culham, Abingdon, Oxfordshire, UK**
Design and Construction Period **1992–1995**

 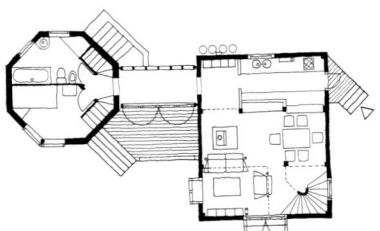

Award RIBA Regional Architecture Award 1996 (Southern Region)
Given by RIBA The Royal Institute of British Architects
Prize Presentation January / 9 / 1997
Design Team Graeme Jones
Structural Engineering Ian Howdill Associates
Approximate Cost £ 30,000

Site Area 12,800 m²
Total Floor Area 125 m²

United Kingdom

Architects **Kennedy FitzGerald and Associates, Belfast**
Award Winning Building **St. Brigid's Church**
Location **Derryvolgie Avenue, Belfast, Northern Ireland, UK**

Award RIBA Regional Architecture Award 1996 (Northern Ireland)
Given by RIBA The Royal Institute of British Architects

United Kingdom

Architect **Roddy Langmuir (Edward Cullinan Architects), London**
Award Winning Building **Clach Mhor**
Location **Avielochan, By Aviemore, Scotland, UK**

Award RIBA Regional Architecture Award 1996 (Scotland)
Given by RIBA The Royal Institute of British Architects
Prize Presentation November / 22 / 1996

United Kingdom

Architects **Lifschutz Davidson, London**
Award Winning Building **J. Sainsbury PLC, Dome Roundabout**
Location **Watford, UK**

Award RIBA Regional Architecture Award 1996 (Eastern Region)
Given by RIBA The Royal Institute of British Architects
Prize Presentation November 1996

United Kingdom

Architects **Rick Mather Architects, London**
Award Winning Building **Arco Building, Keble College**
Location **Oxford, UK**

Award RIBA Regional Architecture Award 1996 (Southern Region)
Given by RIBA The Royal Institute of British Architects
Prize Presentation January / 9 / 1997

United Kingdom

Architects **David Morley Architects, London**

Award Winning Building **MCC Indoor Cricket School, Marylebone**
  Cricket Club

Location **London, UK**

Award 1) RIBA Regional Architecture Award 1996 (London Region);

  2) RIBA Architecture in Sport and Leisure Award 1996

Given by RIBA The Royal Institute of British Architects

Prize Presentation 1) November / 22 / 1996

United Kingdom

Architects **Richard Murphy, Graeme Mitchell, Mark Floate, Edinburgh**

Award Winning Building **17 Royal Terrace Mews**

Award 1) RIBA Regional Architecture Award 1996 (Scotland);

  2) RIBA Ibstock Award 1996

see page 152

United Kingdom

Architects **John Outram Associates, London**

Award Winning Building **Judge Institute of Management Studies,**
  University of Cambridge

Location **Trumpington Street, Cambridge, UK**

Design and Construction Period **1991–1995**

Award RIBA Regional Architecture Award 1996 (Eastern Region)

Given by RIBA The Royal Institute of British Architects

Prize Presentation November 1996

Design Team John Outram (Project Architect Design), Wendy Dellitt
  (Project Architect Conservation), Glen Millar (Project Architect Castle),
  Huw Owen (Project Architect on Site), Alan Smith-Oliver (Project Architect
  Coordinator), David Bass, Natasha Black, Anthony Charnley, Iona Foster,
  Felna Fox, Rebecca Granger, Bill & Elizabeth Gregory, Tim Hall, Nicola Hem,
  Raida Kassim-Bench, Sean Murphy, Nina Noor, Ahir Ramazani, Jeremiah
  Sherhan, Sally MacKay

Structural Engineering Felix Samuely Partnership

Civil Engineering Felix Samuely Partnership

Mechanical Engineering Max Fordham Partners

Electrical Engineering Max Fordham Partners

Environmental Engineering Max Fordham Partners

Acoustic Engineering Max Fordham Partners

Air Conditioning Consultant Max Fordham Partners

Lighting Consultant Max Fordham Partners

Life Safety Consultant Max Fordham Partners

Interior Design John Outram Associates

Landscape Architecture Holden & Liversedge

Quantity Surveying Davis Langdon & Everest (Cambridge)

Approximate Cost £ 11,000,000

Building Area 9,000 m^2

Photographers Peter Cook (architecture), John Outram

United Kingdom

Architects **Page & Park Architects, Glasgow**

Award Winning Building **Port Glasgow Municipal Buildings**

Location **Fore Street, Port Glasgow, Scotland, UK**

Award RIBA Regional Architecture Award 1996 (Scotland)

Given by RIBA The Royal Institute of British Architects

Prize Presentation November / 22 / 1996

United Kingdom

Architects **Perkins Ogden Architects, Alresford**

Award Winning Building **Sparsholt College Library and Information Centre**

Location **Winchester, UK**

Award RIBA Regional Architecture Award 1996 (Southern Region)

Given by RIBA The Royal Institute of British Architects

Prize Presentation January / 9 / 1997

United Kingdom

Architect **Hugh Pilkington, Orford**
Award Winning Building **The New Wing – Well Cottage Orford**
Location **Orford, Suffolk, UK**
Design and Construction Period **1995–1996**

Award RIBA Regional Architecture Award 1996 (Eastern Region)
Given by RIBA The Royal Institute of British Architects
Prize Presentation September 1996
Design Team Hugh Pilkington
Approximate Cost £ 38,000
Site Area 100 m²

Building Area 50 m²
Total Floor Area 50 m²

United Kingdom

Architect **Francis B. Roberts, Preston**
Award Winning Building **St. Peter's Cathedral (Re-Ordering and Restoration)**
Location **East Road, Lancaster, UK**
Design and Construction Period **March–October 1995**

Award RIBA Regional Architecture Award 1996 (North West Region)
Given by RIBA The Royal Institute of British Architects
Prize Presentation 1996
Members of the Jury Joanna van Heyningen (Chair), Ben Johnson,
 Robert Tarbuck (Lay)
Design Team Francis Roberts, James Sanderson, Tom Gaze

Structural Engineering Paul Watson, Sleater & Watson, Preston
Mechanical Engineering Frank Mills, Frank Mills Associates, Leyland
Electrical Engineering J.B. Smith, Leyland
Decoration Bernard Watson, Preston
Stonework S. & J. Whitehead, Oldham
Corona Lucis / Chandeliers / Rood Screen / Refurbish various artefacts /
 Uplighters Cosalt Contract Lighting, Fleetwood
Interior Design Francis B. Roberts
Approximate Cost £ 250,000
Total Floor Area 1,100 m²
Photographer Photogenics

United Kingdom

Architects **Short Ford & Associates, London**
Award Winning Building **The Queen's Building (School of Engineering and Manufacture)**

Award RIBA Regional Architecture Award 1996 (East Midlands)
see page 154

United Kingdom

Architects **Troughton McAslan, London**
Award Winning Building **The Speech, Language and Hearing Centre, Christopher Place**
Location **Kings Cross, London, UK**

Award RIBA Regional Architecture Award 1996 (London Region)
Given by RIBA The Royal Institute of British Architects
Prize Presentation November / 21 / 1996
Members of the Jury Steven Hodder, Valerie Singleton Obe, Richard Brindley
Design Team John McAslan, Piers Smerin, Murray Smith, Hiro Aso
Structural Engineering Ove Arup & Partners
Mechanical Engineering Ove Arup & Partners
Electrical Engineering Ove Arup & Partners
Acoustic Engineering Ove Arup & Partners
Lighting Consultant Ove Arup & Partners
Project Artists Alison Turnbull, Trevor Shearer
Quantity Surveying Boyden and Company
Approximate Cost £ 750,000

Site Area 200 m²
Total Floor Area 350 m²
Photographer Peter Cook

United Kingdom

Architects **Van Heyningen & Haward, London**
Award Winning Building **Wilson Court, Fitzwilliam College**
Location **Cambridge, UK**

Award RIBA Regional Architecture Award 1996 (Eastern Region)
Given by RIBA The Royal Institute of British Architects
Prize Presentation November 1996

United Kingdom

Architect **Adam Voelcker, Garndolbenmaen**
Award Winning Building **TWR Brynkir, Brynkir Home Farm**
Location **CWM Pennant, Garndolbenmaen, Wales, UK**

Award RIBA Regional Architecture Award 1996 (Wales)
Given by RIBA The Royal Institute of British Architects
Prize Presentation 1996

United Kingdom

Architects **YRM Stanton Williams, London**
Award Winning Building **60 Sloane Avenue**
Location **60 Sloane Avenue, Kensington, London, UK**
Design and Construction Period **1991–1994**

Award 1) Royal Borough of Kensington & Chelsea Environmental Award 1995,
Civic Trust; 2) RIBA Regional Architecture Award 1996 (London Region)
Given by 1) Civic Trust; 2) RIBA The Royal Institute of British Architects
Design Team YRM Stanton Williams
Structural Engineering YRM Anthony Hunt Associates
Civil Engineering YRM Anthony Hunt Associates
Mechanical Engineering YRM Engineers
Electrical Engineering YRM Engineers
Acoustic Engineering Arup Acoustics
Air Conditioning Consultant YRM Engineers
Lighting Consultant YRM Engineers
Interior Design YRM Stanton Williams (developer base-building), Fletcher Priest
(office area fit out for Leo Burnett)
Quantity Surveying Leonard Stace Partnership
Approximate Cost £ 15,000,000

Site Area 3,200 m²
Total Floor Area 47,250 m² (155,000 sq. ft.)
Photographer Chris Gascoigne

USA

Architects **Gerald Allen & Jeffrey Harbinson Architects, Inc., New York**
Award Winning Building **Calvary Episcopal Church**
Location **Pittsburgh, Pennsylvania, USA**

Award AIA Religious Art and Architecture Design Award 1995/96
(Architecture Category)
Given by AIA The American Institute of Architects
Prize Presentation September 1996

USA

Architects **Anshen and Allen, Architects, Los Angeles**
Award Winning Building **Bourns Hall College of Engineering, University
of California, Riverside**

Award AIA National Honor Award for Architecture 1996
see page 160

USA

Architects **Errol Barron / Michael Toups Architects, New Orleans**
Award Winning Building **Saint James Episcopal Church**
Location **Fairhope, Alabama, USA**
Design and Construction Period **1993–1996**

Award 1) AIA Religious Art and Architecture Design Award 1995/96
(Architecture Category); 2) Gulf States Region Honor Award; 3) AIA National
Honor Award for Architecture (New Orleans and State of Louisiana)
Given by 1) AIA The American Institute of Architects
Prize Presentation October 1996

Members of the Jury Benjamin H. Weese (Chair), Donald Bruggink,
   Michael Landau, Maureen McGuire, Suzane Reatig
Design Team Errol Barron, Michael Toups, Steve Olson, Dennis Cowart
Structural Engineering D.E. Britt and Associates
Civil Engineering Woolpert and Associates
Mechanical Engineering Sullivan Engineers
Electrical Engineering Guillot-Vogt Associates
Lighting Consultant Errol Barron / Michael Toups Architects
Interior Design EB / MT Interiors
Landscape Architecture Errol Barron / Michael Toups Architects
Approximate Cost US$ 2,500,000
Site Area 44,000 m^2

Building Area 23,000 m^2
Total Floor Area 23,000 m^2
Photographer Alan Karchmer

USA

Architects **Errol Barron / Michael Toups Architects, New Orleans**
Award Winning Building **University of New Orleans / Training, Resource
   and Assistative-Technology Centre**
Location **New Orleans, Louisiana, USA**
Design and Construction Period **1994–1995**

Award AIA Honor Award for Architecture
Given by AIA The American Institute of Architects (New Orleans Chapter)
Prize Presentation January 1997
Members of the Jury Michael Holly (Chair), Mark Beckers, Cassie Ragan
Design Team Errol Barron, Michael Toups, Steve Olson, Dennis Cowart,
   Cindy Garbutt
Structural Engineering Zehner & Bouchon
Mechanical Engineering Goldstein & Goldstein
Electrical Engineering IMC Consulting Engineers
Lighting Consultant Errol Barron / Michael Toups Architects

Interior Design EB / MT Interiors
Landscape Architecture Errol Barron/Michael Toups Architects
Approximate Cost US$ 3,100,000
Site Area 2,700 m^2
Building Area 900 m^2
Total Floor Area 2,518 m^2
Photographer Alan Karchmer

USA

Architects **Bentel & Bentel, Architects / Planners, Locust Valley**
Award Winning Building **St. Stephen Roman Catholic Church**
Location **Warwick, New York, USA**

Award AIA Religious Art and Architecture Design Award 1995/96
(Architecture Category)
Given by AIA The American Institute of Architects
Prize Presentation September 1996

USA

Architects **Bohlin Cywinski Jackson, Wilkes-Barre**
Award Winning Building **Weekend Residence**
Location **Catoctin Mountains, Maryland, USA**

Award AIA National Honor Award for Architecture 1996
Given by AIA The American Institute of Architects
Prize Presentation   May / 12 / 1996

USA

Architects **The Baumgardner Architects, Donald T. Brubeck, Seattle**
Award Winning Building **St. James Cathedral Renovation**
Location **Seattle, Washington, USA**

Award AIA Religious Art and Architecture Design Award 1995/96
   (Architecture Category)
Given by AIA The American Institute of Architects
Prize Presentation September 1996

Architects **DLK Architecture Inc., Chicago**
Award Winning Building **Congress Viaduct and Plaza Reconstruction**
Location **400 to 600 South between Michigan Avenue and Columbus Drive,**
  Chicago, Illinois, USA
Design and Construction Period **January 1995– September1995**

Award AIA National Honor Award 1996 (Urban Design)
Given by AIA The American Institute of Architects
Prize Presentation May / 12 / 1996
Members of the Jury Marilyn J. Taylor (Chair), Gregory S. Baldwin,
  David T. Kahler, Sharon Lee Polledri, Janet Marie Smith
Design Team DLK Architecture Inc.
Structural Engineering H.W. Lochner
Civil Engineering H.W. Lochner

Electrical Engineering H.W. Lochner
Lighting Consultant Schuler & Shook
Landscape Architecture DLK Architecture Inc.
Approximate Cost US$ 10,000,000
Site Area 34,658,579 m²
Photographer Hedrich Blessing

Architects **Ellenzweig Associates, Inc., Cambridge**
Award Winning Building **Joslin Diabetes Centre**
Location **Boston, Massachusetts, USA**

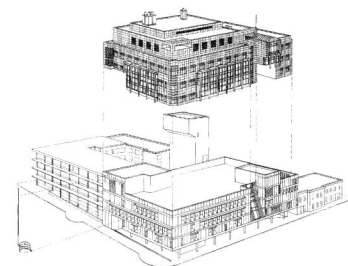 

Award AIA National Honor Award for Architecture 1996
Given by AIA The American Institute of Architects
Prize Presentation May / 12 / 1996
Design Team Harry Ellenzweig (Principal in Charge), Michael Reagan (Project
  Manager), Rob Tullis (Assistant Project Manager), Miltos Cantomeris (Project
  Architect), Arto Kurkjian, Gregory Berndt, Tom Kahmann, Jeffrey Salocks
  (Team)
Structural Engineering LeMessurier Consultants
Mechanical Engineering BR + A Consulting Engineers
Electrical Engineering BR + A Consulting Engineers
Acoustic Engineering Cambridge Acoustical

Air Conditioning Consultant BR + A Consulting Engineers
Lighting Consultant H.M. Brandston
Interior Design Ellenzweig Associates; Lloy Hack (Furnishings)
Landscape Architecture The Halvorson Company
Approximate Cost US$ 18,220,000
Building Area 93,000 GSF (new part), 17,000 GSF (renovation)
Photographer Steve Rosenthal

Architect **Richard C. Frank, Saline**
Award Winning Building **Michigan State Capitol Building**
Location **Capitol Square, Lansing, Michigan, USA**

Award AIA National Honor Award for Architecture 1996
Given by AIA The American Institute of Architects
Prize Presentation May / 12 / 1996

Architect **H. Gary Frank Architect Ltd., Chicago**
Award Winning Building **Temple Jeremiah**
Location **Northfield, Illinois, USA**

Award AIA Religious Art and Architecture Design Award 1995/96
  (Architecture Category)
Given by AIA The American Institute of Architects
Prize Presentation September 1996

Architects **Frank O. Gehry & Associates, Inc., Santa Monica**
Associated Architects **The Collaborative, Inc.**
Award Winning Building **Centre for the Visual Arts, University of Toledo**
Location **Toledo, Ohio, USA**

Award AIA National Honor Award for Architecture 1996
Given by AIA The American Institute of Architects
Prize Presentation May / 12 / 1996

Architects **Hammel Green and Abrahamson, Inc. with Frank Kasmarcik,**
   Liturgical Design Consultant, Minneapolis
Award Winning Building **Mepkin Abbey**
Location **Moncks Corner, South Carolina, USA**
Design and Construction Period **1993**

Award AIA Religious Art and Architecture Design Award 1995/96
   (Architecture Category)
Given by AIA The American Institute of Architects
Prize Presentation September 1996
Design Team Theodore R. Butler, Robert Lundgren
Structural Engineering Hammel, Green and Abrahamson, Inc.
Civil Engineering Hammel, Green and Abrahamson, Inc.
Mechanical Engineering Hammel, Green and Abrahamson, Inc.
Electrical Engineering Hammel, Green and Abrahamson, Inc.
Acoustic Engineering Kvernstoen Kehl and Associates

Lighting Consultant Carla Gallina, HGA
Approximate Cost US$ 800,000
Site Area 7,000 sq. ft.
Building Area 6,400 sq. ft.
Photographer Rick Alexander and Associates, Inc.

Architects **R.M. Kliment & Frances Halsband Architects, New York**
Award Winning Building **Entrance Pavilion – Long Island Rail Road at**
   Pennsylvania Station

Award 1) AIA National Honor Award for Architecture 1996; 2) AIA New York
   City Award for Architecture 1995; 3) AIA New York State Award of
   Excellence 1995
see page 164

Architects **Koning Eizenberg Architecture (Hank Koning, Julie Eizenberg,**
   Tim Andreas), Santa Monica
Award Winning Building **31st Street House**
Location **Santa Monica, California, USA**
Design and Construction Period **1992–1993**

Award 1) AIA National Honor Award for Architecture 1996; 2) AIA Honor
   Award 1994 (California Council)
Given by 1) AIA The American Institute of Architects; 2) AIA The American
   Institute of Architects (California Council)
Design Team Hank Koning, Julie Eizenberg, Tim Andreas
Structural Engineering Ross Downey & Associates

Approximate Cost US$ 200,000
Building Area 1,930 m^2
Photographer Tim Griffith, Images Australia Pty. Ltd.

Architects **Albert C. Martin & Associates, Los Angeles**
Award Winning Building **Padre Serra Parish Church**
Location **5205 Upland Road, Camarillo, California, USA**
Design and Construction Period **1992–1995**

 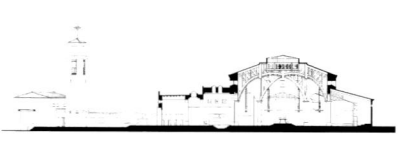

Award AIA Religious Art and Architecture Design Award 1995/96
   (Architecture Category)
Given by AIA The American Institute of Architects
Prize Presentation September 1996
Members of the Jury Benjamin H. Weese (Chair), Donald Bruggink,
   Michael Landau, Maureen McGuire, Suzane Reatig
Design Team David C. Martin (Design Partner), Edward Holakiewicz

(Project Designer), Thomas Emme (Project Architect)
Structural Engineering Tom Nishi, Albert C. Martin & Associates
Civil Engineering Jon Ziegler, P.E., Albert C. Martin & Associates
Mechanical Engineering Wayne Yau, M.E., P.E., Albert C. Martin & Associates

Electrical Engineering Clay Calhoun, P.E., Albert C. Martin & Associates
Acoustic Engineering Purcell and Noppe
Lighting Consultant Tim Thomas, Architectural Lighting
Interior Design Edward Holakiewicz, Darrick Martin (Albert C. Martin &
    Associates)
Liturgical Consultant Daniel Young
Audio Consultant Hughes Sound Engineering

Landscape Architecture Van Atta & Black and Associates
Quantity Surveying Project Cost Management
Approximate Cost US$ 5,200,000 (phase I)
Site Area 47,630 m²
Building Area 2,787 m² (phase I)
Total Floor Area 2,787 m² (phase I)
Photographer Aker / Zvonkovic Photos

USA

Architects **Mitchell / Giurgola Architects, New York**
Award Winning Building **The Belvedere**
Location **Battery Park City, New York City, New York**
Design and Construction Period **1994–1995**

Award AIA National Honor Award 1996 (Urban Design)
Given by AIA The American Institute of Architects
Prize Presentation 1996
Members of the Jury Marilyn Taylor, Gregory Baldwin, David Kahler,
    Sharon Lee Polledri, Janet Marie Smith
Design Consultant Mildred Friedman
Structural Engineering Weidlinger Associates
Construction Manager Raytheon Engineers & Constructors
Mechanical/Plumbing Engineering Lehr Associates
Electrical Engineering Lehr Associates
Artist (Creator of Pylons) Martin Puryear
Lighting Consultant H.M. Brandston & Partners, Inc.
Landscape Architecture Child Associates, Inc. Landscape Architects

Approximate Cost US$ 6,000,000
Site Area 1.6 acres
Photographer Jeff Goldberg, Esto

USA

Architects **Mitchell / Giurgola Architects, New York**
Award Winning Building **The Lighthouse Headquarters
    (renovation and addition)**
Location **New York City, New York, USA**
Design and Construction Period **1993–1994**

 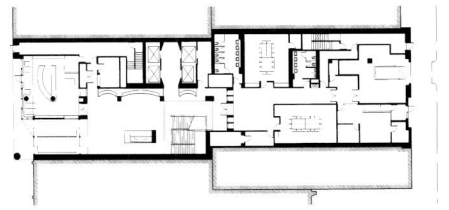

Award AIA National Honor Award 1996 (Interiors)
Given by AIA The American Institute of Architects
Prize Presentation May / 12 / 1996
Members of the Jury J.W. Rainey, Nila Leiserowitz,
    Lamberto Moris, Dianne Pilgrim, Daniella Voith
Design Team Mitchell / Giurgola Architects, LLP
Structural Engineering Severud Associates, New York
Mechanical / Plumbing Engineering Cosentini Associates, New York
Electrical Engineering Cosentini Associates, New York
Acoustic Engineering Robert A. Hansen Associates, Inc., New York
Lighting Consultant H.M. Brandston & Partners, Inc., New York
Theater Consultant Jules Fisher / Joshua Dachs Associates, Inc., New York
Graphics / Wayfinding Consultant Whitehouse & Company, New York

Project Manager Grid Properties, Inc. , New York
Elevator Consultant John A. Van Duesen & Associates, Inc., Livingston,
    New Jersey
Kitchen Consultant Romano / Gatland, Lindenhurst, New York
Construction Manager Barr & Barr, New York
Site Area 170,000 sq. ft.
Photographer Jeff Goldberg, Esto

Architects **M. Mense Architects, Anchorage**

Award Winning Building **Mainstreet Alaska Soldotna '95**

Location **Soldotna, Alaska, USA**

Design and Construction Period **1995**

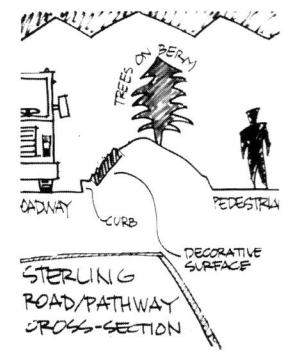

Award AIA National Honor Award 1996 (Urban Design)

Given by AIA The American Institute of Architects

Prize Presentation May 1996

Members of the Jury Barton Myers (Chair), Laurie Beckelmann, Fred Clarke III, James M. Cutler, Laurie D. Olin, Patrick Jones, Carol Shen, Alicia C. Trevino, Frank D. Welch

Design Team Mike Mense (Chair), Steve Izenour, Stephen Peters, Melissa Joyner, Klaus Mayer, Shelah Shauks, Celia Anderson

Planners George Cannelos, Jon Isaacs, Suzanne Little

Landscape Architecture Elise Huggins, Jonathan Schilk, Susan Willhoth

Photographer M Mense Architects

USA

Architects **Murphy / Jahn, Chicago**

Award Winning Building **Kurfürstendamm No. 70**

Award 1) AIA Chicago Chapter Award 1994; 2) AIA National Honor Award for Architecture 1996

see page 166

USA

Architects **Murphy / Jahn, Chicago**

Award Winning Building **Munich Order Centre – M.O.C.**

Award 1) AIA Chicago Chapter Award 1994; 2) AIA National Honor Award for Architecture 1996

see page 168

USA

Architects **Muse Architects (formerly Muse-Wiedemann Architects), Washington D.C.**

Award Winning Building **New Worship Building for Christ Episcopal Church**

Location **Columbia, Maryland, USA**

Design and Construction Period **1992–1994**

 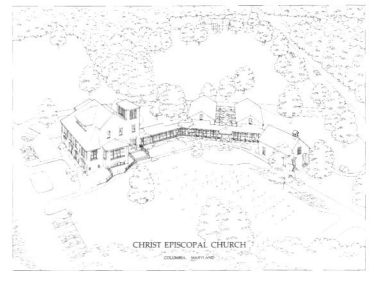

Award AIA Religious Art and Architecture Design Award 1995/96 (Architecture Category)

Given by AIA The American Institute of Architects

Prize Presentation September 1996

Members of the Jury Benjamin H. Weese, Donald Bruggink, Michael Landau, Maureen McGuire, Suzane Reatig

Design Team Stephen Muse, Thomas Ahmann, William Kirwan, Tamar King

Structural Engineering Structron Engineering

Civil Engineering Reimer Muegge and Associates, Inc.

Mechanical Engineering AJ Engineers

Electrical Engineering AJ Engineers

Acoustic Engineering Miller Henning Associates, Inc.

Air Conditioning Consultant AJ Engineers

Interior Design Muse Architects

Approximate Cost US$ 1,022/m²

Site Area 36,365 m²

Building Area 548 m²

Total Floor Area 548 m²

Photographer Alan Karchmer

USA

Architects **Herbert S. Newman and Partners, Architects and Master Planners, New Haven**

Award Winning Building **Ninth Square Redevelopment Project**

Location **New Haven, Connecticut, USA**

Design and Construction Period **1989–1992**

Award AIA National Honor Award 1996 (Urban Design)

Given by AIA The American Institute of Architects

Prize Presentation 1995

Members of the Jury Marilyn Taylor, Gregory Baldwin, David Kahler, Sharon Lee Polledri, Janet Marie Smith

Design Team Herbert S. Newman, Robert Godshall, A. Michael Raso,
Peggy Rubens-Duhl, Joseph Huether, Jeffrey Miles, (Herbert S. Newman
and Partners), Tyler Smith, Jared Edwards, Kent McCoy, Marja Watson,
(Smith Edwards Architects)
Structural Engineering Tor Smolen Calini & Anastos
Civil Engineering Barakos-Landino Design Group
Mechanical Engineering Helenski Zimmerer, Inc.
Electrical Engineering Helenski Zimmerer, Inc.
Environmental Engineering Michael Horton and Associates
Air Conditioning Consultant Helenski Zimmerer, Inc.
Lighting Consultant Helenski Zimmerer, Inc.
Life Safety Consultant Helenski Zimmerer, Inc.
Interior Design Herbert S. Newman and Partners
Landscape Architecture Roland/Towers, PC
Quantity Surveying Barakos-Landino Design Group

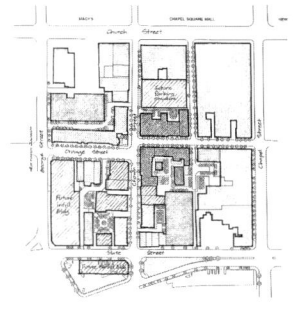 

Approximate Cost US$ 43,000,000
Site Area 4,185 acres (plus parking)
Total Floor Area 285,000 sq. ft.
Photographer Norman McGrath

USA

Architects **Perkins & Will; Burgess & Niple, Ltd., Chicago**
Award Winning Building **Perry Community Education Village**

Award AIA National Honor Award for Architecture 1996
see page 170

USA

Architects **William Rawn Associates, Architects, Inc., Boston**
Associated Architects **Hanbury Evans Newill Vlattas & Co., Norfolk; Metcalf
Tobey & Partners, Reston**
Award Winning Building **West Main Street Corridor Urban Design Plan,
University of Virginia**
Location **Charlotteville, Virginia, USA**
Design and Construction Period **1992–1993**

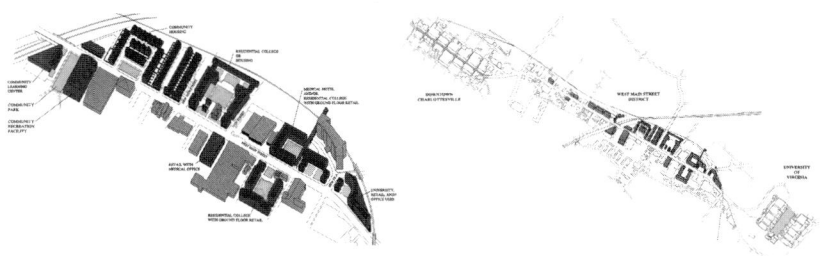

Award AIA National Honor Award 1996 (Urban Design)
Given by AIA The American Institute of Architects
Prize Presentation May / 12 / 1996
Members of the Jury Marilyn Taylor, Gregory Baldwin, David Kahler,
Sharon Lee Polledri, Janet Marie Smith
Design Team William Rawn Associates: William L. Rawn III (Principal),
Clifford V. Gayley (Project Architect), Craig Mutter (Project Team); Metcalf
Tobey & Partners: Philip Tobey (Principal), Alan Flora (Project Team); Hambury
Evans Newill Vlattas & Co., Michael Evans and Jane Wright (Principals),
Wesley Page (Renderer)

Economic Consultant Halcyon Real Estate Advisors, Ernst & Young: Patrick
Philips, Paul Sehnert
Real Estate Consultant Real Estate Enterprises, Inc: Reese Fayde, Greta Harris
Approximate Cost US$ 60,000,000–80,000,000
Site Area approximately 1 mile long and some 150 ft. to 500 ft.wide
Photographer William Rawn Associates

USA

Architects **Rios Associates, Inc., Los Angeles**
Award Winning Building **Warner Bros. Children's Centre**
Location **3901 W. Oak Street, Burbank, California, USA**

Award AIA National Honor Award for Architecture 1996
Given by AIA The American Institute of Architects
Prize Presentation May / 12 / 1996

USA

Architects **Sasaki Associates Inc., Watertown**
Award Winning Building **Cleveland Gateway**

Award 1) AIA National Honor Award 1996 (Urban Design);
2) Honor Award 1994 (Planning and Urban Design)
see page 172

Architects **Skidmore, Owings & Merrill LLP (Joseph A. Gonzalez), Chicago**
Award Winning Building **Martin Theatre at Ravinia Festival**
Location **Highland Park, Illinois, USA**
Design and Construction Period **1991–1992**

Award AIA National Honor Award for Architecture 1996
Given by AIA The American Institute of Architects
Prize Presentation May / 12 / 1996
Members of the Jury Barton Myers, Laurie Beckelmann, Fred Clarke III,
  James M. Cutler, Laurie D. Olin, Patrick Jones, Carol Shen, Alicia C. Trevino,
  Frank D. Welch
Design Team Joseph A. Gonzalez, Jeffrey McCarthy, Charles Hasbrouck,
  David Kennedy
Civil Engineering Brian J. Schirmer
Mechanical Engineering Ray J. Clark
Electrical Engineering Ray J. Clark
Acoustic Engineering Kirkegaard & Associates

Air Conditioning Consultant Ray J. Clark
Lighting Consultant Schuler & Shook, Inc.
Landscape Architecture Ted Wolf
Approximate Cost US$ 2,500,000
Building Area 1,134 m^2
Total Floor Area 837 m^2
Photographer Jon Miller, Hedrich Blessing

Architects **Skidmore, Owings & Merrill, Chicago**
Award Winning Building **United States Air Force Academy Cadet Chapel**
Location **United States Air Force Academy, Colorado Springs,
  Colorado, USA**

Award AIA The 1996 Twenty-Five-Year Award
Given by AIA The American Institute of Architects
Prize Presentation 1996

Architects **Harry Weese Associates, Chicago**
Award Winning Building **Clarence F. Buckingham Memorial Fountain**
Location **Chicago, Illinois, USA**
Design and Construction Period **1994–1995**

Award 1) AIA National Honor Award for Architecture 1996; 2) Bricks and
  Mortar Award
Given by 1) AIA The American Institute of Architects; 2) Landmarks
  Preservation Council of Illinois
Prize Presentation May / 12 / 1996
Members of the Jury Andrea Leers, Frederic Schwartz, Allison Williams
Design Team Harry Weese Associates
Structural Engineering Rubinos & Mesia Engineers
Mechanical Engineering Environmental Systems Design
Electrical Engineering Environmental Systems Design
Materials Testing Construction Technology Laboratories

General Contractor E.W. Corrigan
  Construction Co.
Archival Reserach Ann McGuire &
  Associates
Cost Control Construction Cost
  Systems
Fund Trustee and Project Manager
  The Art Institute of Chicago
Approximate Cost US$ 2,900,000
Photographer Bob Harr, Hedrich
  Blessing

Architects **Weinstein Copeland Architects, Seattle**
Award Winning Building **Banner Building**
Location **2600 Western Avenue, Seattle, Washington, USA**

Award AIA National Honor Award for Architecture 1996
Given by AIA The American Institute of Architects
Prize Presentation May / 12 / 1996

INDEXES

Sections of the UIA (International Union of Architects) and Awards

Algeria
Union des Architectes Algériens, Kouba

Argentina
Federación Argentina de Sociedades de Arquitectos, Buenos Aires

Azerbaijan
Union of Architects of Azerbaijan, Baku

Australia
The Royal Australian Institute of Architects, Canberra
Awards Robin Boyd Award for Housing, International Citation, Commercial Architecture Award, International Award, Environmental Citation, National Interiors Architecture Award, Sir Zelman Cowen Award for Public Buildings, Lachlan Macquarie Award for Conservation, Access Citation, Walter Burley Griffin Award for Urban Design (National Award), Victorian Architecture Medal, Merit Award for Outstanding Architecture – Multiple Residential Category, Merit Award for Civic Design

Austria
Bundeskammer der Architekten und Ingenieurkonsulenten, Wien
Award Staatspreis für Consulting

Baltic States
Association of Unions of Baltic Architects Esthonia, Latvia, Lithuania, Riga (Latvia)

Bangladesh
Institute of Architects of Bangladesh, Dacca Award: IAB Gold Medal

Belgium
Fédération Royale des Sociétés d'Architectes de Belgique, Bruxelles (without any Prize Presentation)
Recommendation of the institution: Fondation Philippe Rotthier pour l'architecture
Awards Prix Européen de la Reconstruction de la Ville – Category: Espace Public et Projet Urbain

Bolivia
The College of Architects of Bolivia, La Paz

Brazil
Instituto de Arquitetos do Brasil, São Paulo
Awards Prêmio Habitação / Premiação IAB, Annual Award of the Instituto de Arquitetos do Brasil – Departamento de São Paulo – one person residence, Premiação Instituto de Arquitetos do Brasil, Premio Fachada (Best Façade), Premiação IAB / SP – Best Building, Premiação IAB – Category: Edificações-Projeto, Premiação IAB / SP Building for Educational Activities, Premiação IAB / SP Building for Healthcare Services, Premio ex-aequo IAB – Category: Arquitetura de Interiores-Ohra Executada

Bulgaria
Union des Architectes Bulgares, Sofia

Cameroun
Ordre des Architectes du Cameroun, Yaunde

Canada
The Royal Architectural Institute of Canada, Ontario

Award Governor General's Award for Architecture

Central America
Federación Centroamericana de Arquitectos (Costa Rica, Guatemala, Honduras, Nicaragua, El Salvador), Guatemala
Award Mayor de la Ciudad

Chile
Colegio de Arquitectos de Chile, Santiago de Chile

People's Republic of China
The Architectural Society of China, Beijing
Awards Creation Awards of the Architectural Society of China between 1984-1993, Creation Awards of the Architectural Society of China between 1988-1992, National Excellent Design (Gold Award), World Habitat Awards

Colombia
Sociedad Colombiana de Arquitectos, Bogotá
Award Award of the ›Bienal Colombiana‹

Croatia
Association of Croatian Architects, Zagreb

Cuba
Unión Nacional de Arquitectos e Ingenieros de la Construcción de Cuba, La Habana

Czech Republic
Society of Czech Architects, Prague
Award Grand Prix of the Association of Czech Architects

Denmark
Danske Arkitekters Landsforbund, Copenhagen
Awards Den Grønne Nål, The Architectural Prize

Ecuador
Colegio Nacional de Arquitectos del Ecuador, Quito
Awards IX Bienal Panamericana de Arquitectura de Quito - Categoria de Conservacion, Preservacion, Restauracion y Adaptacion a Nuevo Uso del Patrimonio Edificado, IX Bienal Panamericana de Arquitectura de Quito, Mencion de Honor, Architectural Design Grand Award, Gran Premio Internacional IX Bienal Panamericana de Arquitectura de Quito

Egypt
Society of Egyptian Architects, Cairo

Eurasian Group
(Armenia, Bielorussia, Kirgizia, Tadjikistan, Ubekistan), Moscow
Awards II. Prize and Medal at the International Contest ›Best Architectural Work of 1993‹, Grand Prix of Architecture, Construction and Design

Finland
The Finnish Association of Architects, Helsinki
Award Alvar Aalto Medal

France
Conseil National de l'Ordre des Architectes, Paris (without any Prize Presentation)
Recommendation of the institution: Ministère du Logement, Paris
Awards Equerre d'Argent, Prize for Town Planning, Grand Prix National d'Architecture, Yearly ›Moniteur de l'Architecture‹ Award

Gabun
Ordre des Architectes du Gabon, Libreville

Germany
Bund Deutscher Architekten BDA, Bonn
Award Der Große BDA-Preis

Greece
Chambre Technique de Grèce, Athènes

Hong Kong
The Hong Kong Institute of Architects, Wanchai
Awards Annual Award (President's Prize), ARCASIA Award, HKIA Medal

Hungary
Chamber and Association of Hungarian Architects, Budapest
Awards Pro Architectura Prize, YBL Miklós Prize

Iceland
Arkitektafelag Islands, Reykjavik

India
The Indian Institute of Architects, Bombay

Indonesia
The Institute of Architects of Indonesia, Jakarta
Awards IAI Award for Architects and their Buildings, IAI Award for Individuals (Architects and Non-Architects) & Institutions

Ireland
The Royal Institute of the Architects of Ireland, Dublin
Awards Award for Architectural Excellence, RIAI Regional Award - Dublin - Northern - Eastern - Western - Southern

Israel
Association of Engineers & Architects in Israel, Tel Aviv
Awards Zeev Rechter Prize, Architecture Prize on 1st of July

Italy
Consiglio nazionale degli Architetti, Roma

Ivory Coast
Conseil national de l'Ordre des Architectes de Côte d'Ivoire, Abidjan, Jamaica
The Jamaican Institute of Architects, Kingston

Japan
Japan Institute of Architects,Tokyo
Awards JIA Prize for the Best Young Architect of the Year, Annual Architectural Design Commendation of the Japan Institute of Architects, Special Award for Design Excellence

Kazakhstan
Union of Architects of Kazakhstan, Alma Ata
Award Le Prix de l'Union des Architectes de la République du Kazakhstan

Kenya
The Architectural Association of Kenya, Nairobi
Award Shilling Award

Korea
The Korean Institute of Architects, Seoul

Republic of Korea
Union des Architects de la R.P. de Corée, Pyong-Yang

Kuwait
Kuwait Society of Engineers, Safat

Lebanon
Order of Engineers and Architects, Beirut

Luxembourg
Ordre des Architectes et des Ingénieurs du Luxembourg, Luxembourg
Award Prix Luxembourgeois d'Architecture

Macau
Associacao dos Arquitectos de Macau, South East Asia

Macedonia
Association of Architects of the Former Yougoslavian Republic of Macedonia, Skopje

Malaysia
Malaysian Institute of Architects, Kuala Lumpur

Malta
Chamber of Architects and Civil Engineers, Pembroke
Award Recommendation of Chamber of Architects and Civil Engineers of Malta

Mauritius
The Mauritius Association of Architects MAA, Port Louis

Mexico
Federación de Colegios de Arquitectos de la República Mexicana, Mexico

Mongolia
Union of Mongolian Architects, Ulan Bator

Morocco
Section Marocaine de l'UIA, Rabat
Award Award of the Ministère de l'Habitat / ERAC Oriental

Republic of Namibia
Namibia Institute of Architects, Windhoek
Award Award of Merit: Engraved Plaque & Certificate of Merit

The Netherlands
Bond van Nederlandse Architekten, Amsterdam
Awards Grand Prix Rhénan d'Architecture, National Steel Award, BNA Kubus, A.J. van Eyck Prize

Nigeria
The Nigerian Institute of Architects, Lagos

Norway
Norske Arkitekters Landsforbund, Oslo
Awards Anton Christian Houens Fonds Diplom, European Steel Design Award

Pakistan
Institute of Architects of Pakistan, Lahore

Panama
Sociedad Panamena de Ingenieros y Arquitectos, Panama
Awards Best Midsize Apartment Building of the Year, Best Large Apartment Building of the Year

Paraguay
Associación Paraguaya de Arquitectos, Asunción

Peru
Colegio de Arquitectos del Perú, Lima
Awards Hexagono de Oro – Bienal de Arquitectura, Hexagono de Plata a Mejor Estructura, Hexagono de Plata a Mejor Uso Materiales

Republic of the Philippines
United Architects of the Philippines, Metro Manila
Award Likha Award on Gold Medal

Indexes

Architects
of AWA 1996 and 1997